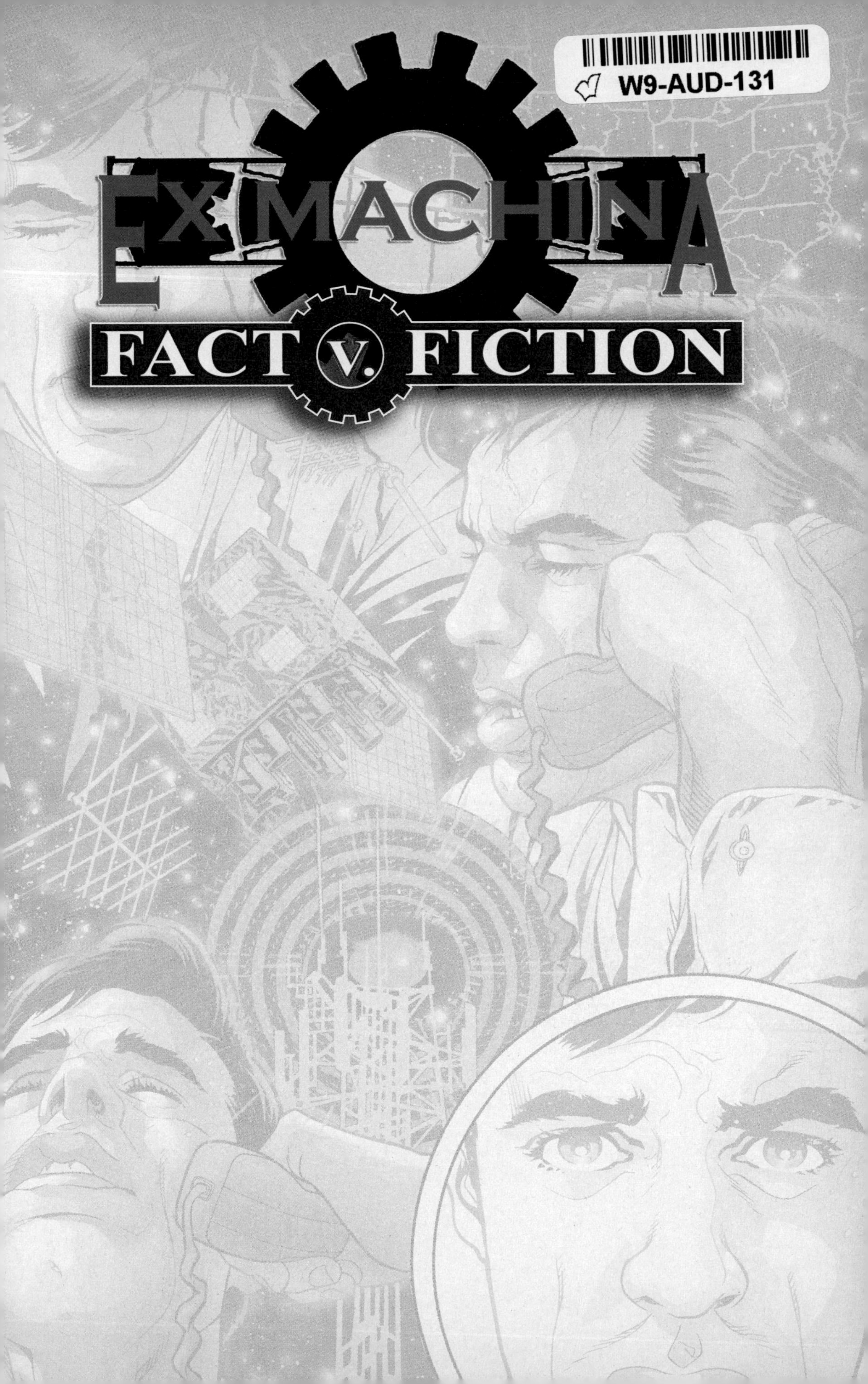
EX MACHINA
FACT v. FICTION

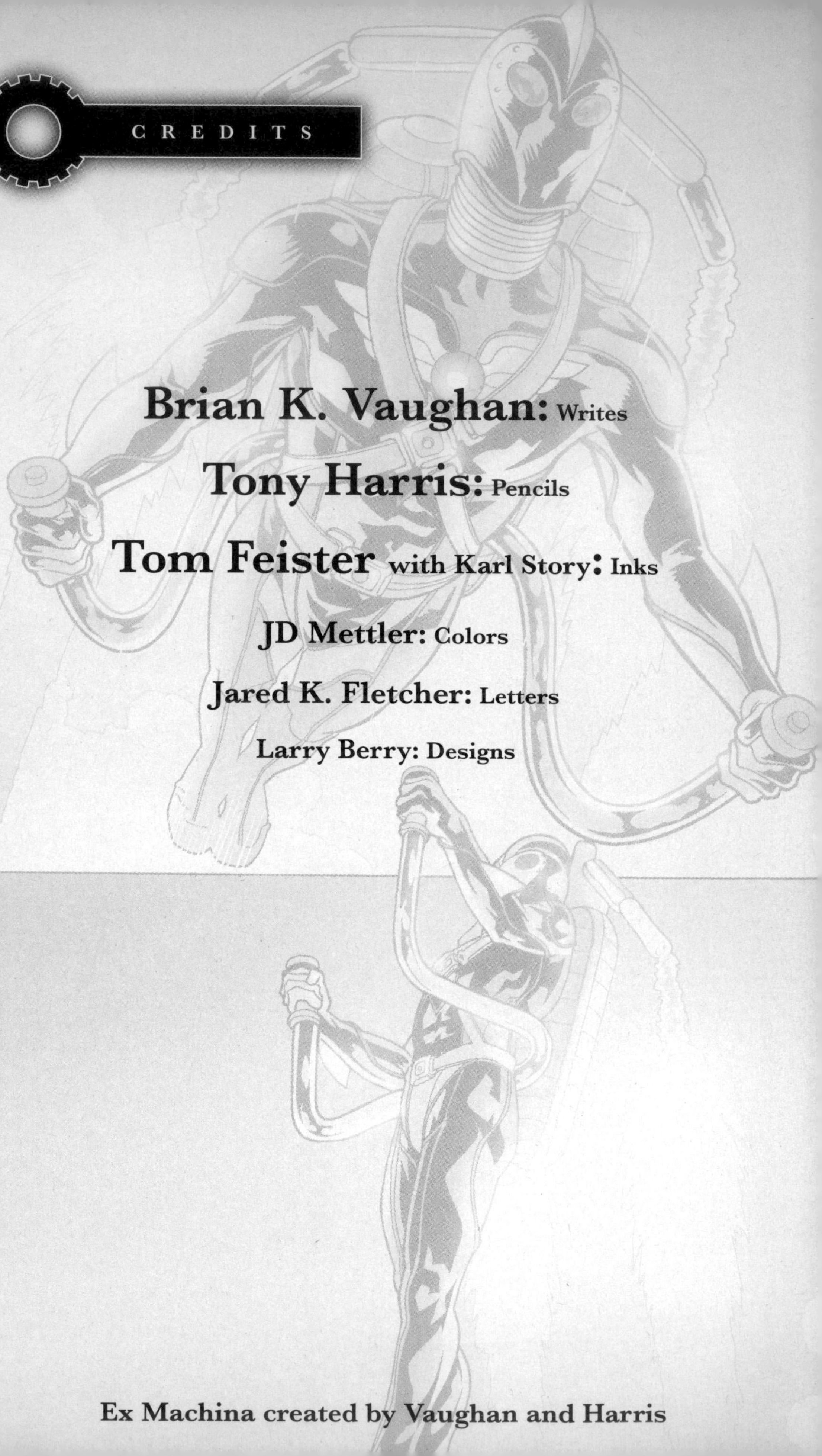

CREDITS

Brian K. Vaughan: Writes

Tony Harris: Pencils

Tom Feister with Karl Story: Inks

JD Mettler: Colors

Jared K. Fletcher: Letters

Larry Berry: Designs

Ex Machina created by Vaughan and Harris

LEGAL

Jim Lee, Editorial Director **John Nee,** VP—Business Development **Scott Dunbier,** Executive Editor
Ben Abernathy, Editor **Kristy Quinn,** Assistant Editor **Ed Roeder,** Art Director **Paul Levitz,** President & Publisher
Georg Brewer, VP—Design & DC Direct Creative **Richard Bruning,** Senior VP—Creative Director
Patrick Caldon, Executive VP—Finance & Operations **Chris Caramalis,** VP—Finance **John Cunningham,** VP—Marketing
Terri Cunningham, VP—Managing Editor **Stephanie Fierman,** Senior VP—Sales & Marketing **Alison Gill,** VP—Manufacturing
Rich Johnson, VP—Book Trade Sales **Hank Kanalz,** VP—General Manager, WildStorm
Lillian Laserson, Senior VP & General Counsel **Paula Lowitt,** Senior VP—Business & Legal Affairs
David McKillips, VP—Advertising & Custom Publishing **Gregory Noveck,** Senior VP—Creative Affairs
Cheryl Rubin, Senior VP—Brand Management **Jeff Trojan,** VP—Business Development, DC Direct **Bob Wayne,** VP—Sales

DEDICATIONS

"For Ruth, my New York City." - Brian K. Vaughan

"I would like to dedicate this volume to two dear friends, Eric and his wife Mimi.

"They are first my friends and second my fans, but it didn't start out that way. It's a rare thing in the entertainment industry to meet folks at a show and become such fast friends, but that's what happened. Over the years you guys have supported me personally, professionally, and emotionally. You will always have a fan in me."

- Tony Harris

"To Jack, my hope. To Sonya, my love."

-Tom Feister

"To my wife Amy, for your love and white magic; to my mother Darlene, for teaching me that creativity and practicality can coexist; and to my father George, for teaching me that although it's possible to color completely within the lines, it is more interesting not to."

- JD Mettler

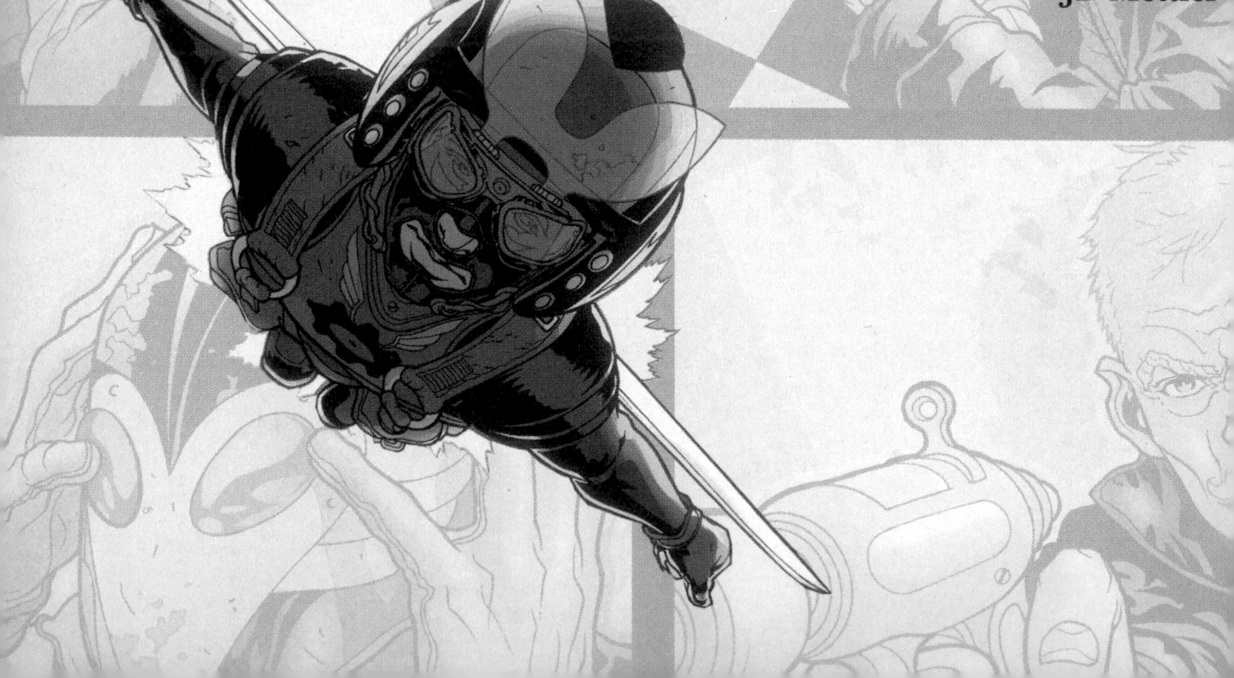

CHAPTER 1 Fortune Favors

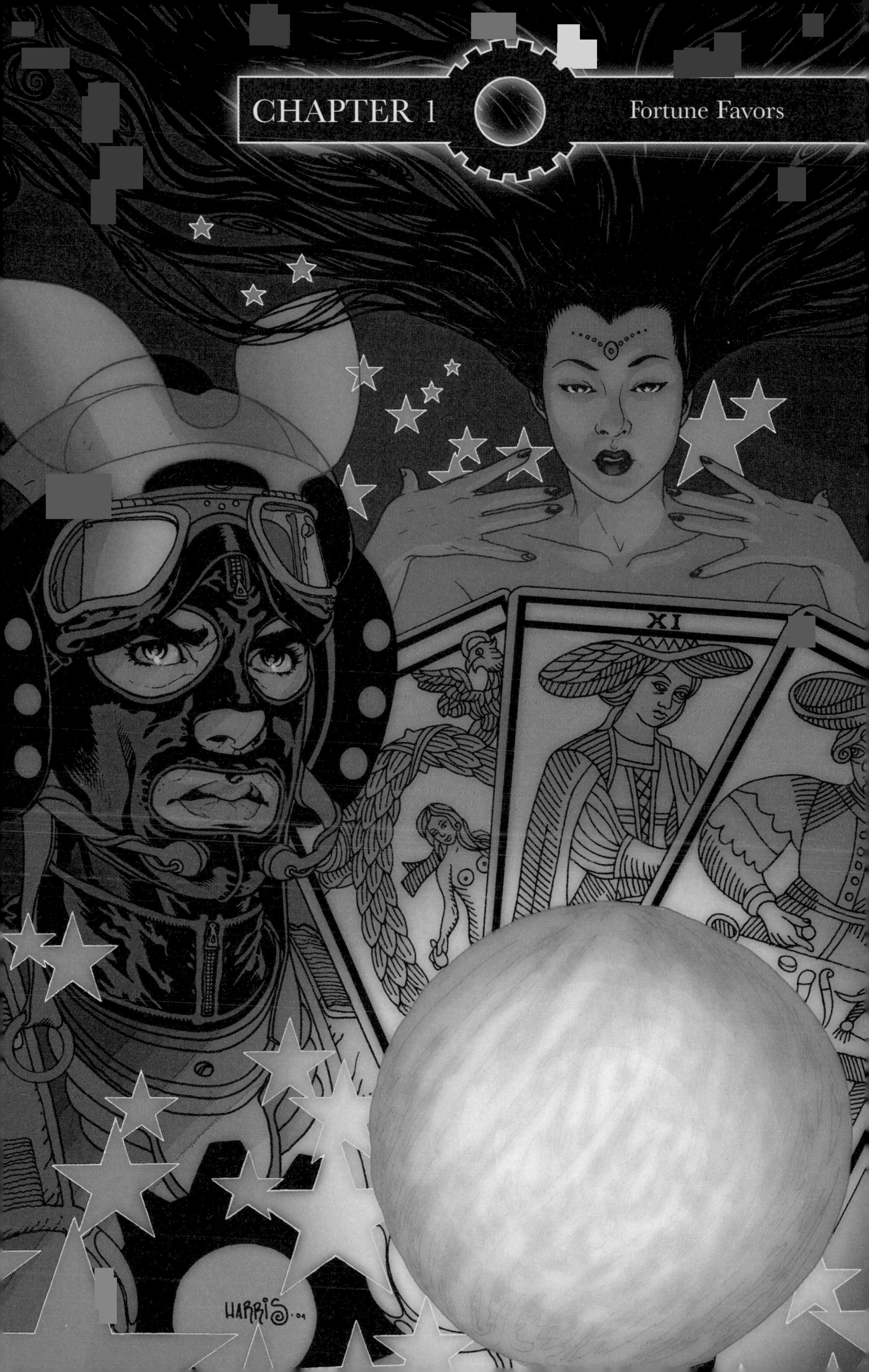

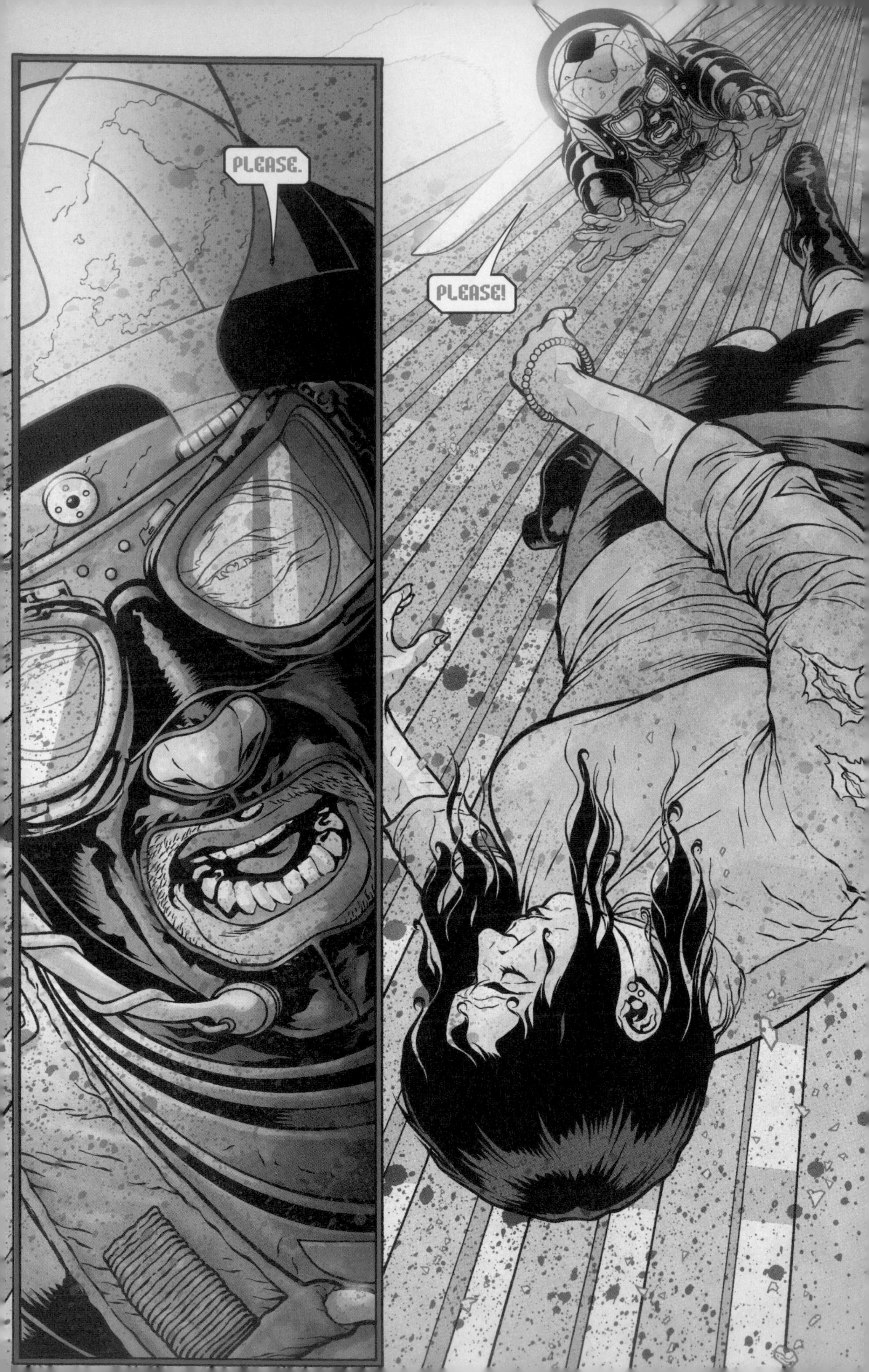
PLEASE.
PLEASE!

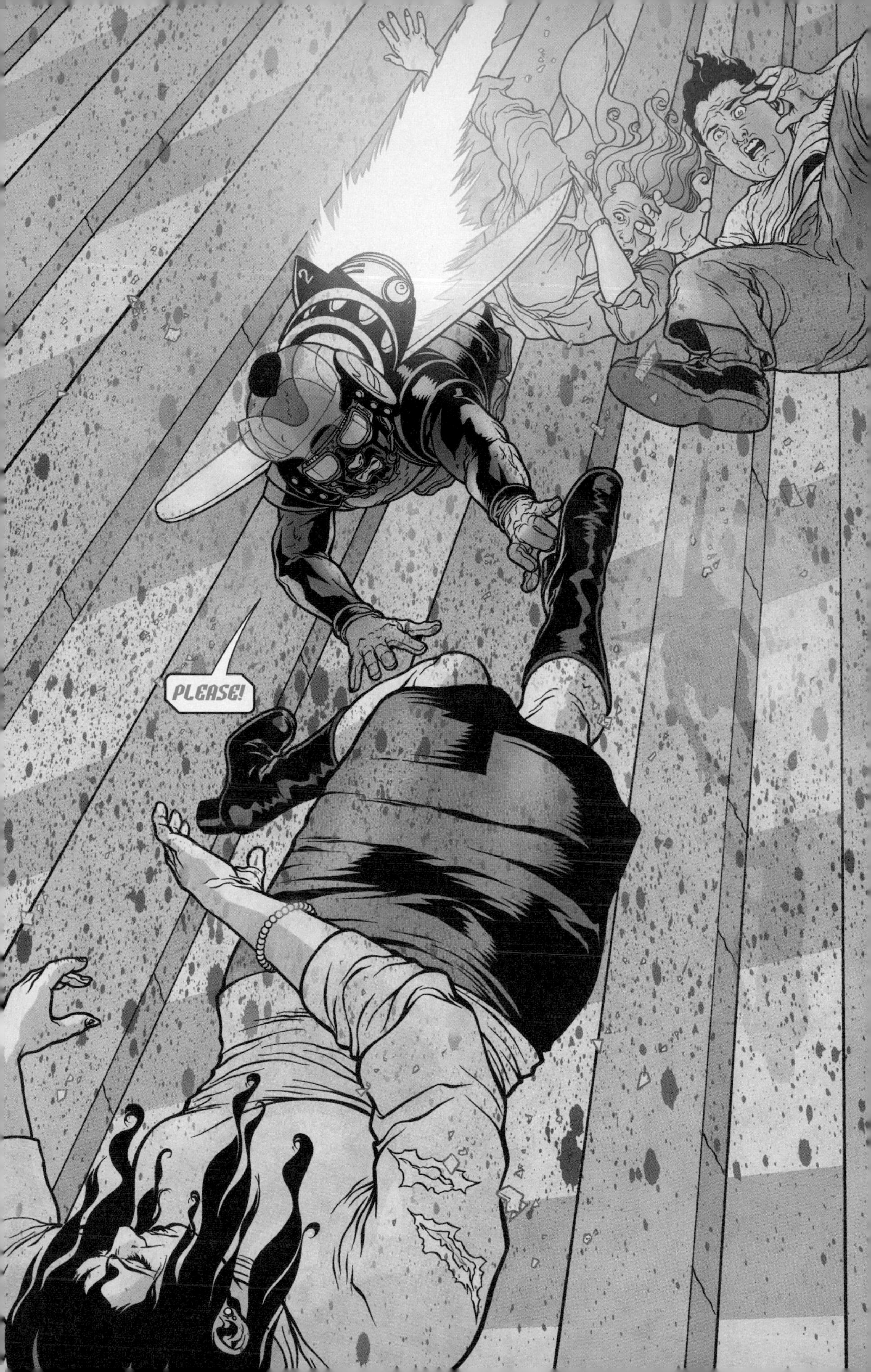
PLEASE!

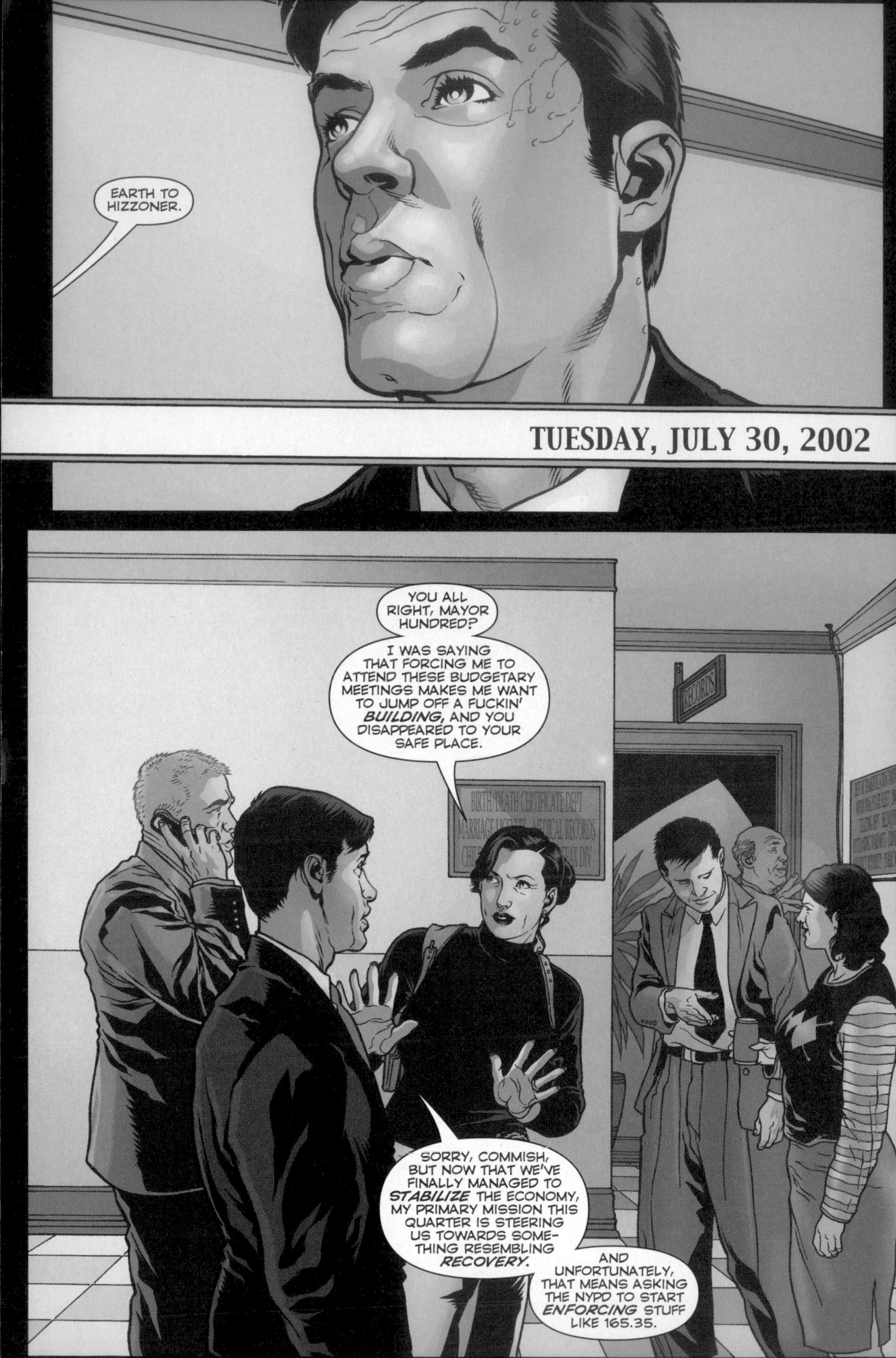
EARTH TO HIZZONER.
TUESDAY, JULY 30, 2002
YOU ALL RIGHT, MAYOR HUNDRED?
I WAS SAYING THAT FORCING ME TO ATTEND THESE BUDGETARY MEETINGS MAKES ME WANT TO JUMP OFF A FUCKIN' *BUILDING,* AND YOU DISAPPEARED TO YOUR SAFE PLACE.
RECORDS
BIRTH/DEATH CERTIFICATE DEPT
SORRY, COMMISH, BUT NOW THAT WE'VE FINALLY MANAGED TO *STABILIZE* THE ECONOMY, MY PRIMARY MISSION THIS QUARTER IS STEERING US TOWARDS SOMETHING RESEMBLING *RECOVERY.*
AND UNFORTUNATELY, THAT MEANS ASKING THE NYPD TO START *ENFORCING* STUFF LIKE 165.35.

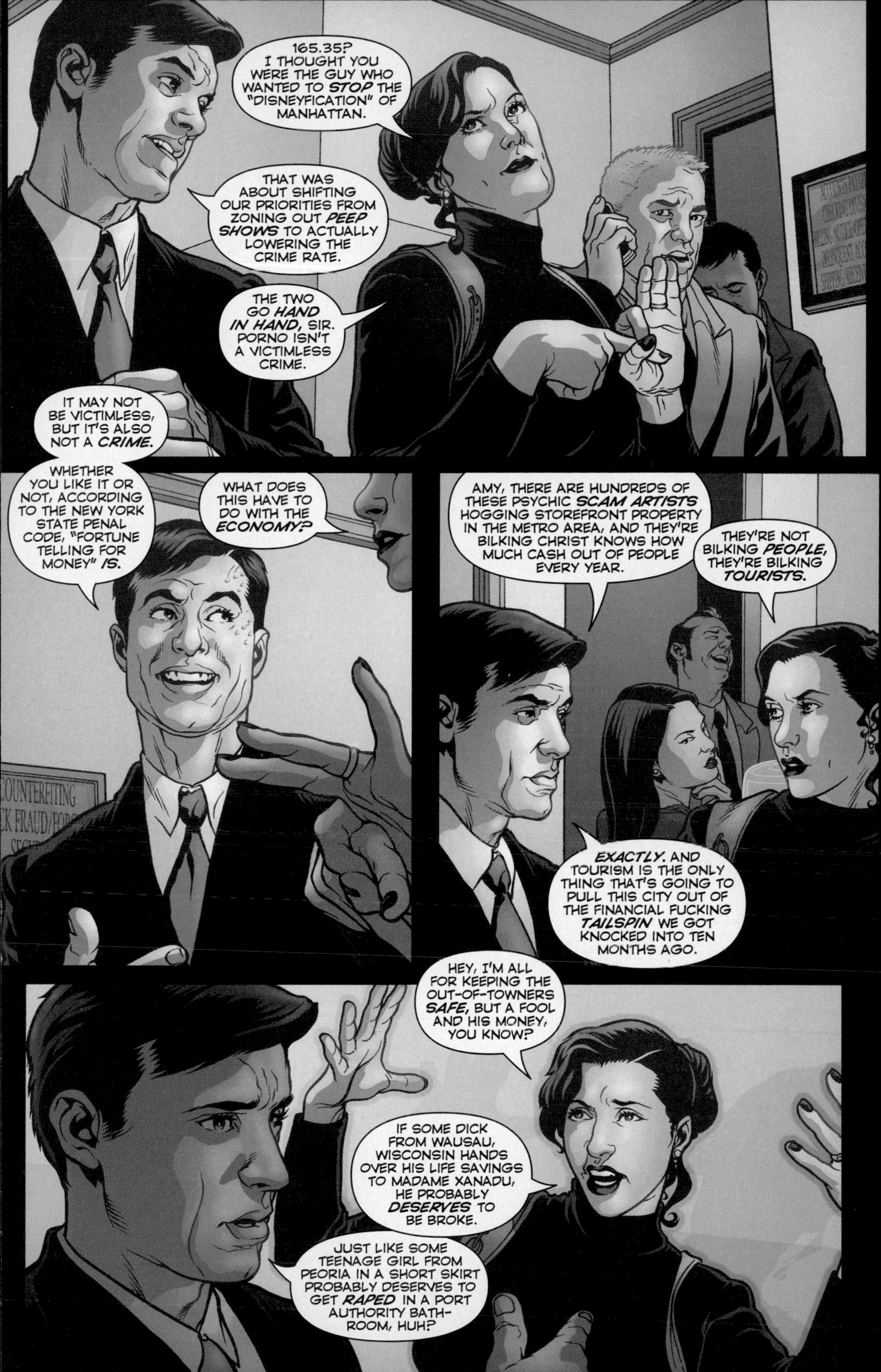
165.35? I THOUGHT YOU WERE THE GUY WHO WANTED TO *STOP* THE "DISNEYFICATION" OF MANHATTAN.
THAT WAS ABOUT SHIFTING OUR PRIORITIES FROM ZONING OUT *PEEP SHOWS* TO ACTUALLY LOWERING THE CRIME RATE.
THE TWO GO *HAND IN HAND,* SIR. PORNO ISN'T A VICTIMLESS CRIME.
IT MAY NOT BE VICTIMLESS, BUT IT'S ALSO NOT A *CRIME*.
WHETHER YOU LIKE IT OR NOT, ACCORDING TO THE NEW YORK STATE PENAL CODE, "FORTUNE TELLING FOR MONEY" *IS*.
WHAT DOES THIS HAVE TO DO WITH THE *ECONOMY?*
AMY, THERE ARE HUNDREDS OF THESE PSYCHIC *SCAM ARTISTS* HOGGING STOREFRONT PROPERTY IN THE METRO AREA, AND THEY'RE BILKING CHRIST KNOWS HOW MUCH CASH OUT OF PEOPLE EVERY YEAR.
THEY'RE NOT BILKING *PEOPLE,* THEY'RE BILKING *TOURISTS*.
EXACTLY. AND TOURISM IS THE ONLY THING THAT'S GOING TO PULL THIS CITY OUT OF THE FINANCIAL FUCKING *TAILSPIN* WE GOT KNOCKED INTO TEN MONTHS AGO.
HEY, I'M ALL FOR KEEPING THE OUT-OF-TOWNERS *SAFE,* BUT A FOOL AND HIS MONEY, YOU KNOW?
IF SOME DICK FROM WAUSAU, WISCONSIN HANDS OVER HIS LIFE SAVINGS TO MADAME XANADU, HE PROBABLY *DESERVES* TO BE BROKE.
JUST LIKE SOME TEENAGE GIRL FROM PEORIA IN A SHORT SKIRT PROBABLY DESERVES TO GET *RAPED* IN A PORT AUTHORITY BATH-ROOM, HUH?

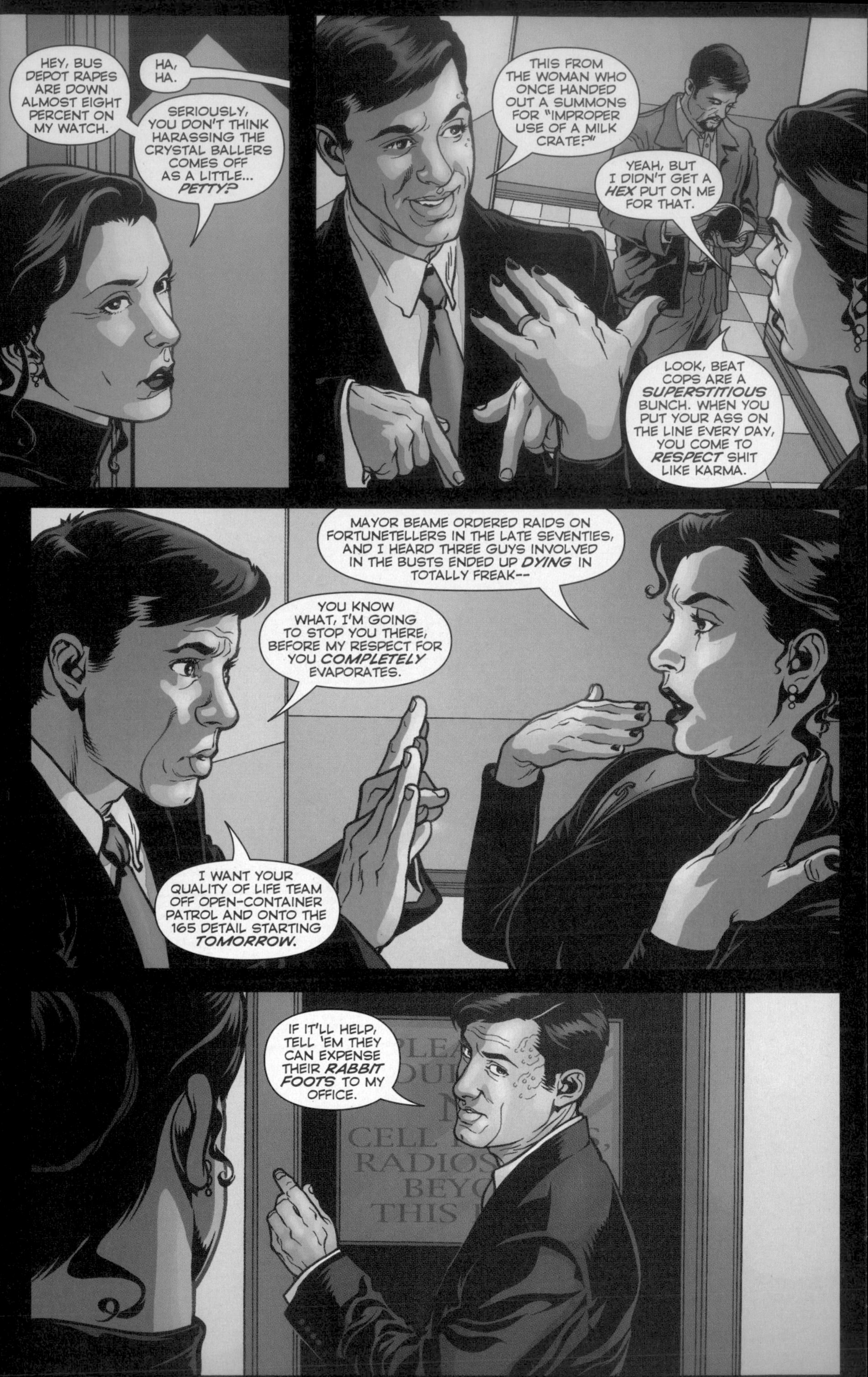
HEY, BUS DEPOT RAPES ARE DOWN ALMOST EIGHT PERCENT ON MY WATCH.
HA, HA.
SERIOUSLY, YOU DON'T THINK HARASSING THE CRYSTAL BALLERS COMES OFF AS A LITTLE... PETTY?
THIS FROM THE WOMAN WHO ONCE HANDED OUT A SUMMONS FOR "IMPROPER USE OF A MILK CRATE?"
YEAH, BUT I DIDN'T GET A HEX PUT ON ME FOR THAT.
LOOK, BEAT COPS ARE A SUPERSTITIOUS BUNCH. WHEN YOU PUT YOUR ASS ON THE LINE EVERY DAY, YOU COME TO RESPECT SHIT LIKE KARMA.
MAYOR BEAME ORDERED RAIDS ON FORTUNETELLERS IN THE LATE SEVENTIES, AND I HEARD THREE GUYS INVOLVED IN THE BUSTS ENDED UP DYING IN TOTALLY FREAK--
YOU KNOW WHAT, I'M GOING TO STOP YOU THERE, BEFORE MY RESPECT FOR YOU COMPLETELY EVAPORATES.
I WANT YOUR QUALITY OF LIFE TEAM OFF OPEN-CONTAINER PATROL AND ONTO THE 165 DETAIL STARTING TOMORROW.
IF IT'LL HELP, TELL 'EM THEY CAN EXPENSE THEIR RABBIT FOOTS TO MY OFFICE.

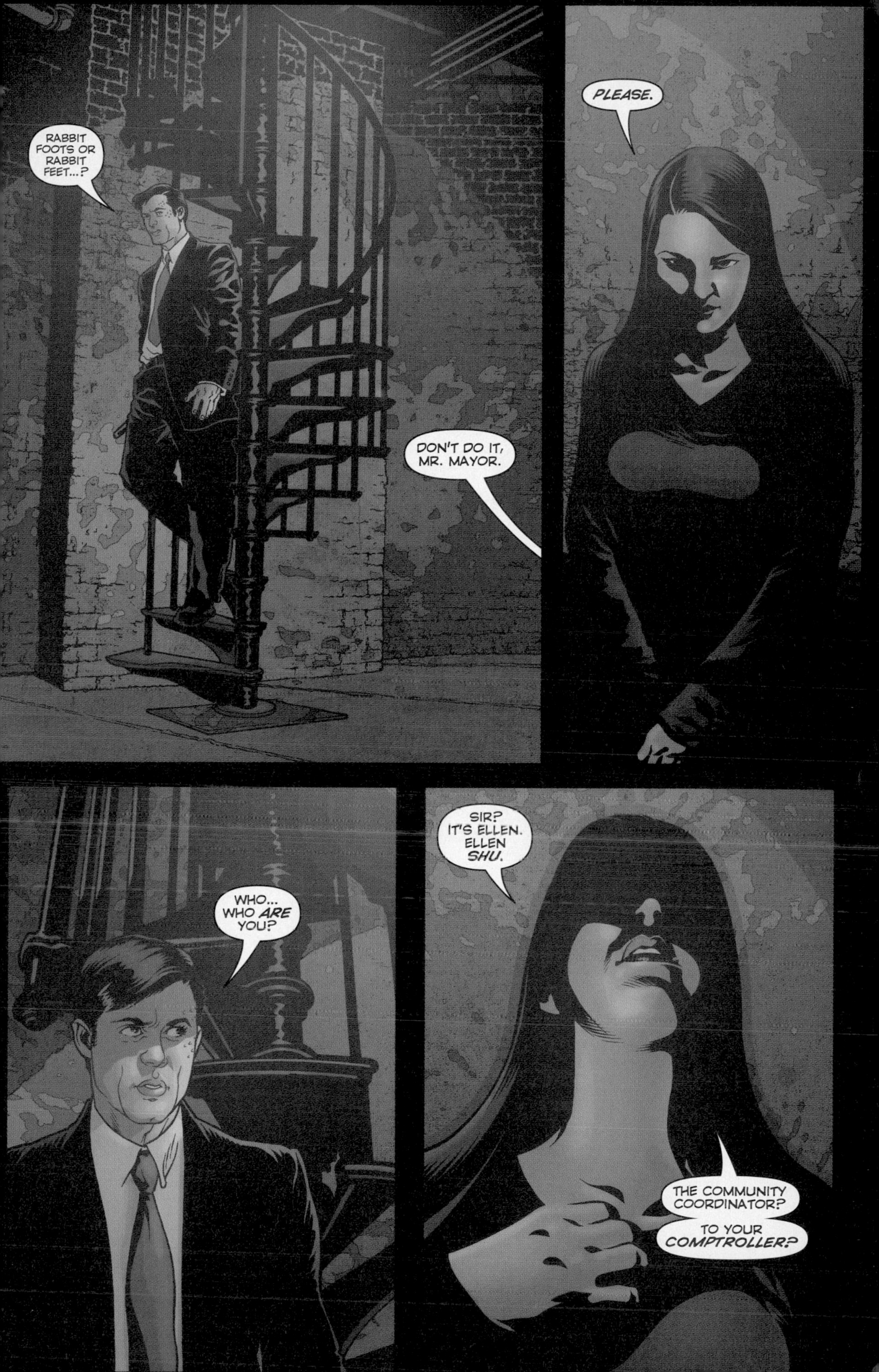
RABBIT FOOTS OR RABBIT FEET...?
PLEASE.
DON'T DO IT, MR. MAYOR.
SIR? IT'S ELLEN. ELLEN SHU.
WHO... WHO ARE YOU?
THE COMMUNITY COORDINATOR?
TO YOUR COMPTROLLER?

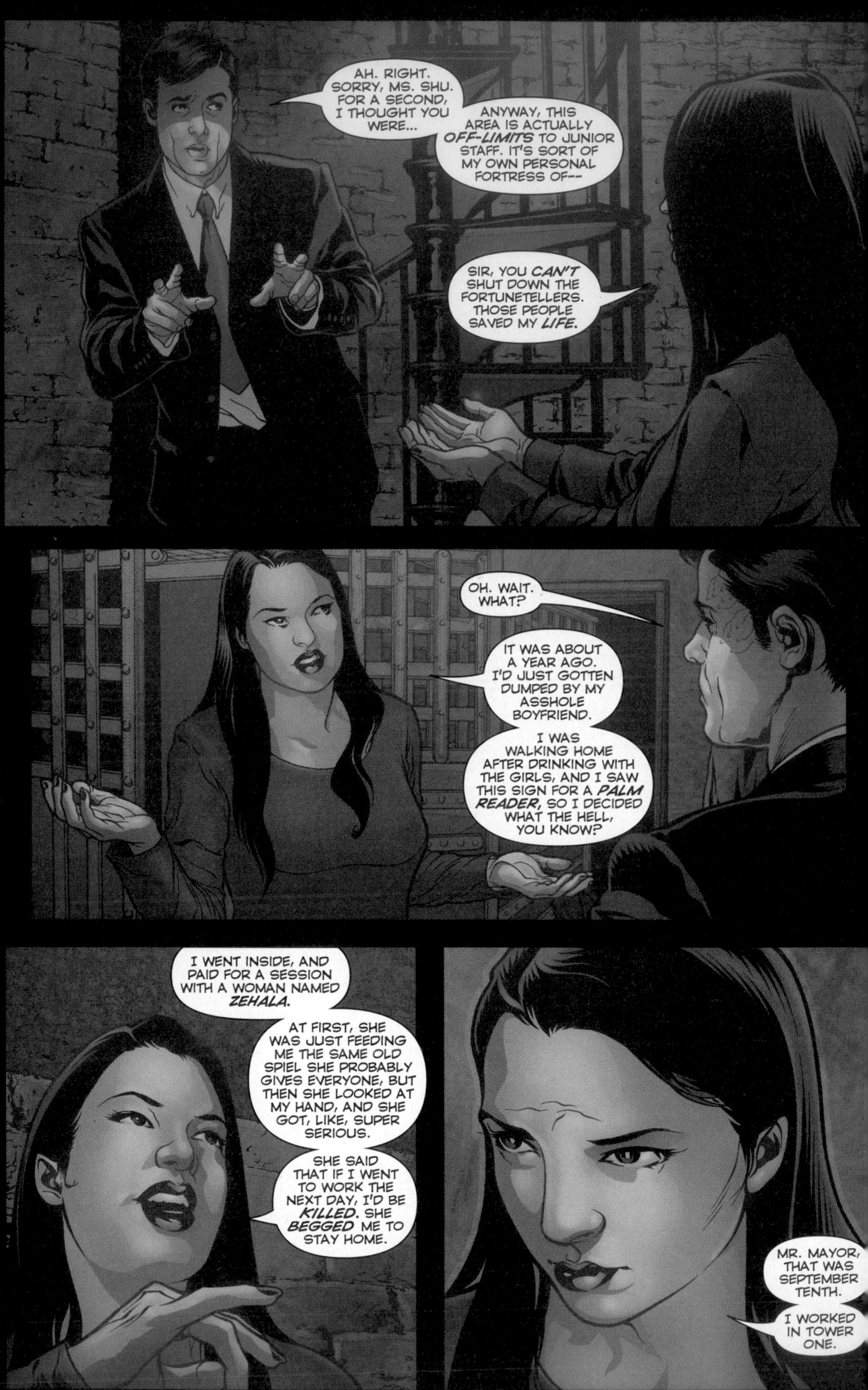
AH. RIGHT. SORRY, MS. SHU. FOR A SECOND, I THOUGHT YOU WERE...
ANYWAY, THIS AREA IS ACTUALLY *OFF-LIMITS* TO JUNIOR STAFF. IT'S SORT OF MY OWN PERSONAL FORTRESS OF--
SIR, YOU *CAN'T* SHUT DOWN THE FORTUNETELLERS. THOSE PEOPLE SAVED MY *LIFE*.
OH. WAIT. WHAT?
IT WAS ABOUT A YEAR AGO. I'D JUST GOTTEN DUMPED BY MY ASSHOLE BOYFRIEND.
I WAS WALKING HOME AFTER DRINKING WITH THE GIRLS, AND I SAW THIS SIGN FOR A *PALM READER*, SO I DECIDED WHAT THE HELL, YOU KNOW?
I WENT INSIDE, AND PAID FOR A SESSION WITH A WOMAN NAMED *ZEHALA*.
AT FIRST, SHE WAS JUST FEEDING ME THE SAME OLD SPIEL SHE PROBABLY GIVES EVERYONE, BUT THEN SHE LOOKED AT MY HAND, AND SHE GOT, LIKE, SUPER SERIOUS.
SHE SAID THAT IF I WENT TO WORK THE NEXT DAY, I'D BE *KILLED*. SHE *BEGGED* ME TO STAY HOME.
MR. MAYOR, THAT WAS SEPTEMBER TENTH.
I WORKED IN TOWER ONE.

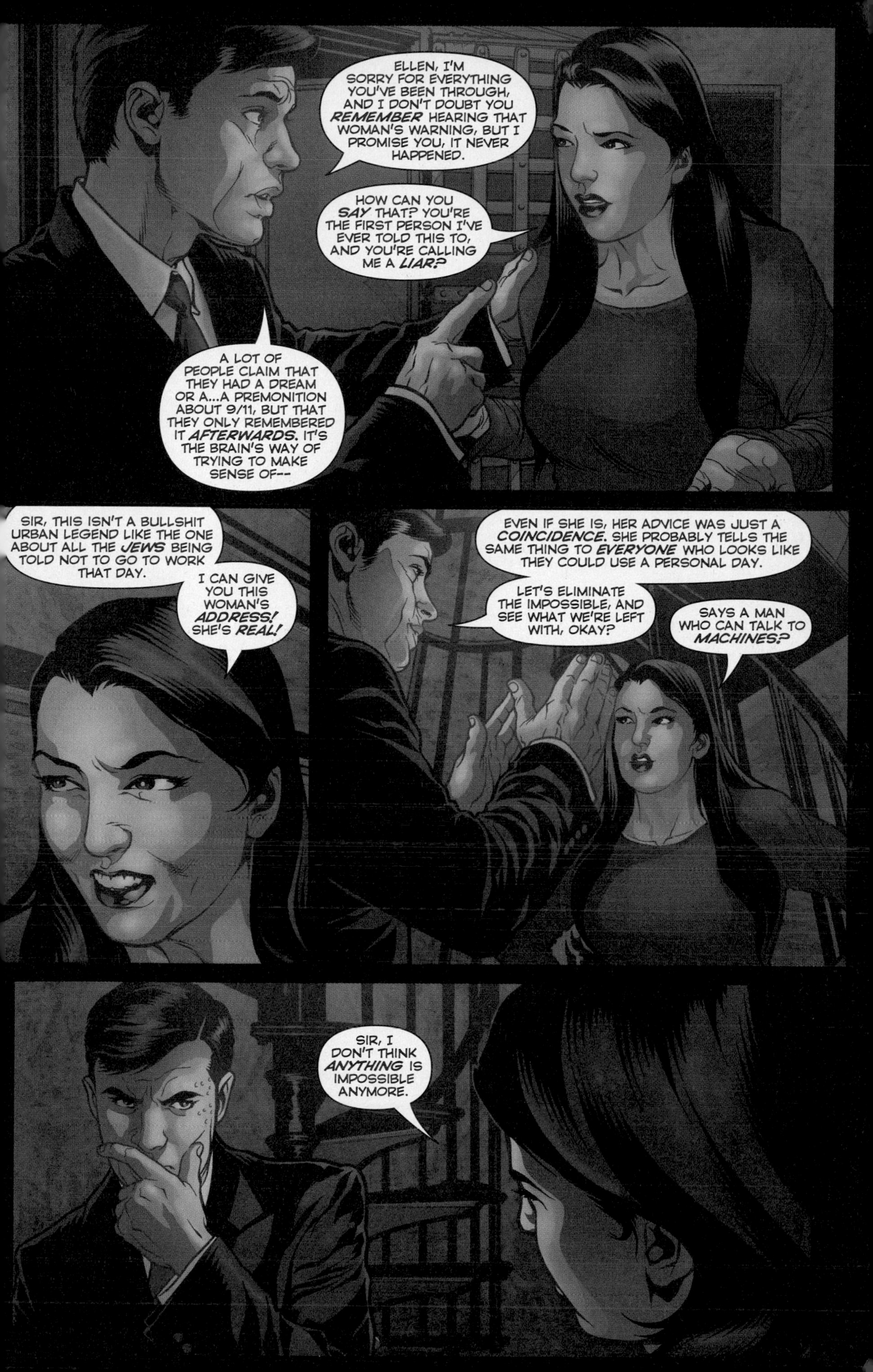
ELLEN, I'M SORRY FOR EVERYTHING YOU'VE BEEN THROUGH, AND I DON'T DOUBT YOU *REMEMBER* HEARING THAT WOMAN'S WARNING, BUT I PROMISE YOU, IT NEVER HAPPENED.
HOW CAN YOU *SAY* THAT? YOU'RE THE FIRST PERSON I'VE EVER TOLD THIS TO, AND YOU'RE CALLING ME A *LIAR?*
A LOT OF PEOPLE CLAIM THAT THEY HAD A DREAM OR A...A PREMONITION ABOUT 9/11, BUT THAT THEY ONLY REMEMBERED IT *AFTERWARDS.* IT'S THE BRAIN'S WAY OF TRYING TO MAKE SENSE OF--
SIR, THIS ISN'T A BULLSHIT URBAN LEGEND LIKE THE ONE ABOUT ALL THE *JEWS* BEING TOLD NOT TO GO TO WORK THAT DAY.
I CAN GIVE YOU THIS WOMAN'S *ADDRESS!* SHE'S *REAL!*
EVEN IF SHE IS, HER ADVICE WAS JUST A *COINCIDENCE.* SHE PROBABLY TELLS THE SAME THING TO *EVERYONE* WHO LOOKS LIKE THEY COULD USE A PERSONAL DAY.
LET'S ELIMINATE THE IMPOSSIBLE, AND SEE WHAT WE'RE LEFT WITH, OKAY?
SAYS A MAN WHO CAN TALK TO *MACHINES?*
SIR, I DON'T THINK *ANYTHING* IS IMPOSSIBLE ANYMORE.

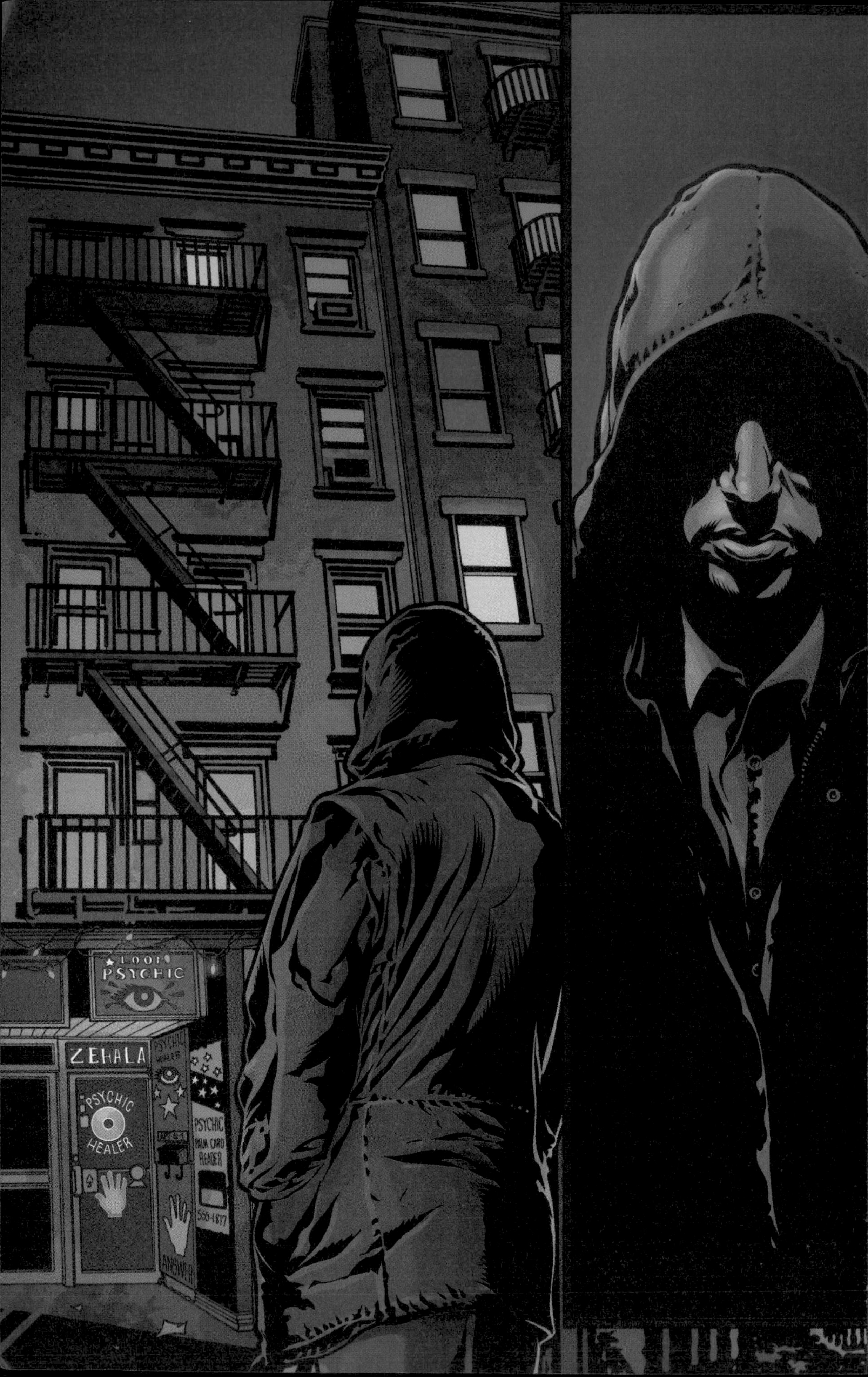
PSYCHIC
ZEHALA
PSYCHIC HEALER
PSYCHIC
PSYCHIC
PALM CARD
READER
555-1817

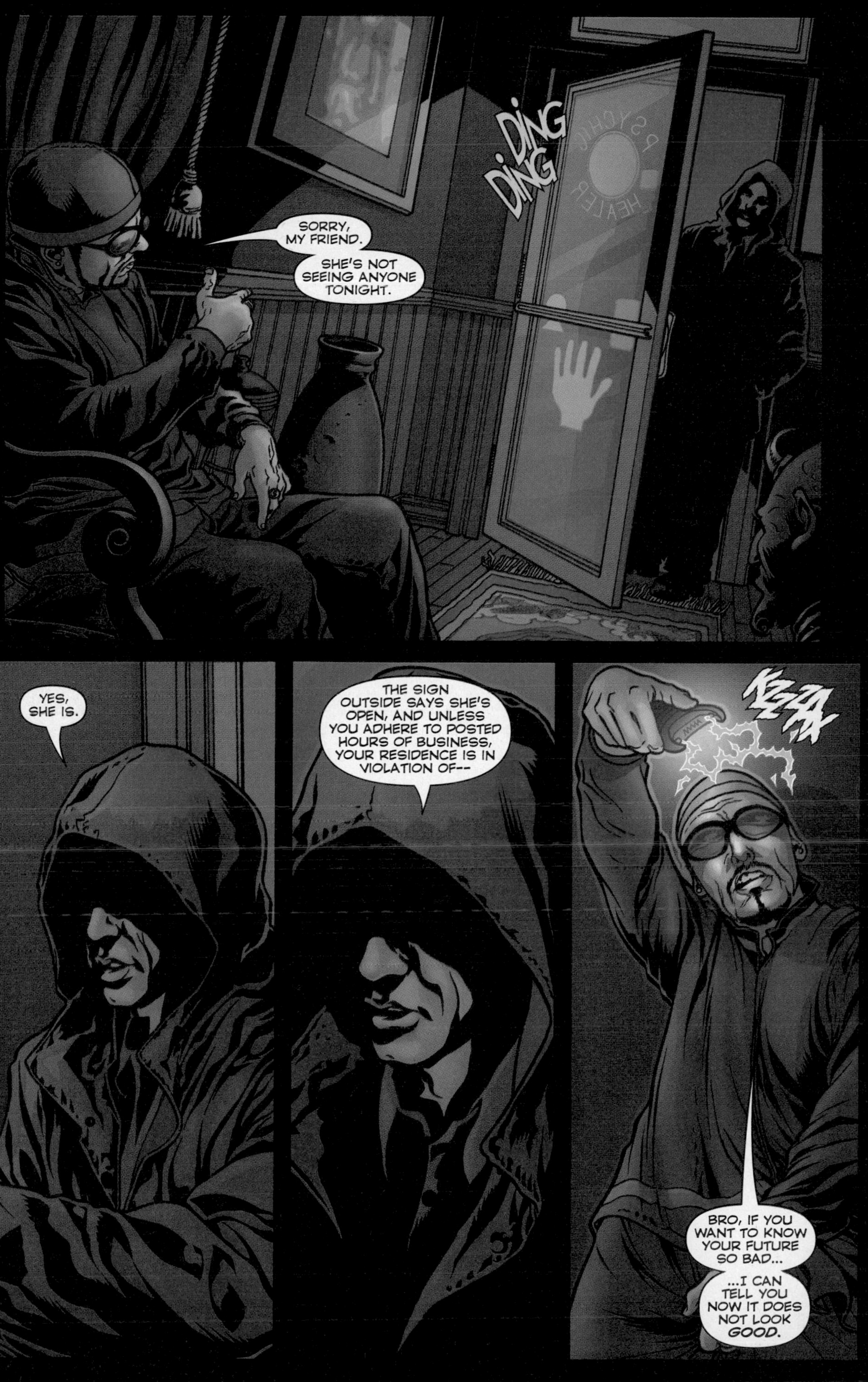
DING DING
SORRY, MY FRIEND.
SHE'S NOT SEEING ANYONE TONIGHT.
YES, SHE IS.
THE SIGN OUTSIDE SAYS SHE'S OPEN, AND UNLESS YOU ADHERE TO POSTED HOURS OF BUSINESS, YOUR RESIDENCE IS IN VIOLATION OF--
KZZAK
BRO, IF YOU WANT TO KNOW YOUR FUTURE SO BAD...
...I CAN TELL YOU NOW IT DOES NOT LOOK GOOD.

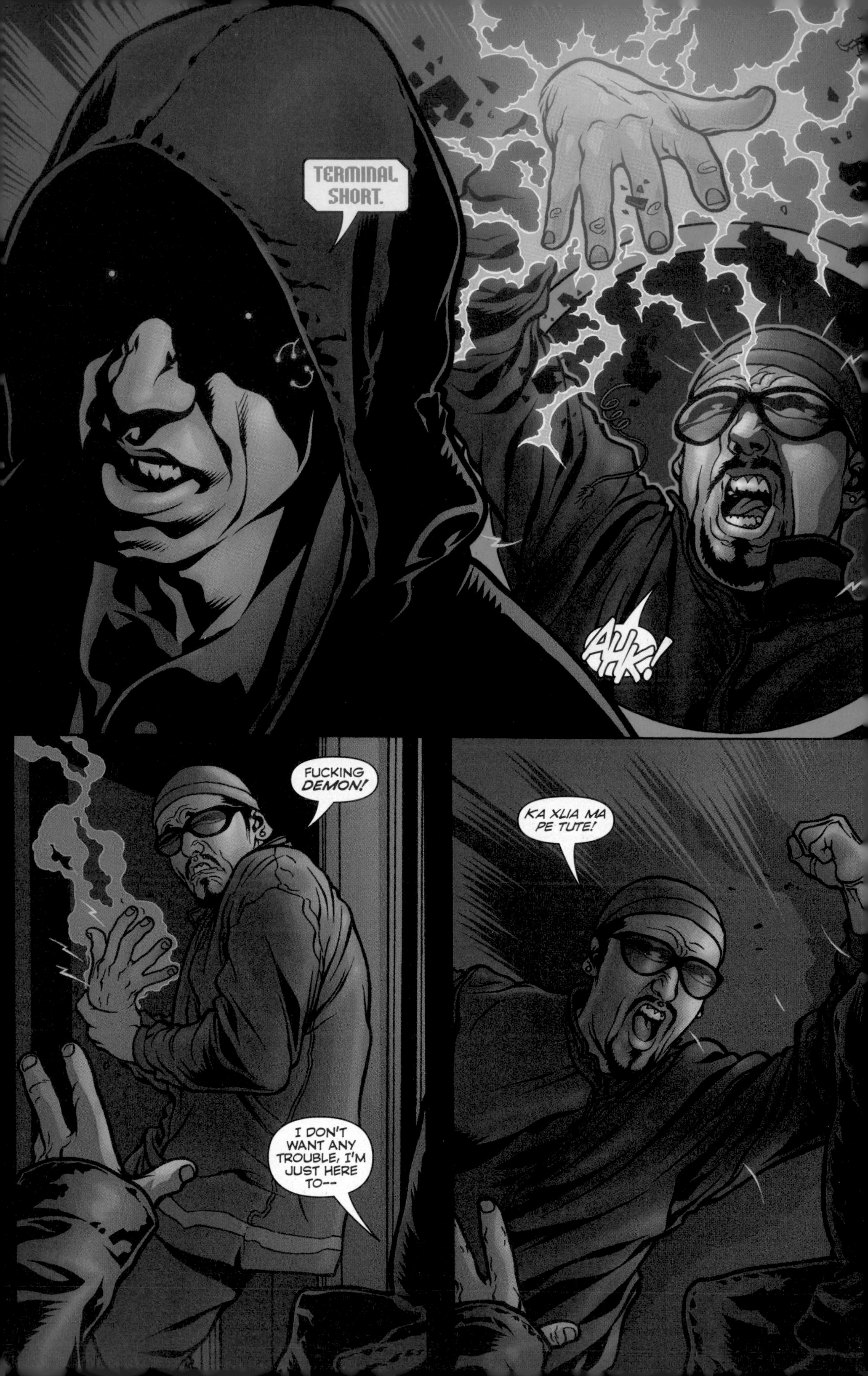
TERMINAL SHORT.
AHK!
FUCKING *DEMON!*
I DON'T WANT ANY TROUBLE, I'M JUST HERE TO--
KA XLIA MA PE TUTE!

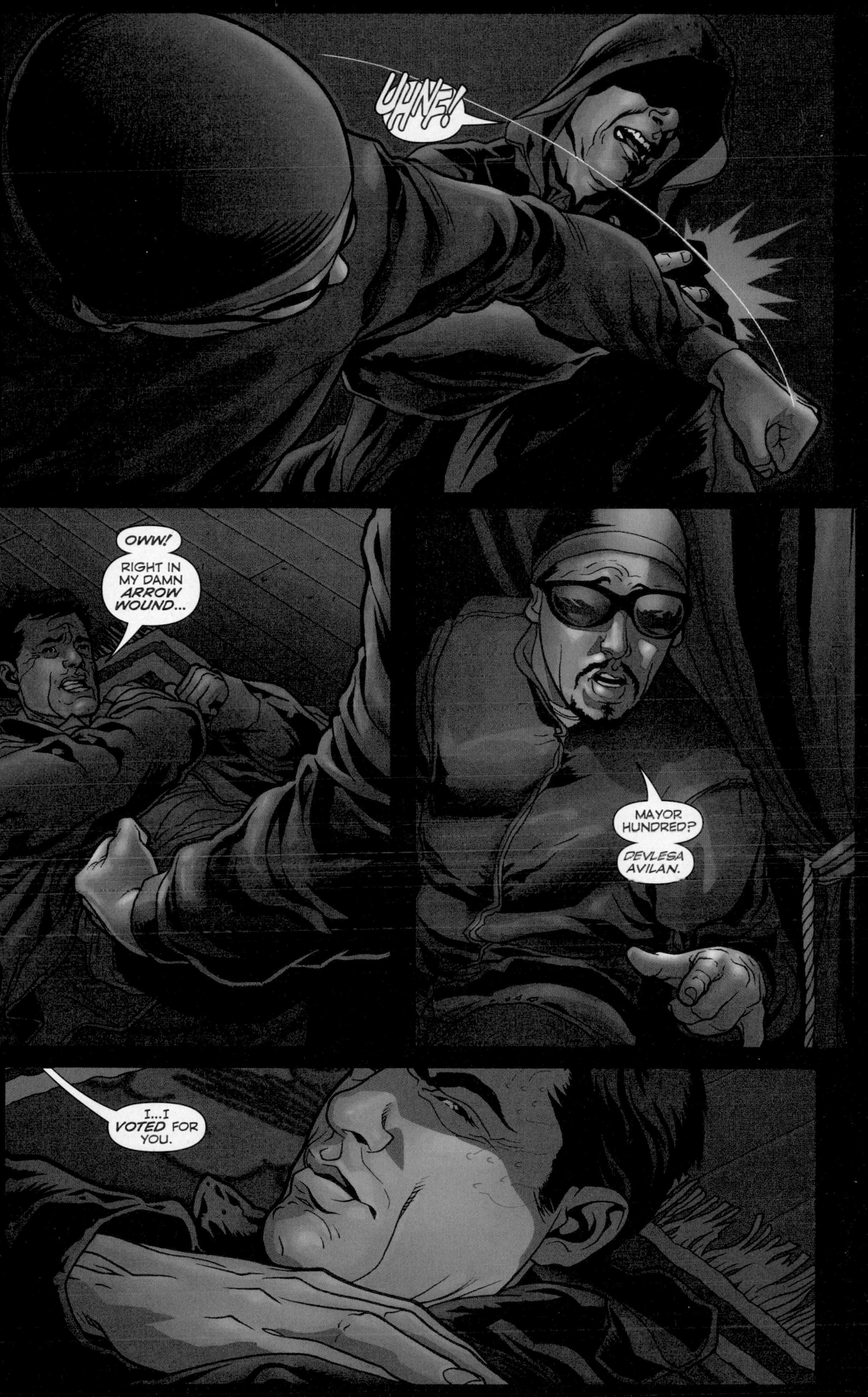

UHNF!
OWW!
RIGHT IN MY DAMN ARROW WOUND...
MAYOR HUNDRED?
DEVLESA AVILAN.
I...I VOTED FOR YOU.

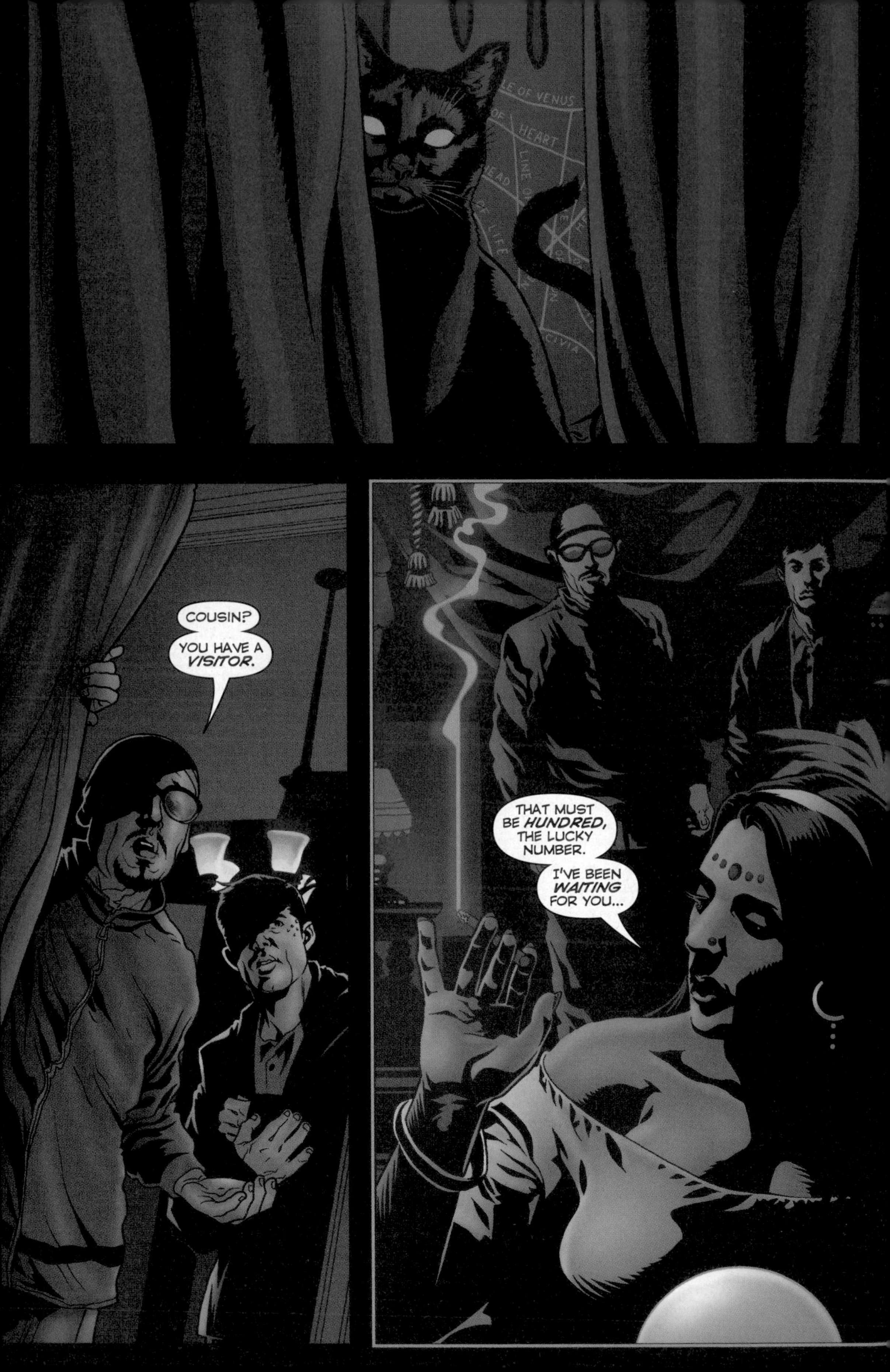
COUSIN?
YOU HAVE A *VISITOR*.
THAT MUST BE *HUNDRED*, THE LUCKY NUMBER.
I'VE BEEN *WAITING* FOR YOU...

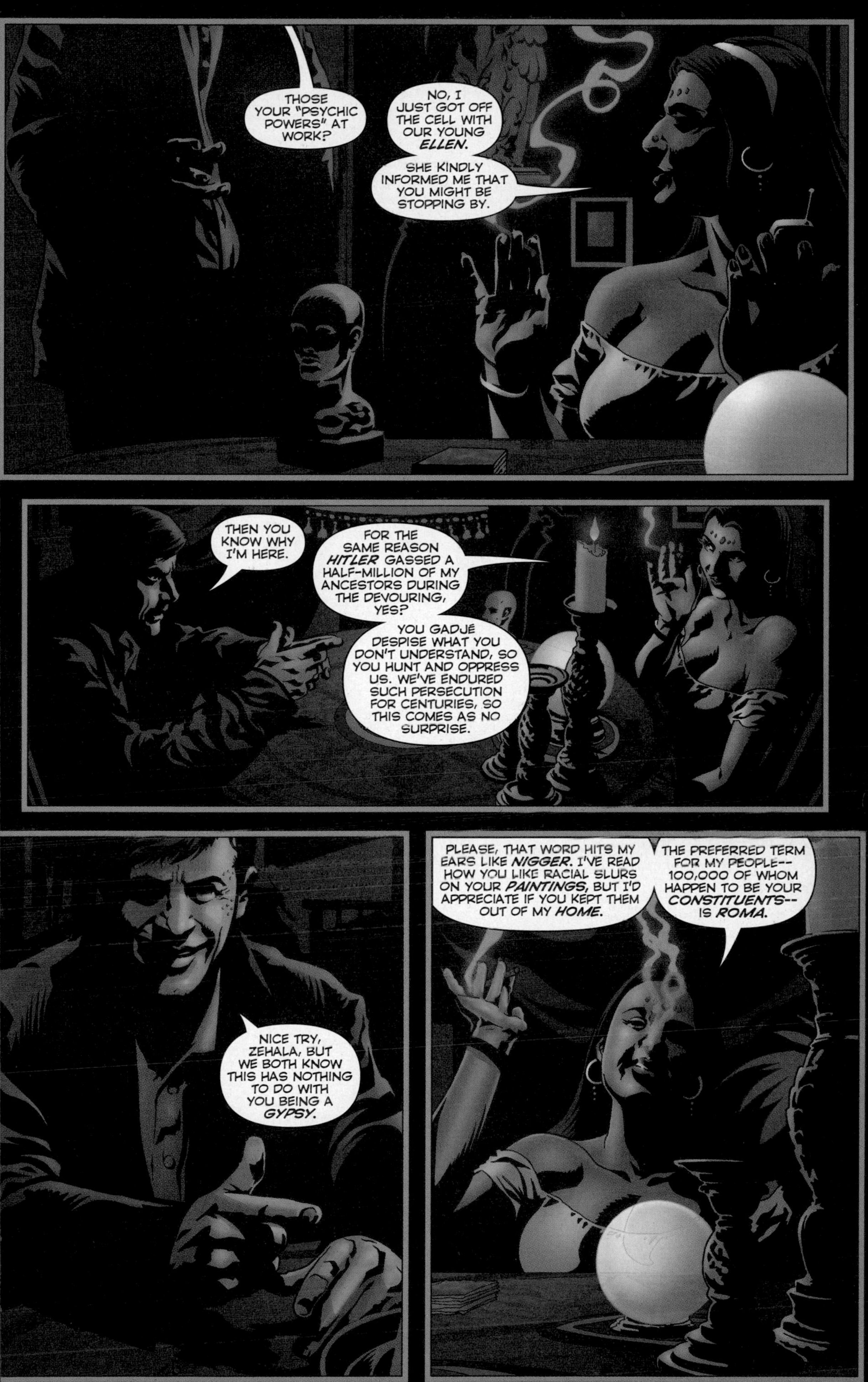
THOSE YOUR "PSYCHIC POWERS" AT WORK?
NO, I JUST GOT OFF THE CELL WITH OUR YOUNG *ELLEN*.
SHE KINDLY INFORMED ME THAT YOU MIGHT BE STOPPING BY.
THEN YOU KNOW WHY I'M HERE.
FOR THE SAME REASON *HITLER* GASSED A HALF-MILLION OF MY ANCESTORS DURING THE DEVOURING, YES?
YOU GADJÉ DESPISE WHAT YOU DON'T UNDERSTAND, SO YOU HUNT AND OPPRESS US. WE'VE ENDURED SUCH PERSECUTION FOR CENTURIES, SO THIS COMES AS NO SURPRISE.
NICE TRY, ZEHALA, BUT WE BOTH KNOW THIS HAS NOTHING TO DO WITH YOU BEING A *GYPSY*.
PLEASE, THAT WORD HITS MY EARS LIKE *NIGGER*. I'VE READ HOW YOU LIKE RACIAL SLURS ON YOUR *PAINTINGS*, BUT I'D APPRECIATE IF YOU KEPT THEM OUT OF MY *HOME*.
THE PREFERRED TERM FOR MY PEOPLE-- 100,000 OF WHOM HAPPEN TO BE YOUR *CONSTITUENTS*-- IS *ROMA*.

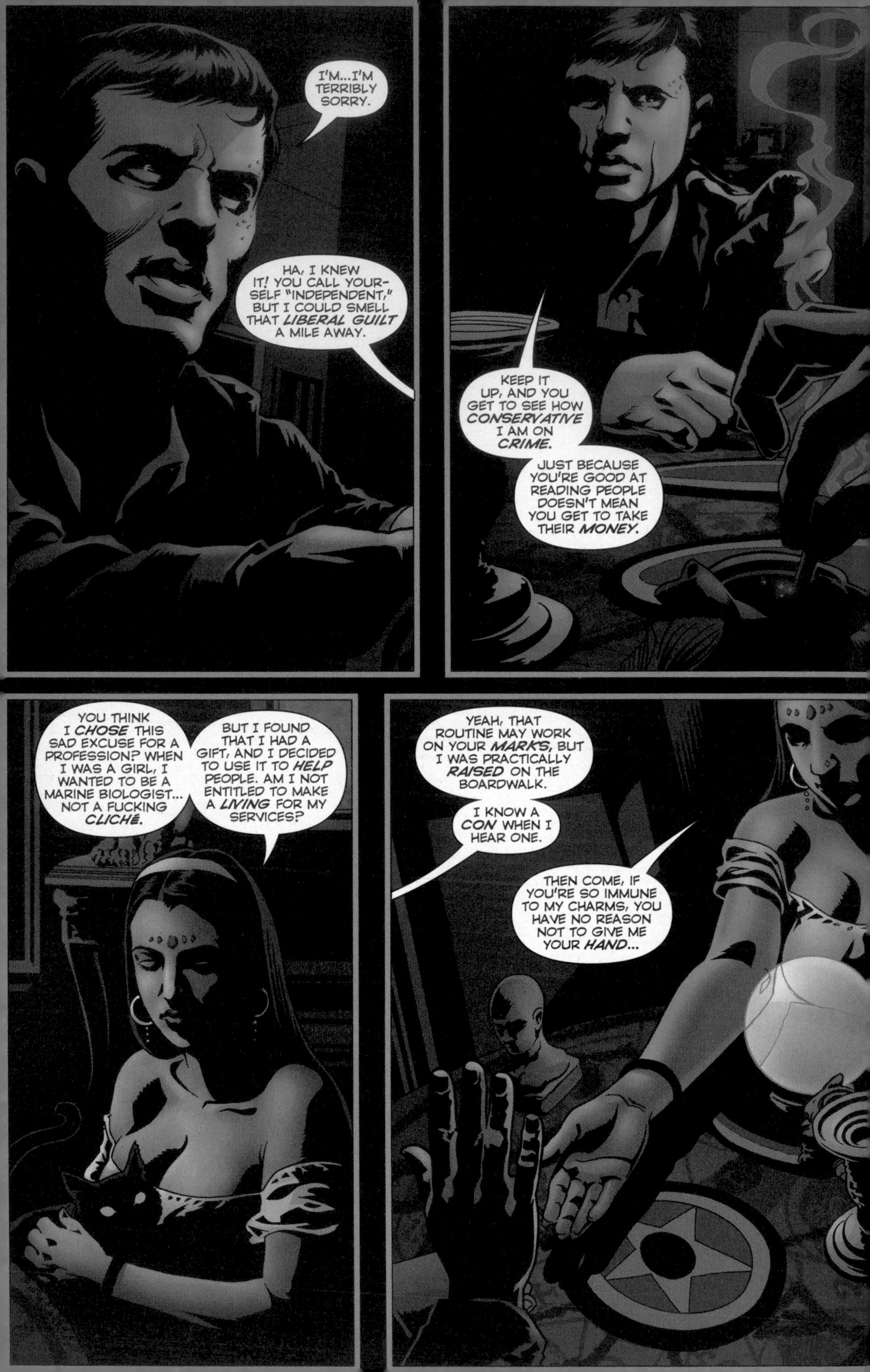

I'M...I'M TERRIBLY SORRY.
HA, I KNEW IT! YOU CALL YOURSELF "INDEPENDENT," BUT I COULD SMELL THAT LIBERAL GUILT A MILE AWAY.
KEEP IT UP, AND YOU GET TO SEE HOW CONSERVATIVE I AM ON CRIME.
JUST BECAUSE YOU'RE GOOD AT READING PEOPLE DOESN'T MEAN YOU GET TO TAKE THEIR MONEY.
YOU THINK I CHOSE THIS SAD EXCUSE FOR A PROFESSION? WHEN I WAS A GIRL, I WANTED TO BE A MARINE BIOLOGIST... NOT A FUCKING CLICHÉ.
BUT I FOUND THAT I HAD A GIFT, AND I DECIDED TO USE IT TO HELP PEOPLE. AM I NOT ENTITLED TO MAKE A LIVING FOR MY SERVICES?
YEAH, THAT ROUTINE MAY WORK ON YOUR MARKS, BUT I WAS PRACTICALLY RAISED ON THE BOARDWALK.
I KNOW A CON WHEN I HEAR ONE.
THEN COME, IF YOU'RE SO IMMUNE TO MY CHARMS, YOU HAVE NO REASON NOT TO GIVE ME YOUR HAND...

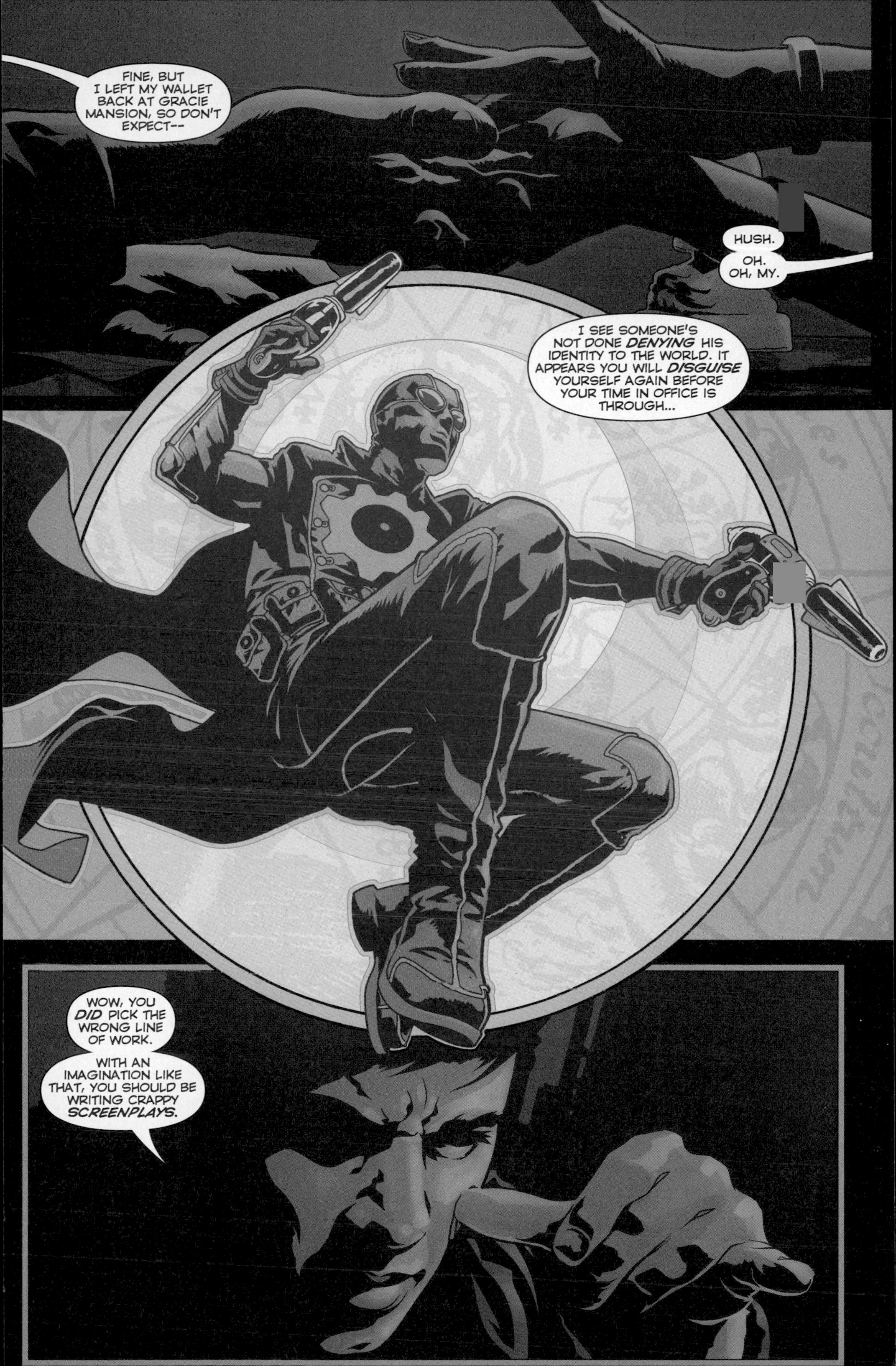
FINE, BUT I LEFT MY WALLET BACK AT GRACIE MANSION, SO DON'T EXPECT--
HUSH.
OH. OH, MY.
I SEE SOMEONE'S NOT DONE *DENYING* HIS IDENTITY TO THE WORLD. IT APPEARS YOU WILL *DISGUISE* YOURSELF AGAIN BEFORE YOUR TIME IN OFFICE IS THROUGH...
WOW, YOU *DID* PICK THE WRONG LINE OF WORK.
WITH AN IMAGINATION LIKE THAT, YOU SHOULD BE WRITING CRAPPY *SCREENPLAYS*.

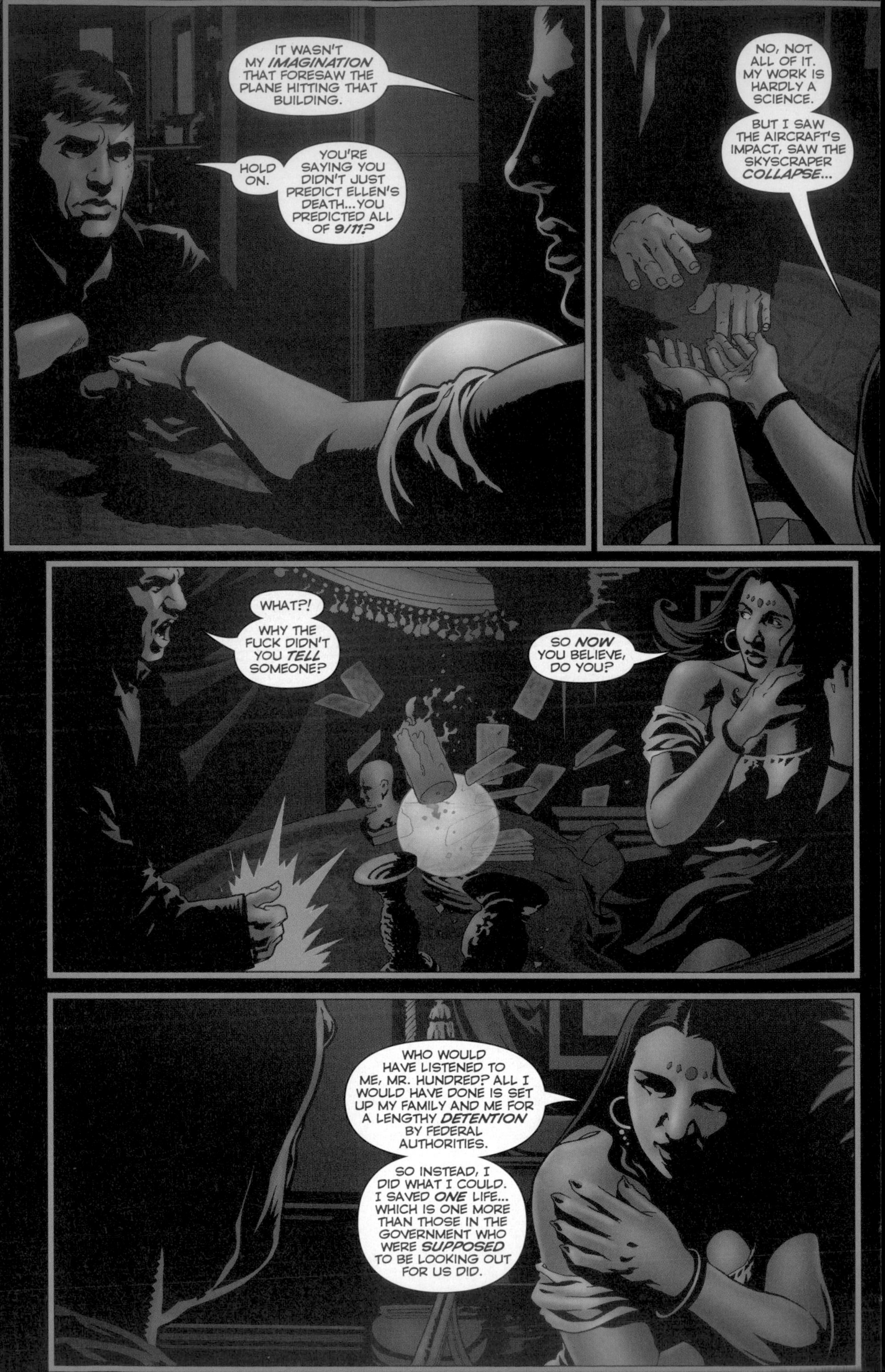
IT WASN'T MY IMAGINATION THAT FORESAW THE PLANE HITTING THAT BUILDING.
HOLD ON.
YOU'RE SAYING YOU DIDN'T JUST PREDICT ELLEN'S DEATH...YOU PREDICTED ALL OF 9/11?
NO, NOT ALL OF IT. MY WORK IS HARDLY A SCIENCE.
BUT I SAW THE AIRCRAFT'S IMPACT, SAW THE SKYSCRAPER COLLAPSE...
WHAT?!
WHY THE FUCK DIDN'T YOU TELL SOMEONE?
SO NOW YOU BELIEVE, DO YOU?
WHO WOULD HAVE LISTENED TO ME, MR. HUNDRED? ALL I WOULD HAVE DONE IS SET UP MY FAMILY AND ME FOR A LENGTHY DETENTION BY FEDERAL AUTHORITIES.
SO INSTEAD, I DID WHAT I COULD. I SAVED ONE LIFE... WHICH IS ONE MORE THAN THOSE IN THE GOVERNMENT WHO WERE SUPPOSED TO BE LOOKING OUT FOR US DID.

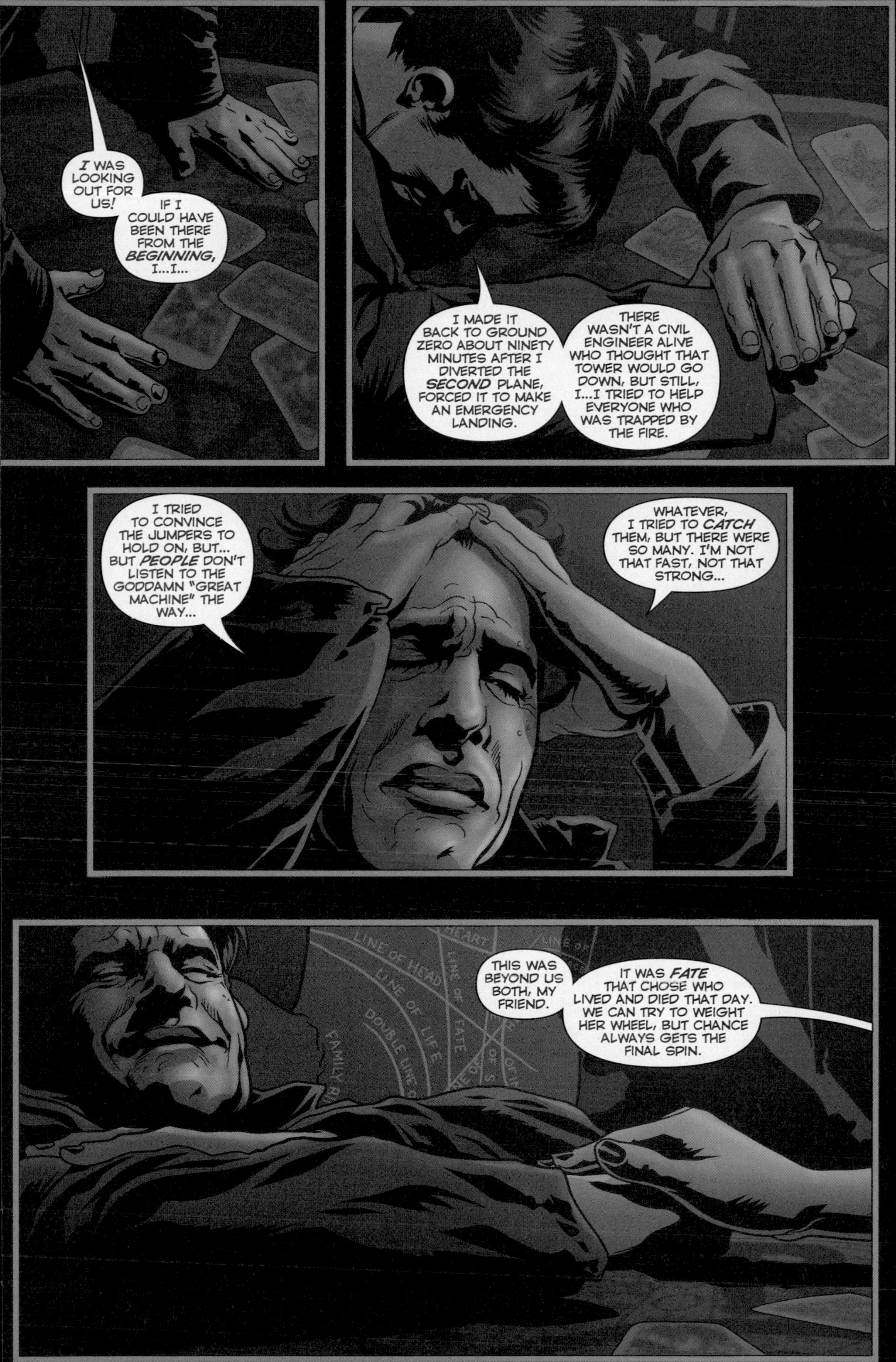
I WAS LOOKING OUT FOR US!
IF I COULD HAVE BEEN THERE FROM THE BEGINNING, I...I...
I MADE IT BACK TO GROUND ZERO ABOUT NINETY MINUTES AFTER I DIVERTED THE SECOND PLANE, FORCED IT TO MAKE AN EMERGENCY LANDING.
THERE WASN'T A CIVIL ENGINEER ALIVE WHO THOUGHT THAT TOWER WOULD GO DOWN, BUT STILL, I...I TRIED TO HELP EVERYONE WHO WAS TRAPPED BY THE FIRE.
I TRIED TO CONVINCE THE JUMPERS TO HOLD ON, BUT... BUT PEOPLE DON'T LISTEN TO THE GODDAMN "GREAT MACHINE" THE WAY...
WHATEVER, I TRIED TO CATCH THEM, BUT THERE WERE SO MANY. I'M NOT THAT FAST, NOT THAT STRONG...
HEART
LINE OF HEAD
LINE OF FATE
LINE OF LIFE
DOUBLE LINE OF LIFE
THIS WAS BEYOND US BOTH, MY FRIEND.
IT WAS FATE THAT CHOSE WHO LIVED AND DIED THAT DAY. WE CAN TRY TO WEIGHT HER WHEEL, BUT CHANCE ALWAYS GETS THE FINAL SPIN.

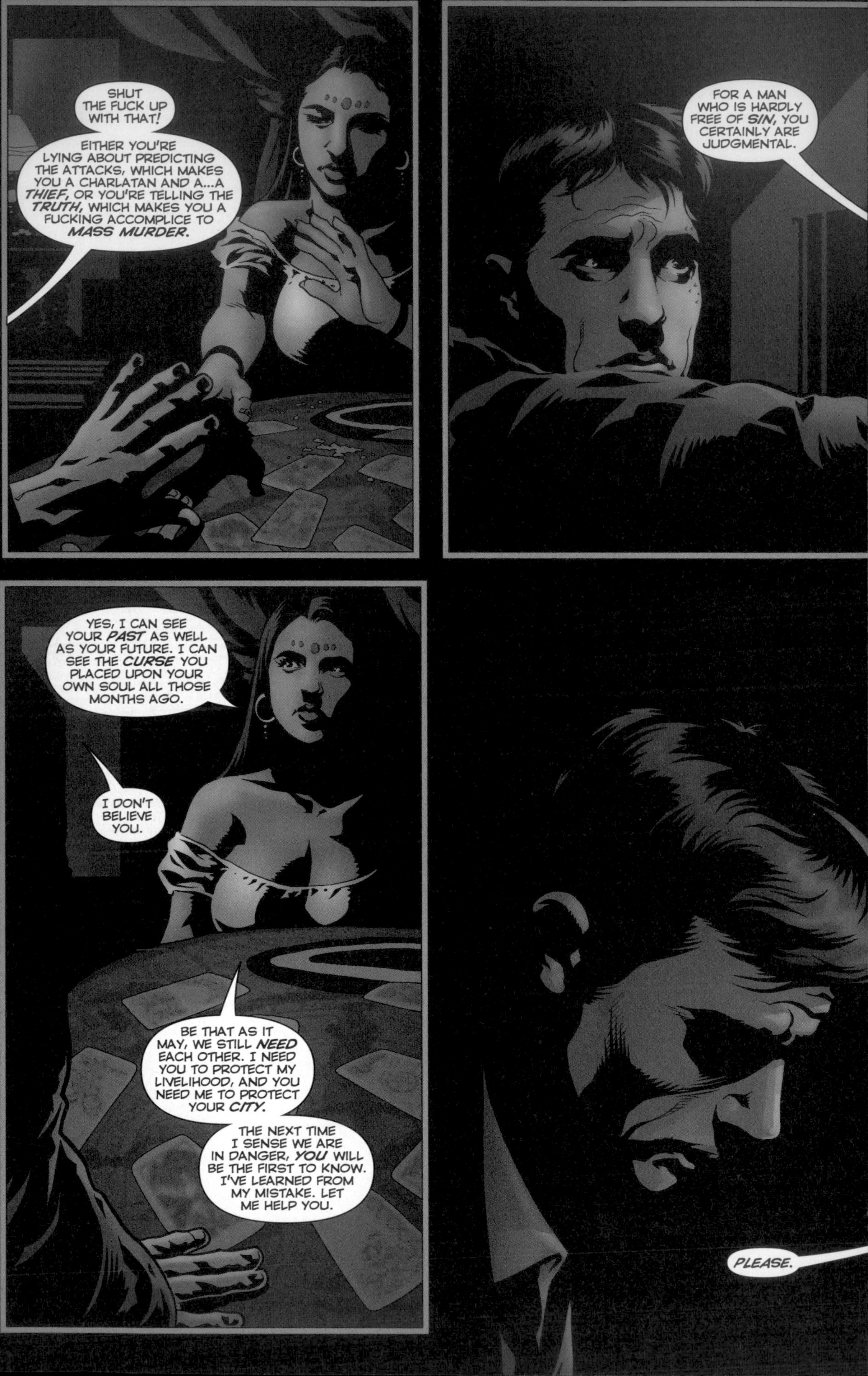
SHUT THE FUCK UP WITH THAT!
EITHER YOU'RE LYING ABOUT PREDICTING THE ATTACKS, WHICH MAKES YOU A CHARLATAN AND A...A *THIEF*, OR YOU'RE TELLING THE *TRUTH*, WHICH MAKES YOU A FUCKING ACCOMPLICE TO *MASS MURDER*.
FOR A MAN WHO IS HARDLY FREE OF *SIN*, YOU CERTAINLY ARE JUDGMENTAL.
YES, I CAN SEE YOUR *PAST* AS WELL AS YOUR FUTURE. I CAN SEE THE *CURSE* YOU PLACED UPON YOUR OWN SOUL ALL THOSE MONTHS AGO.
I DON'T BELIEVE YOU.
BE THAT AS IT MAY, WE STILL *NEED* EACH OTHER. I NEED YOU TO PROTECT MY LIVELIHOOD, AND YOU NEED ME TO PROTECT YOUR *CITY*.
THE NEXT TIME I SENSE WE ARE IN DANGER, *YOU* WILL BE THE FIRST TO KNOW. I'VE LEARNED FROM MY MISTAKE. LET ME HELP YOU.
PLEASE.

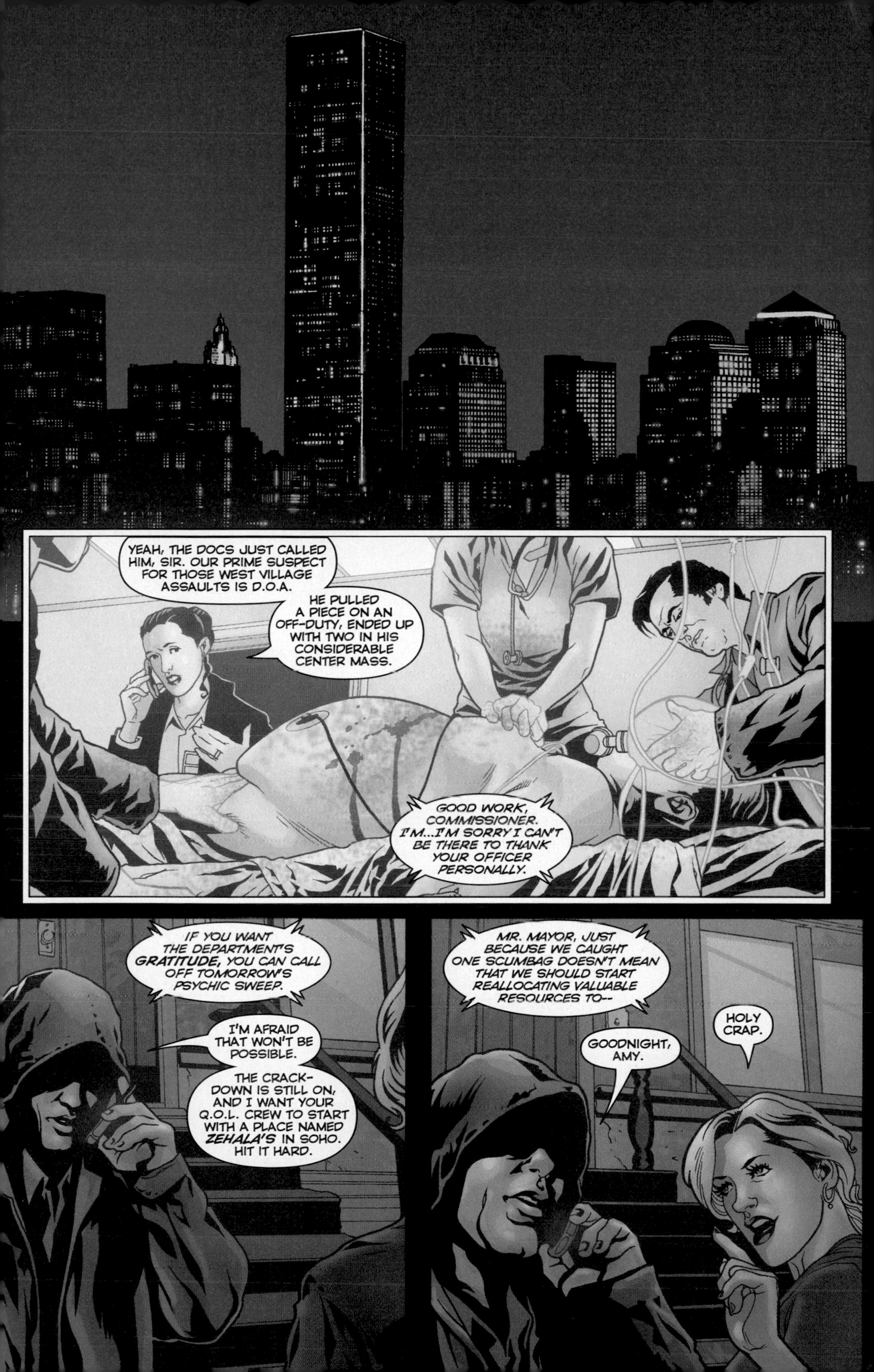
YEAH, THE DOCS JUST CALLED HIM, SIR. OUR PRIME SUSPECT FOR THOSE WEST VILLAGE ASSAULTS IS D.O.A.
HE PULLED A PIECE ON AN OFF-DUTY, ENDED UP WITH TWO IN HIS CONSIDERABLE CENTER MASS.
GOOD WORK, COMMISSIONER. I'M...I'M SORRY I CAN'T BE THERE TO THANK YOUR OFFICER PERSONALLY.
IF YOU WANT THE DEPARTMENT'S GRATITUDE, YOU CAN CALL OFF TOMORROW'S PSYCHIC SWEEP.
I'M AFRAID THAT WON'T BE POSSIBLE.
THE CRACK-DOWN IS STILL ON, AND I WANT YOUR Q.O.L. CREW TO START WITH A PLACE NAMED ZEHALA'S IN SOHO. HIT IT HARD.
MR. MAYOR, JUST BECAUSE WE CAUGHT ONE SCUMBAG DOESN'T MEAN THAT WE SHOULD START REALLOCATING VALUABLE RESOURCES TO--
GOODNIGHT, AMY.
HOLY CRAP.

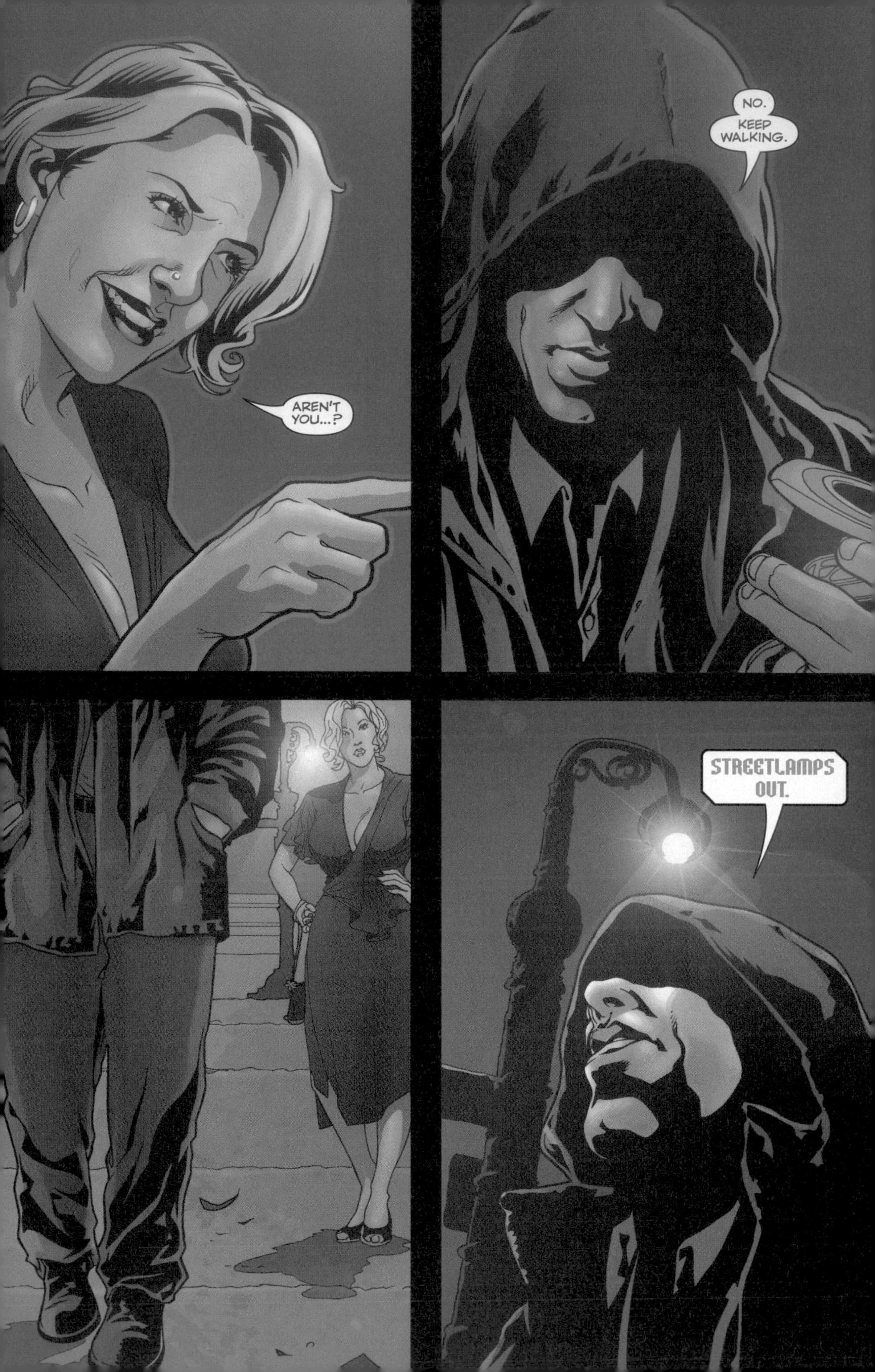
AREN'T YOU...?
NO. KEEP WALKING.
STREETLAMPS OUT.

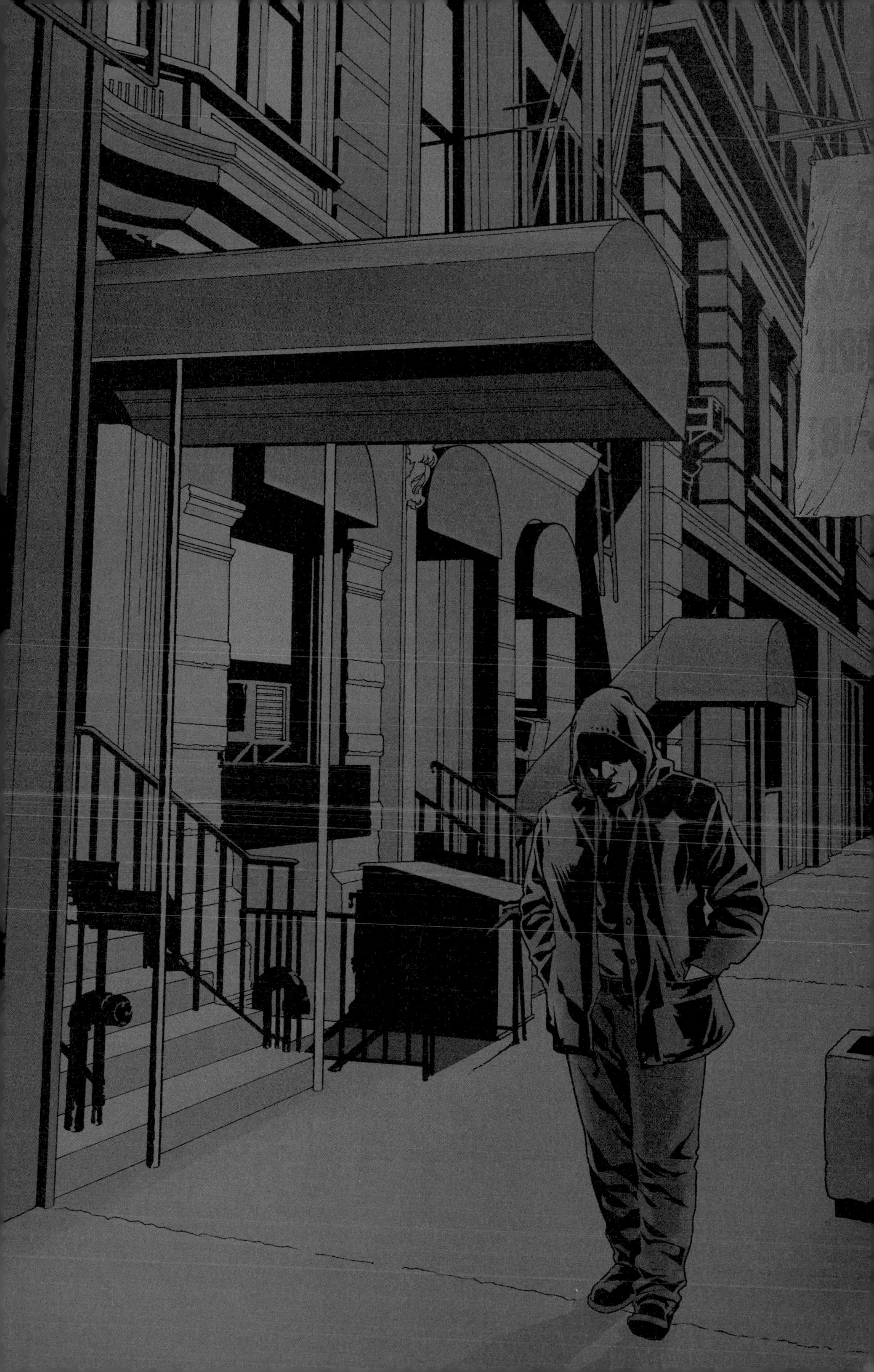

CHAPTER 2

Fact v. Fiction part 1

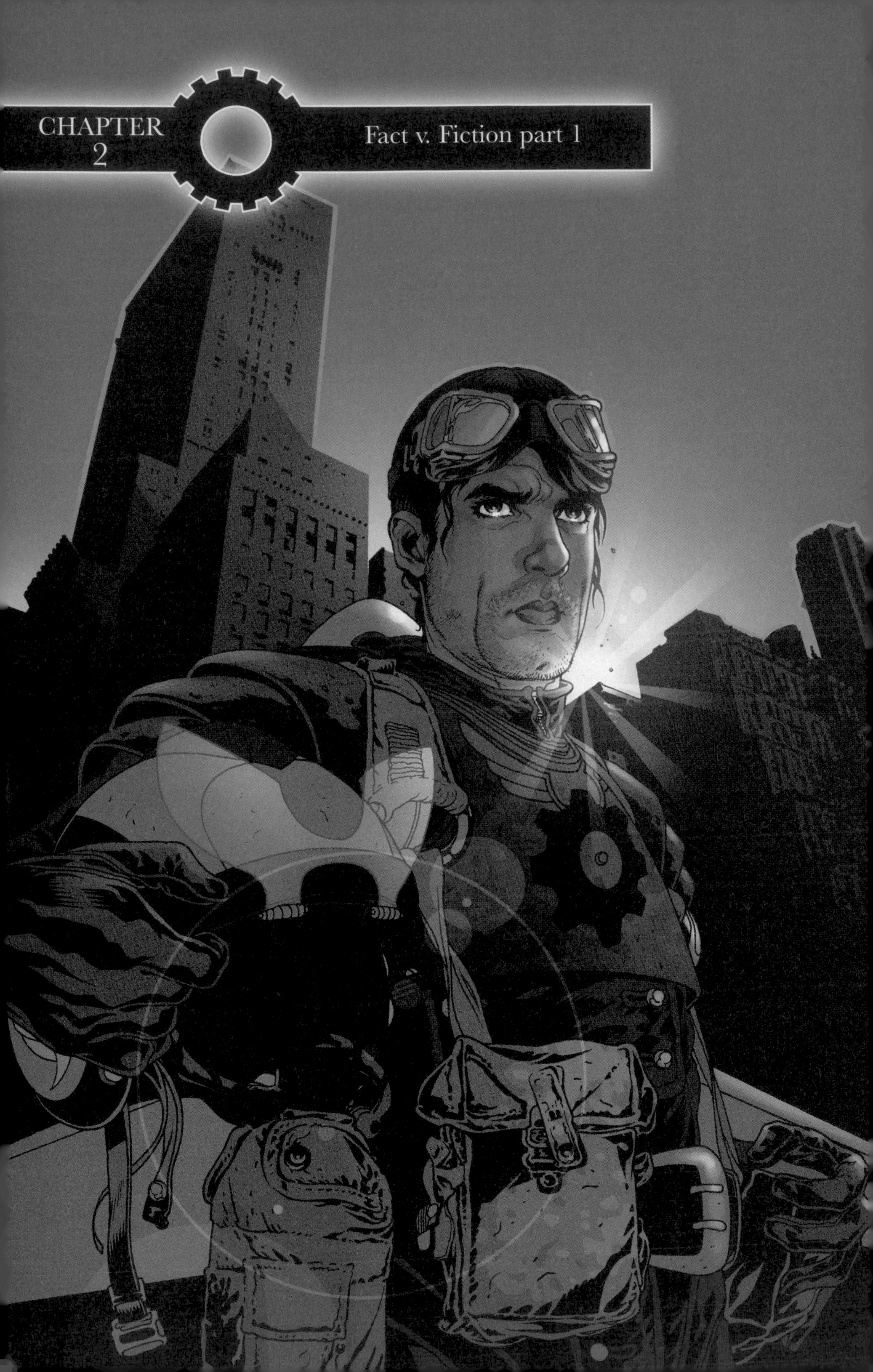

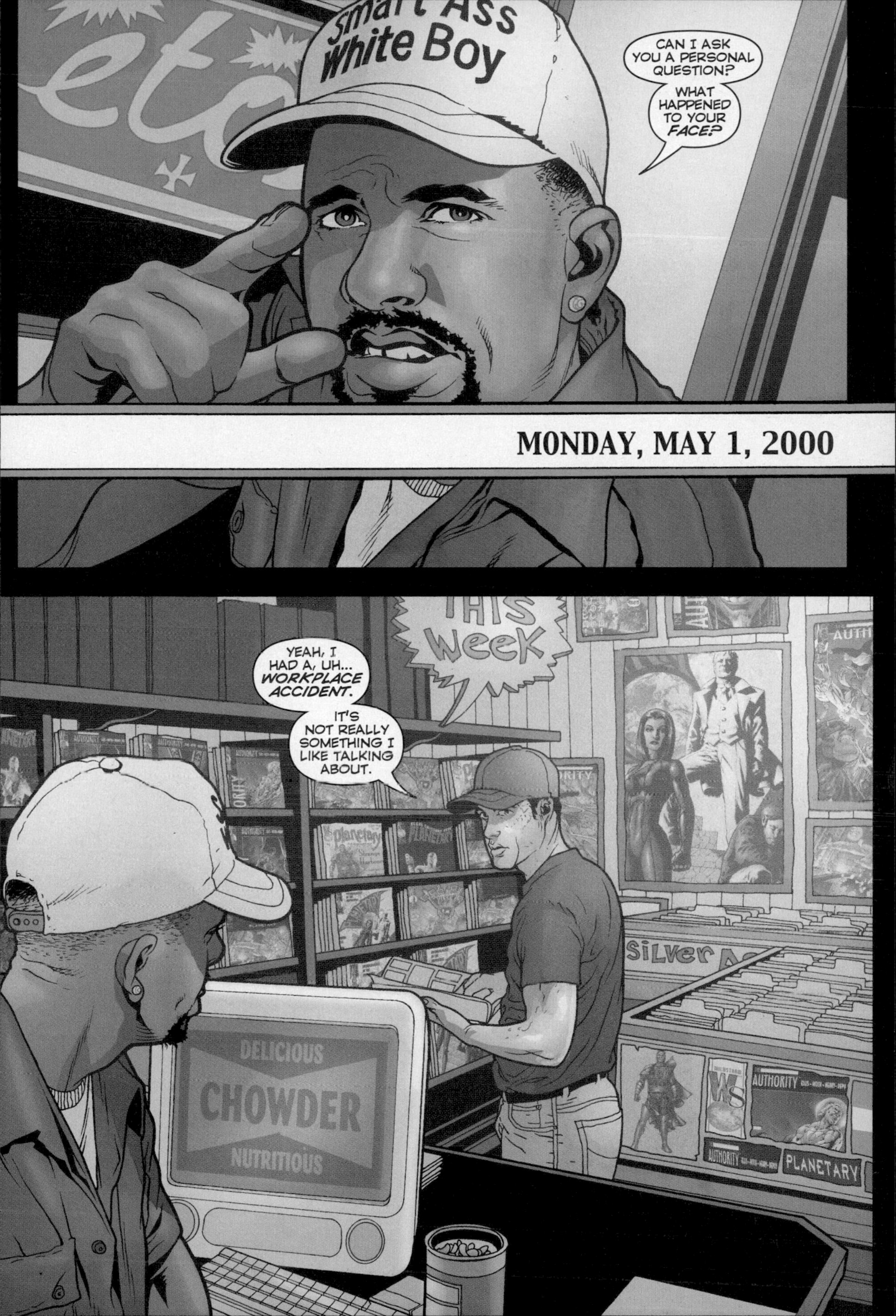
Smart Ass White Boy
CAN I ASK YOU A PERSONAL QUESTION?
WHAT HAPPENED TO YOUR *FACE?*
MONDAY, MAY 1, 2000
THIS week
YEAH, I HAD A, UH... *WORKPLACE ACCIDENT*.
IT'S NOT REALLY SOMETHING I LIKE TALKING ABOUT.
DELICIOUS
CHOWDER
NUTRITIOUS
AUTHORITY
PLANETARY

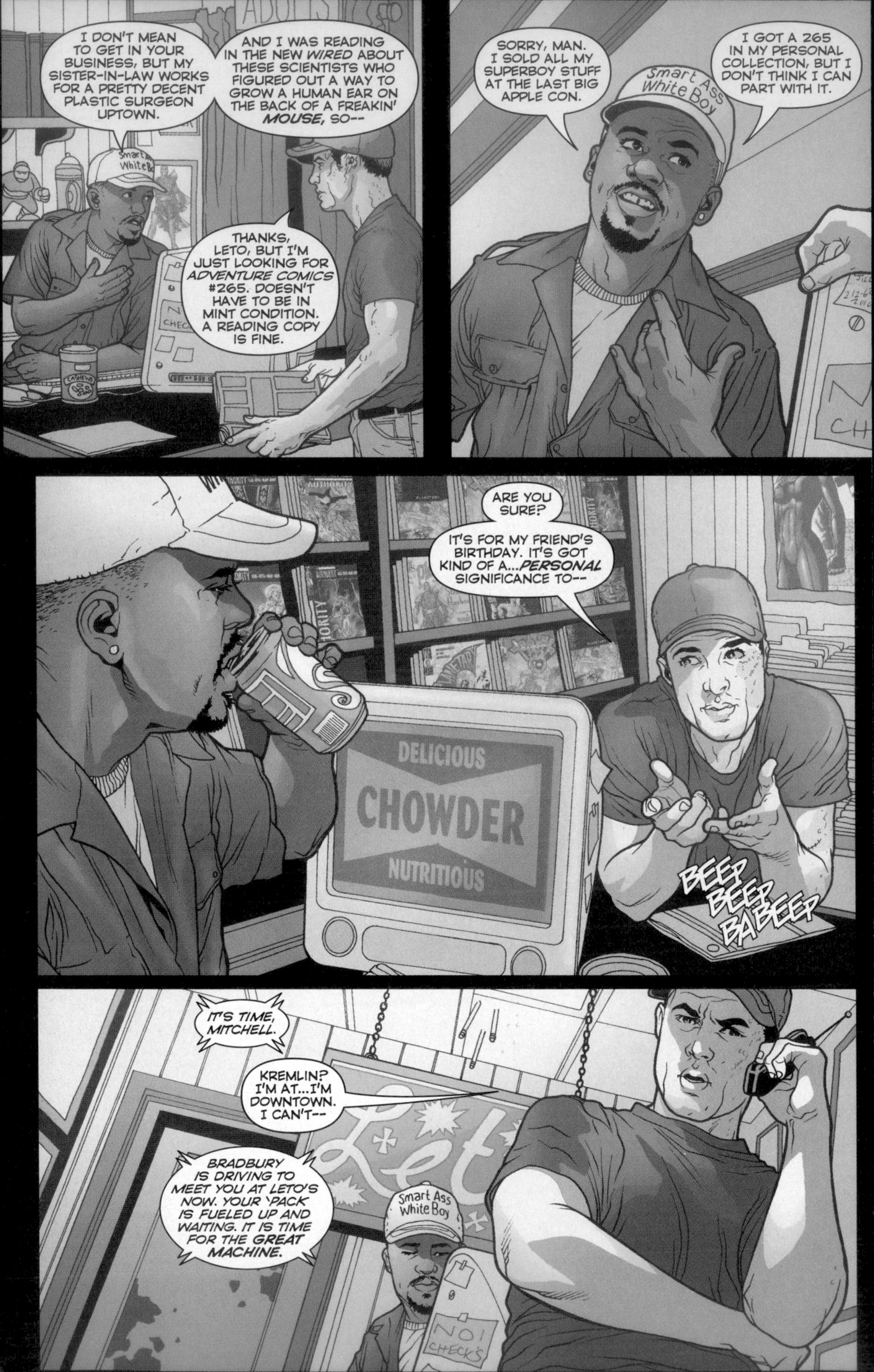
I DON'T MEAN TO GET IN YOUR BUSINESS, BUT MY SISTER-IN-LAW WORKS FOR A PRETTY DECENT PLASTIC SURGEON UPTOWN.
AND I WAS READING IN THE NEW *WIRED* ABOUT THESE SCIENTISTS WHO FIGURED OUT A WAY TO GROW A HUMAN EAR ON THE BACK OF A FREAKIN' ***MOUSE***, SO--
Smart Ass White Boy
THANKS, LETO, BUT I'M JUST LOOKING FOR *ADVENTURE COMICS* #265. DOESN'T HAVE TO BE IN MINT CONDITION. A READING COPY IS FINE.
CASHEWS
SORRY, MAN. I SOLD ALL MY SUPERBOY STUFF AT THE LAST BIG APPLE CON.
I GOT A 265 IN MY PERSONAL COLLECTION, BUT I DON'T THINK I CAN PART WITH IT.
Smart Ass White Boy
ARE YOU SURE?
IT'S FOR MY FRIEND'S BIRTHDAY. IT'S GOT KIND OF A...***PERSONAL*** SIGNIFICANCE TO--
DELICIOUS
CHOWDER
NUTRITIOUS
BEEP BEEP BABEEP
IT'S TIME, MITCHELL.
KREMLIN? I'M AT...I'M DOWNTOWN. I CAN'T--
*BRADBURY IS DRIVING TO MEET YOU AT LETO'S NOW. YOUR 'PACK IS FUELED UP AND WAITING. IT IS TIME FOR THE **GREAT MACHINE**.*
Smart Ass White Boy
NO! CHECKS

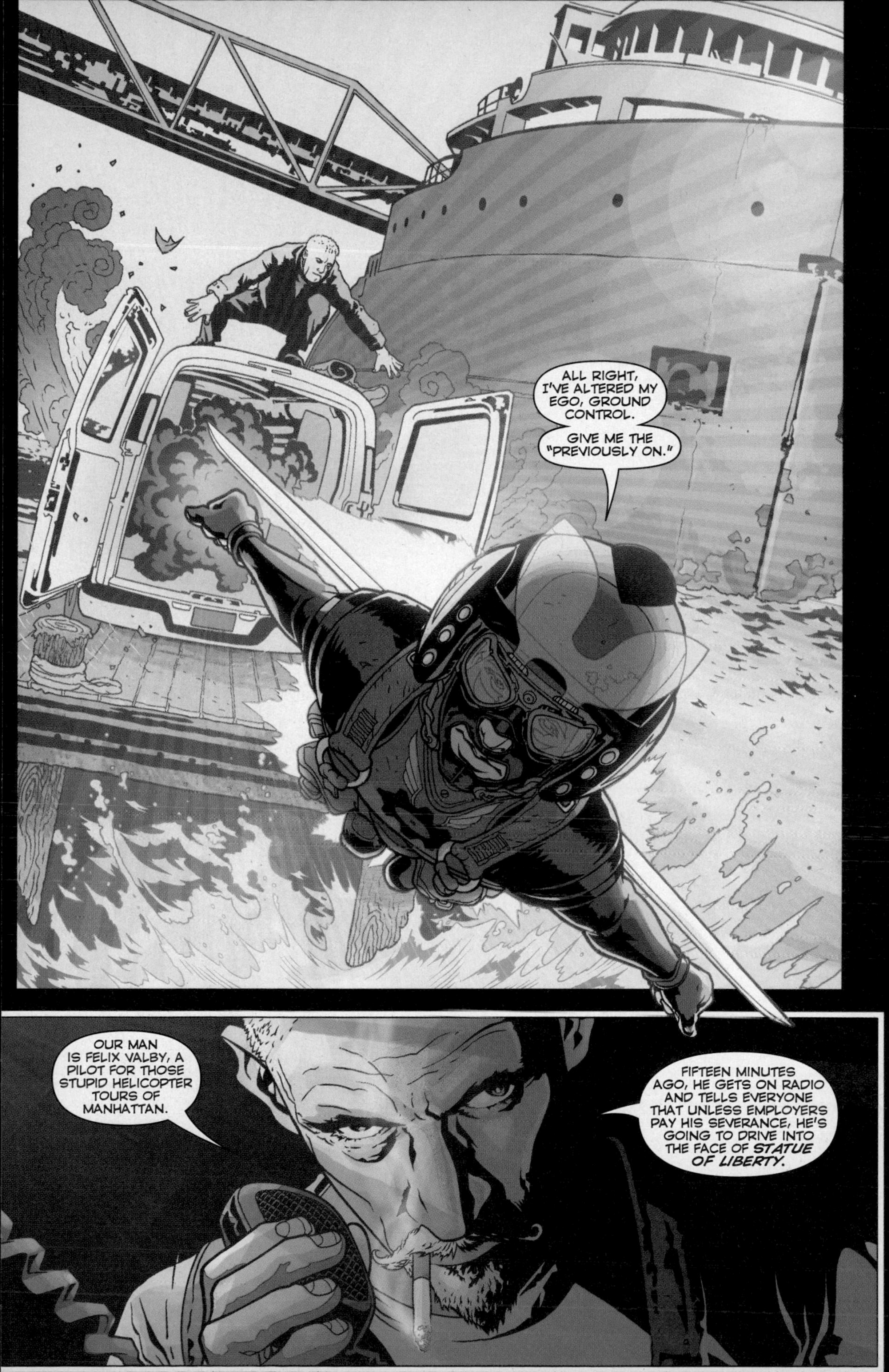
ALL RIGHT, I'VE ALTERED MY EGO, GROUND CONTROL.
GIVE ME THE "PREVIOUSLY ON."
OUR MAN IS FELIX VALBY, A PILOT FOR THOSE STUPID HELICOPTER TOURS OF MANHATTAN.
FIFTEEN MINUTES AGO, HE GETS ON RADIO AND TELLS EVERYONE THAT UNLESS EMPLOYERS PAY HIS SEVERANCE, HE'S GOING TO DRIVE INTO THE FACE OF ***STATUE OF LIBERTY.***

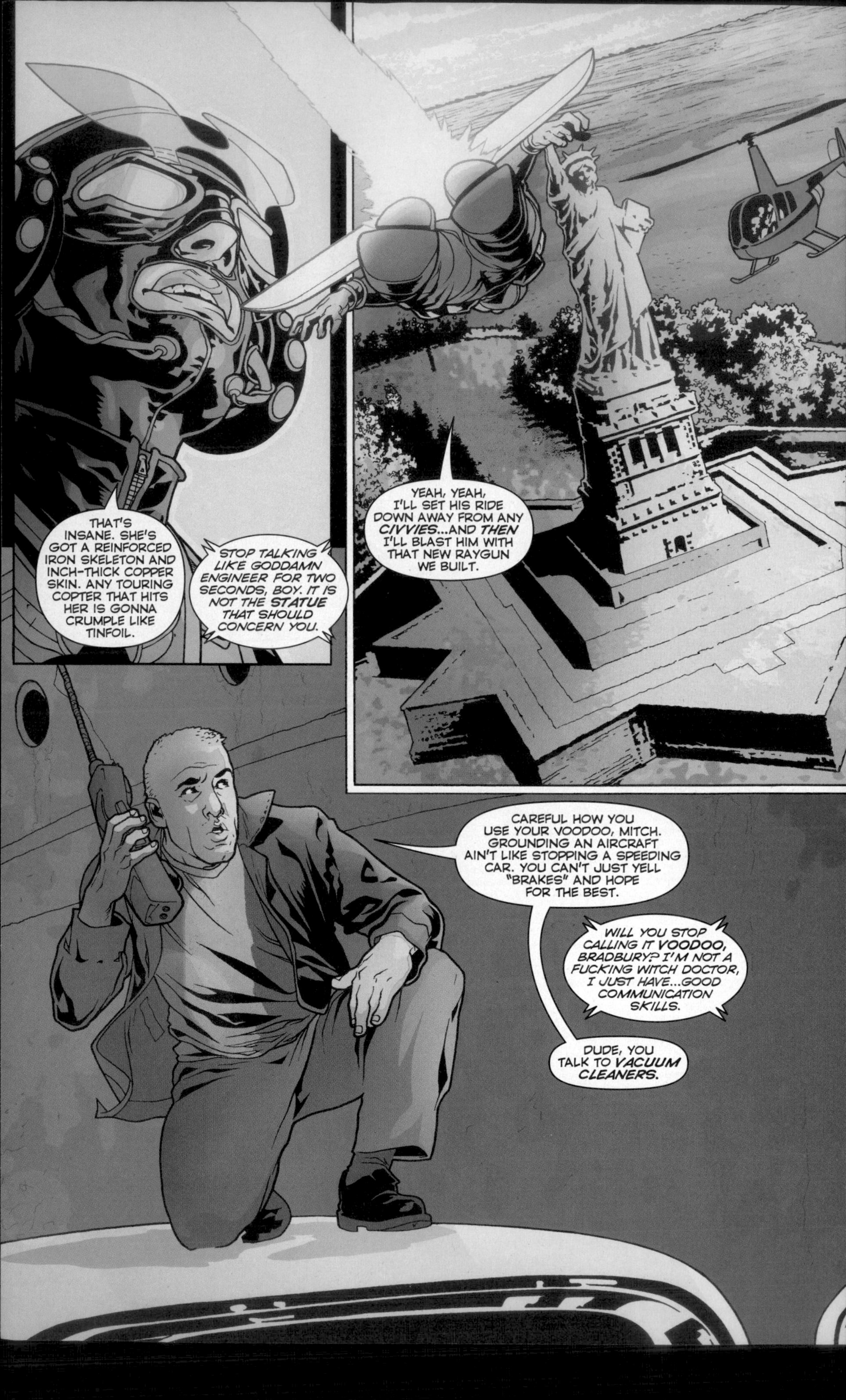
THAT'S INSANE. SHE'S GOT A REINFORCED IRON SKELETON AND INCH-THICK COPPER SKIN. ANY TOURING COPTER THAT HITS HER IS GONNA CRUMPLE LIKE TINFOIL.
STOP TALKING LIKE GODDAMN ENGINEER FOR TWO SECONDS, BOY. IT IS NOT THE STATUE THAT SHOULD CONCERN YOU.
YEAH, YEAH, I'LL SET HIS RIDE DOWN AWAY FROM ANY CIVVIES...AND THEN I'LL BLAST HIM WITH THAT NEW RAYGUN WE BUILT.
CAREFUL HOW YOU USE YOUR VOODOO, MITCH. GROUNDING AN AIRCRAFT AIN'T LIKE STOPPING A SPEEDING CAR. YOU CAN'T JUST YELL "BRAKES" AND HOPE FOR THE BEST.
WILL YOU STOP CALLING IT VOODOO, BRADBURY? I'M NOT A FUCKING WITCH DOCTOR, I JUST HAVE...GOOD COMMUNICATION SKILLS.
DUDE, YOU TALK TO VACUUM CLEANERS.

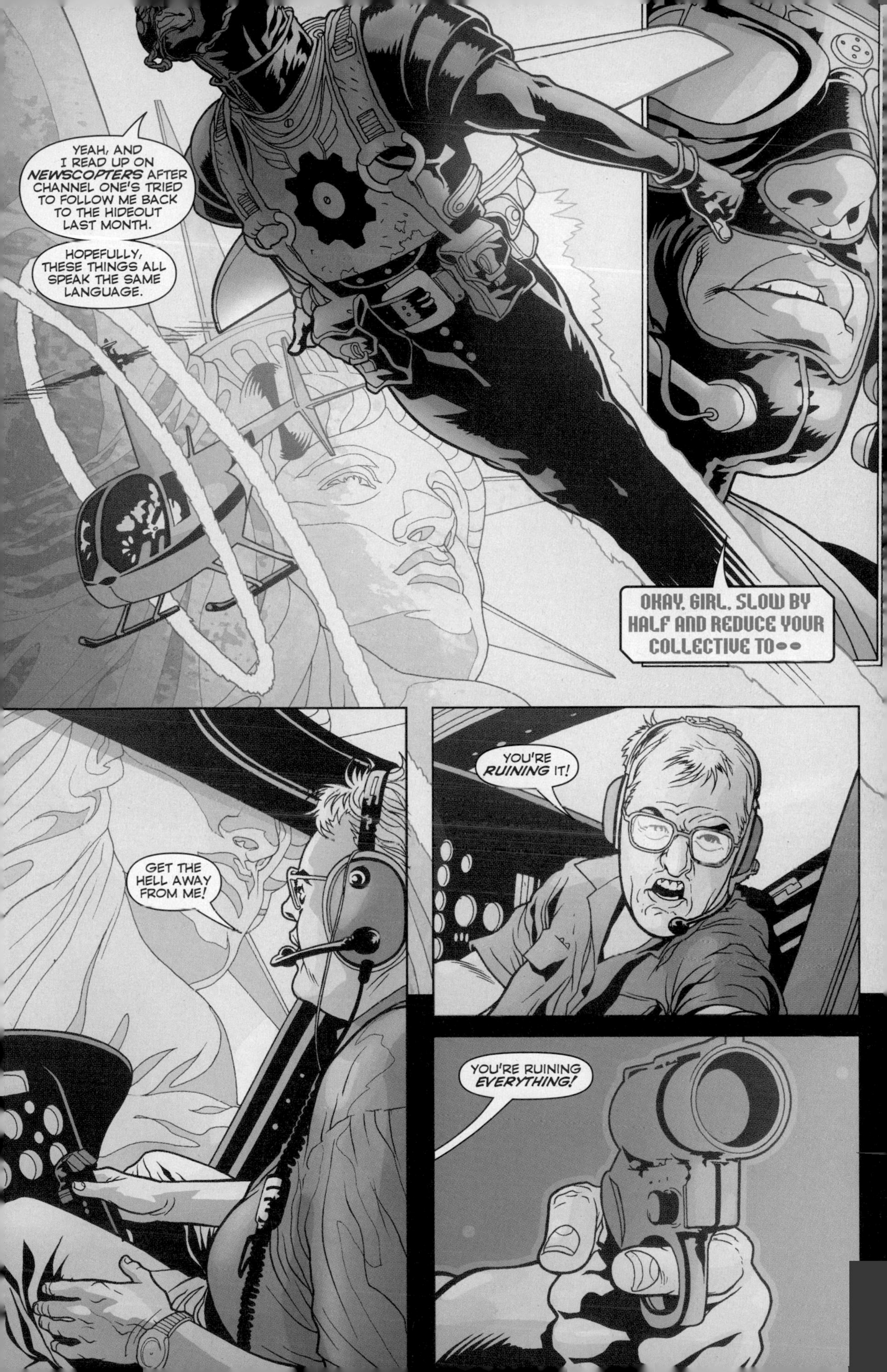
YEAH, AND I READ UP ON *NEWSCOPTERS* AFTER CHANNEL ONE'S TRIED TO FOLLOW ME BACK TO THE HIDEOUT LAST MONTH.
HOPEFULLY, THESE THINGS ALL SPEAK THE SAME LANGUAGE.
OKAY, GIRL, SLOW BY HALF AND REDUCE YOUR COLLECTIVE TO--
GET THE HELL AWAY FROM ME!
YOU'RE *RUINING* IT!
YOU'RE RUINING *EVERYTHING!*

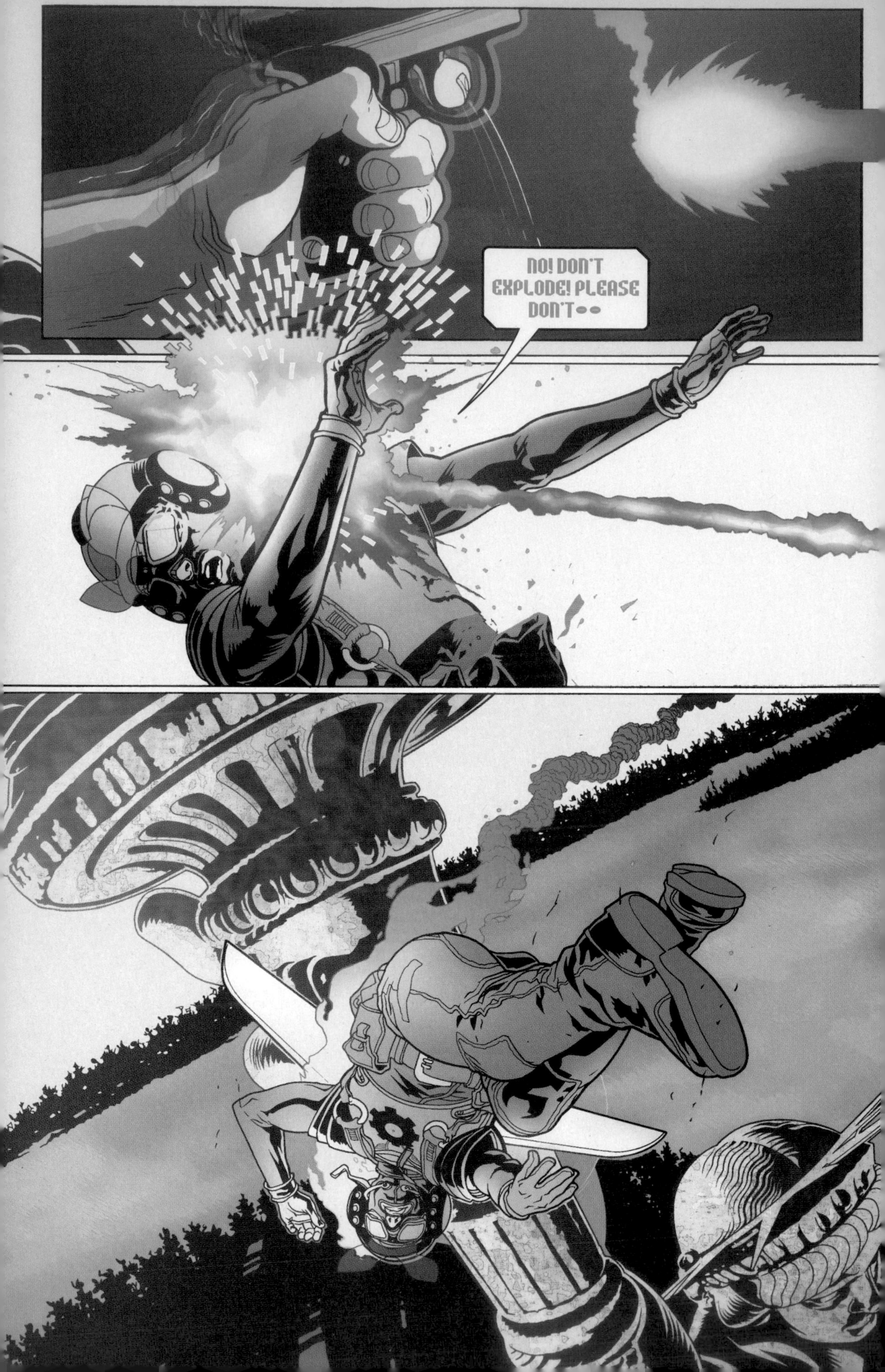
NO! DON'T EXPLODE! PLEASE DON'T--

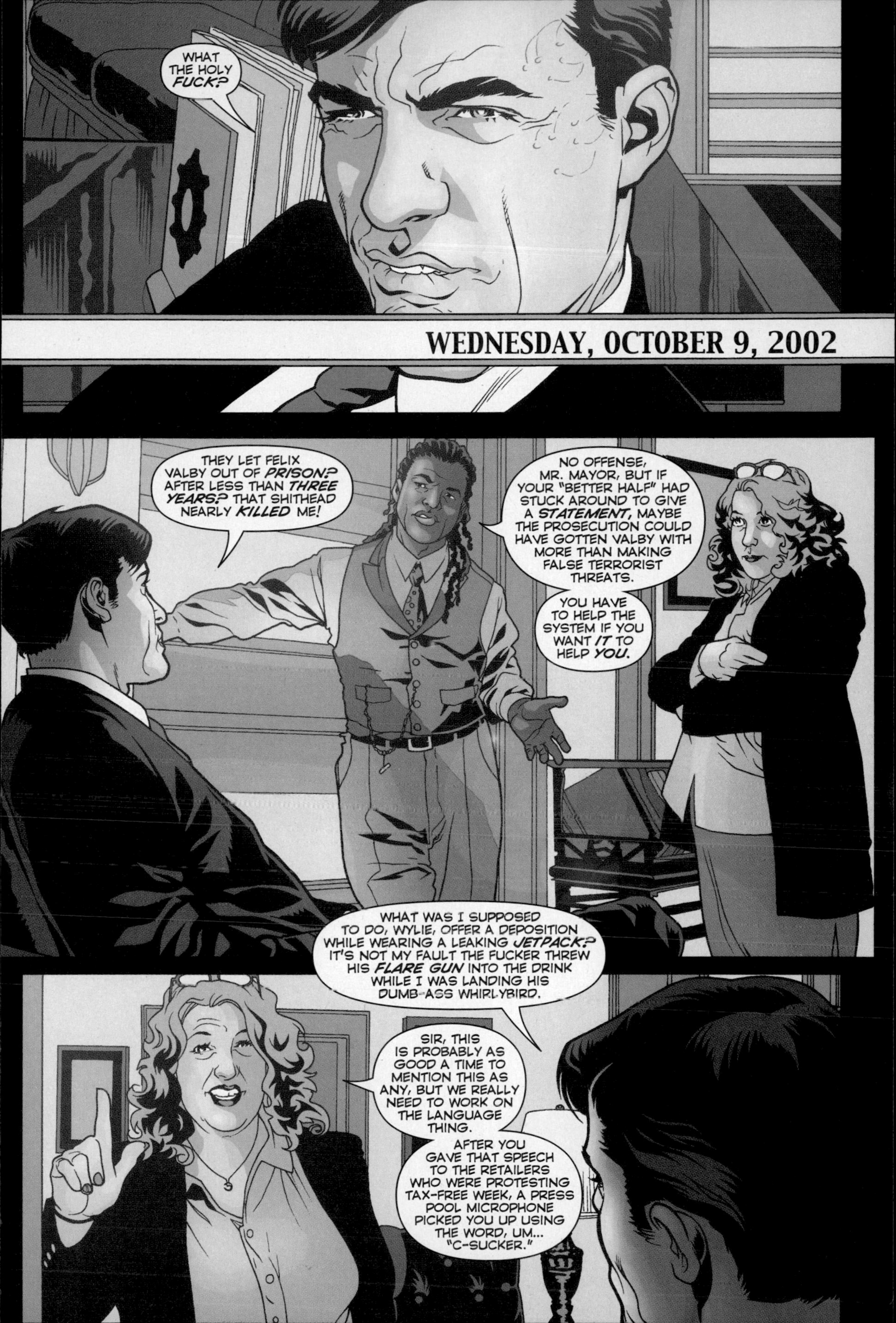

WHAT THE HOLY FUCK?
WEDNESDAY, OCTOBER 9, 2002
THEY LET FELIX VALBY OUT OF PRISON? AFTER LESS THAN THREE YEARS? THAT SHITHEAD NEARLY KILLED ME!
NO OFFENSE, MR. MAYOR, BUT IF YOUR "BETTER HALF" HAD STUCK AROUND TO GIVE A STATEMENT, MAYBE THE PROSECUTION COULD HAVE GOTTEN VALBY WITH MORE THAN MAKING FALSE TERRORIST THREATS.
YOU HAVE TO HELP THE SYSTEM IF YOU WANT IT TO HELP YOU.
WHAT WAS I SUPPOSED TO DO, WYLIE, OFFER A DEPOSITION WHILE WEARING A LEAKING JETPACK? IT'S NOT MY FAULT THE FUCKER THREW HIS FLARE GUN INTO THE DRINK WHILE I WAS LANDING HIS DUMB-ASS WHIRLYBIRD.
SIR, THIS IS PROBABLY AS GOOD A TIME TO MENTION THIS AS ANY, BUT WE REALLY NEED TO WORK ON THE LANGUAGE THING.
AFTER YOU GAVE THAT SPEECH TO THE RETAILERS WHO WERE PROTESTING TAX-FREE WEEK, A PRESS POOL MICROPHONE PICKED YOU UP USING THE WORD, UM... "C-SUCKER."

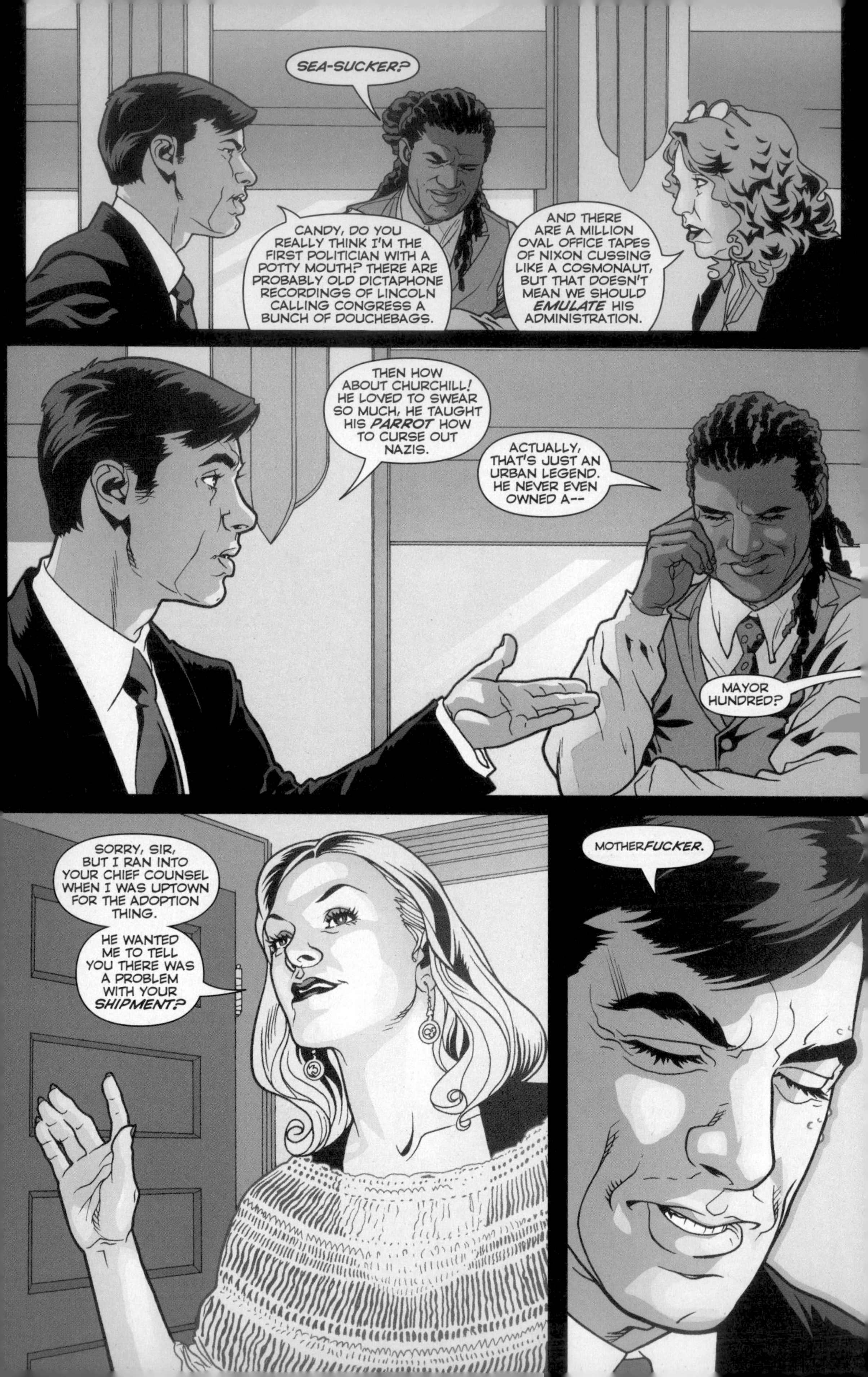
SEA-SUCKER?
CANDY, DO YOU REALLY THINK I'M THE FIRST POLITICIAN WITH A POTTY MOUTH? THERE ARE PROBABLY OLD DICTAPHONE RECORDINGS OF LINCOLN CALLING CONGRESS A BUNCH OF DOUCHEBAGS.
AND THERE ARE A MILLION OVAL OFFICE TAPES OF NIXON CUSSING LIKE A COSMONAUT, BUT THAT DOESN'T MEAN WE SHOULD EMULATE HIS ADMINISTRATION.
THEN HOW ABOUT CHURCHILL! HE LOVED TO SWEAR SO MUCH, HE TAUGHT HIS PARROT HOW TO CURSE OUT NAZIS.
ACTUALLY, THAT'S JUST AN URBAN LEGEND. HE NEVER EVEN OWNED A--
MAYOR HUNDRED?
SORRY, SIR, BUT I RAN INTO YOUR CHIEF COUNSEL WHEN I WAS UPTOWN FOR THE ADOPTION THING.
HE WANTED ME TO TELL YOU THERE WAS A PROBLEM WITH YOUR SHIPMENT?
MOTHERFUCKER.

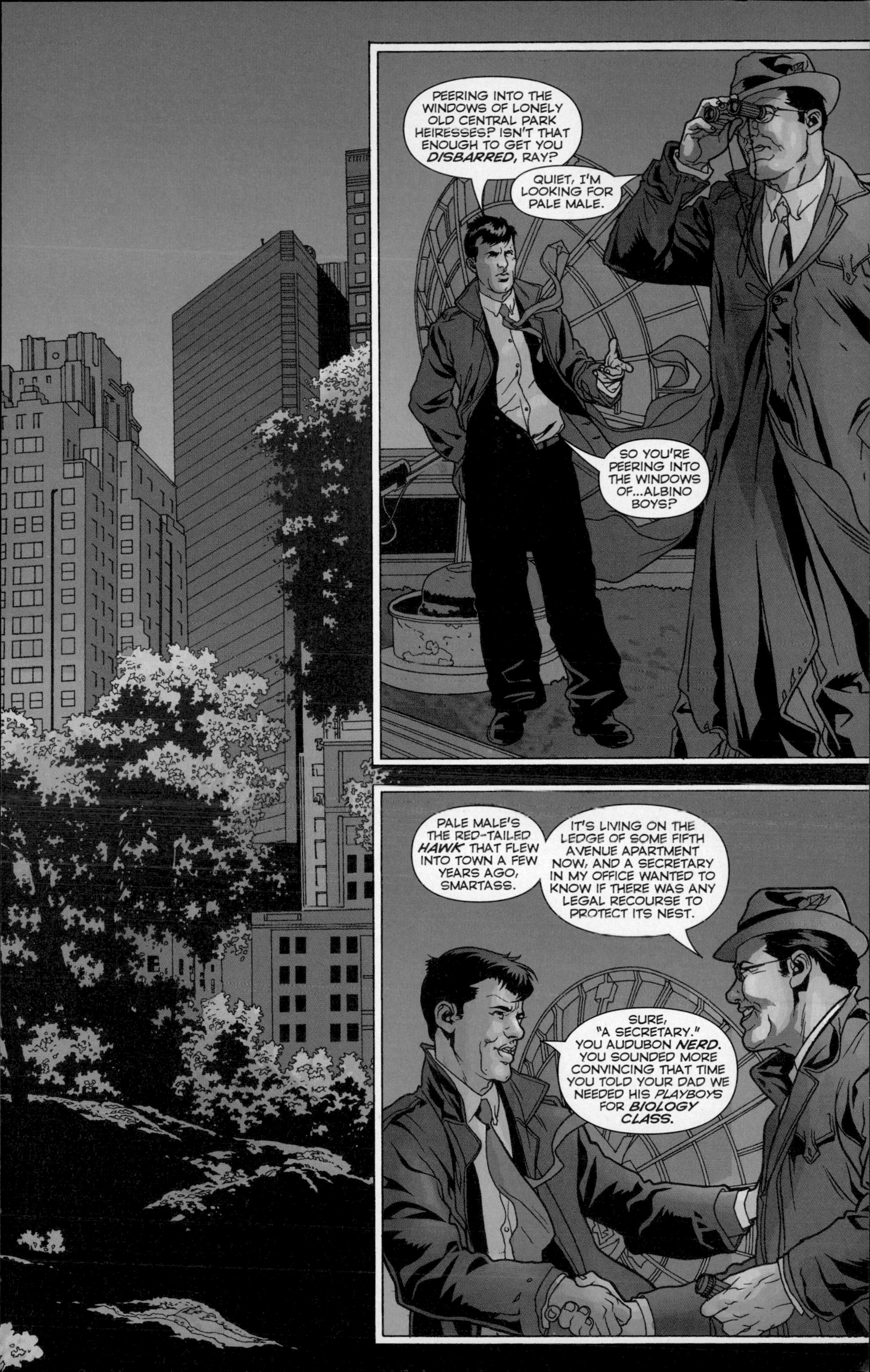
PEERING INTO THE WINDOWS OF LONELY OLD CENTRAL PARK HEIRESSES? ISN'T THAT ENOUGH TO GET YOU *DISBARRED*, RAY?
QUIET, I'M LOOKING FOR PALE MALE.
SO YOU'RE PEERING INTO THE WINDOWS OF...ALBINO BOYS?
PALE MALE'S THE RED-TAILED *HAWK* THAT FLEW INTO TOWN A FEW YEARS AGO, SMARTASS.
IT'S LIVING ON THE LEDGE OF SOME FIFTH AVENUE APARTMENT NOW, AND A SECRETARY IN MY OFFICE WANTED TO KNOW IF THERE WAS ANY LEGAL RECOURSE TO PROTECT ITS NEST.
SURE, "A SECRETARY." YOU AUDUBON *NERD*. YOU SOUNDED MORE CONVINCING THAT TIME YOU TOLD YOUR DAD WE NEEDED HIS *PLAYBOYS* FOR *BIOLOGY CLASS*.

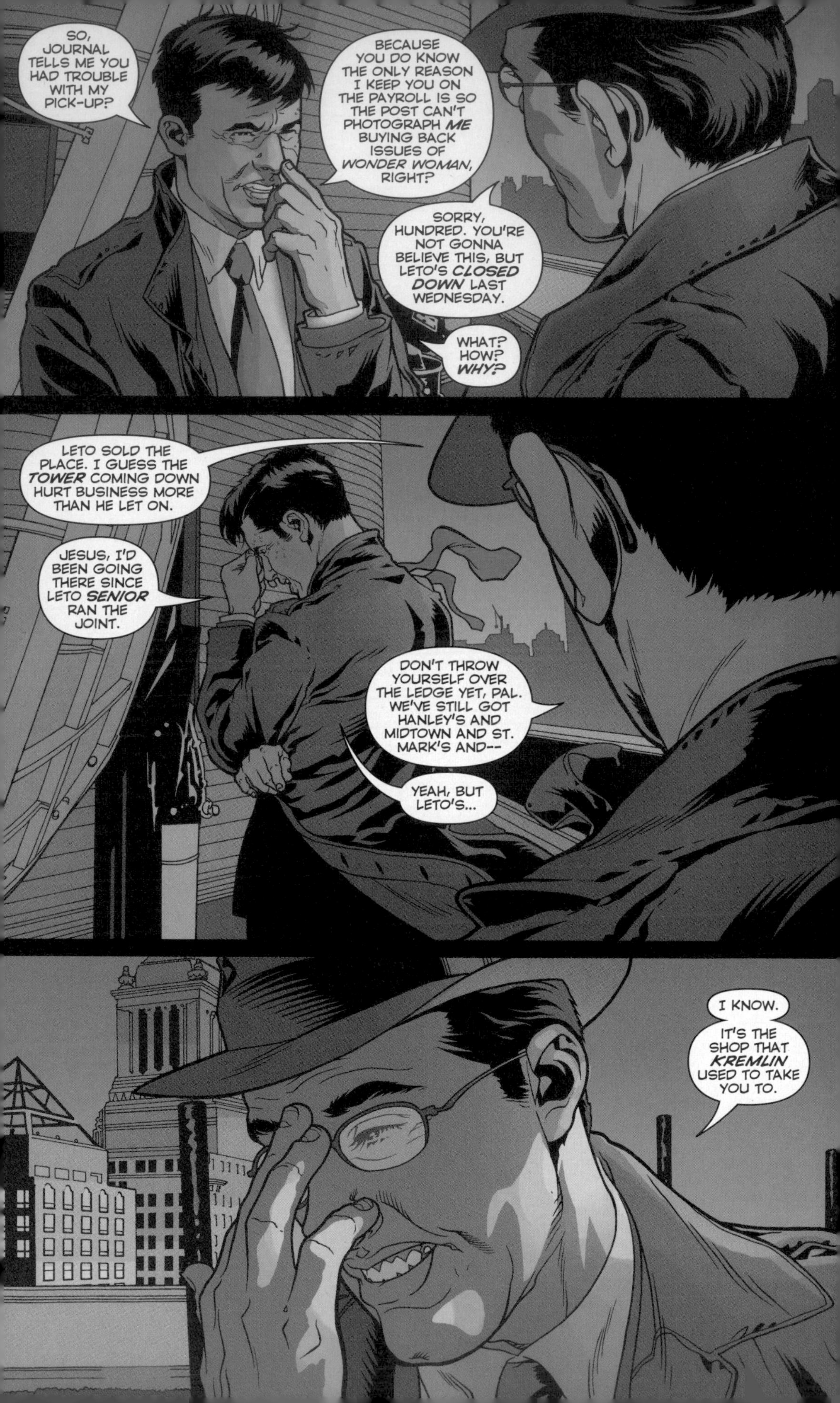
SO, JOURNAL TELLS ME YOU HAD TROUBLE WITH MY PICK-UP?
BECAUSE YOU DO KNOW THE ONLY REASON I KEEP YOU ON THE PAYROLL IS SO THE POST CAN'T PHOTOGRAPH *ME* BUYING BACK ISSUES OF *WONDER WOMAN*, RIGHT?
SORRY, HUNDRED. YOU'RE NOT GONNA BELIEVE THIS, BUT LETO'S *CLOSED DOWN* LAST WEDNESDAY.
WHAT? HOW? *WHY?*
LETO SOLD THE PLACE. I GUESS THE *TOWER* COMING DOWN HURT BUSINESS MORE THAN HE LET ON.
JESUS, I'D BEEN GOING THERE SINCE LETO *SENIOR* RAN THE JOINT.
DON'T THROW YOURSELF OVER THE LEDGE YET, PAL. WE'VE STILL GOT HANLEY'S AND MIDTOWN AND ST. MARK'S AND--
YEAH, BUT LETO'S...
I KNOW.
IT'S THE SHOP THAT *KREMLIN* USED TO TAKE YOU TO.

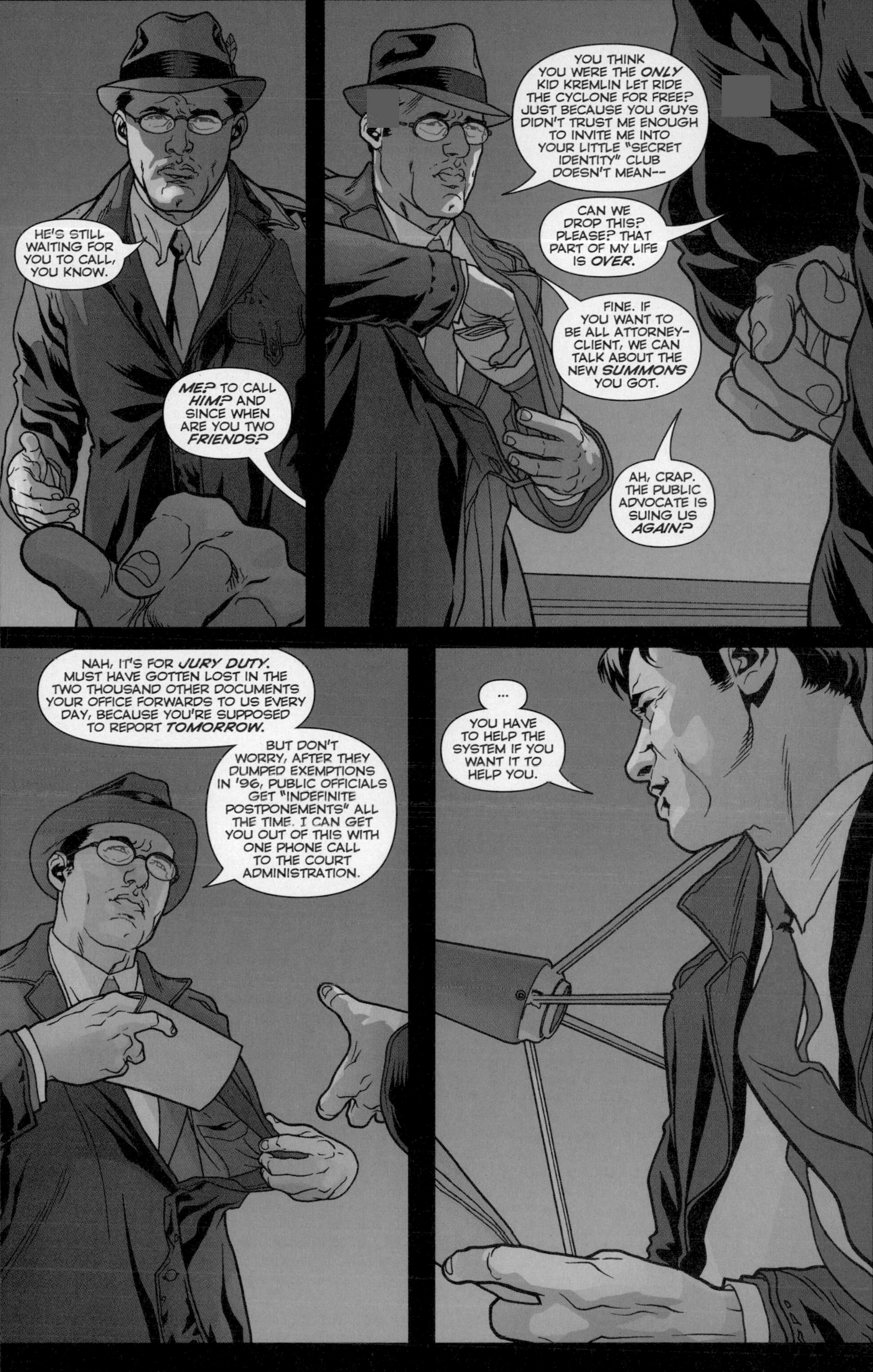

HE'S STILL WAITING FOR YOU TO CALL, YOU KNOW.
ME? TO CALL HIM? AND SINCE WHEN ARE YOU TWO FRIENDS?
YOU THINK YOU WERE THE ONLY KID KREMLIN LET RIDE THE CYCLONE FOR FREE? JUST BECAUSE YOU GUYS DIDN'T TRUST ME ENOUGH TO INVITE ME INTO YOUR LITTLE "SECRET IDENTITY" CLUB DOESN'T MEAN--
CAN WE DROP THIS? PLEASE? THAT PART OF MY LIFE IS OVER.
FINE. IF YOU WANT TO BE ALL ATTORNEY-CLIENT, WE CAN TALK ABOUT THE NEW SUMMONS YOU GOT.
AH, CRAP. THE PUBLIC ADVOCATE IS SUING US AGAIN?
NAH, IT'S FOR JURY DUTY. MUST HAVE GOTTEN LOST IN THE TWO THOUSAND OTHER DOCUMENTS YOUR OFFICE FORWARDS TO US EVERY DAY, BECAUSE YOU'RE SUPPOSED TO REPORT TOMORROW.
BUT DON'T WORRY, AFTER THEY DUMPED EXEMPTIONS IN '96, PUBLIC OFFICIALS GET "INDEFINITE POSTPONEMENTS" ALL THE TIME. I CAN GET YOU OUT OF THIS WITH ONE PHONE CALL TO THE COURT ADMINISTRATION.
...
YOU HAVE TO HELP THE SYSTEM IF YOU WANT IT TO HELP YOU.

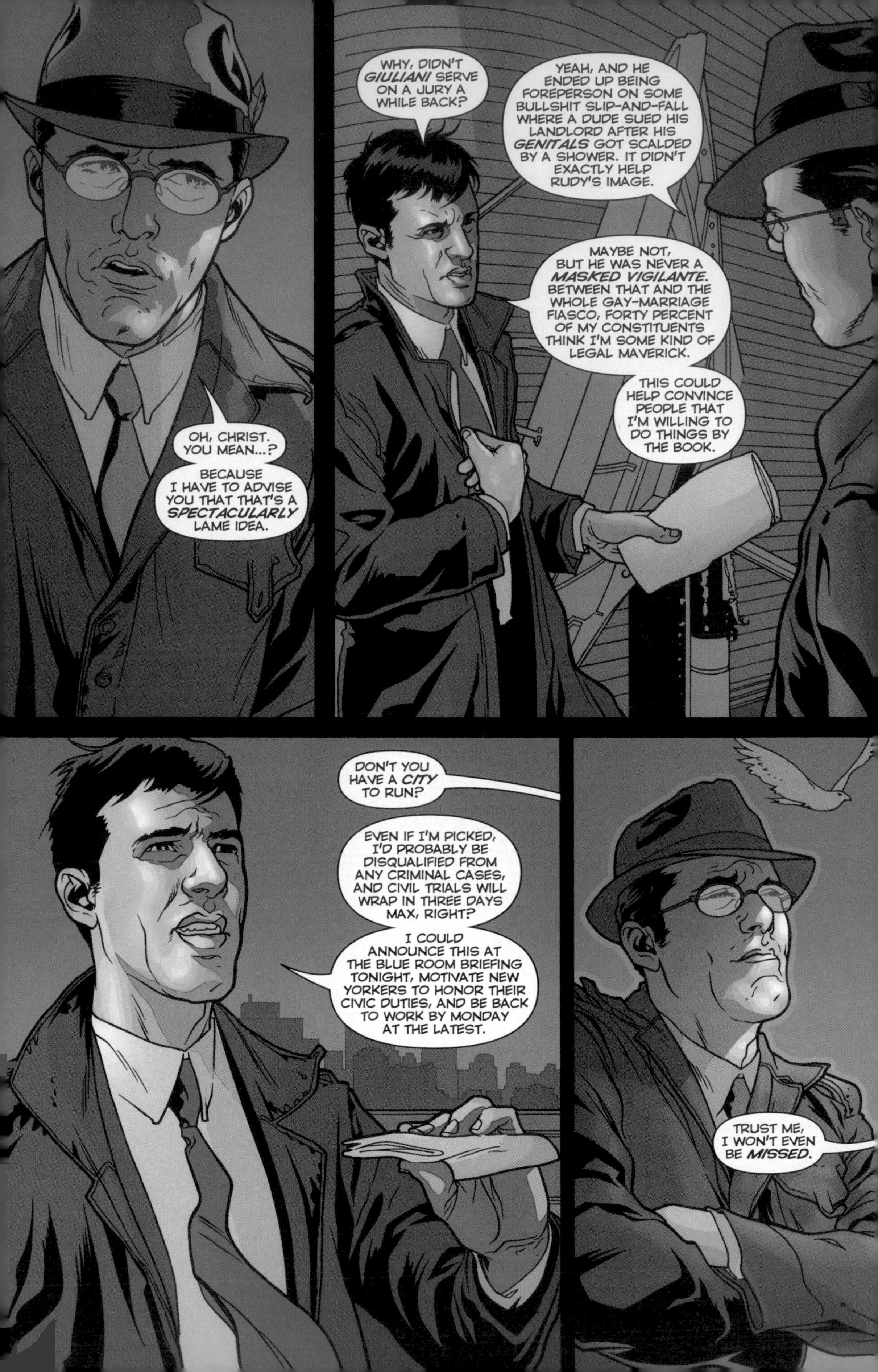
OH, CHRIST. YOU MEAN...?
BECAUSE I HAVE TO ADVISE YOU THAT THAT'S A *SPECTACULARLY* LAME IDEA.
WHY, DIDN'T *GIULIANI* SERVE ON A JURY A WHILE BACK?
YEAH, AND HE ENDED UP BEING FOREPERSON ON SOME BULLSHIT SLIP-AND-FALL WHERE A DUDE SUED HIS LANDLORD AFTER HIS *GENITALS* GOT SCALDED BY A SHOWER. IT DIDN'T EXACTLY HELP RUDY'S IMAGE.
MAYBE NOT, BUT HE WAS NEVER A ***MASKED VIGILANTE***. BETWEEN THAT AND THE WHOLE GAY-MARRIAGE FIASCO, FORTY PERCENT OF MY CONSTITUENTS THINK I'M SOME KIND OF LEGAL MAVERICK.
THIS COULD HELP CONVINCE PEOPLE THAT I'M WILLING TO DO THINGS BY THE BOOK.
DON'T YOU HAVE A *CITY* TO RUN?
EVEN IF I'M PICKED, I'D PROBABLY BE DISQUALIFIED FROM ANY CRIMINAL CASES, AND CIVIL TRIALS WILL WRAP IN THREE DAYS MAX, RIGHT?
I COULD ANNOUNCE THIS AT THE BLUE ROOM BRIEFING TONIGHT, MOTIVATE NEW YORKERS TO HONOR THEIR CIVIC DUTIES, AND BE BACK TO WORK BY MONDAY AT THE LATEST.
TRUST ME, I WON'T EVEN BE ***MISSED***.

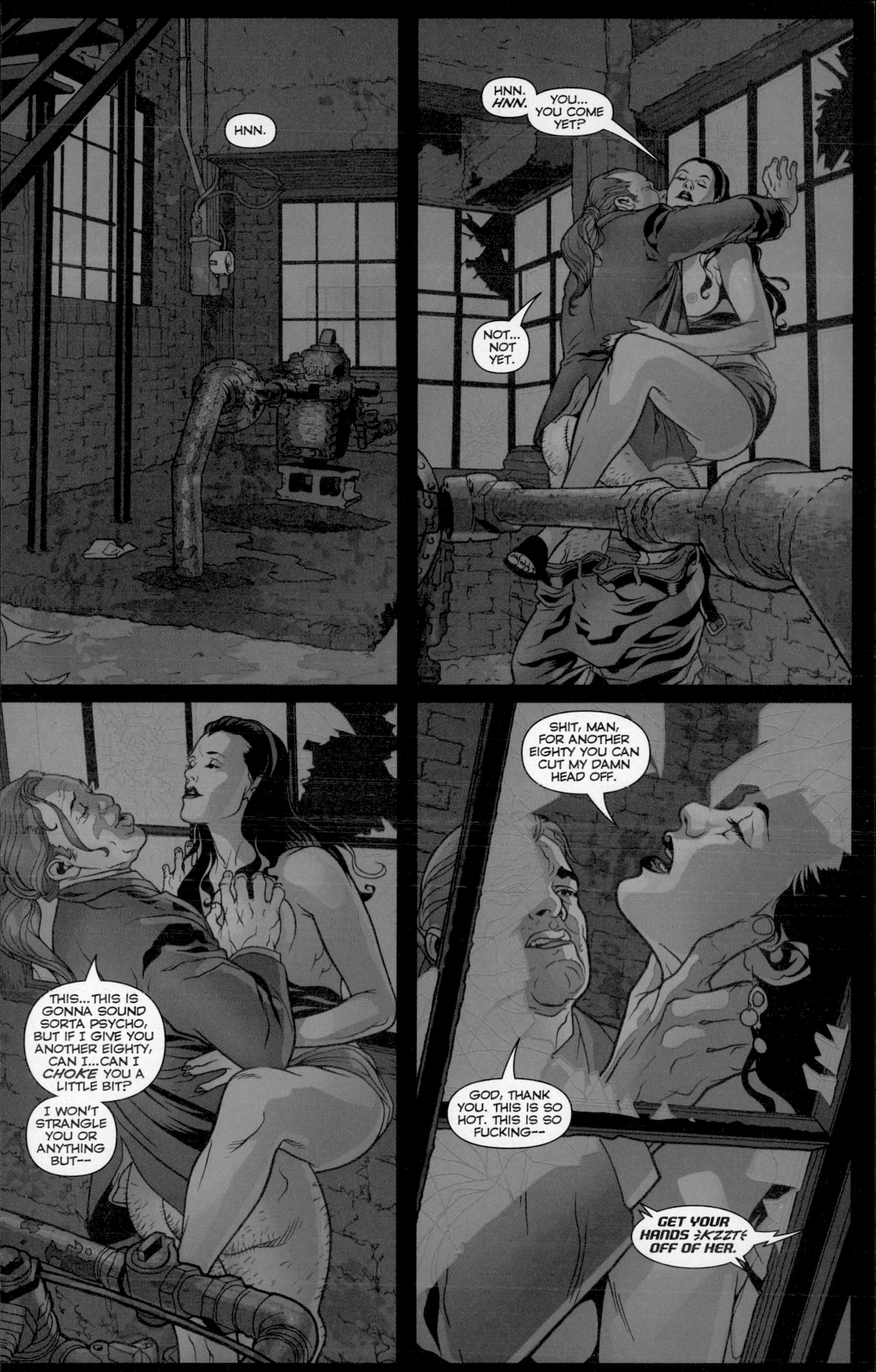
HNN.
HNN. HNN.
YOU... YOU COME YET?
NOT... NOT YET.
THIS...THIS IS GONNA SOUND SORTA PSYCHO, BUT IF I GIVE YOU ANOTHER EIGHTY, CAN I...CAN I CHOKE YOU A LITTLE BIT?
I WON'T STRANGLE YOU OR ANYTHING BUT--
SHIT, MAN, FOR ANOTHER EIGHTY YOU CAN CUT MY DAMN HEAD OFF.
GOD, THANK YOU. THIS IS SO HOT. THIS IS SO FUCKING--
GET YOUR HANDS KZZT OFF OF HER.

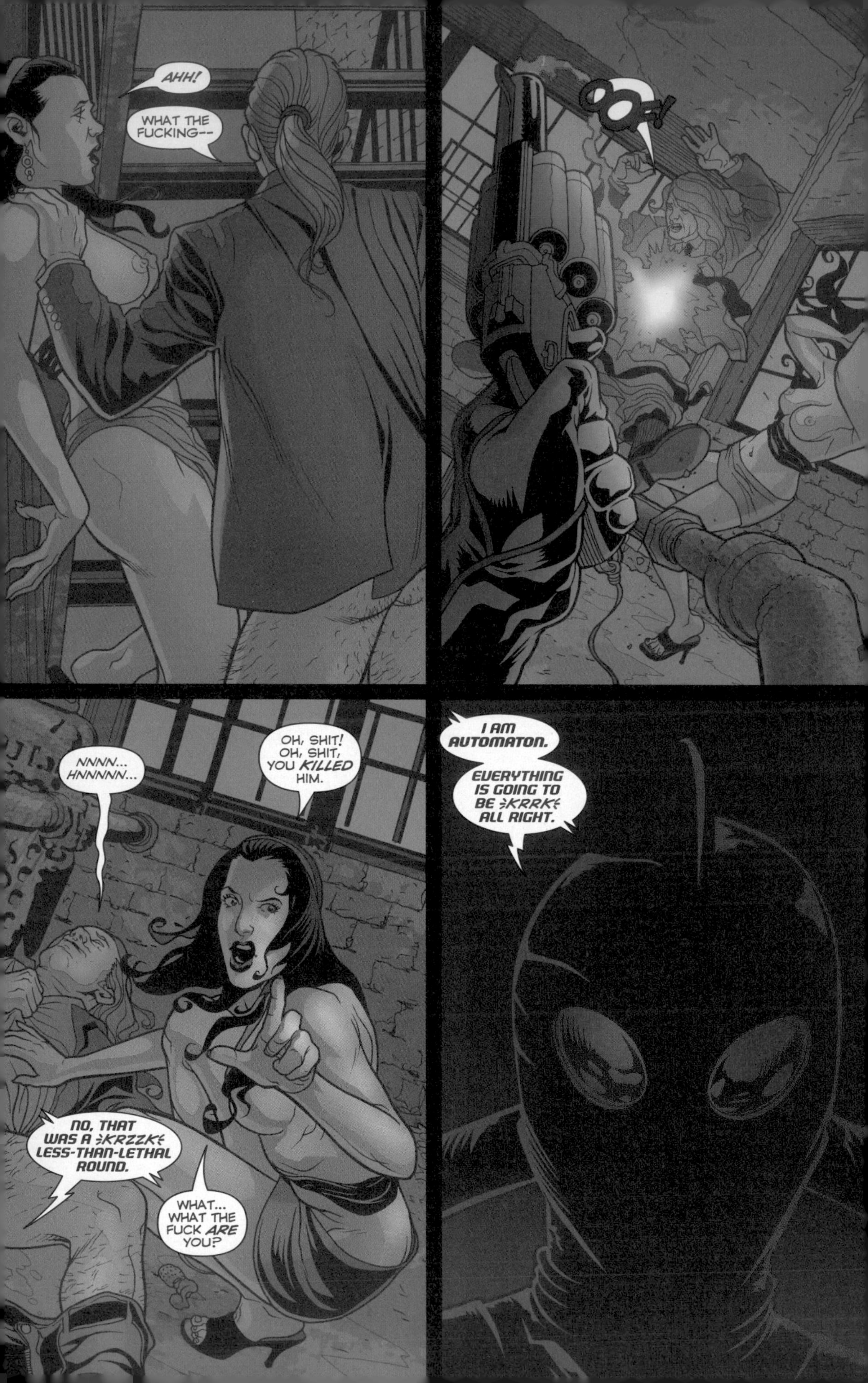
AHH!
WHAT THE FUCKING--
OOF!
NNNN... HNNNNN...
OH, SHIT! OH, SHIT, YOU *KILLED* HIM.
NO, THAT WAS A KRZZK LESS-THAN-LETHAL ROUND.
WHAT... WHAT THE FUCK *ARE* YOU?
I AM AUTOMATON.
EVERYTHING IS GOING TO BE KRRK ALL RIGHT.

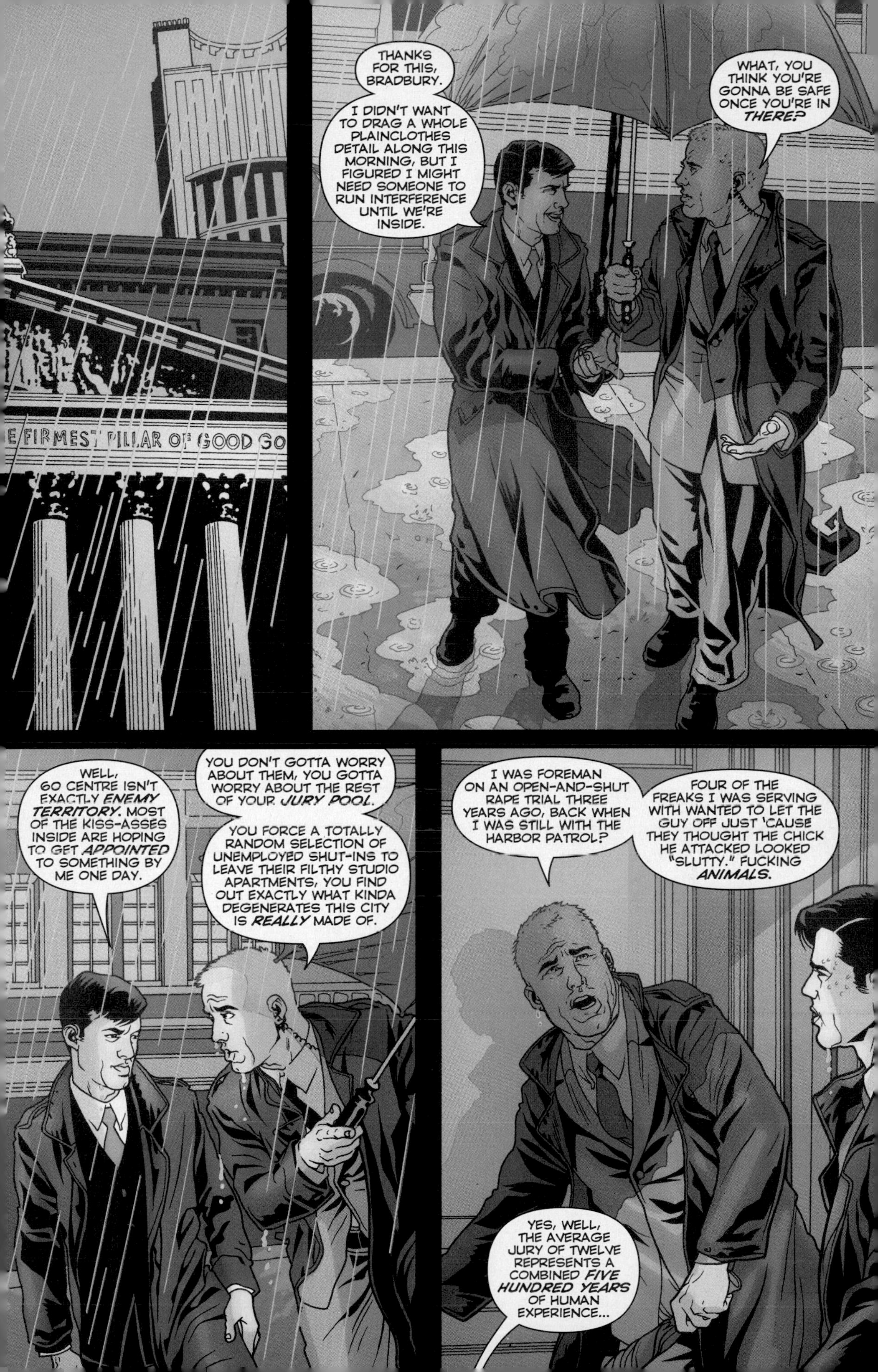
E FIRMEST PILLAR OF GOOD GO
THANKS FOR THIS, BRADBURY.
I DIDN'T WANT TO DRAG A WHOLE PLAINCLOTHES DETAIL ALONG THIS MORNING, BUT I FIGURED I MIGHT NEED SOMEONE TO RUN INTERFERENCE UNTIL WE'RE INSIDE.
WHAT, YOU THINK YOU'RE GONNA BE SAFE ONCE YOU'RE IN *THERE?*
WELL, 60 CENTRE ISN'T EXACTLY *ENEMY TERRITORY.* MOST OF THE KISS-ASSES INSIDE ARE HOPING TO GET *APPOINTED* TO SOMETHING BY ME ONE DAY.
YOU DON'T GOTTA WORRY ABOUT THEM, YOU GOTTA WORRY ABOUT THE REST OF YOUR *JURY POOL*.
YOU FORCE A TOTALLY RANDOM SELECTION OF UNEMPLOYED SHUT-INS TO LEAVE THEIR FILTHY STUDIO APARTMENTS, YOU FIND OUT EXACTLY WHAT KINDA DEGENERATES THIS CITY IS *REALLY* MADE OF.
I WAS FOREMAN ON AN OPEN-AND-SHUT RAPE TRIAL THREE YEARS AGO, BACK WHEN I WAS STILL WITH THE HARBOR PATROL?
FOUR OF THE FREAKS I WAS SERVING WITH WANTED TO LET THE GUY OFF JUST 'CAUSE THEY THOUGHT THE CHICK HE ATTACKED LOOKED "SLUTTY." FUCKING *ANIMALS*.
YES, WELL, THE AVERAGE JURY OF TWELVE REPRESENTS A COMBINED *FIVE HUNDRED YEARS* OF HUMAN EXPERIENCE...

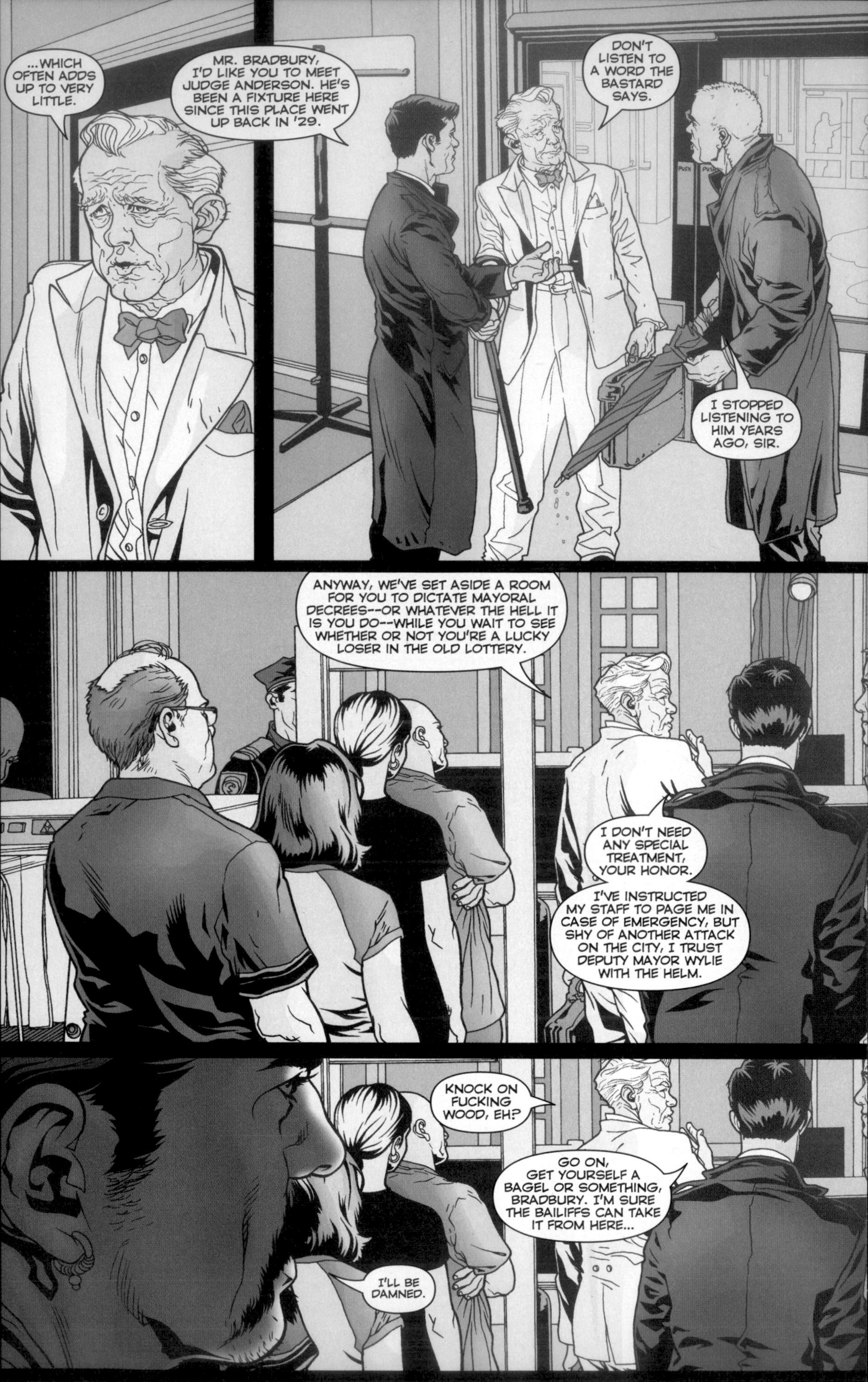
...WHICH OFTEN ADDS UP TO VERY LITTLE.
MR. BRADBURY, I'D LIKE YOU TO MEET JUDGE ANDERSON. HE'S BEEN A FIXTURE HERE SINCE THIS PLACE WENT UP BACK IN '29.
DON'T LISTEN TO A WORD THE BASTARD SAYS.
I STOPPED LISTENING TO HIM YEARS AGO, SIR.
ANYWAY, WE'VE SET ASIDE A ROOM FOR YOU TO DICTATE MAYORAL DECREES--OR WHATEVER THE HELL IT IS YOU DO--WHILE YOU WAIT TO SEE WHETHER OR NOT YOU'RE A LUCKY LOSER IN THE OLD LOTTERY.
I DON'T NEED ANY SPECIAL TREATMENT, YOUR HONOR.
I'VE INSTRUCTED MY STAFF TO PAGE ME IN CASE OF EMERGENCY, BUT SHY OF ANOTHER ATTACK ON THE CITY, I TRUST DEPUTY MAYOR WYLIE WITH THE HELM.
KNOCK ON FUCKING WOOD, EH?
GO ON, GET YOURSELF A BAGEL OR SOMETHING, BRADBURY. I'M SURE THE BAILIFFS CAN TAKE IT FROM HERE...
I'LL BE DAMNED.

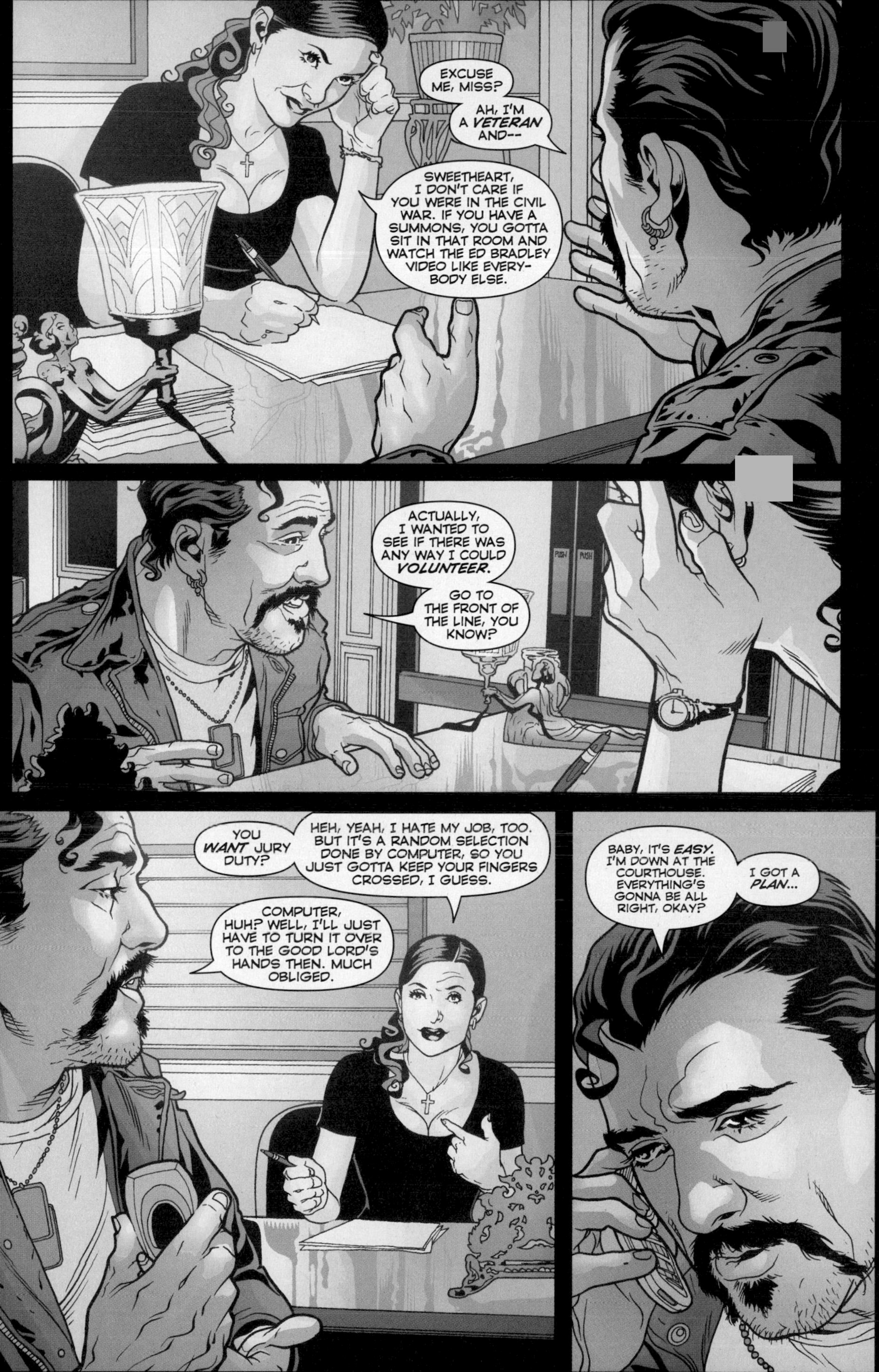
EXCUSE ME, MISS?
AH, I'M A *VETERAN* AND--
SWEETHEART, I DON'T CARE IF YOU WERE IN THE CIVIL WAR. IF YOU HAVE A SUMMONS, YOU GOTTA SIT IN THAT ROOM AND WATCH THE ED BRADLEY VIDEO LIKE EVERY-BODY ELSE.
ACTUALLY, I WANTED TO SEE IF THERE WAS ANY WAY I COULD ***VOLUNTEER***.
GO TO THE FRONT OF THE LINE, YOU KNOW?
PUSH
PUSH
YOU *WANT* JURY DUTY?
HEH, YEAH, I HATE MY JOB, TOO. BUT IT'S A RANDOM SELECTION DONE BY COMPUTER, SO YOU JUST GOTTA KEEP YOUR FINGERS CROSSED, I GUESS.
COMPUTER, HUH? WELL, I'LL JUST HAVE TO TURN IT OVER TO THE GOOD LORD'S HANDS THEN. MUCH OBLIGED.
BABY, IT'S *EASY*. I'M DOWN AT THE COURTHOUSE. EVERYTHING'S GONNA BE ALL RIGHT, OKAY?
I GOT A *PLAN*...

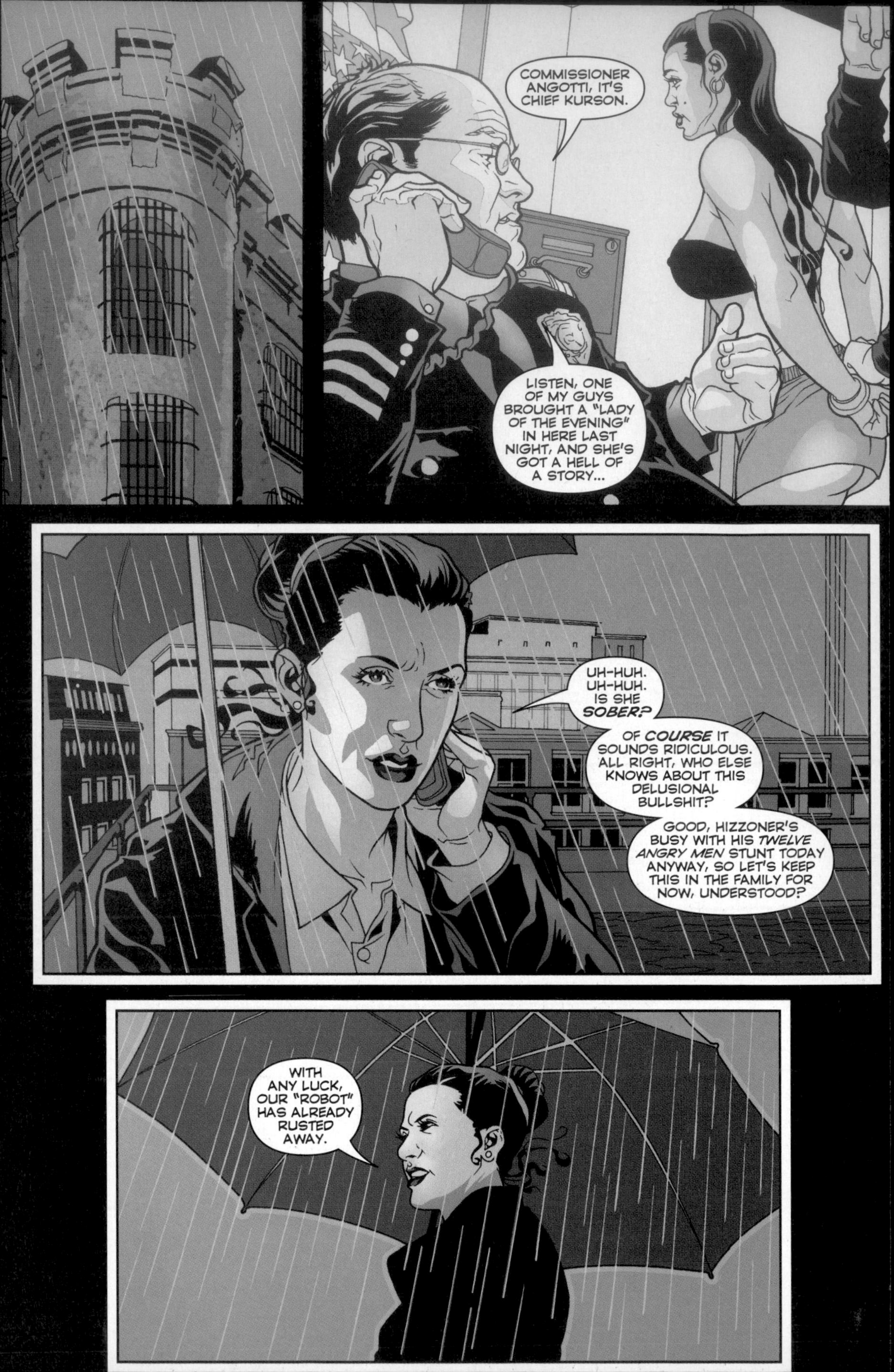
COMMISSIONER ANGOTTI, IT'S CHIEF KURSON.
LISTEN, ONE OF MY GUYS BROUGHT A "LADY OF THE EVENING" IN HERE LAST NIGHT, AND SHE'S GOT A HELL OF A STORY...
UH-HUH. UH-HUH. IS SHE *SOBER?*
OF *COURSE* IT SOUNDS RIDICULOUS. ALL RIGHT, WHO ELSE KNOWS ABOUT THIS DELUSIONAL BULLSHIT?
GOOD, HIZZONER'S BUSY WITH HIS *TWELVE ANGRY MEN* STUNT TODAY ANYWAY, SO LET'S KEEP THIS IN THE FAMILY FOR NOW, UNDERSTOOD?
WITH ANY LUCK, OUR "ROBOT" HAS ALREADY RUSTED AWAY.

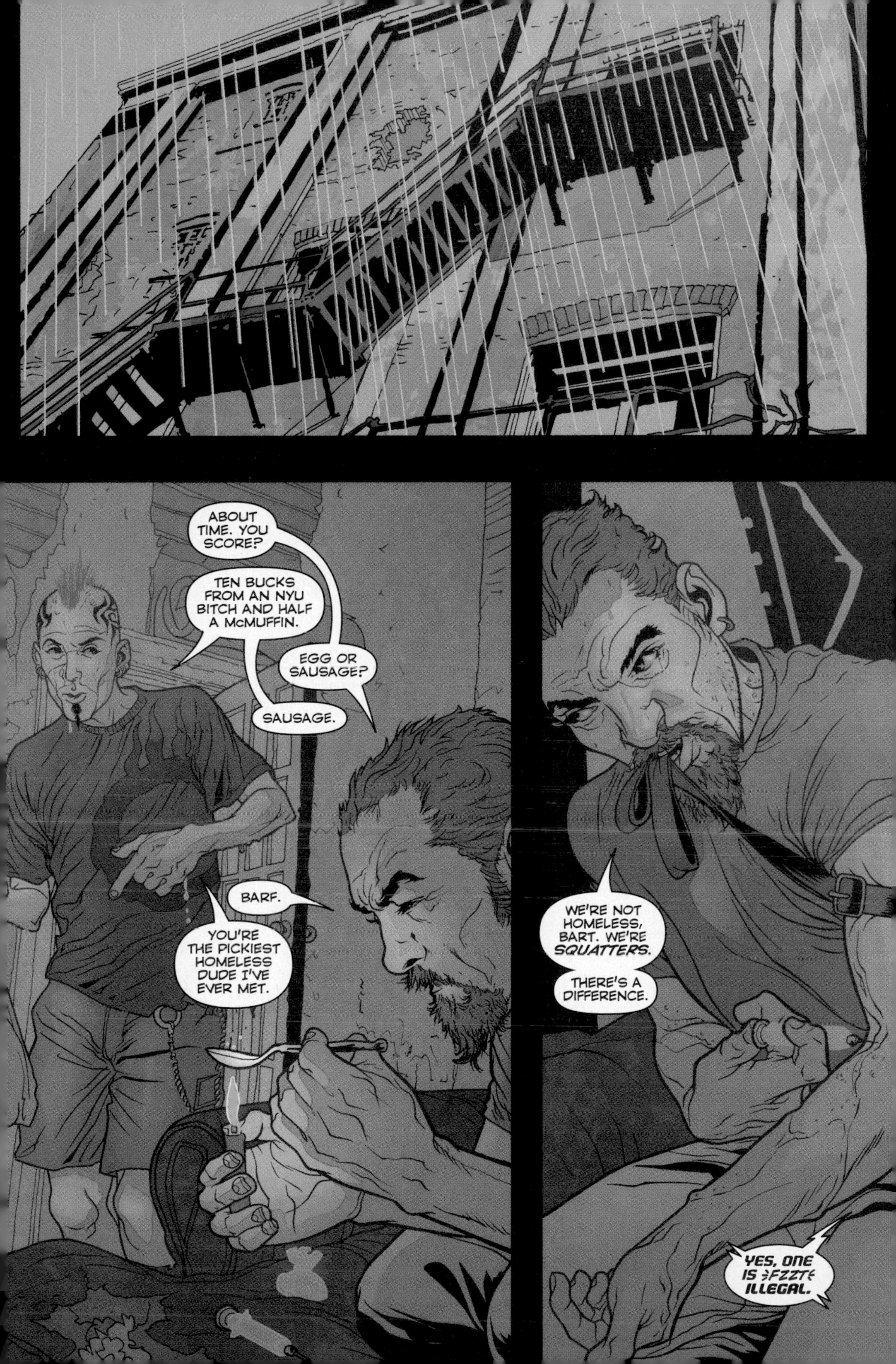
ABOUT TIME. YOU SCORE?
TEN BUCKS FROM AN NYU BITCH AND HALF A McMUFFIN.
EGG OR SAUSAGE?
SAUSAGE.
BARF.
YOU'RE THE PICKIEST HOMELESS DUDE I'VE EVER MET.
WE'RE NOT HOMELESS, BART. WE'RE *SQUATTERS*.
THERE'S A DIFFERENCE.
YES, ONE IS ƎFZZTƐ ILLEGAL.

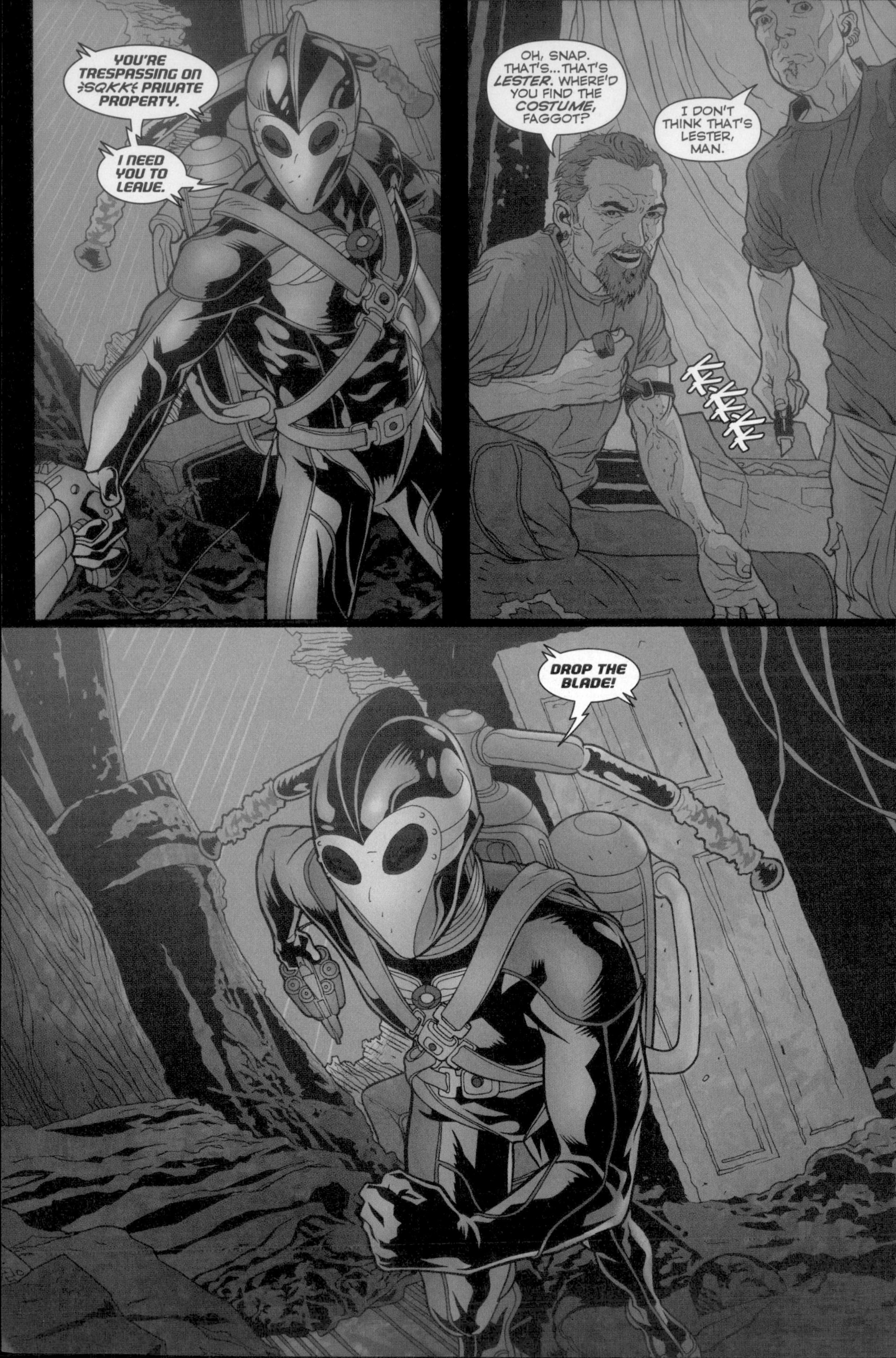
YOU'RE TRESPASSING ON ⚡SQKK⚡ PRIVATE PROPERTY.
I NEED YOU TO LEAVE.
OH, SNAP. THAT'S...THAT'S LESTER. WHERE'D YOU FIND THE COSTUME, FAGGOT?
I DON'T THINK THAT'S LESTER, MAN.
KKKKK
DROP THE BLADE!

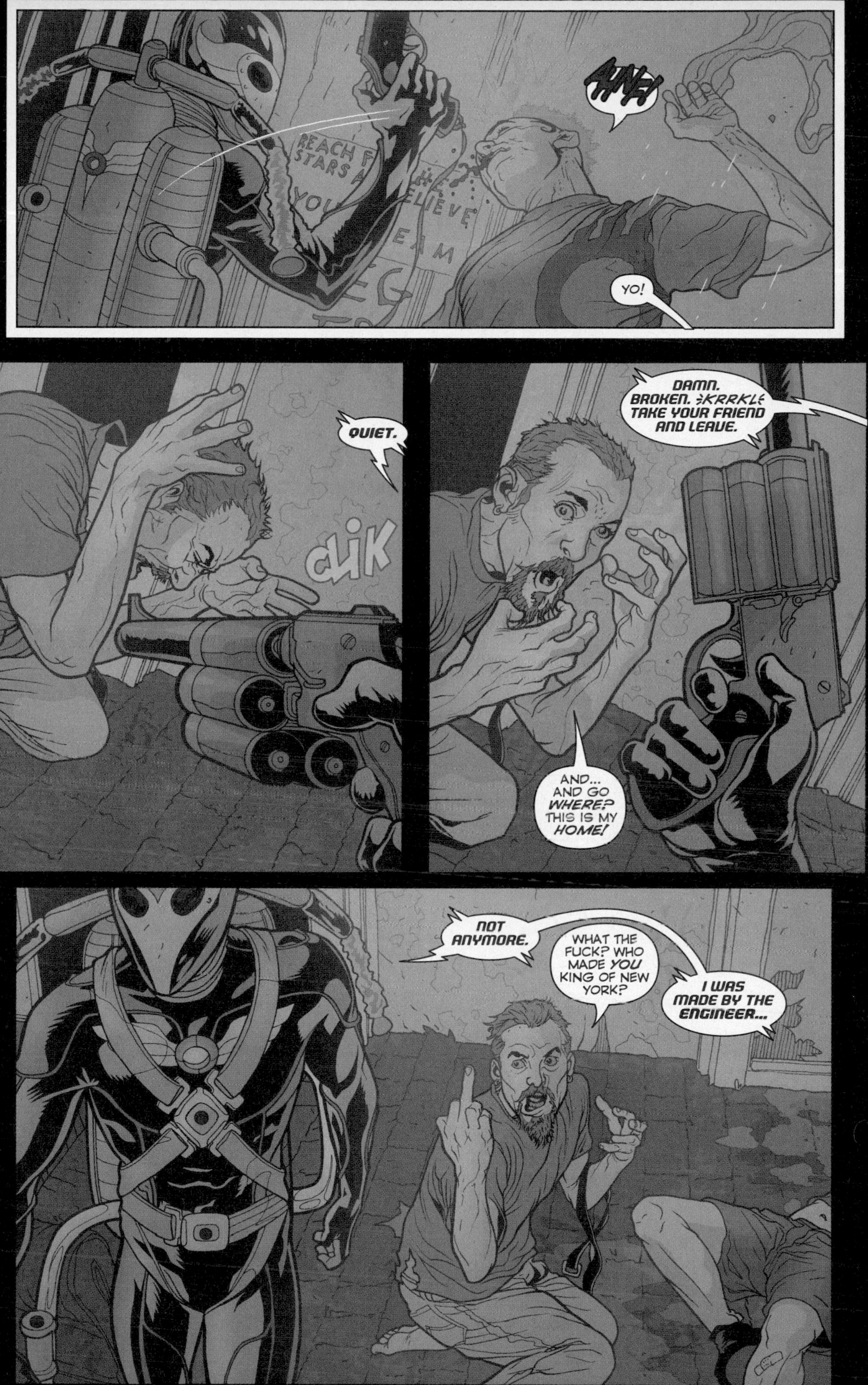
AWK!
REACH F... STARS A... YOU ...ELIEVE ...EAM
YO!
QUIET.
CLIK
DAMN. BROKEN. ⩥KRRKL⩤ TAKE YOUR FRIEND AND LEAVE.
AND... AND GO WHERE? THIS IS MY HOME!
NOT ANYMORE.
WHAT THE FUCK? WHO MADE YOU KING OF NEW YORK?
I WAS MADE BY THE ENGINEER...

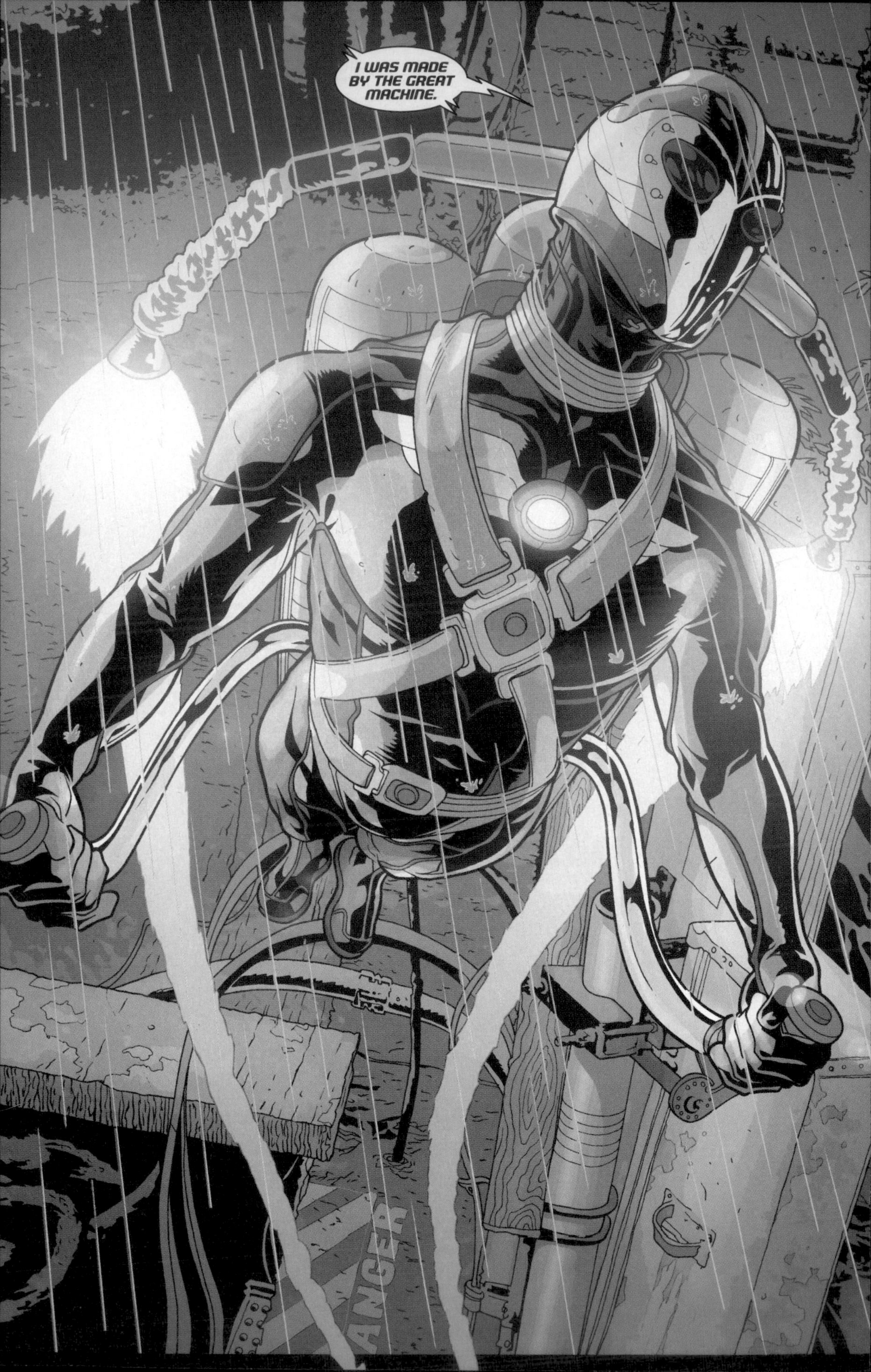
I WAS MADE BY THE GREAT MACHINE.
ANGER

CHAPTER 3 Fact v. Fiction part 2

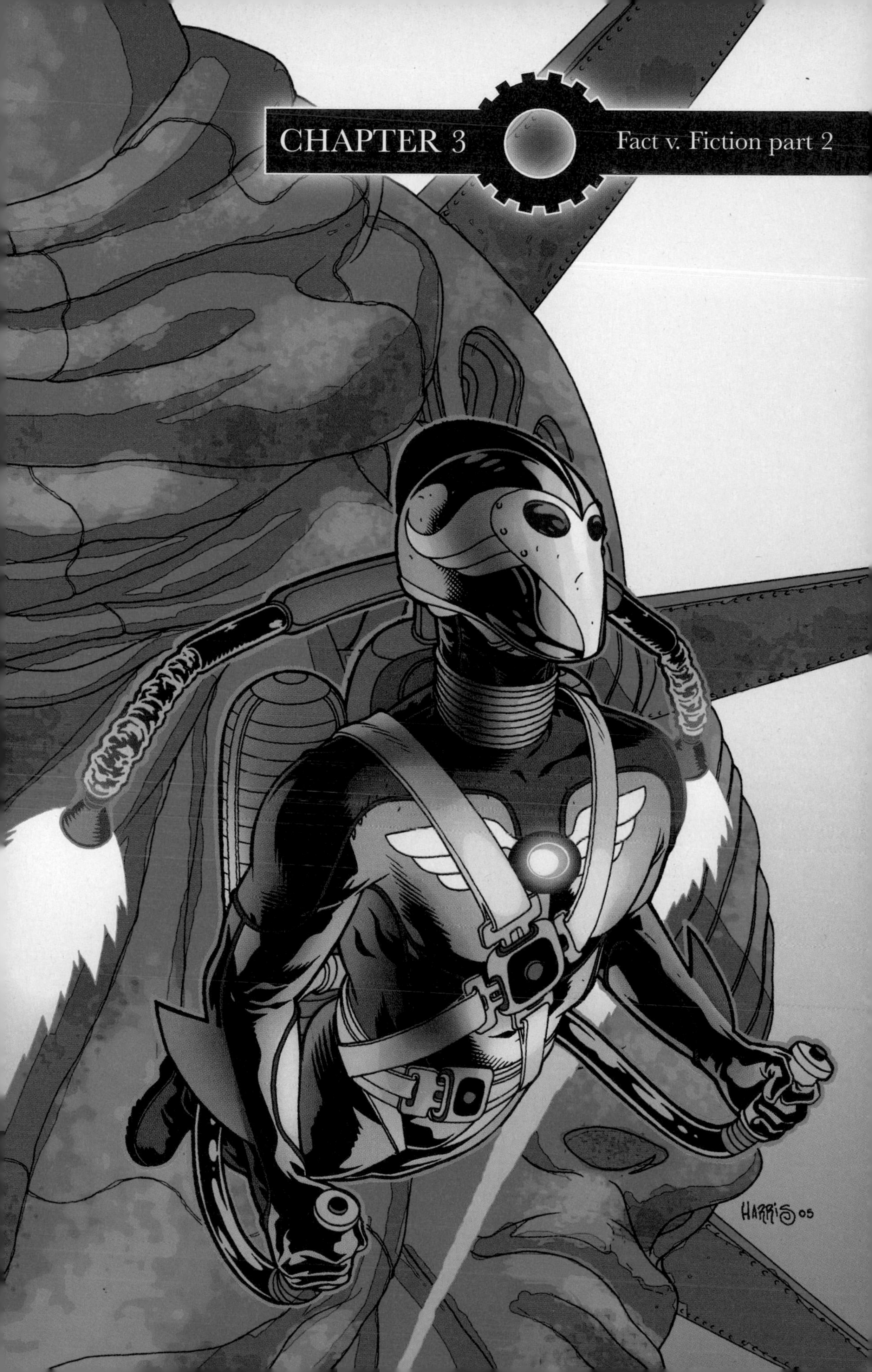
HARRIS 05

GO ON, MITCH.
BUT YOU MAY ONLY BE HAVING *ONE*, SO CHOOSE CAREFULLY.
COMICS ETC
TUESDAY, JULY 26, 1977
WHY JUST *ONE*, KREMLIN?
COMICS ONLY COST THIRTY-FIVE CENTS.
YES, ALMOST *THREE TIMES* WHAT THEY COST WHEN I FIRST COME HERE ONLY TEN YEARS AGO. *DISGUSTING*.
KUNG FU

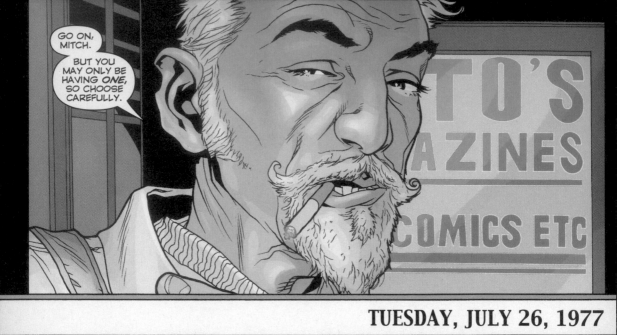

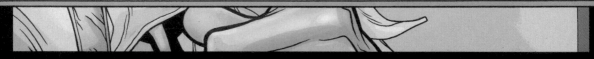

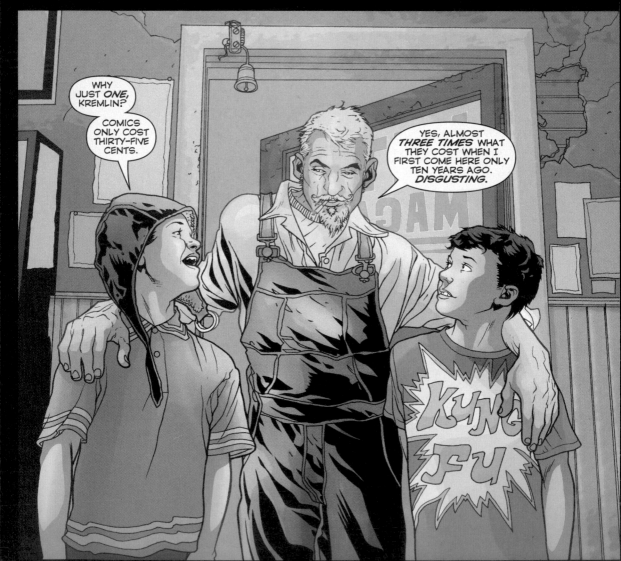

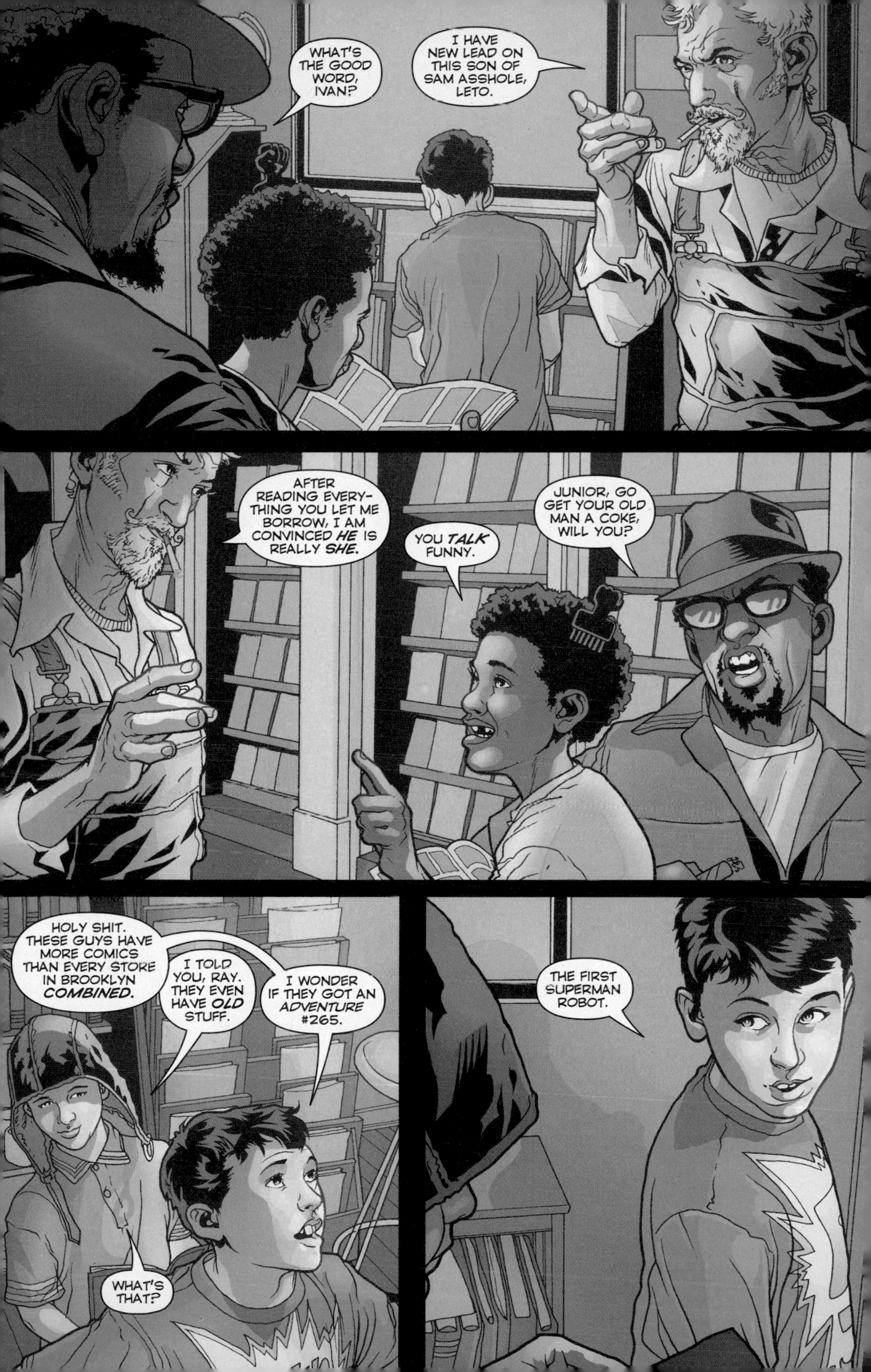
WHAT'S THE GOOD WORD, IVAN?
I HAVE NEW LEAD ON THIS SON OF SAM ASSHOLE, LETO.
AFTER READING EVERYTHING YOU LET ME BORROW, I AM CONVINCED *HE* IS REALLY *SHE*.
YOU *TALK* FUNNY.
JUNIOR, GO GET YOUR OLD MAN A COKE, WILL YOU?
HOLY SHIT. THESE GUYS HAVE MORE COMICS THAN EVERY STORE IN BROOKLYN *COMBINED*.
I TOLD YOU, RAY. THEY EVEN HAVE *OLD* STUFF.
I WONDER IF THEY GOT AN *ADVENTURE* #265.
WHAT'S THAT?
THE FIRST SUPERMAN ROBOT.

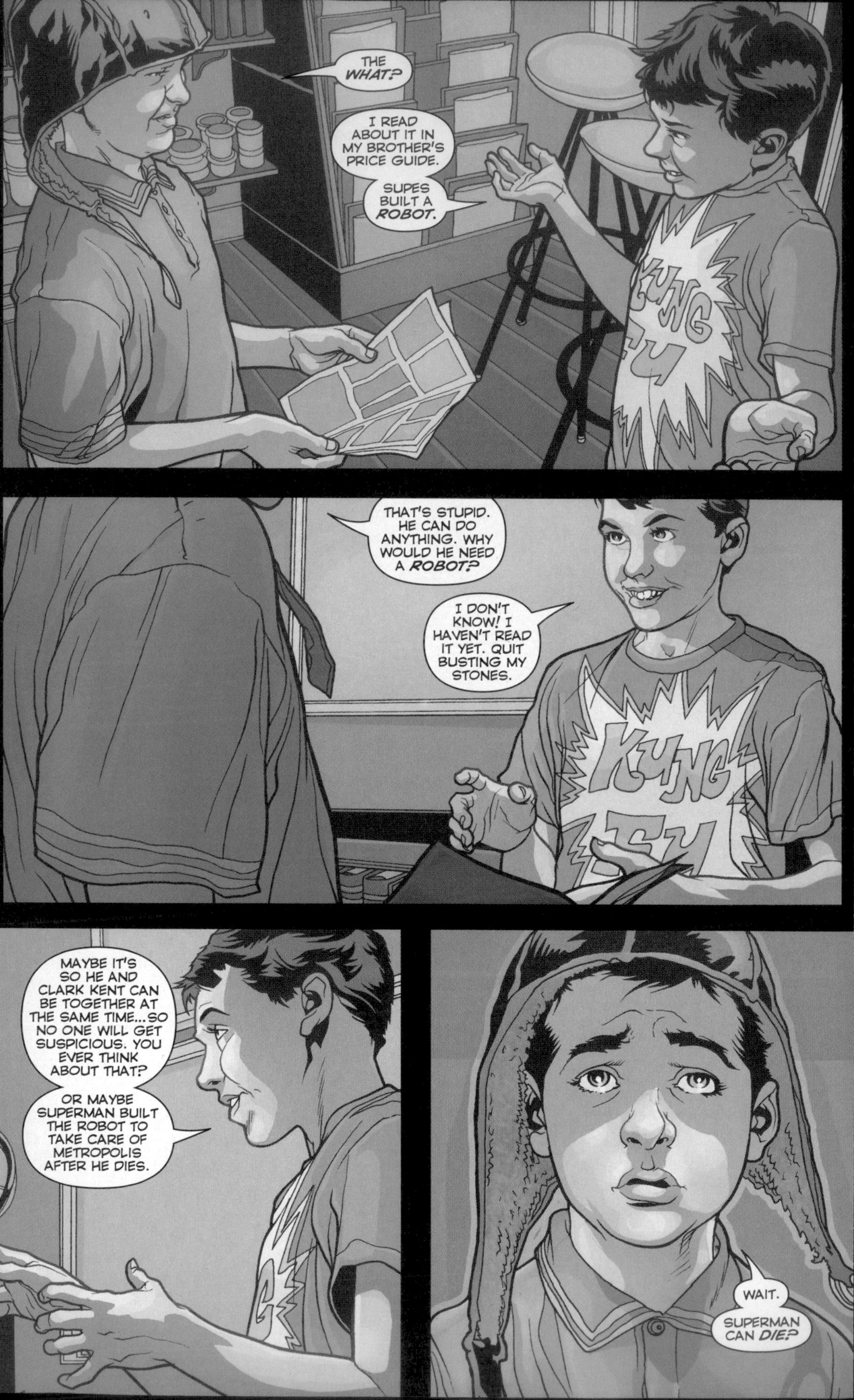
THE *WHAT?*
I READ ABOUT IT IN MY BROTHER'S PRICE GUIDE.
SUPES BUILT A *ROBOT*.
KUNG FU
THAT'S STUPID. HE CAN DO ANYTHING. WHY WOULD HE NEED A *ROBOT?*
I DON'T KNOW*!* I HAVEN'T READ IT YET. QUIT BUSTING MY STONES.
KUNG
MAYBE IT'S SO HE AND CLARK KENT CAN BE TOGETHER AT THE SAME TIME...SO NO ONE WILL GET SUSPICIOUS. YOU EVER THINK ABOUT THAT?
OR MAYBE SUPERMAN BUILT THE ROBOT TO TAKE CARE OF METROPOLIS AFTER HE DIES.
WAIT.
SUPERMAN CAN *DIE?*

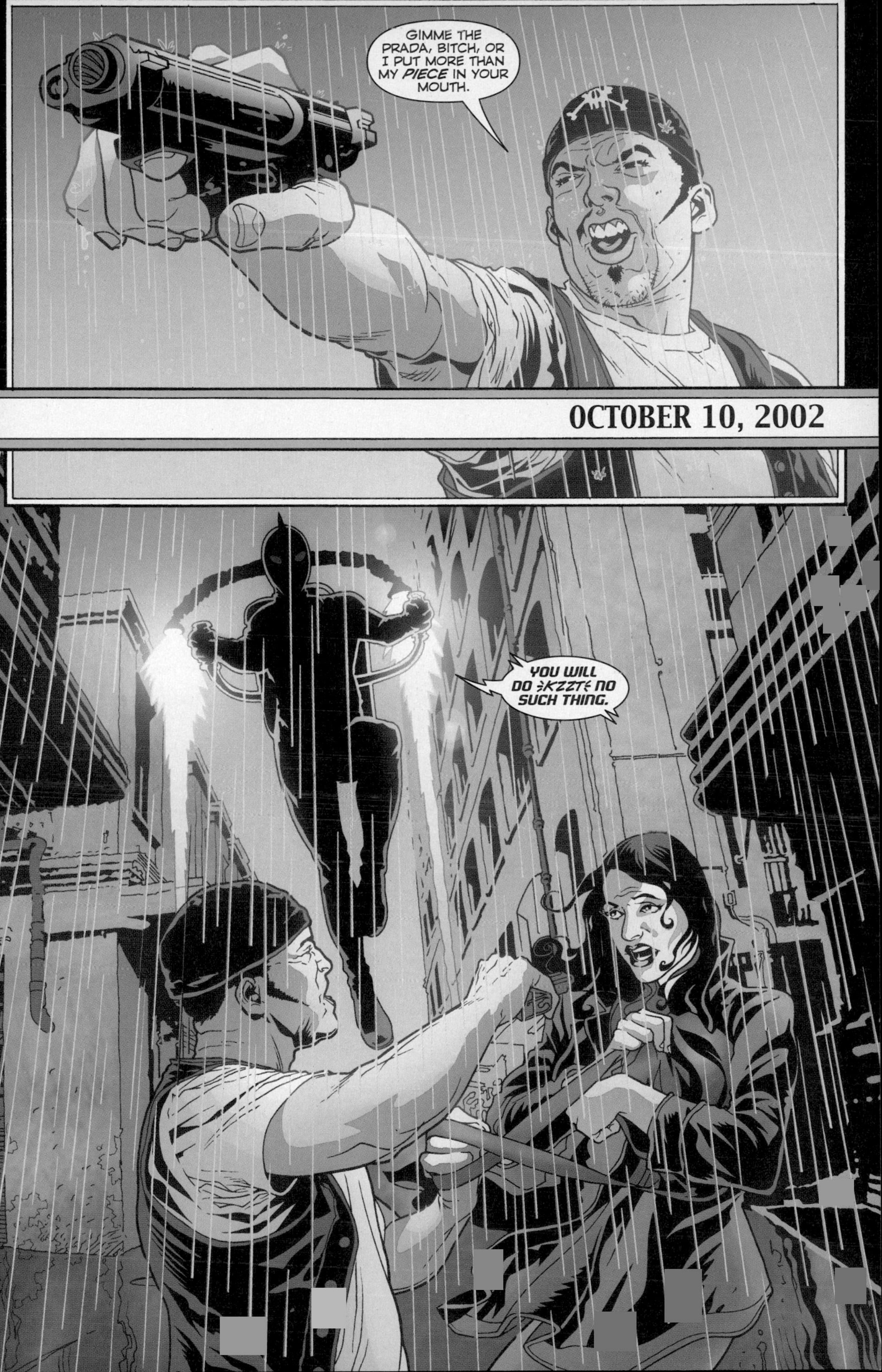
GIMME THE PRADA, BITCH, OR I PUT MORE THAN MY *PIECE* IN YOUR MOUTH.
OCTOBER 10, 2002
YOU WILL DO KZZT NO SUCH THING.

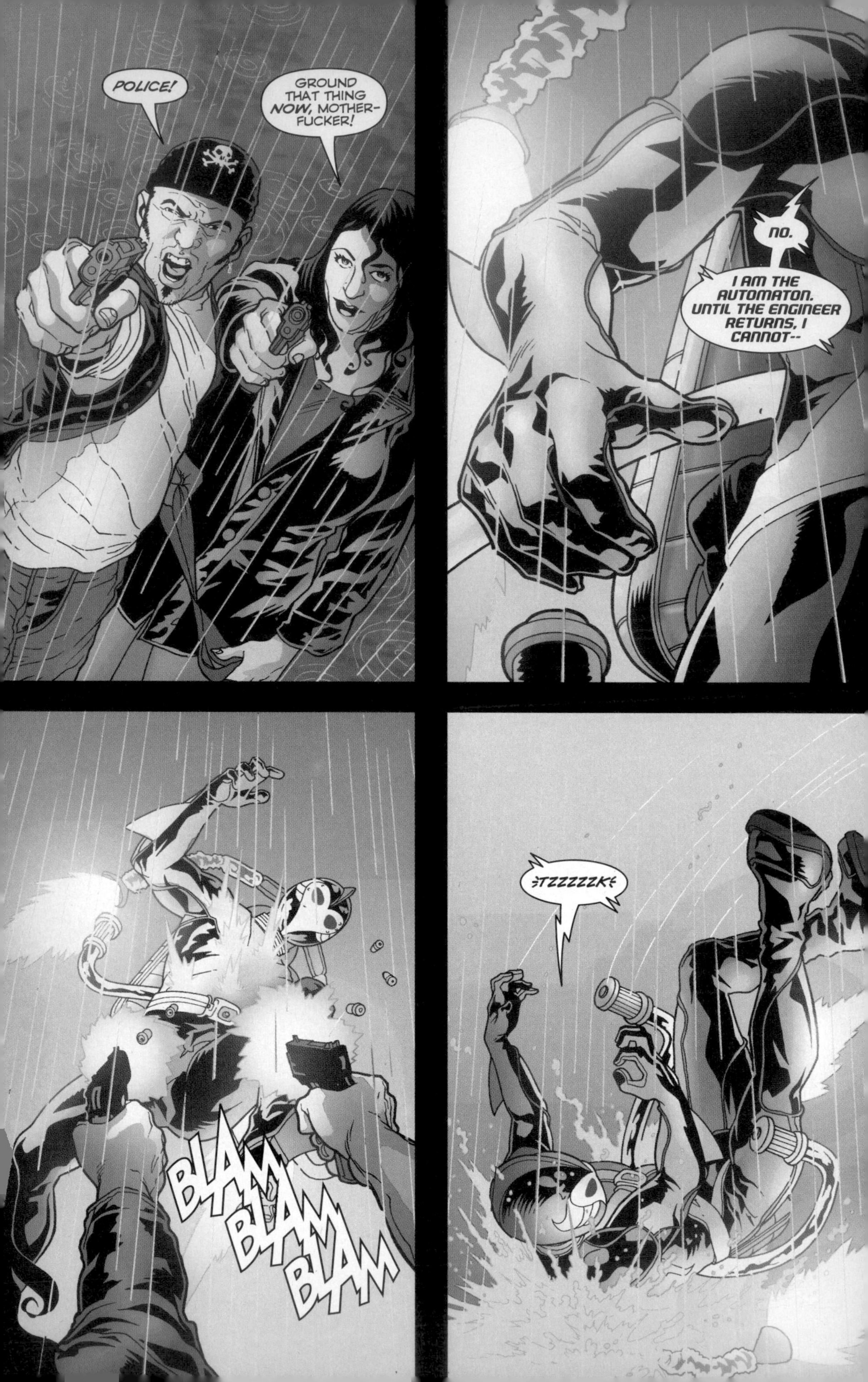
POLICE!
GROUND THAT THING *NOW*, MOTHER-FUCKER!
no.
I AM THE AUTOMATON. UNTIL THE ENGINEER RETURNS, I CANNOT--
BLAM BLAM BLAM
TZZZZZK

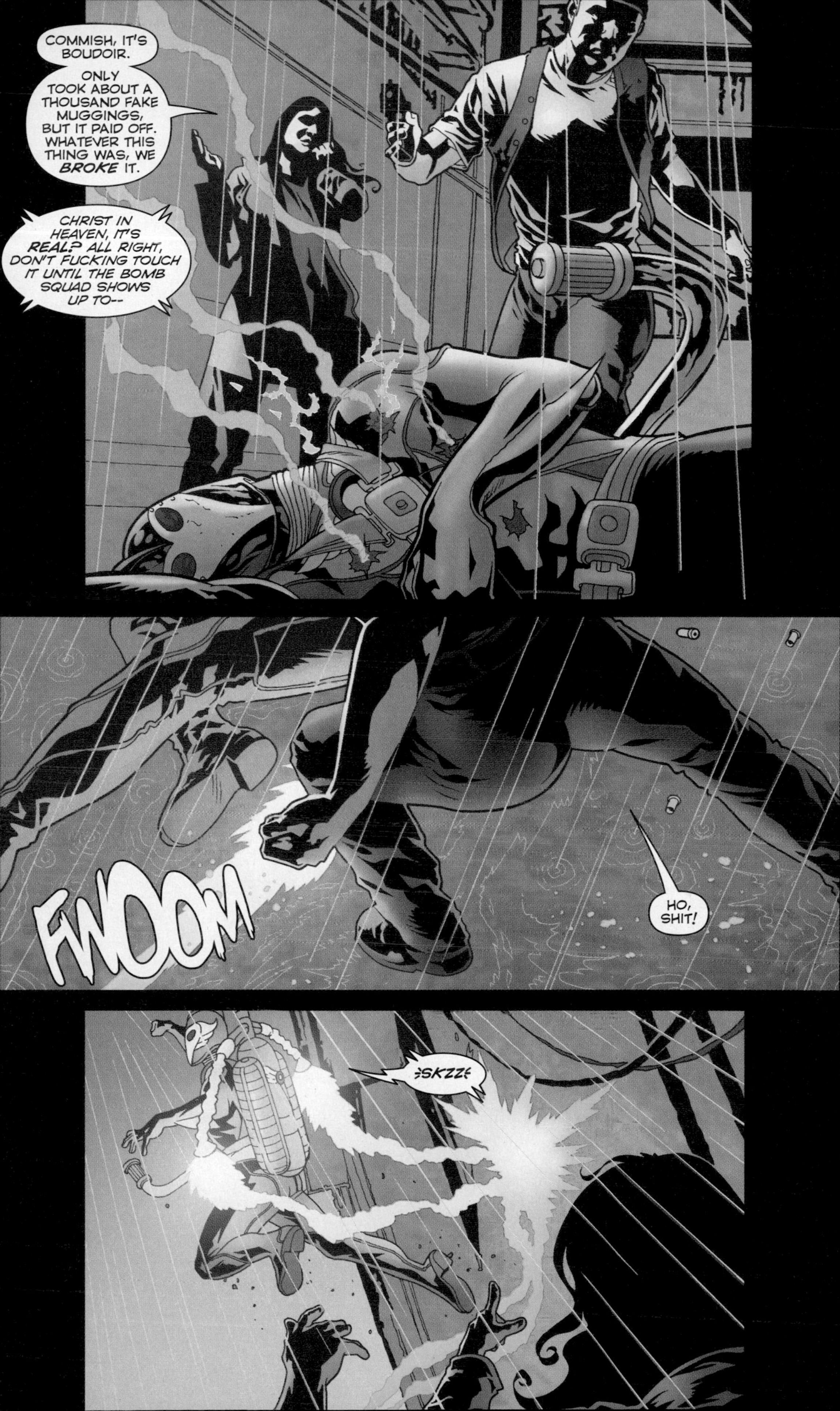
COMMISH, IT'S BOUDOIR.
ONLY TOOK ABOUT A THOUSAND FAKE MUGGINGS, BUT IT PAID OFF. WHATEVER THIS THING WAS, WE BROKE IT.
CHRIST IN HEAVEN, IT'S REAL? ALL RIGHT, DON'T FUCKING TOUCH IT UNTIL THE BOMB SQUAD SHOWS UP TO--
FWOOM
HO, SHIT!
SKZZ

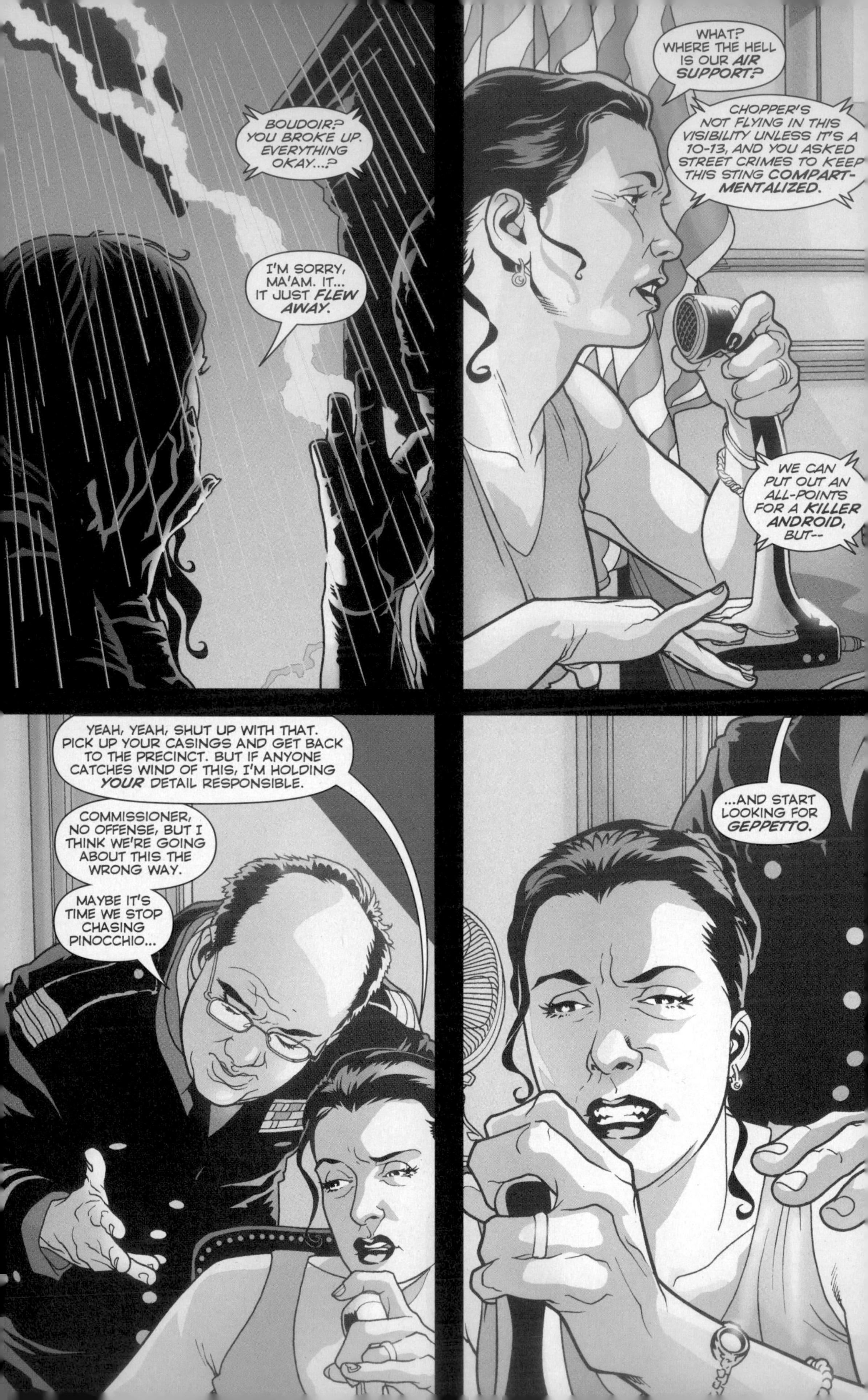
BOUDOIR? YOU BROKE UP. EVERYTHING OKAY...?
I'M SORRY, MA'AM. IT... IT JUST FLEW AWAY.
WHAT? WHERE THE HELL IS OUR AIR SUPPORT?
CHOPPER'S NOT FLYING IN THIS VISIBILITY UNLESS IT'S A 10-13, AND YOU ASKED STREET CRIMES TO KEEP THIS STING COMPART-MENTALIZED.
WE CAN PUT OUT AN ALL-POINTS FOR A KILLER ANDROID, BUT--
YEAH, YEAH, SHUT UP WITH THAT. PICK UP YOUR CASINGS AND GET BACK TO THE PRECINCT. BUT IF ANYONE CATCHES WIND OF THIS, I'M HOLDING YOUR DETAIL RESPONSIBLE.
COMMISSIONER, NO OFFENSE, BUT I THINK WE'RE GOING ABOUT THIS THE WRONG WAY.
MAYBE IT'S TIME WE STOP CHASING PINOCCHIO...
...AND START LOOKING FOR GEPPETTO.

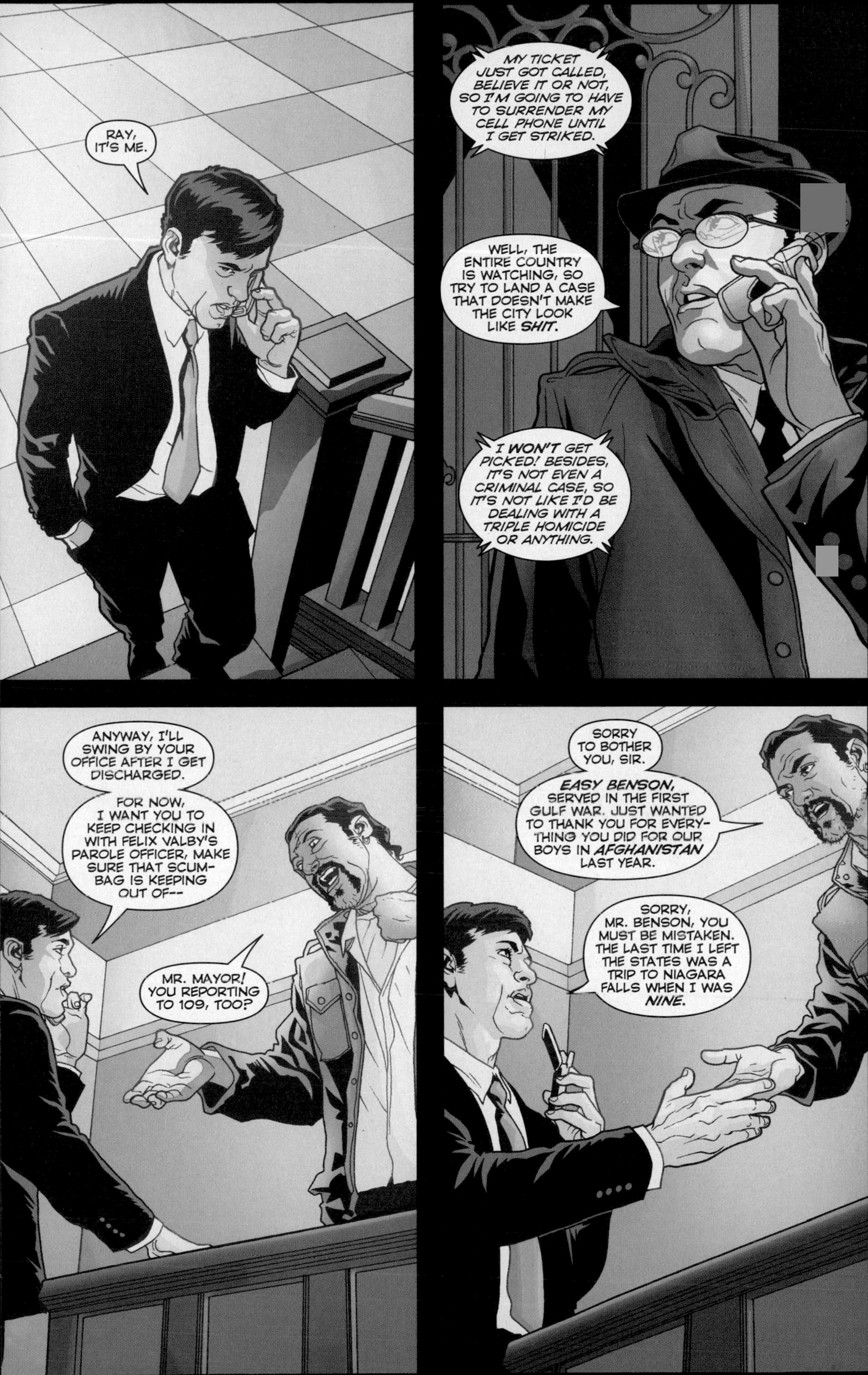
RAY, IT'S ME.
MY TICKET JUST GOT CALLED, BELIEVE IT OR NOT, SO I'M GOING TO HAVE TO SURRENDER MY CELL PHONE UNTIL I GET STRIKED.
WELL, THE ENTIRE COUNTRY IS WATCHING, SO TRY TO LAND A CASE THAT DOESN'T MAKE THE CITY LOOK LIKE SHIT.
I WON'T GET PICKED! BESIDES, IT'S NOT EVEN A CRIMINAL CASE, SO IT'S NOT LIKE I'D BE DEALING WITH A TRIPLE HOMICIDE OR ANYTHING.
ANYWAY, I'LL SWING BY YOUR OFFICE AFTER I GET DISCHARGED.
FOR NOW, I WANT YOU TO KEEP CHECKING IN WITH FELIX VALBY'S PAROLE OFFICER, MAKE SURE THAT SCUM-BAG IS KEEPING OUT OF--
MR. MAYOR! YOU REPORTING TO 109, TOO?
SORRY TO BOTHER YOU, SIR.
EASY BENSON, SERVED IN THE FIRST GULF WAR. JUST WANTED TO THANK YOU FOR EVERY-THING YOU DID FOR OUR BOYS IN AFGHANISTAN LAST YEAR.
SORRY, MR. BENSON, YOU MUST BE MISTAKEN. THE LAST TIME I LEFT THE STATES WAS A TRIP TO NIAGARA FALLS WHEN I WAS NINE.

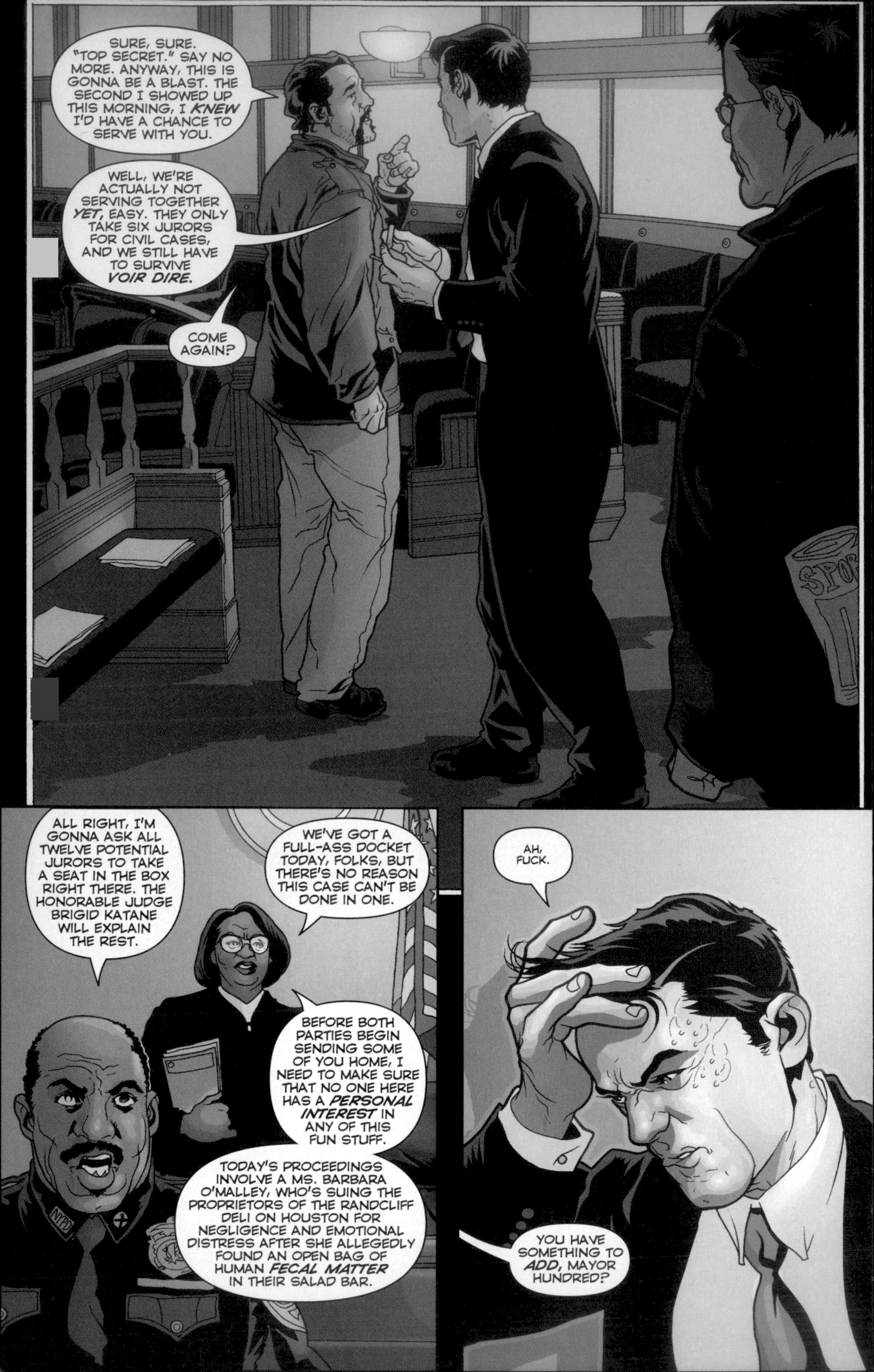

SURE, SURE. "TOP SECRET." SAY NO MORE. ANYWAY, THIS IS GONNA BE A BLAST. THE SECOND I SHOWED UP THIS MORNING, I KNEW I'D HAVE A CHANCE TO SERVE WITH YOU.
WELL, WE'RE ACTUALLY NOT SERVING TOGETHER YET, EASY. THEY ONLY TAKE SIX JURORS FOR CIVIL CASES, AND WE STILL HAVE TO SURVIVE VOIR DIRE.
COME AGAIN?
ALL RIGHT, I'M GONNA ASK ALL TWELVE POTENTIAL JURORS TO TAKE A SEAT IN THE BOX RIGHT THERE. THE HONORABLE JUDGE BRIGID KATANE WILL EXPLAIN THE REST.
WE'VE GOT A FULL-ASS DOCKET TODAY, FOLKS, BUT THERE'S NO REASON THIS CASE CAN'T BE DONE IN ONE.
BEFORE BOTH PARTIES BEGIN SENDING SOME OF YOU HOME, I NEED TO MAKE SURE THAT NO ONE HERE HAS A PERSONAL INTEREST IN ANY OF THIS FUN STUFF.
TODAY'S PROCEEDINGS INVOLVE A MS. BARBARA O'MALLEY, WHO'S SUING THE PROPRIETORS OF THE RANDCLIFF DELI ON HOUSTON FOR NEGLIGENCE AND EMOTIONAL DISTRESS AFTER SHE ALLEGEDLY FOUND AN OPEN BAG OF HUMAN FECAL MATTER IN THEIR SALAD BAR.
AH, FUCK.
YOU HAVE SOMETHING TO ADD, MAYOR HUNDRED?

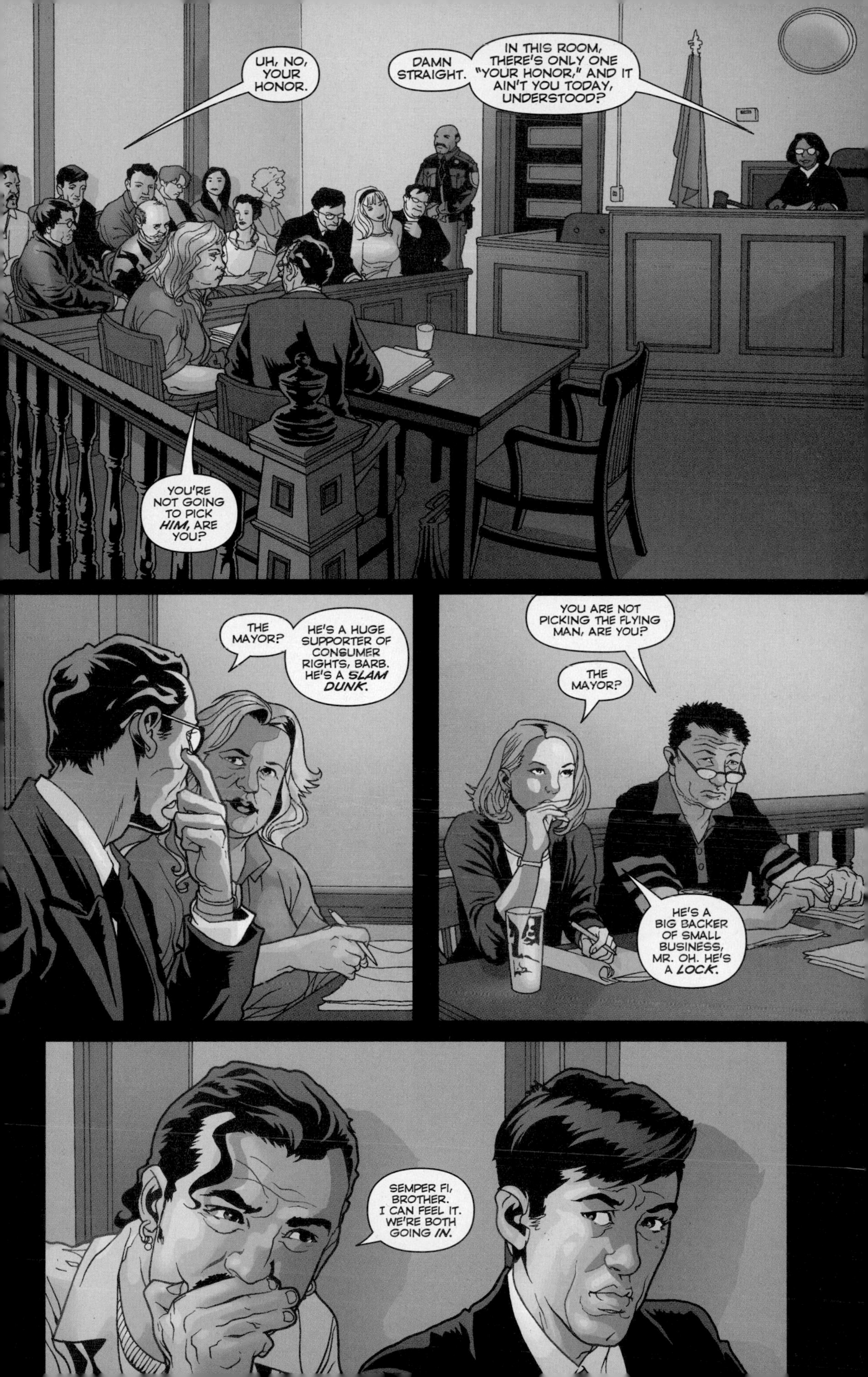
UH, NO, YOUR HONOR.
DAMN STRAIGHT.
IN THIS ROOM, THERE'S ONLY ONE "YOUR HONOR," AND IT AIN'T YOU TODAY, UNDERSTOOD?
YOU'RE NOT GOING TO PICK *HIM*, ARE YOU?
THE MAYOR?
HE'S A HUGE SUPPORTER OF CONSUMER RIGHTS, BARB. HE'S A *SLAM DUNK*.
YOU ARE NOT PICKING THE FLYING MAN, ARE YOU?
THE MAYOR?
HE'S A BIG BACKER OF SMALL BUSINESS, MR. OH. HE'S A *LOCK*.
SEMPER FI, BROTHER. I CAN FEEL IT. WE'RE BOTH GOING *IN*.

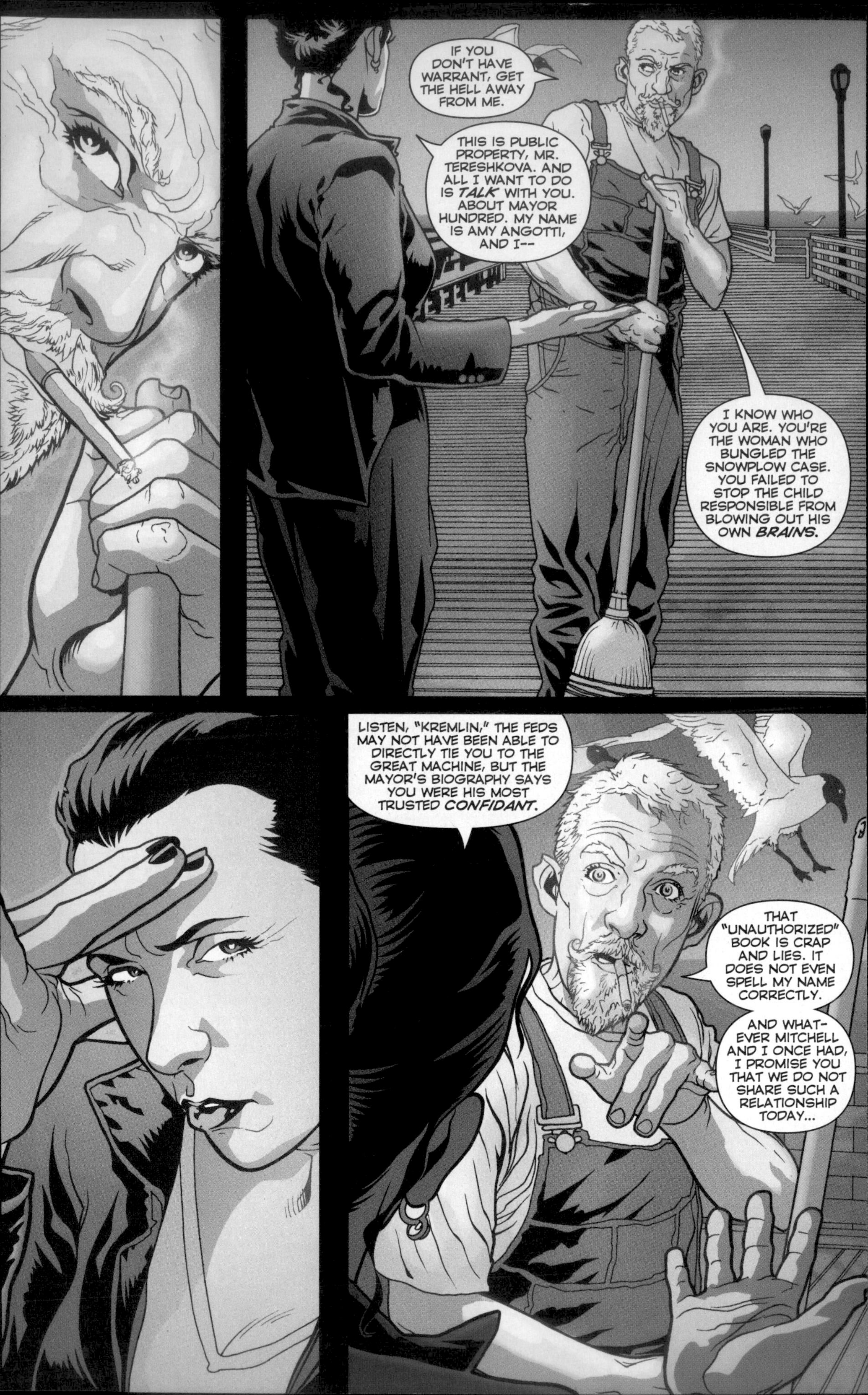
IF YOU DON'T HAVE WARRANT, GET THE HELL AWAY FROM ME.
THIS IS PUBLIC PROPERTY, MR. TERESHKOVA. AND ALL I WANT TO DO IS TALK WITH YOU. ABOUT MAYOR HUNDRED. MY NAME IS AMY ANGOTTI, AND I--
I KNOW WHO YOU ARE. YOU'RE THE WOMAN WHO BUNGLED THE SNOWPLOW CASE. YOU FAILED TO STOP THE CHILD RESPONSIBLE FROM BLOWING OUT HIS OWN BRAINS.
LISTEN, "KREMLIN," THE FEDS MAY NOT HAVE BEEN ABLE TO DIRECTLY TIE YOU TO THE GREAT MACHINE, BUT THE MAYOR'S BIOGRAPHY SAYS YOU WERE HIS MOST TRUSTED CONFIDANT.
THAT "UNAUTHORIZED" BOOK IS CRAP AND LIES. IT DOES NOT EVEN SPELL MY NAME CORRECTLY.
AND WHAT-EVER MITCHELL AND I ONCE HAD, I PROMISE YOU THAT WE DO NOT SHARE SUCH A RELATIONSHIP TODAY...

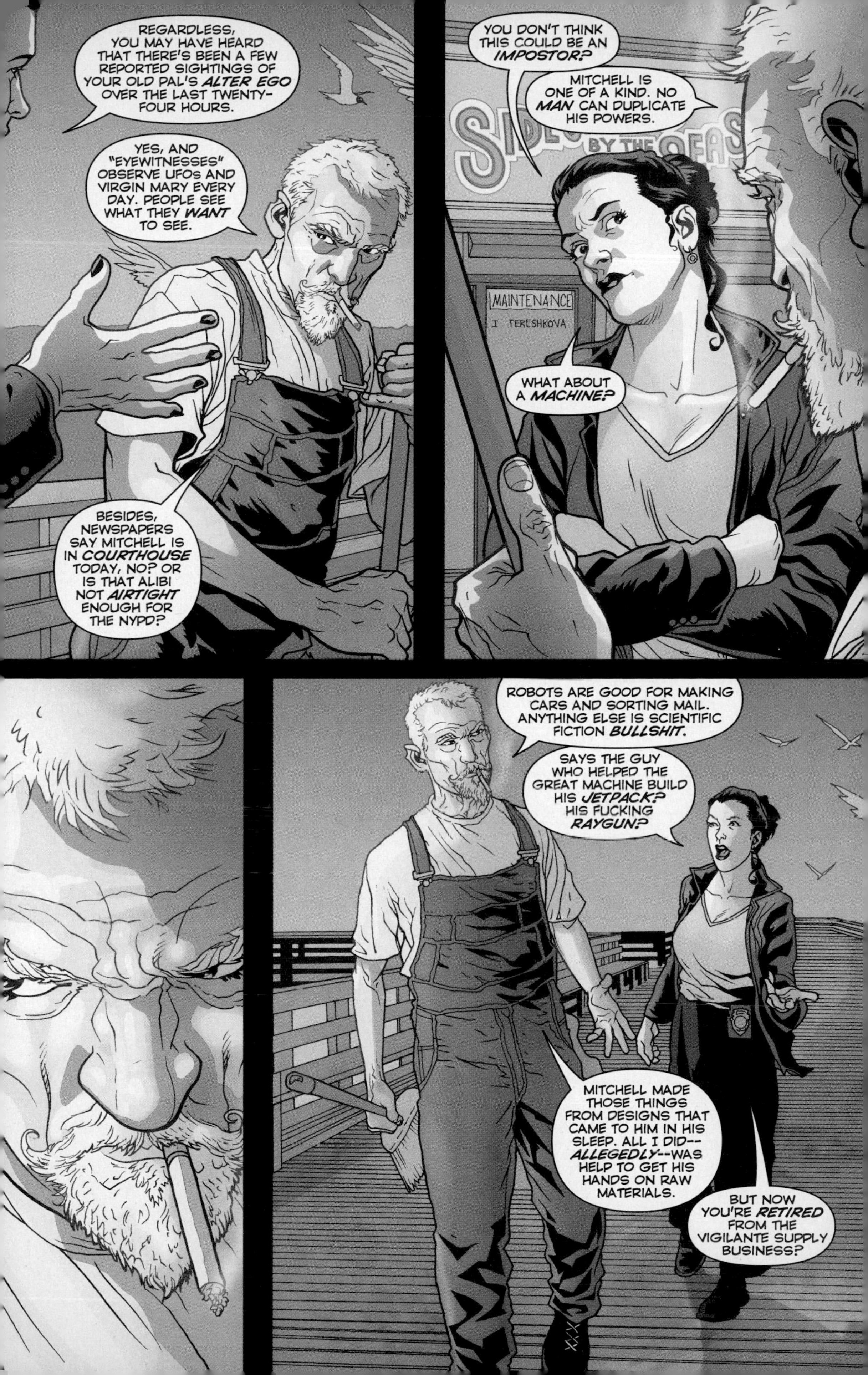
REGARDLESS, YOU MAY HAVE HEARD THAT THERE'S BEEN A FEW REPORTED SIGHTINGS OF YOUR OLD PAL'S ALTER EGO OVER THE LAST TWENTY-FOUR HOURS.
YES, AND "EYEWITNESSES" OBSERVE UFOs AND VIRGIN MARY EVERY DAY. PEOPLE SEE WHAT THEY WANT TO SEE.
BESIDES, NEWSPAPERS SAY MITCHELL IS IN COURTHOUSE TODAY, NO? OR IS THAT ALIBI NOT AIRTIGHT ENOUGH FOR THE NYPD?
YOU DON'T THINK THIS COULD BE AN IMPOSTOR?
MITCHELL IS ONE OF A KIND. NO MAN CAN DUPLICATE HIS POWERS.
MAINTENANCE
I. TERESHKOVA
WHAT ABOUT A MACHINE?
ROBOTS ARE GOOD FOR MAKING CARS AND SORTING MAIL. ANYTHING ELSE IS SCIENTIFIC FICTION BULLSHIT.
SAYS THE GUY WHO HELPED THE GREAT MACHINE BUILD HIS JETPACK? HIS FUCKING RAYGUN?
MITCHELL MADE THOSE THINGS FROM DESIGNS THAT CAME TO HIM IN HIS SLEEP. ALL I DID--ALLEGEDLY--WAS HELP TO GET HIS HANDS ON RAW MATERIALS.
BUT NOW YOU'RE RETIRED FROM THE VIGILANTE SUPPLY BUSINESS?

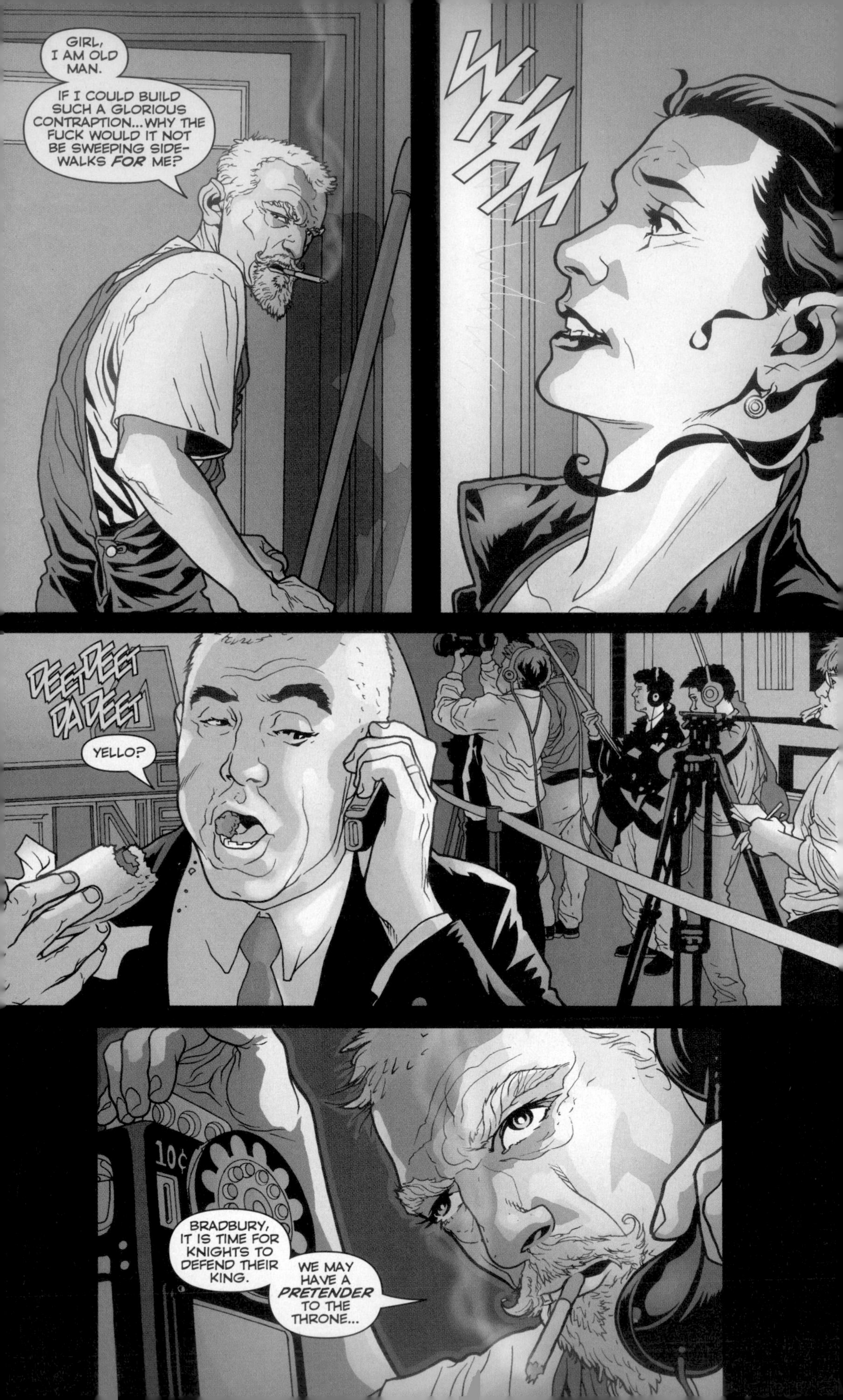

GIRL, I AM OLD MAN.
IF I COULD BUILD SUCH A GLORIOUS CONTRAPTION...WHY THE FUCK WOULD IT NOT BE SWEEPING SIDE-WALKS *FOR* ME?
WHAM
DEET-DEET DA DEET
YELLO?
BRADBURY, IT IS TIME FOR KNIGHTS TO DEFEND THEIR KING.
WE MAY HAVE A *PRETENDER* TO THE THRONE...

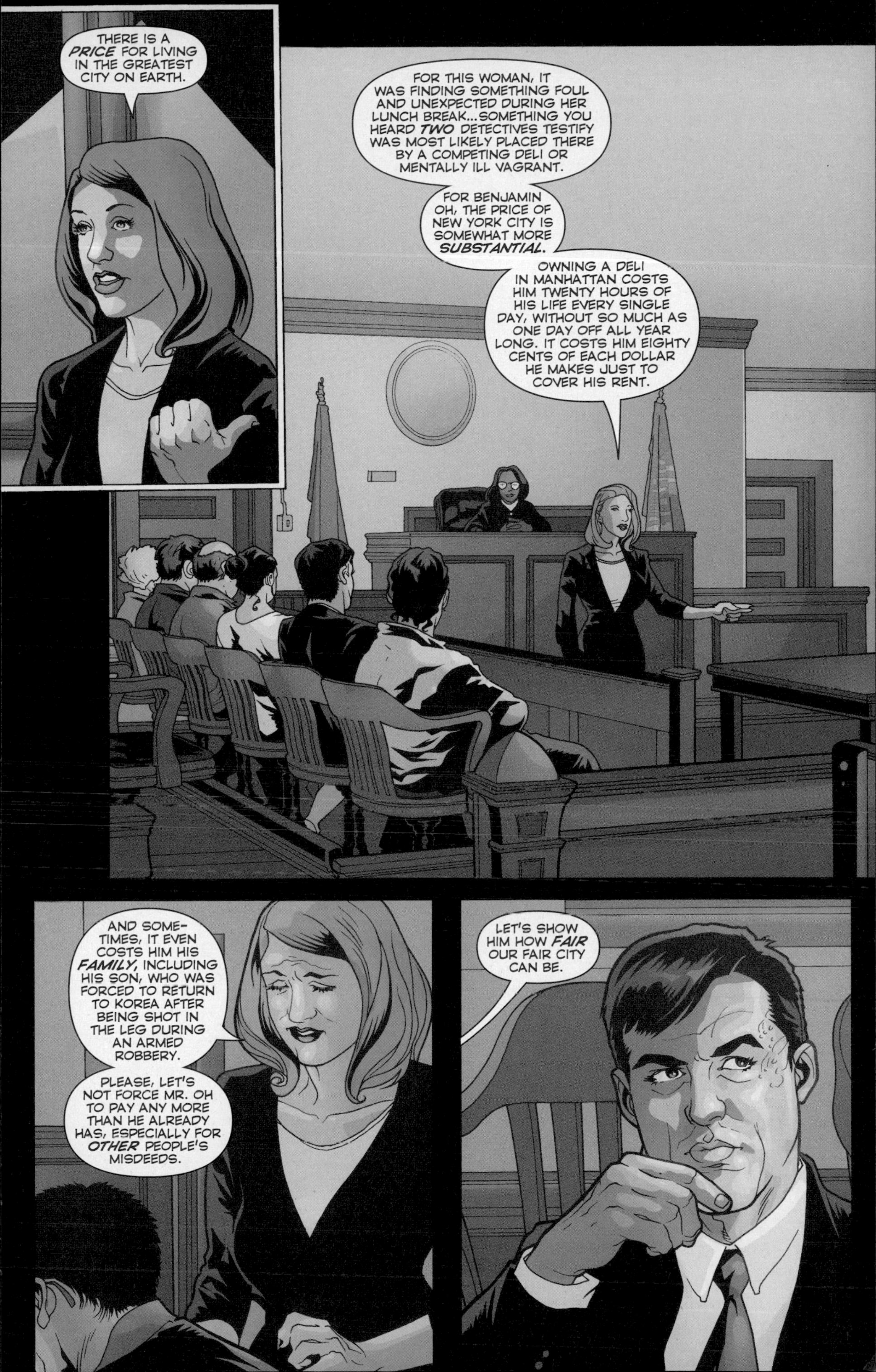
THERE IS A PRICE FOR LIVING IN THE GREATEST CITY ON EARTH.
FOR THIS WOMAN, IT WAS FINDING SOMETHING FOUL AND UNEXPECTED DURING HER LUNCH BREAK...SOMETHING YOU HEARD TWO DETECTIVES TESTIFY WAS MOST LIKELY PLACED THERE BY A COMPETING DELI OR MENTALLY ILL VAGRANT.
FOR BENJAMIN OH, THE PRICE OF NEW YORK CITY IS SOMEWHAT MORE SUBSTANTIAL.
OWNING A DELI IN MANHATTAN COSTS HIM TWENTY HOURS OF HIS LIFE EVERY SINGLE DAY, WITHOUT SO MUCH AS ONE DAY OFF ALL YEAR LONG. IT COSTS HIM EIGHTY CENTS OF EACH DOLLAR HE MAKES JUST TO COVER HIS RENT.
AND SOME-TIMES, IT EVEN COSTS HIM HIS FAMILY, INCLUDING HIS SON, WHO WAS FORCED TO RETURN TO KOREA AFTER BEING SHOT IN THE LEG DURING AN ARMED ROBBERY.
PLEASE, LET'S NOT FORCE MR. OH TO PAY ANY MORE THAN HE ALREADY HAS, ESPECIALLY FOR OTHER PEOPLE'S MISDEEDS.
LET'S SHOW HIM HOW FAIR OUR FAIR CITY CAN BE.

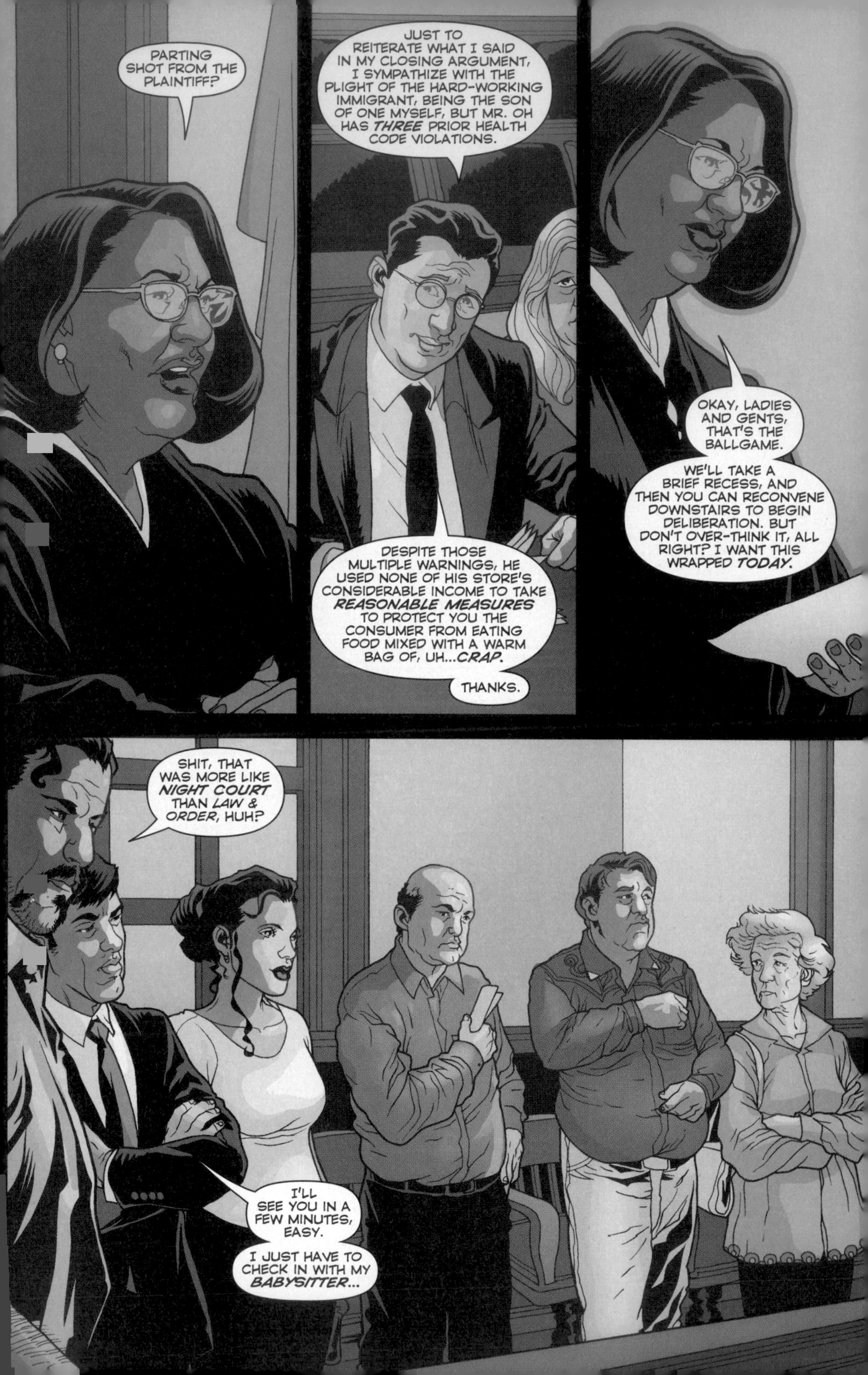
PARTING SHOT FROM THE PLAINTIFF?
JUST TO REITERATE WHAT I SAID IN MY CLOSING ARGUMENT, I SYMPATHIZE WITH THE PLIGHT OF THE HARD-WORKING IMMIGRANT, BEING THE SON OF ONE MYSELF, BUT MR. OH HAS THREE PRIOR HEALTH CODE VIOLATIONS.
DESPITE THOSE MULTIPLE WARNINGS, HE USED NONE OF HIS STORE'S CONSIDERABLE INCOME TO TAKE REASONABLE MEASURES TO PROTECT YOU THE CONSUMER FROM EATING FOOD MIXED WITH A WARM BAG OF, UH...CRAP.
THANKS.
OKAY, LADIES AND GENTS, THAT'S THE BALLGAME.
WE'LL TAKE A BRIEF RECESS, AND THEN YOU CAN RECONVENE DOWNSTAIRS TO BEGIN DELIBERATION. BUT DON'T OVER-THINK IT, ALL RIGHT? I WANT THIS WRAPPED TODAY.
SHIT, THAT WAS MORE LIKE NIGHT COURT THAN LAW & ORDER, HUH?
I'LL SEE YOU IN A FEW MINUTES, EASY.
I JUST HAVE TO CHECK IN WITH MY BABYSITTER...

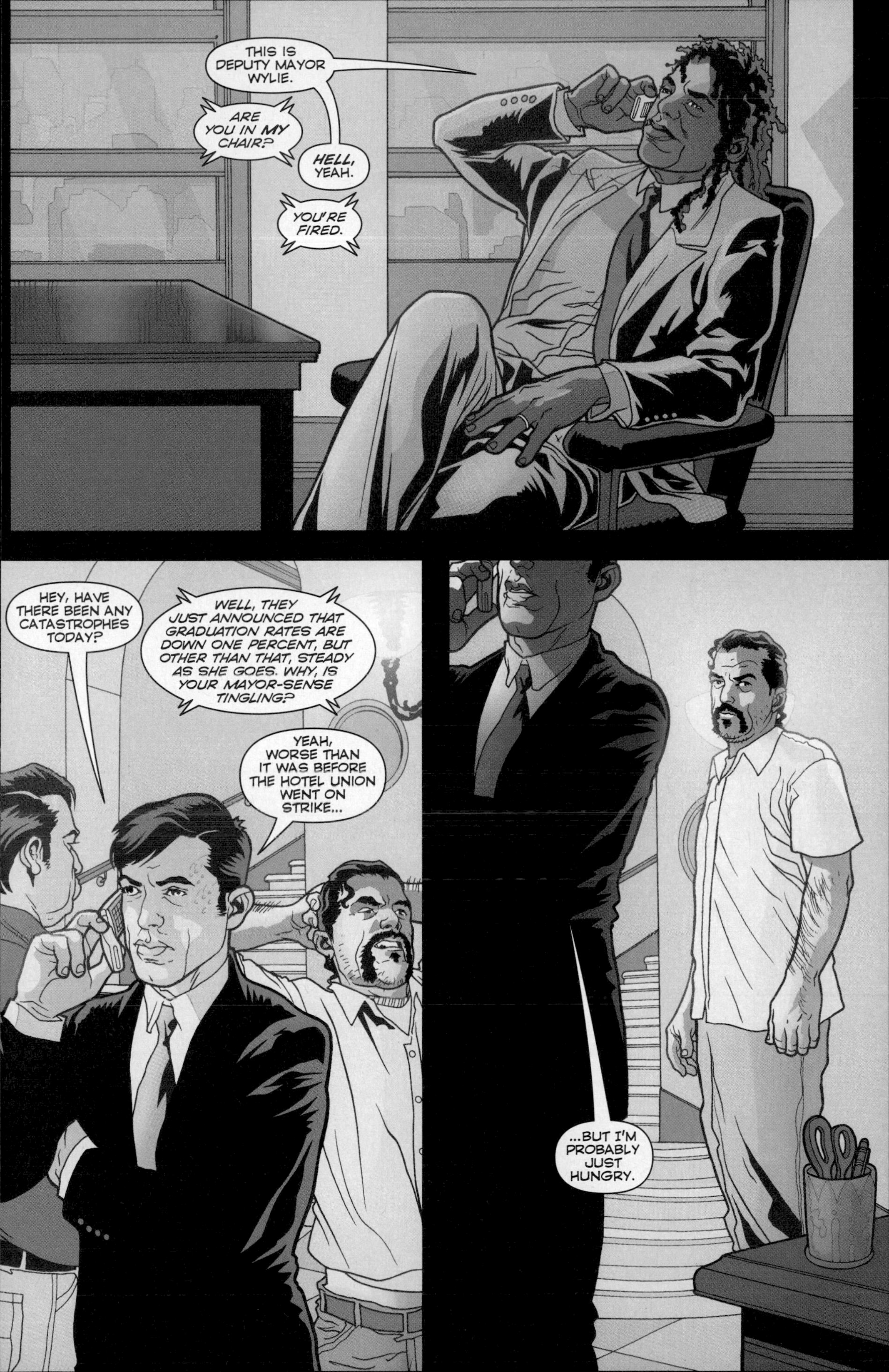
THIS IS DEPUTY MAYOR WYLIE.
ARE YOU IN MY CHAIR?
HELL, YEAH.
YOU'RE FIRED.
HEY, HAVE THERE BEEN ANY CATASTROPHES TODAY?
WELL, THEY JUST ANNOUNCED THAT GRADUATION RATES ARE DOWN ONE PERCENT, BUT OTHER THAN THAT, STEADY AS SHE GOES. WHY, IS YOUR MAYOR-SENSE TINGLING?
YEAH, WORSE THAN IT WAS BEFORE THE HOTEL UNION WENT ON STRIKE...
...BUT I'M PROBABLY JUST HUNGRY.

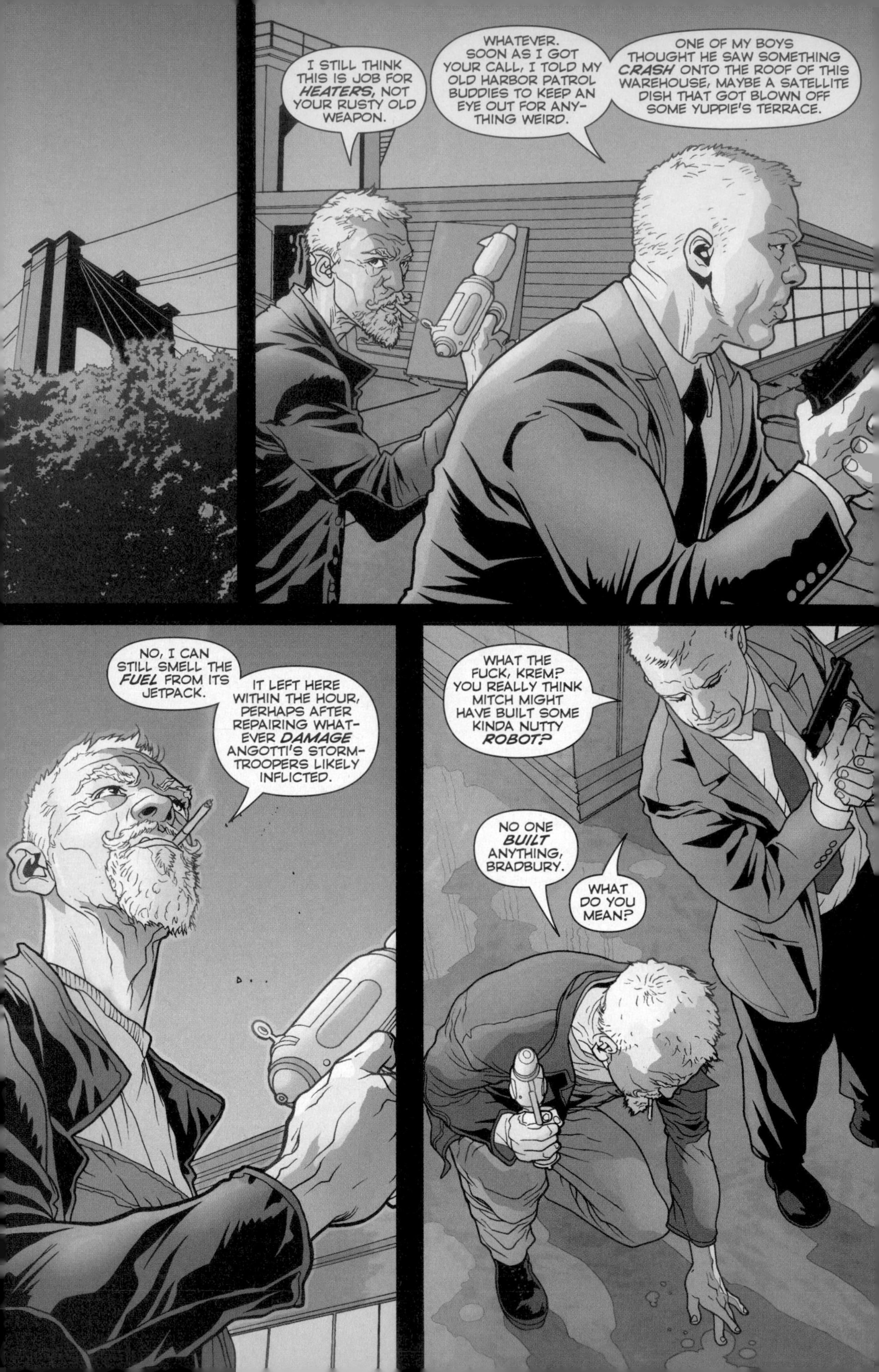
I STILL THINK THIS IS JOB FOR HEATERS, NOT YOUR RUSTY OLD WEAPON.
WHATEVER. SOON AS I GOT YOUR CALL, I TOLD MY OLD HARBOR PATROL BUDDIES TO KEEP AN EYE OUT FOR ANY-THING WEIRD.
ONE OF MY BOYS THOUGHT HE SAW SOMETHING CRASH ONTO THE ROOF OF THIS WAREHOUSE, MAYBE A SATELLITE DISH THAT GOT BLOWN OFF SOME YUPPIE'S TERRACE.
NO, I CAN STILL SMELL THE FUEL FROM ITS JETPACK.
IT LEFT HERE WITHIN THE HOUR, PERHAPS AFTER REPAIRING WHAT-EVER DAMAGE ANGOTTI'S STORM-TROOPERS LIKELY INFLICTED.
WHAT THE FUCK, KREM? YOU REALLY THINK MITCH MIGHT HAVE BUILT SOME KINDA NUTTY ROBOT?
NO ONE BUILT ANYTHING, BRADBURY.
WHAT DO YOU MEAN?

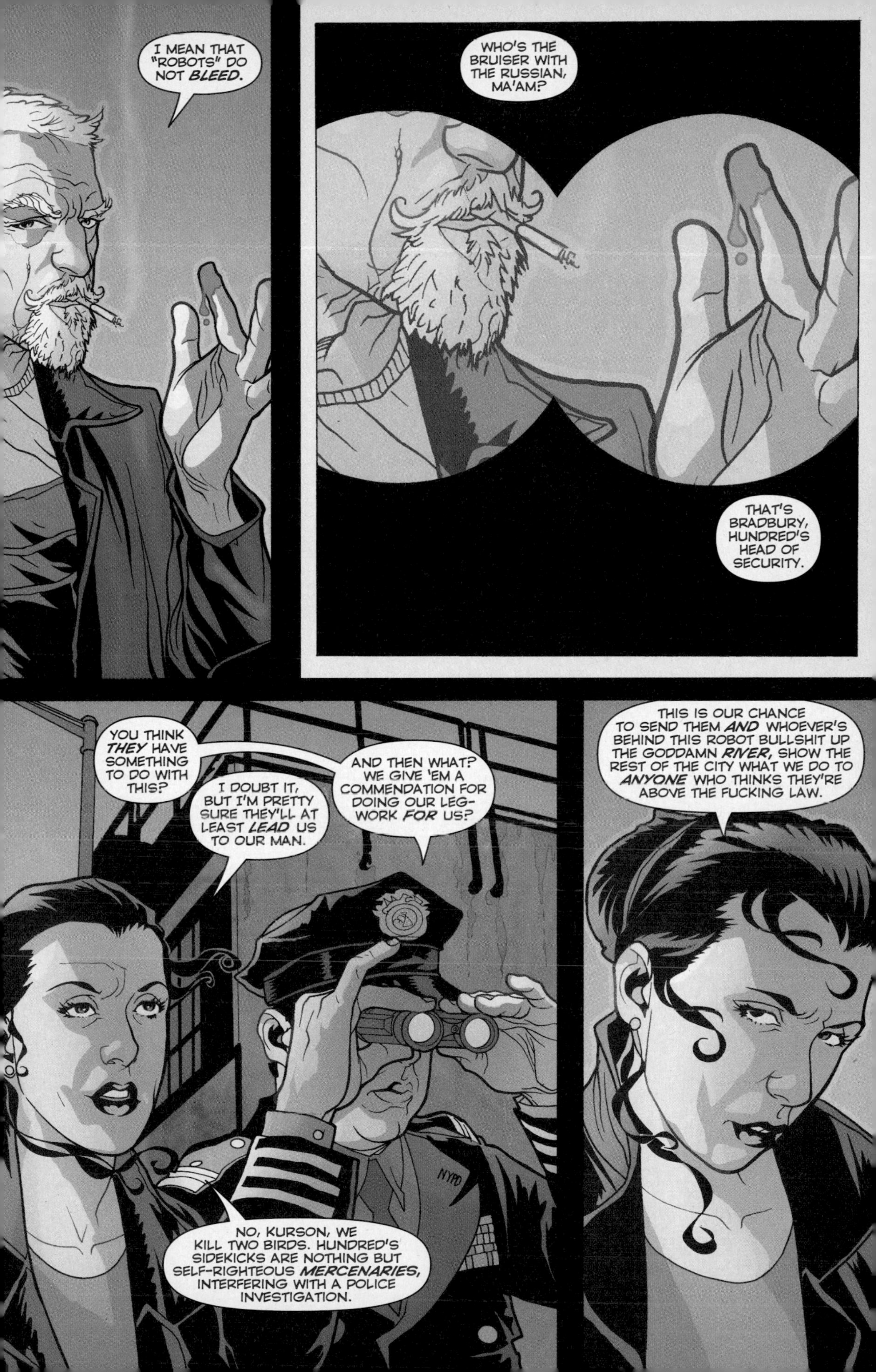
I MEAN THAT "ROBOTS" DO NOT BLEED.
WHO'S THE BRUISER WITH THE RUSSIAN, MA'AM?
THAT'S BRADBURY, HUNDRED'S HEAD OF SECURITY.
YOU THINK THEY HAVE SOMETHING TO DO WITH THIS?
I DOUBT IT, BUT I'M PRETTY SURE THEY'LL AT LEAST LEAD US TO OUR MAN.
AND THEN WHAT? WE GIVE 'EM A COMMENDATION FOR DOING OUR LEG-WORK FOR US?
NO, KURSON, WE KILL TWO BIRDS. HUNDRED'S SIDEKICKS ARE NOTHING BUT SELF-RIGHTEOUS MERCENARIES, INTERFERING WITH A POLICE INVESTIGATION.
NYPD
THIS IS OUR CHANCE TO SEND THEM AND WHOEVER'S BEHIND THIS ROBOT BULLSHIT UP THE GODDAMN RIVER, SHOW THE REST OF THE CITY WHAT WE DO TO ANYONE WHO THINKS THEY'RE ABOVE THE FUCKING LAW.

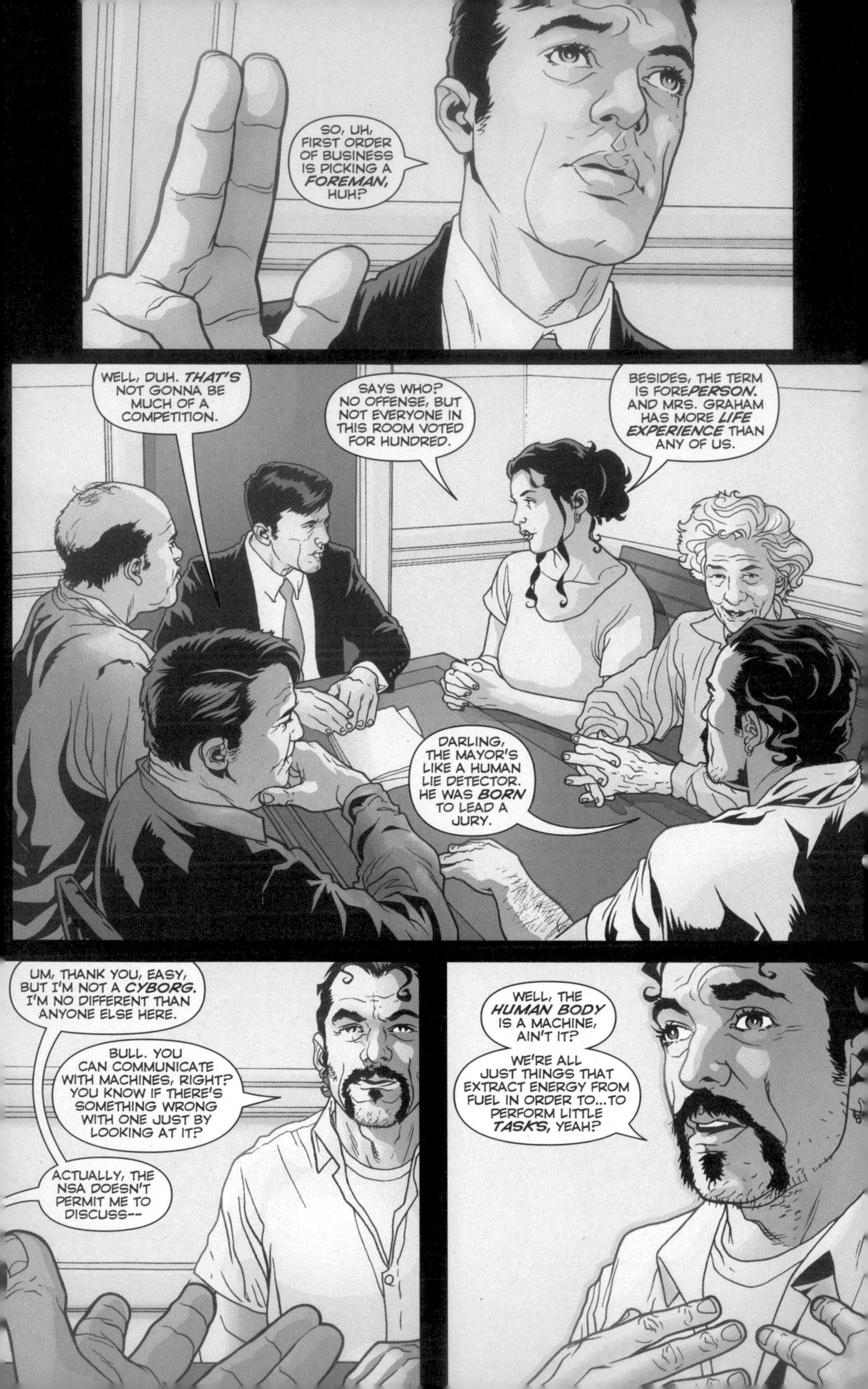
SO, UH, FIRST ORDER OF BUSINESS IS PICKING A FOREMAN, HUH?
WELL, DUH. THAT'S NOT GONNA BE MUCH OF A COMPETITION.
SAYS WHO? NO OFFENSE, BUT NOT EVERYONE IN THIS ROOM VOTED FOR HUNDRED.
BESIDES, THE TERM IS FOREPERSON. AND MRS. GRAHAM HAS MORE LIFE EXPERIENCE THAN ANY OF US.
DARLING, THE MAYOR'S LIKE A HUMAN LIE DETECTOR. HE WAS BORN TO LEAD A JURY.
UM, THANK YOU, EASY, BUT I'M NOT A CYBORG. I'M NO DIFFERENT THAN ANYONE ELSE HERE.
BULL. YOU CAN COMMUNICATE WITH MACHINES, RIGHT? YOU KNOW IF THERE'S SOMETHING WRONG WITH ONE JUST BY LOOKING AT IT?
ACTUALLY, THE NSA DOESN'T PERMIT ME TO DISCUSS--
WELL, THE HUMAN BODY IS A MACHINE, AIN'T IT?
WE'RE ALL JUST THINGS THAT EXTRACT ENERGY FROM FUEL IN ORDER TO...TO PERFORM LITTLE TASKS, YEAH?

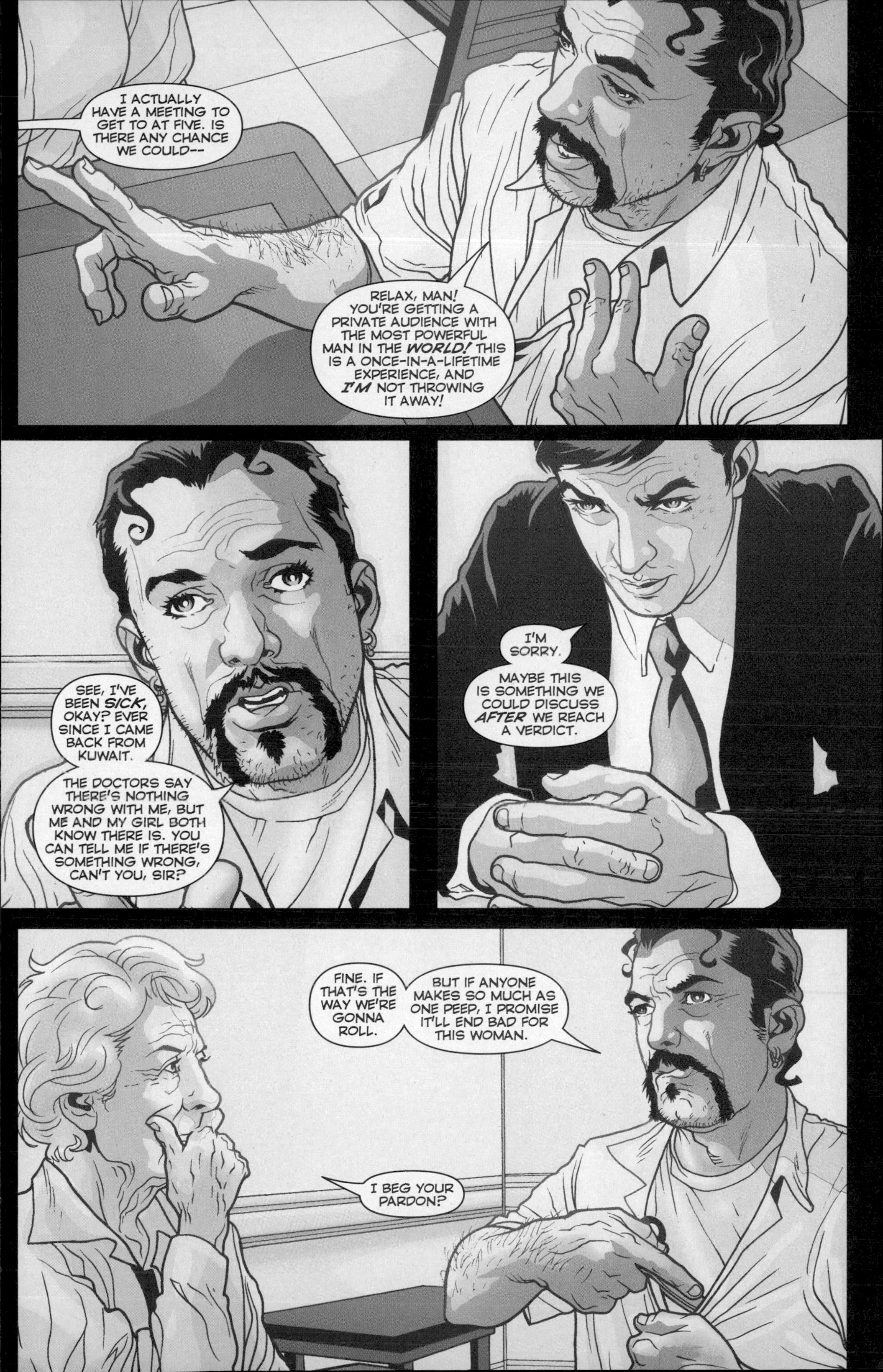
I ACTUALLY HAVE A MEETING TO GET TO AT FIVE. IS THERE ANY CHANCE WE COULD--
RELAX, MAN! YOU'RE GETTING A PRIVATE AUDIENCE WITH THE MOST POWERFUL MAN IN THE *WORLD!* THIS IS A ONCE-IN-A-LIFETIME EXPERIENCE, AND *I'M* NOT THROWING IT AWAY!
SEE, I'VE BEEN *SICK*, OKAY? EVER SINCE I CAME BACK FROM KUWAIT.
THE DOCTORS SAY THERE'S NOTHING WRONG WITH ME, BUT ME AND MY GIRL BOTH KNOW THERE IS. YOU CAN TELL ME IF THERE'S SOMETHING WRONG, CAN'T YOU, SIR?
I'M SORRY.
MAYBE THIS IS SOMETHING WE COULD DISCUSS *AFTER* WE REACH A VERDICT.
FINE. IF THAT'S THE WAY WE'RE GONNA ROLL.
BUT IF ANYONE MAKES SO MUCH AS ONE PEEP, I PROMISE IT'LL END BAD FOR THIS WOMAN.
I BEG YOUR PARDON?

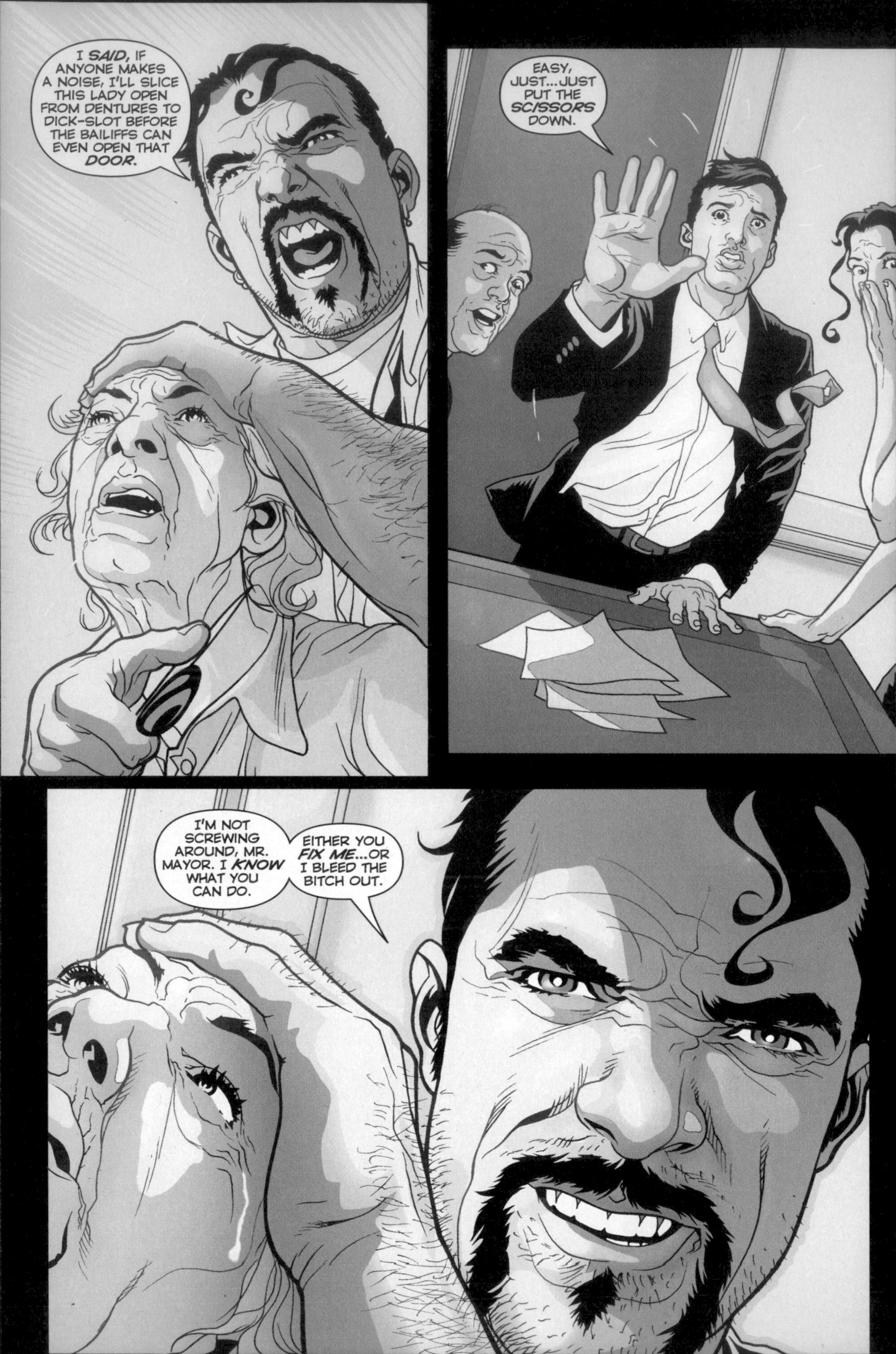
I SAID, IF ANYONE MAKES A NOISE, I'LL SLICE THIS LADY OPEN FROM DENTURES TO DICK-SLOT BEFORE THE BAILIFFS CAN EVEN OPEN THAT DOOR.
EASY, JUST...JUST PUT THE SCISSORS DOWN.
I'M NOT SCREWING AROUND, MR. MAYOR. I KNOW WHAT YOU CAN DO.
EITHER YOU FIX ME...OR I BLEED THE BITCH OUT.

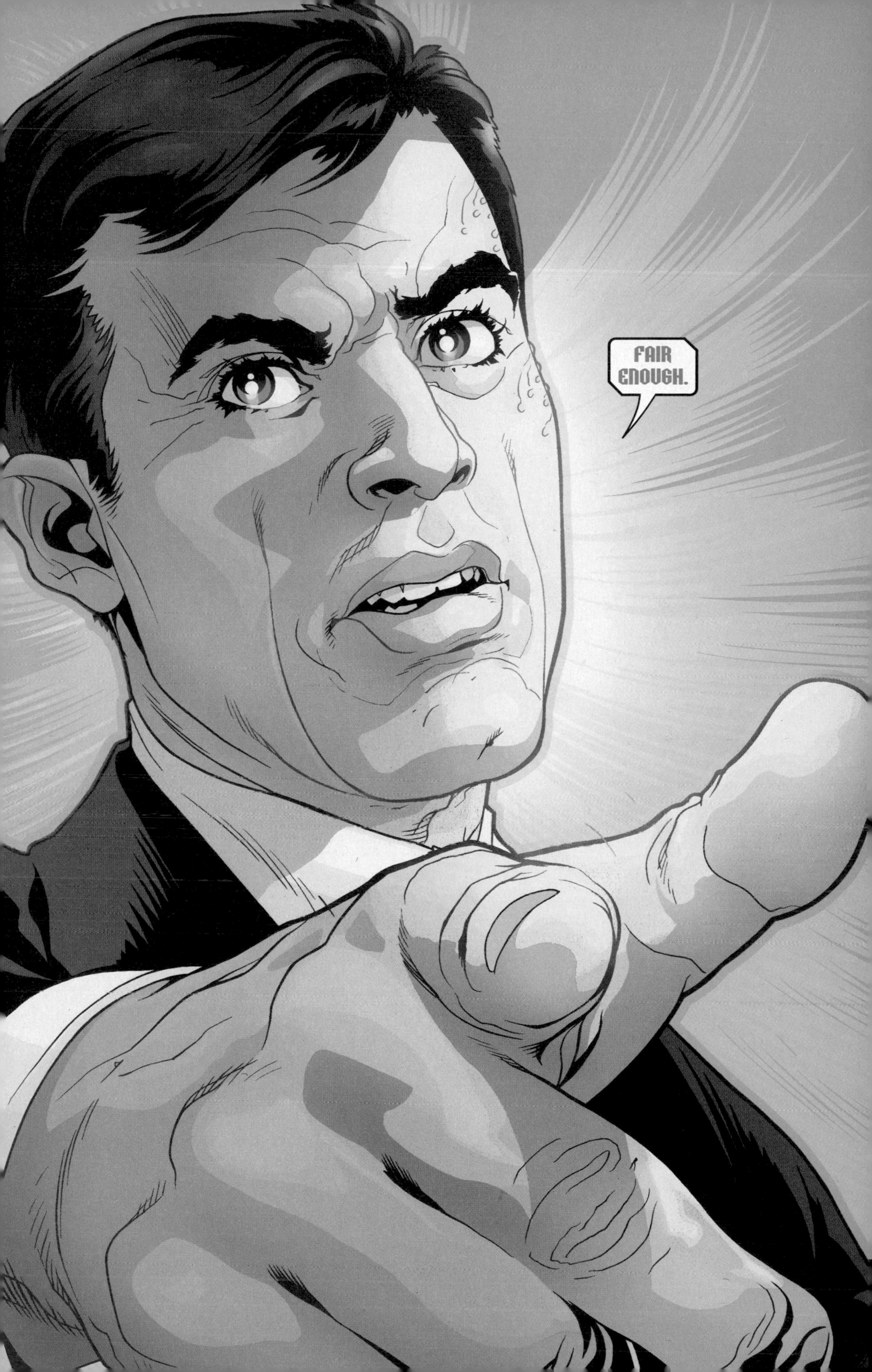
FAIR ENOUGH.

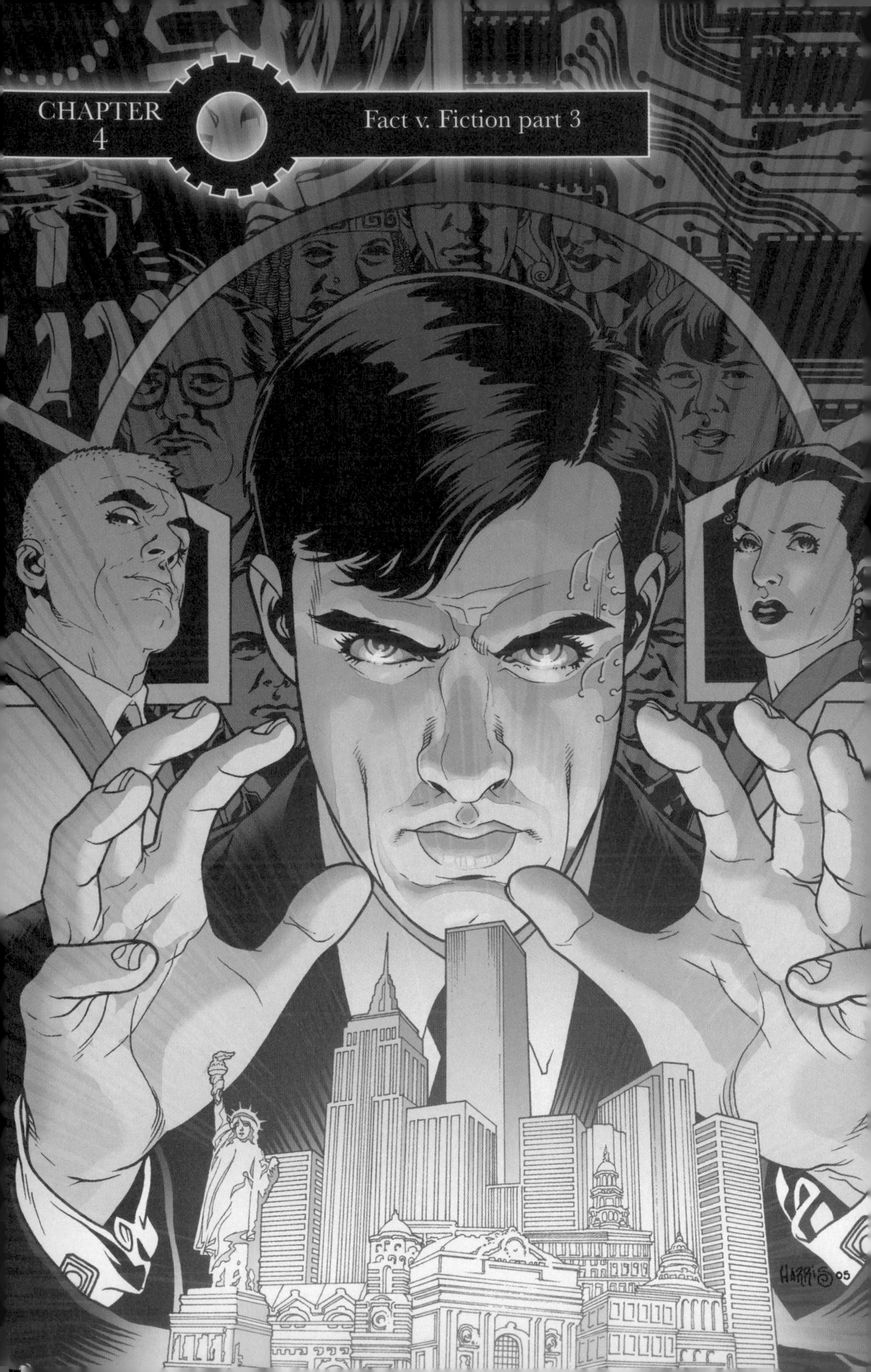
CHAPTER
4
Fact v. Fiction part 3
HARRIS 05

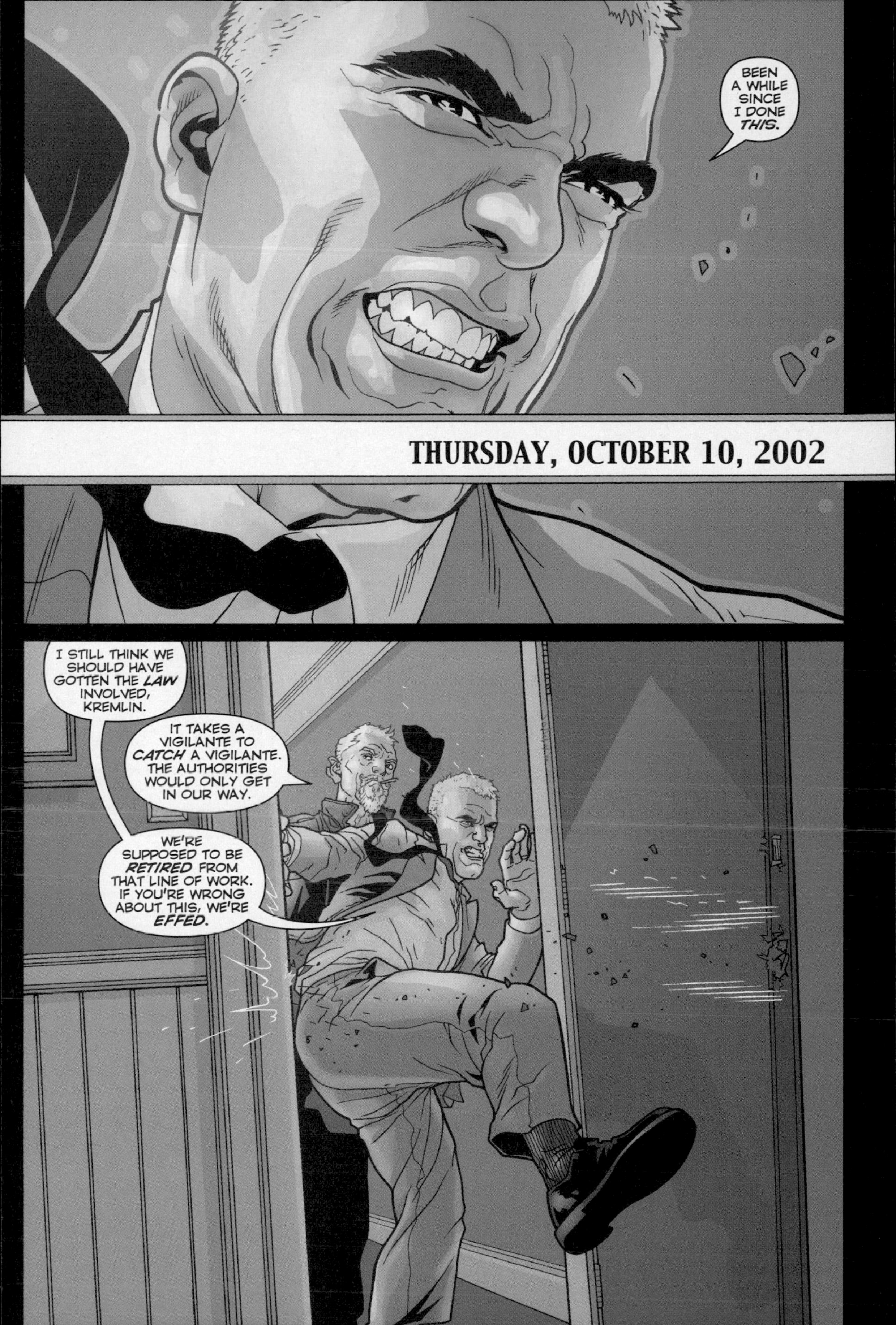
BEEN A WHILE SINCE I DONE *THIS*.
THURSDAY, OCTOBER 10, 2002
I STILL THINK WE SHOULD HAVE GOTTEN THE *LAW* INVOLVED, KREMLIN.
IT TAKES A VIGILANTE TO *CATCH* A VIGILANTE. THE AUTHORITIES WOULD ONLY GET IN OUR WAY.
WE'RE SUPPOSED TO BE *RETIRED* FROM THAT LINE OF WORK. IF YOU'RE WRONG ABOUT THIS, WE'RE *EFFED*.

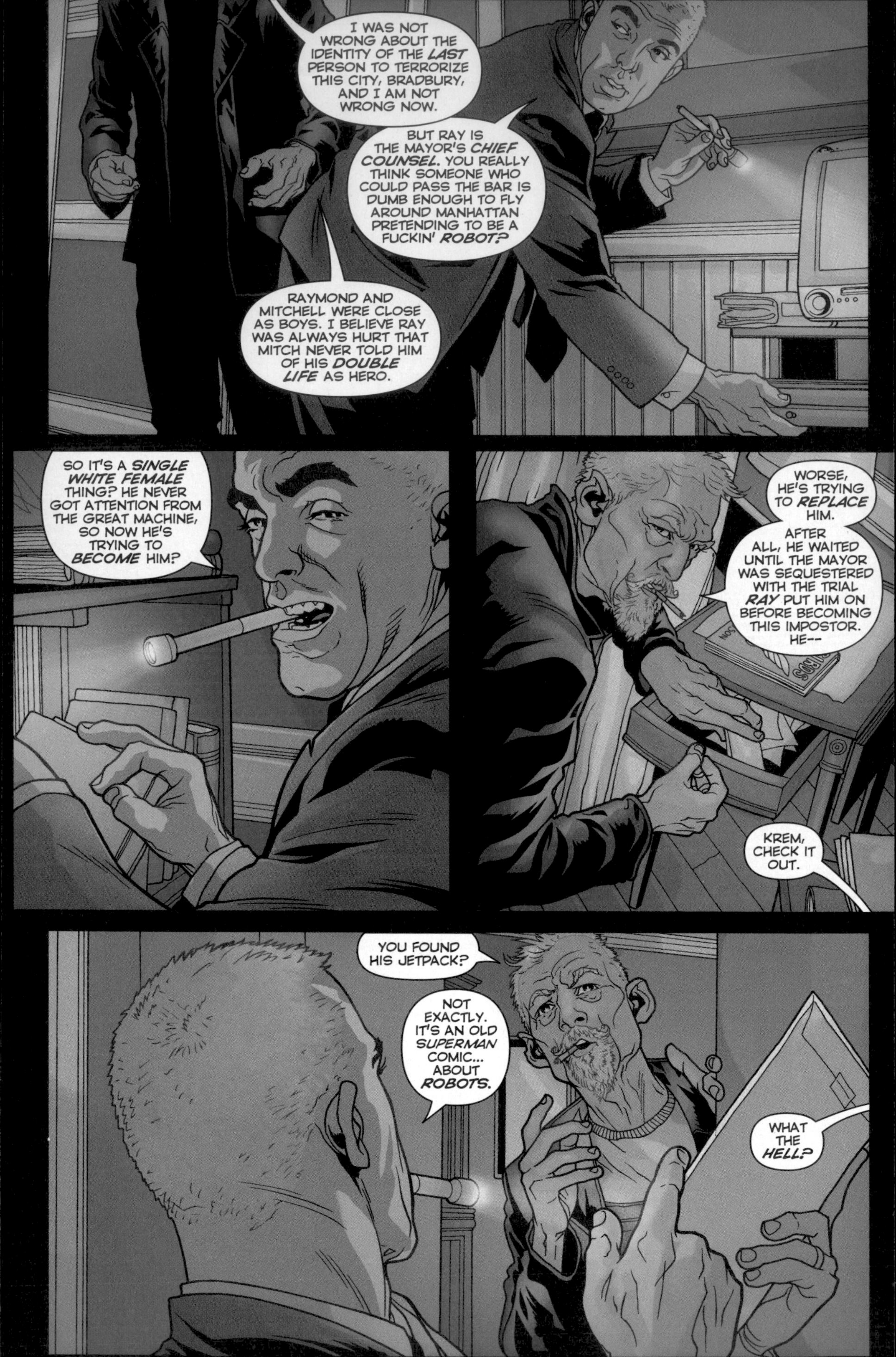
I WAS NOT WRONG ABOUT THE IDENTITY OF THE LAST PERSON TO TERRORIZE THIS CITY, BRADBURY, AND I AM NOT WRONG NOW.
BUT RAY IS THE MAYOR'S CHIEF COUNSEL. YOU REALLY THINK SOMEONE WHO COULD PASS THE BAR IS DUMB ENOUGH TO FLY AROUND MANHATTAN PRETENDING TO BE A FUCKIN' ROBOT?
RAYMOND AND MITCHELL WERE CLOSE AS BOYS. I BELIEVE RAY WAS ALWAYS HURT THAT MITCH NEVER TOLD HIM OF HIS DOUBLE LIFE AS HERO.
SO IT'S A SINGLE WHITE FEMALE THING? HE NEVER GOT ATTENTION FROM THE GREAT MACHINE, SO NOW HE'S TRYING TO BECOME HIM?
WORSE, HE'S TRYING TO REPLACE HIM.
AFTER ALL, HE WAITED UNTIL THE MAYOR WAS SEQUESTERED WITH THE TRIAL RAY PUT HIM ON BEFORE BECOMING THIS IMPOSTOR. HE--
KREM, CHECK IT OUT.
YOU FOUND HIS JETPACK?
NOT EXACTLY. IT'S AN OLD SUPERMAN COMIC... ABOUT ROBOTS.
WHAT THE HELL?

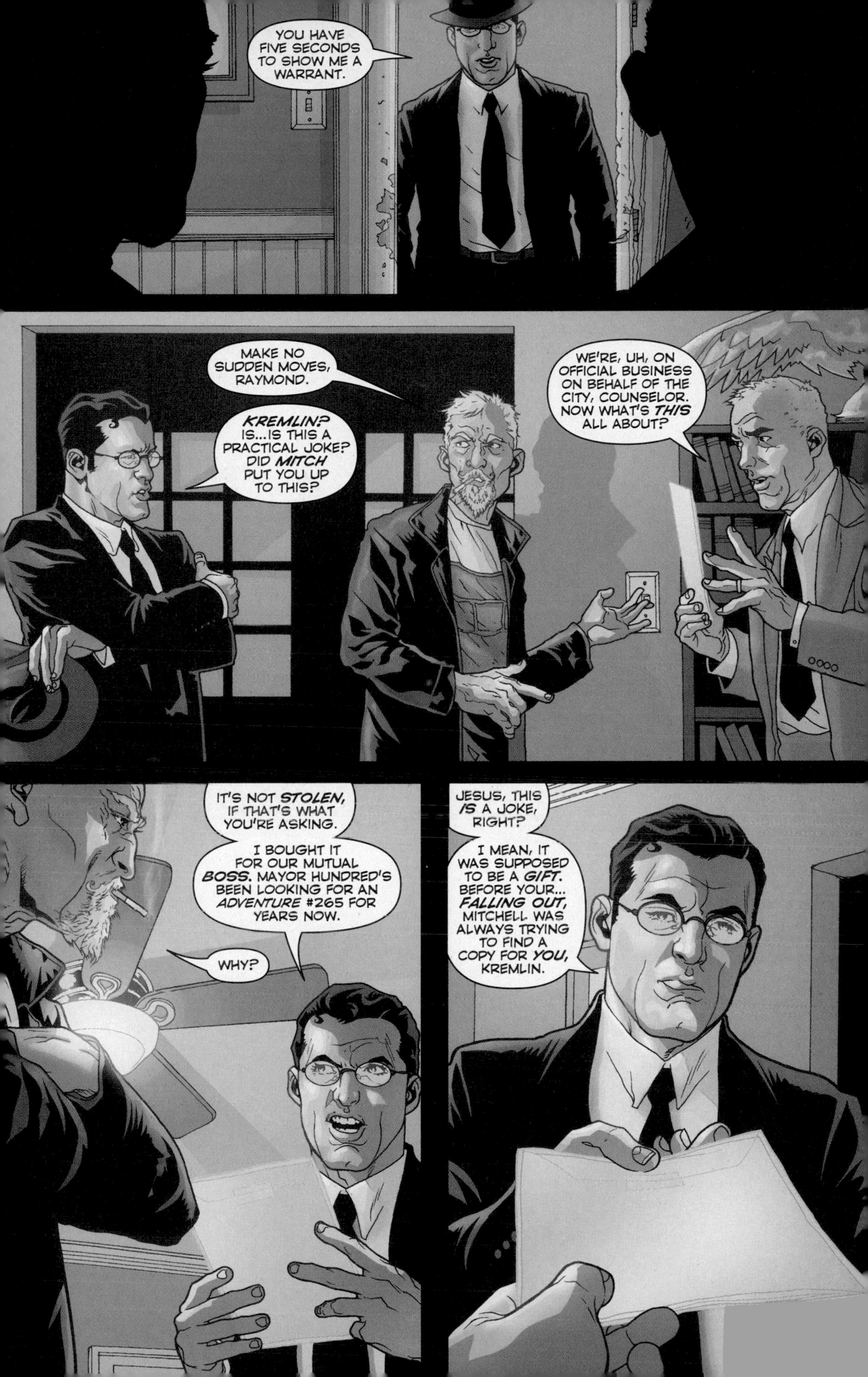
YOU HAVE FIVE SECONDS TO SHOW ME A WARRANT.
MAKE NO SUDDEN MOVES, RAYMOND.
KREMLIN? IS...IS THIS A PRACTICAL JOKE? DID MITCH PUT YOU UP TO THIS?
WE'RE, UH, ON OFFICIAL BUSINESS ON BEHALF OF THE CITY, COUNSELOR. NOW WHAT'S THIS ALL ABOUT?
IT'S NOT STOLEN, IF THAT'S WHAT YOU'RE ASKING.
I BOUGHT IT FOR OUR MUTUAL BOSS. MAYOR HUNDRED'S BEEN LOOKING FOR AN ADVENTURE #265 FOR YEARS NOW.
WHY?
JESUS, THIS IS A JOKE, RIGHT?
I MEAN, IT WAS SUPPOSED TO BE A GIFT. BEFORE YOUR... FALLING OUT, MITCHELL WAS ALWAYS TRYING TO FIND A COPY FOR YOU, KREMLIN.

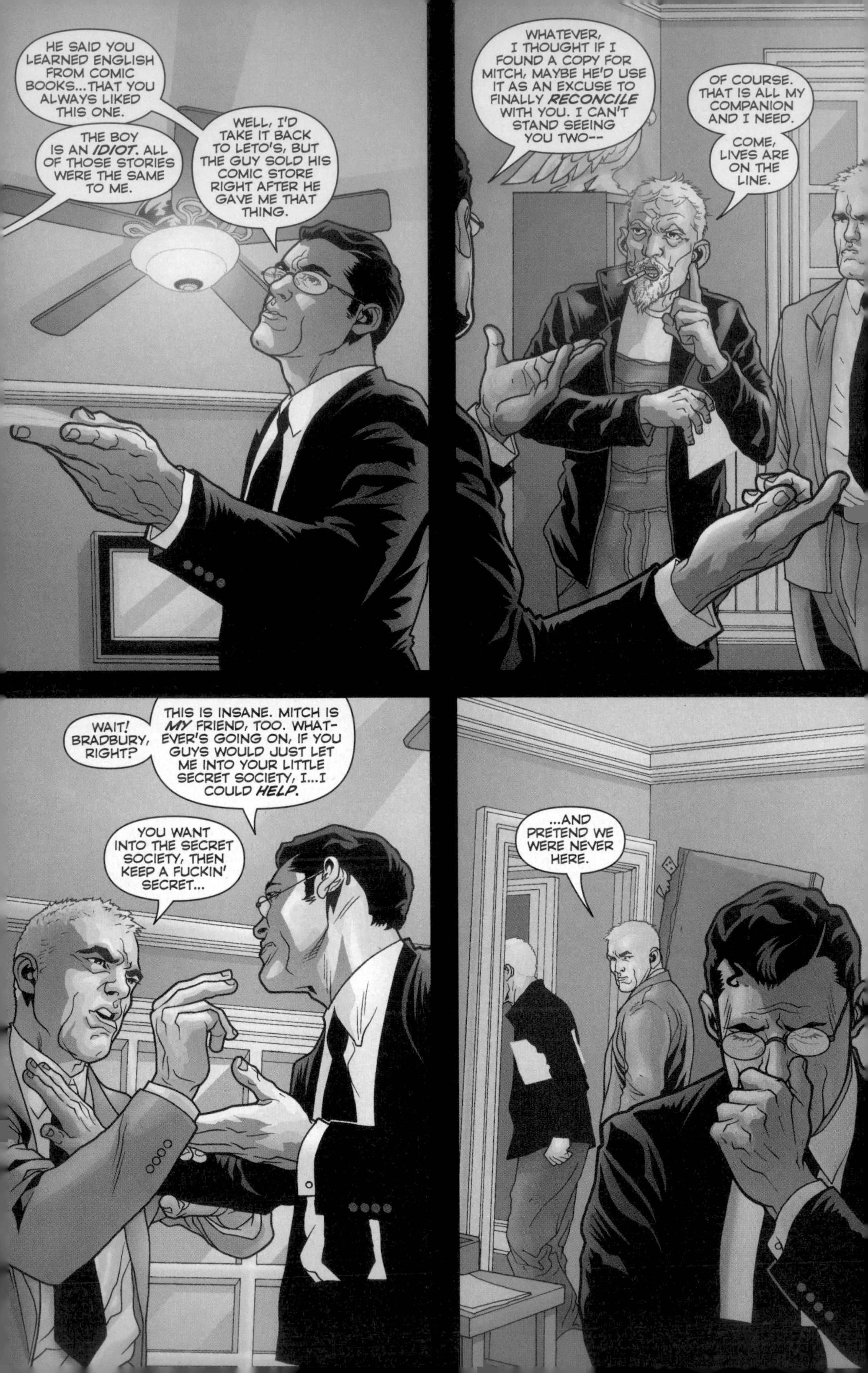
HE SAID YOU LEARNED ENGLISH FROM COMIC BOOKS...THAT YOU ALWAYS LIKED THIS ONE.
THE BOY IS AN *IDIOT*. ALL OF THOSE STORIES WERE THE SAME TO ME.
WELL, I'D TAKE IT BACK TO LETO'S, BUT THE GUY SOLD HIS COMIC STORE RIGHT AFTER HE GAVE ME THAT THING.
WHATEVER, I THOUGHT IF I FOUND A COPY FOR MITCH, MAYBE HE'D USE IT AS AN EXCUSE TO FINALLY *RECONCILE* WITH YOU. I CAN'T STAND SEEING YOU TWO--
OF COURSE. THAT IS ALL MY COMPANION AND I NEED.
COME, LIVES ARE ON THE LINE.
WAIT! BRADBURY, RIGHT?
THIS IS INSANE. MITCH IS *MY* FRIEND, TOO. WHATEVER'S GOING ON, IF YOU GUYS WOULD JUST LET ME INTO YOUR LITTLE SECRET SOCIETY, I...I COULD *HELP*.
YOU WANT INTO THE SECRET SOCIETY, THEN KEEP A FUCKIN' SECRET...
...AND PRETEND WE WERE NEVER HERE.

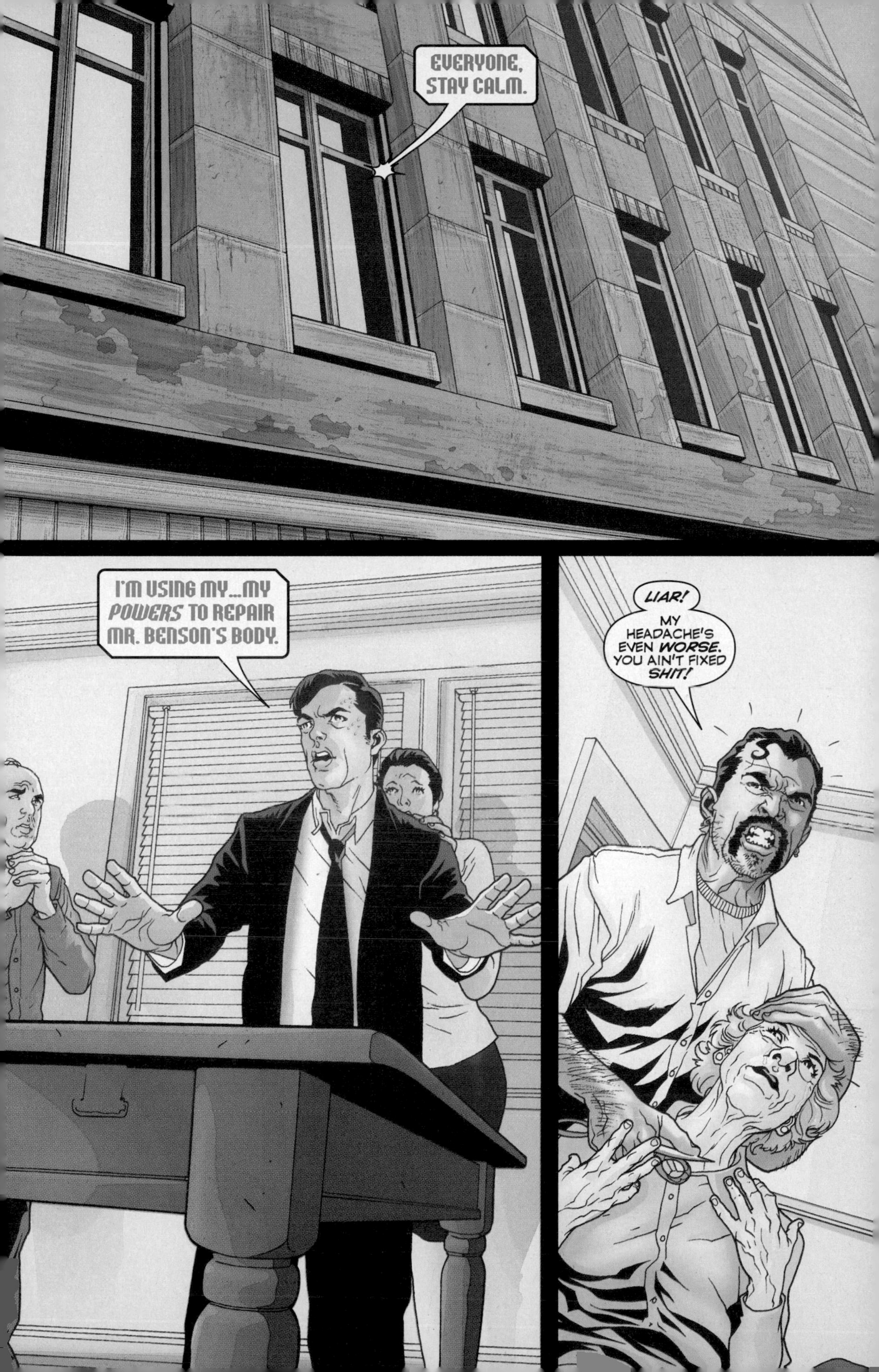
EVERYONE, STAY CALM.
I'M USING MY...MY *POWERS* TO REPAIR MR. BENSON'S BODY.
LIAR!
MY HEADACHE'S EVEN *WORSE*. YOU AIN'T FIXED *SHIT!*

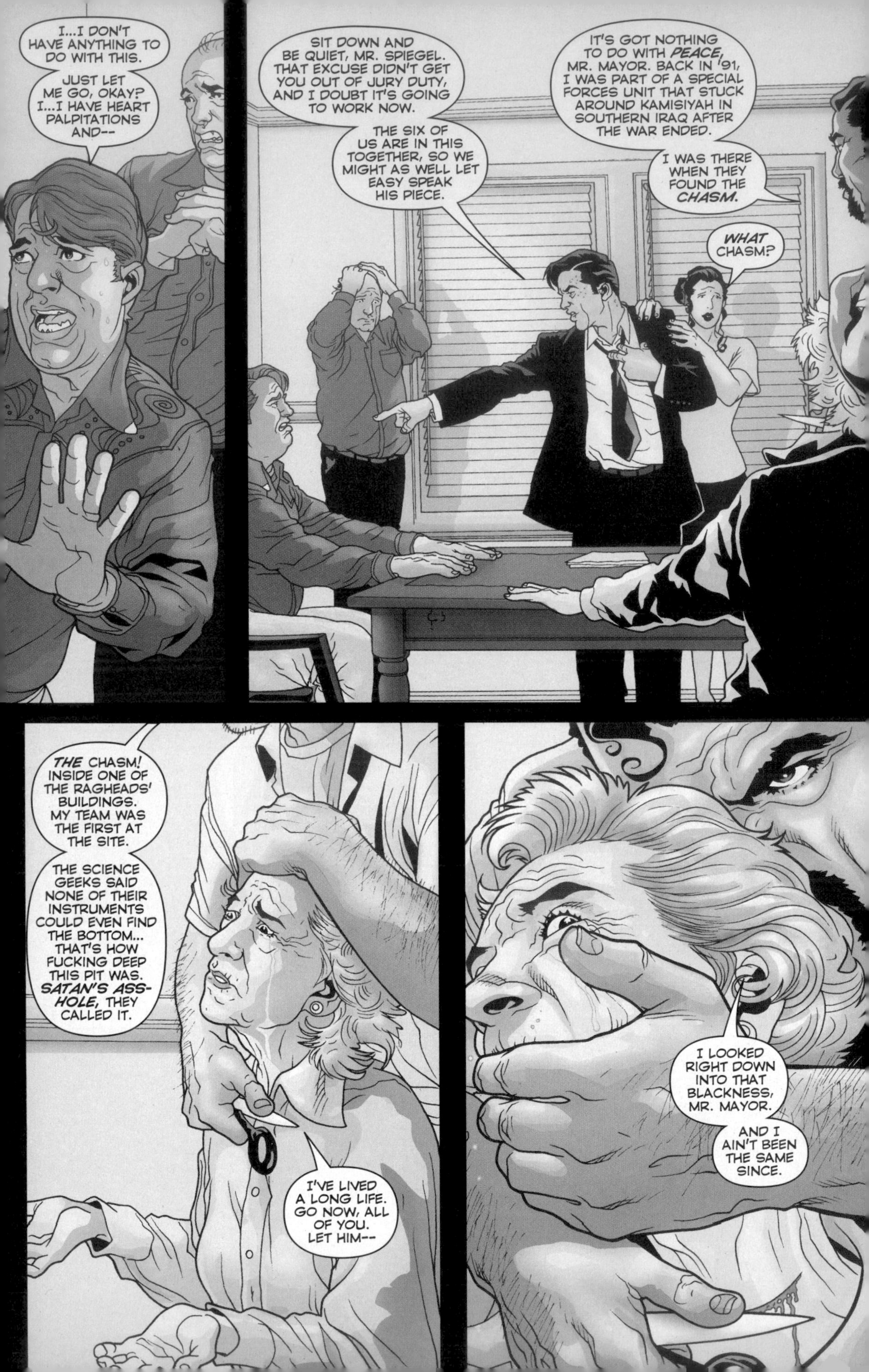
I...I DON'T HAVE ANYTHING TO DO WITH THIS.
JUST LET ME GO, OKAY? I...I HAVE HEART PALPITATIONS AND--
SIT DOWN AND BE QUIET, MR. SPIEGEL. THAT EXCUSE DIDN'T GET YOU OUT OF JURY DUTY, AND I DOUBT IT'S GOING TO WORK NOW.
THE SIX OF US ARE IN THIS TOGETHER, SO WE MIGHT AS WELL LET EASY SPEAK HIS PIECE.
IT'S GOT NOTHING TO DO WITH PEACE, MR. MAYOR. BACK IN '91, I WAS PART OF A SPECIAL FORCES UNIT THAT STUCK AROUND KAMISIYAH IN SOUTHERN IRAQ AFTER THE WAR ENDED.
I WAS THERE WHEN THEY FOUND THE CHASM.
WHAT CHASM?
THE CHASM! INSIDE ONE OF THE RAGHEADS' BUILDINGS. MY TEAM WAS THE FIRST AT THE SITE.
THE SCIENCE GEEKS SAID NONE OF THEIR INSTRUMENTS COULD EVEN FIND THE BOTTOM... THAT'S HOW FUCKING DEEP THIS PIT WAS. SATAN'S ASS-HOLE, THEY CALLED IT.
I'VE LIVED A LONG LIFE. GO NOW, ALL OF YOU. LET HIM--
I LOOKED RIGHT DOWN INTO THAT BLACKNESS, MR. MAYOR.
AND I AIN'T BEEN THE SAME SINCE.

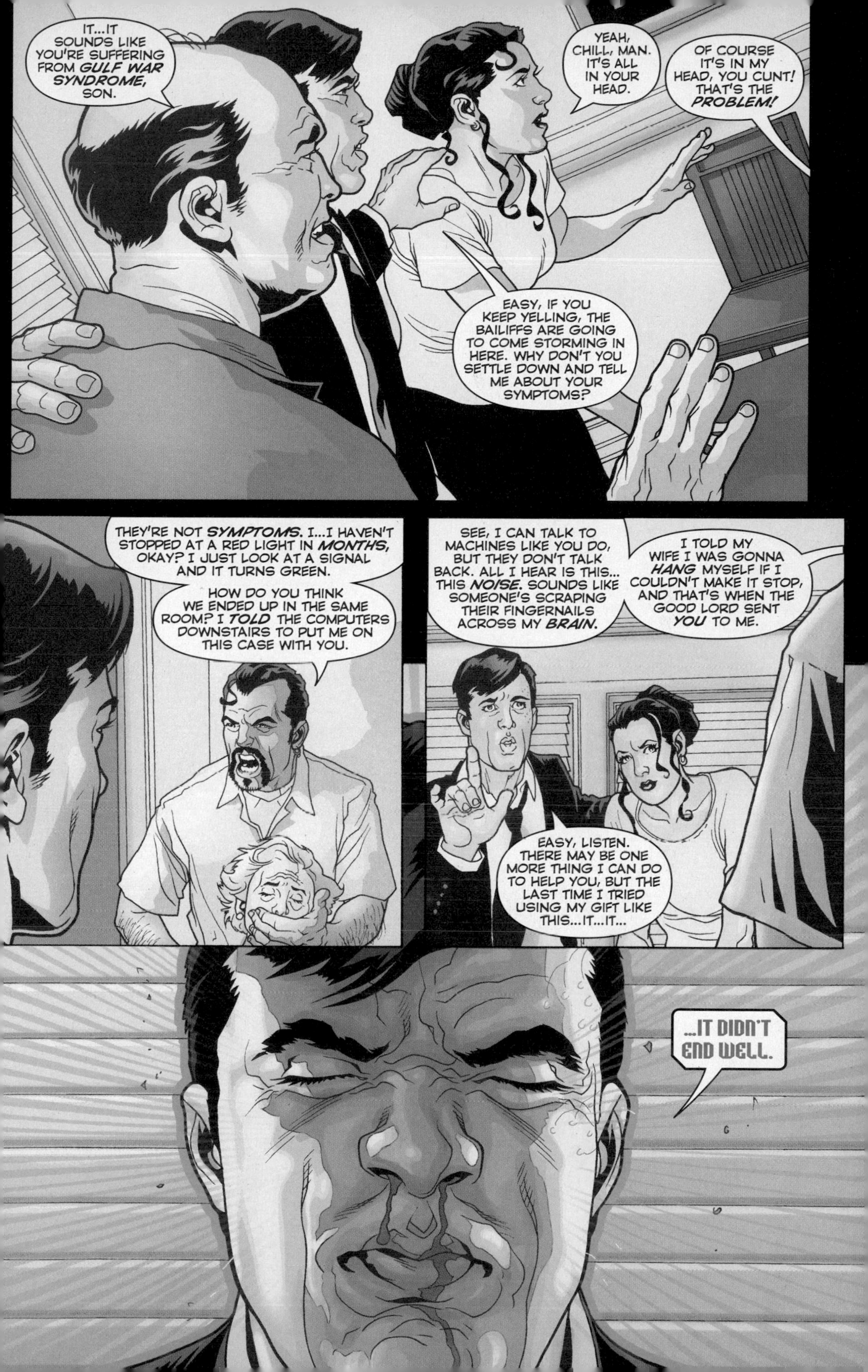
IT...IT SOUNDS LIKE YOU'RE SUFFERING FROM GULF WAR SYNDROME, SON.
YEAH, CHILL, MAN. IT'S ALL IN YOUR HEAD.
OF COURSE IT'S IN MY HEAD, YOU CUNT! THAT'S THE PROBLEM!
EASY, IF YOU KEEP YELLING, THE BAILIFFS ARE GOING TO COME STORMING IN HERE. WHY DON'T YOU SETTLE DOWN AND TELL ME ABOUT YOUR SYMPTOMS?
THEY'RE NOT SYMPTOMS. I...I HAVEN'T STOPPED AT A RED LIGHT IN MONTHS, OKAY? I JUST LOOK AT A SIGNAL AND IT TURNS GREEN.
HOW DO YOU THINK WE ENDED UP IN THE SAME ROOM? I TOLD THE COMPUTERS DOWNSTAIRS TO PUT ME ON THIS CASE WITH YOU.
SEE, I CAN TALK TO MACHINES LIKE YOU DO, BUT THEY DON'T TALK BACK. ALL I HEAR IS THIS... THIS NOISE. SOUNDS LIKE SOMEONE'S SCRAPING THEIR FINGERNAILS ACROSS MY BRAIN.
I TOLD MY WIFE I WAS GONNA HANG MYSELF IF I COULDN'T MAKE IT STOP, AND THAT'S WHEN THE GOOD LORD SENT YOU TO ME.
EASY, LISTEN. THERE MAY BE ONE MORE THING I CAN DO TO HELP YOU, BUT THE LAST TIME I TRIED USING MY GIFT LIKE THIS...IT...IT...
...IT DIDN'T END WELL.

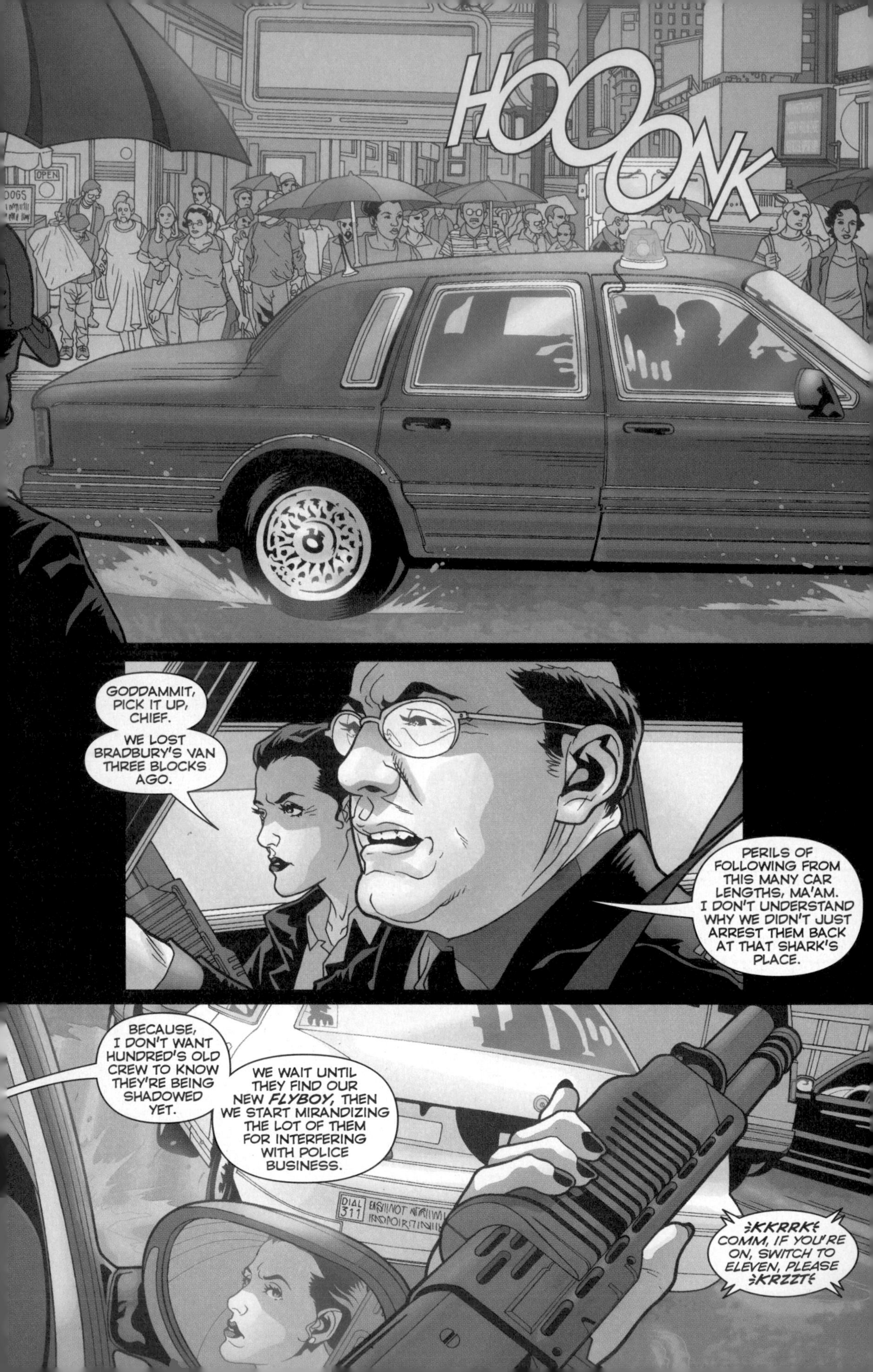
HOOONK
GODDAMMIT, PICK IT UP, CHIEF.
WE LOST BRADBURY'S VAN THREE BLOCKS AGO.
PERILS OF FOLLOWING FROM THIS MANY CAR LENGTHS, MA'AM. I DON'T UNDERSTAND WHY WE DIDN'T JUST ARREST THEM BACK AT THAT SHARK'S PLACE.
BECAUSE, I DON'T WANT HUNDRED'S OLD CREW TO KNOW THEY'RE BEING SHADOWED YET.
WE WAIT UNTIL THEY FIND OUR NEW *FLYBOY,* THEN WE START MIRANDIZING THE LOT OF THEM FOR INTERFERING WITH POLICE BUSINESS.
DIAL 311
KKRRK COMM, IF YOU'RE ON, SWITCH TO ELEVEN, PLEASE *KRZZT*

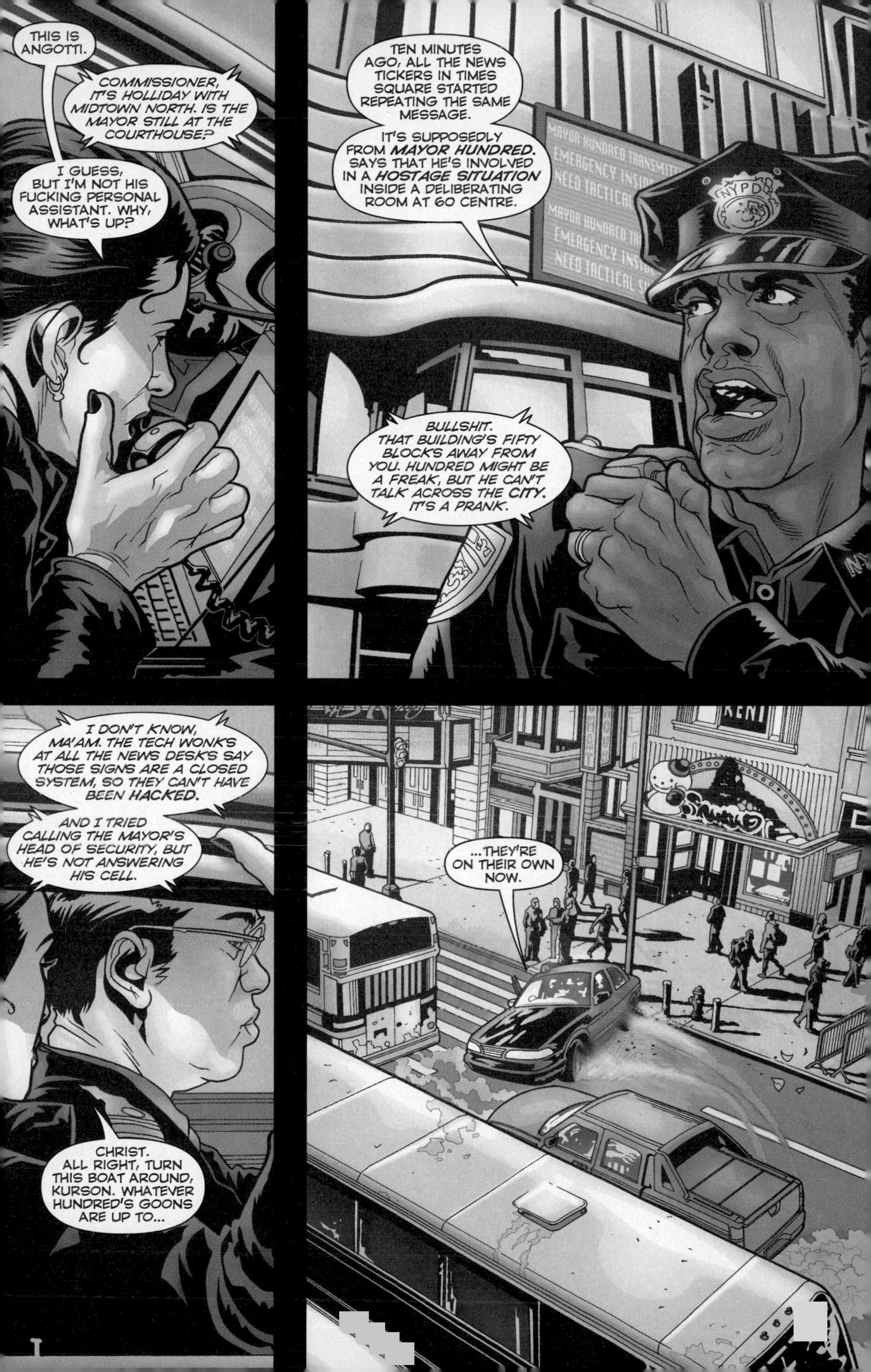
THIS IS ANGOTTI.
COMMISSIONER, IT'S HOLLIDAY WITH MIDTOWN NORTH. IS THE MAYOR STILL AT THE COURTHOUSE?
I GUESS, BUT I'M NOT HIS FUCKING PERSONAL ASSISTANT. WHY, WHAT'S UP?
TEN MINUTES AGO, ALL THE NEWS TICKERS IN TIMES SQUARE STARTED REPEATING THE SAME MESSAGE.
IT'S SUPPOSEDLY FROM MAYOR HUNDRED. SAYS THAT HE'S INVOLVED IN A HOSTAGE SITUATION INSIDE A DELIBERATING ROOM AT 60 CENTRE.
MAYOR HUNDRED TRANSMITTI
EMERGENCY INSIDE
NEED TACTICAL
BULLSHIT. THAT BUILDING'S FIFTY BLOCKS AWAY FROM YOU. HUNDRED MIGHT BE A FREAK, BUT HE CAN'T TALK ACROSS THE CITY. IT'S A PRANK.
I DON'T KNOW, MA'AM. THE TECH WONKS AT ALL THE NEWS DESKS SAY THOSE SIGNS ARE A CLOSED SYSTEM, SO THEY CAN'T HAVE BEEN HACKED.
AND I TRIED CALLING THE MAYOR'S HEAD OF SECURITY, BUT HE'S NOT ANSWERING HIS CELL.
CHRIST. ALL RIGHT, TURN THIS BOAT AROUND, KURSON. WHATEVER HUNDRED'S GOONS ARE UP TO...
...THEY'RE ON THEIR OWN NOW.
RENT

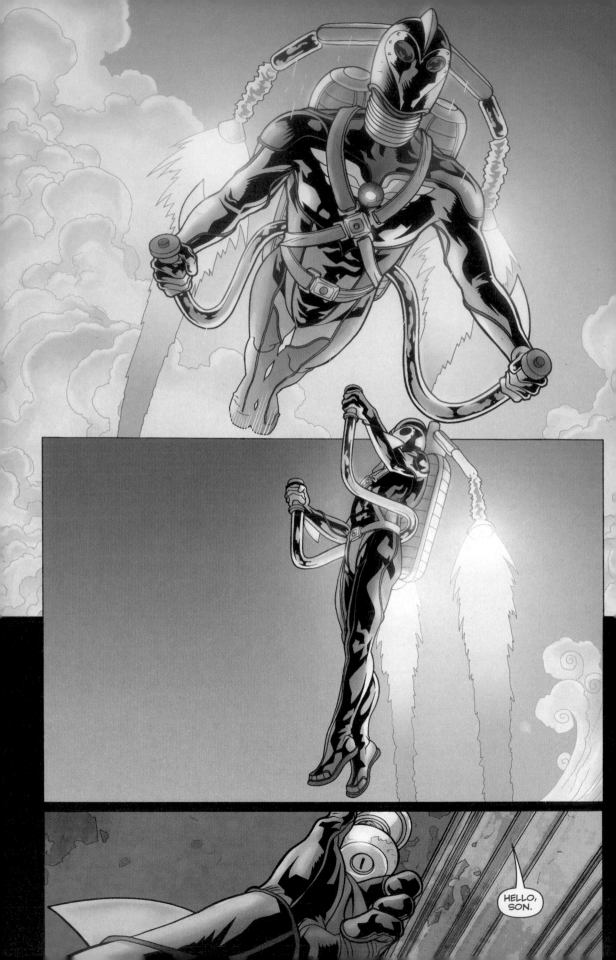

HELLO,
SON.

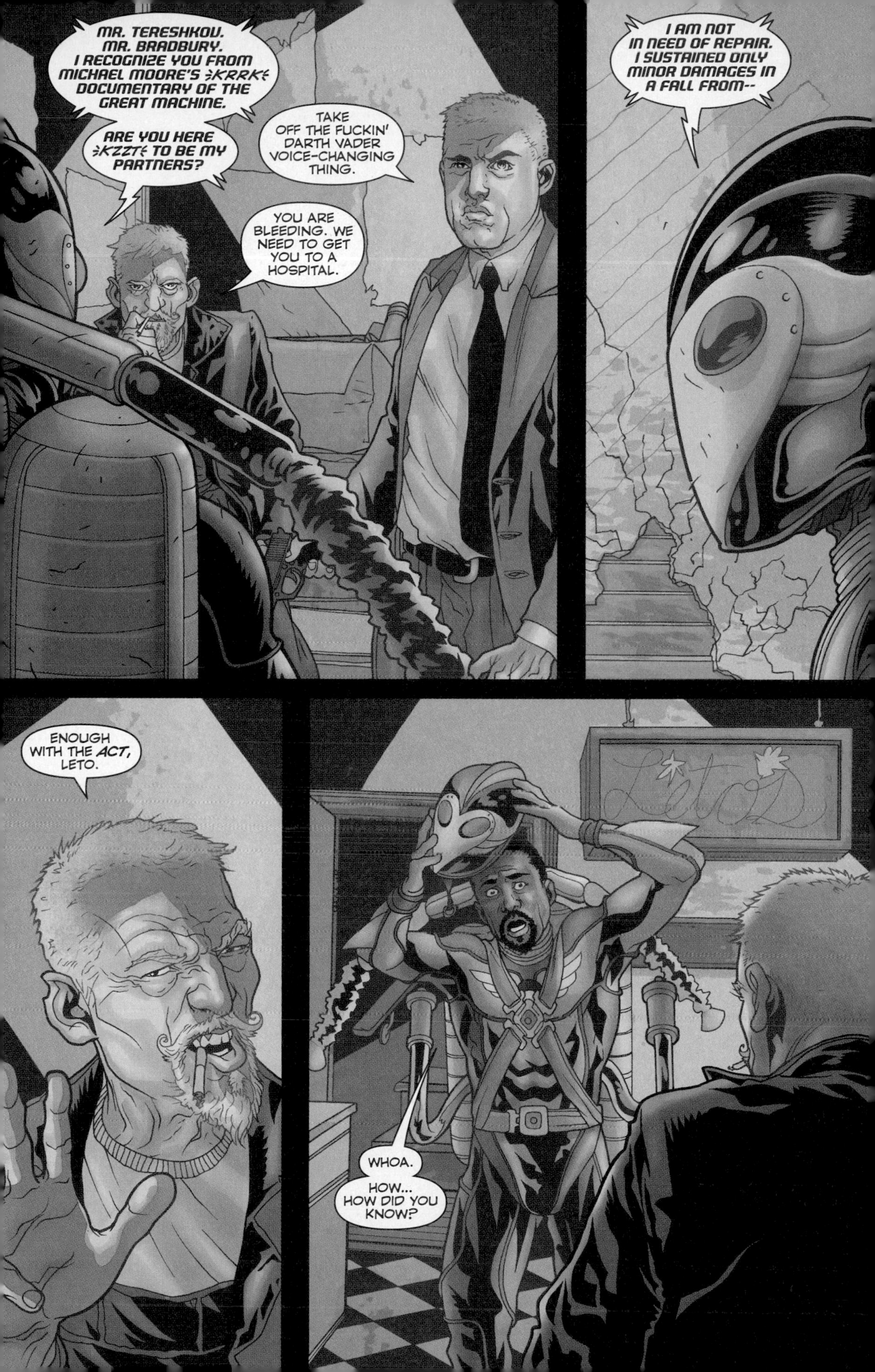
MR. TERESHKOV. MR. BRADBURY. I RECOGNIZE YOU FROM MICHAEL MOORE'S KRRK DOCUMENTARY OF THE GREAT MACHINE.
ARE YOU HERE KZZT TO BE MY PARTNERS?
TAKE OFF THE FUCKIN' DARTH VADER VOICE-CHANGING THING.
YOU ARE BLEEDING. WE NEED TO GET YOU TO A HOSPITAL.
I AM NOT IN NEED OF REPAIR. I SUSTAINED ONLY MINOR DAMAGES IN A FALL FROM--
ENOUGH WITH THE ACT, LETO.
WHOA. HOW... HOW DID YOU KNOW?

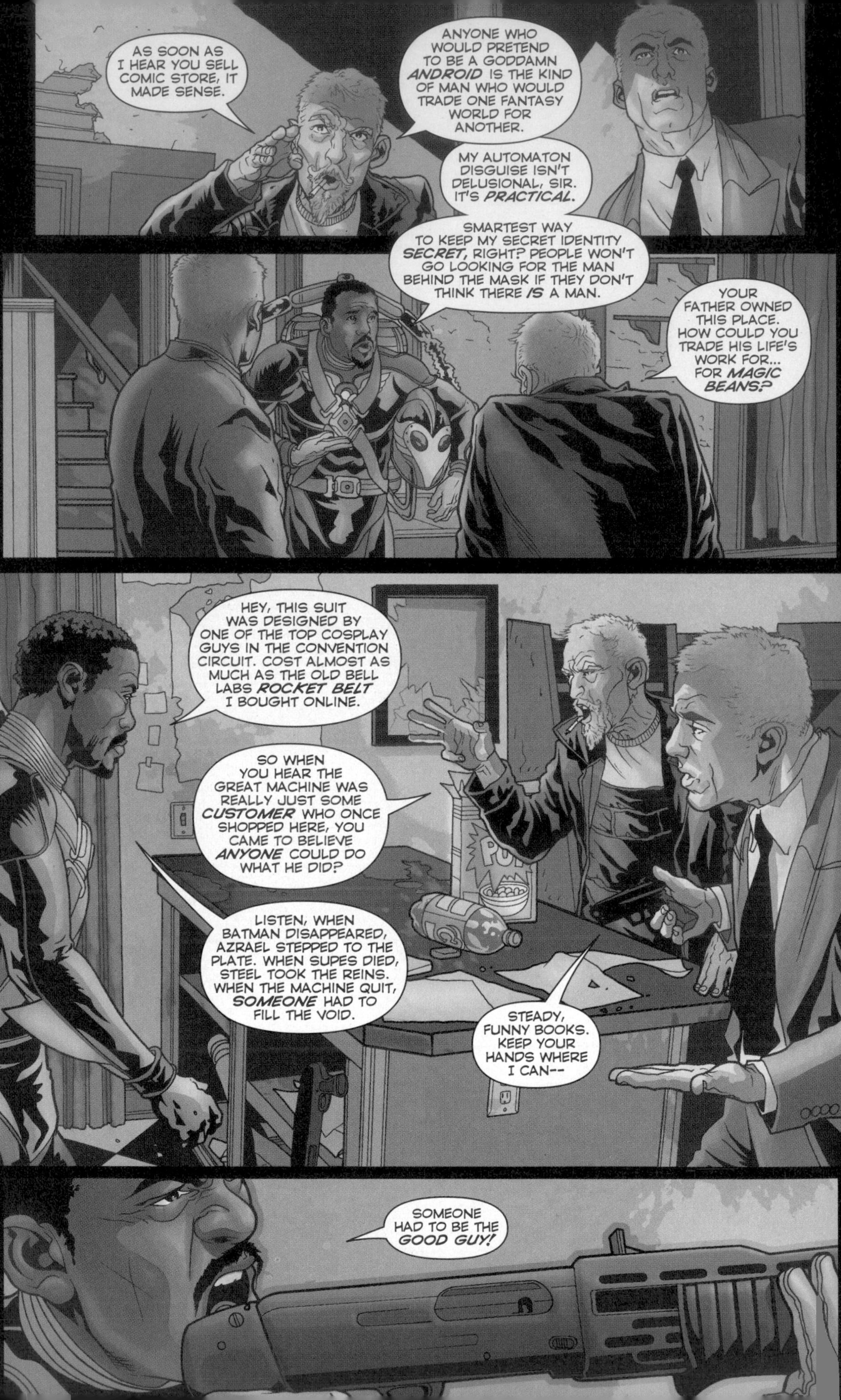
AS SOON AS I HEAR YOU SELL COMIC STORE, IT MADE SENSE.
ANYONE WHO WOULD PRETEND TO BE A GODDAMN ANDROID IS THE KIND OF MAN WHO WOULD TRADE ONE FANTASY WORLD FOR ANOTHER.
MY AUTOMATON DISGUISE ISN'T DELUSIONAL, SIR. IT'S PRACTICAL.
SMARTEST WAY TO KEEP MY SECRET IDENTITY SECRET, RIGHT? PEOPLE WON'T GO LOOKING FOR THE MAN BEHIND THE MASK IF THEY DON'T THINK THERE IS A MAN.
YOUR FATHER OWNED THIS PLACE. HOW COULD YOU TRADE HIS LIFE'S WORK FOR... FOR MAGIC BEANS?
HEY, THIS SUIT WAS DESIGNED BY ONE OF THE TOP COSPLAY GUYS IN THE CONVENTION CIRCUIT. COST ALMOST AS MUCH AS THE OLD BELL LABS ROCKET BELT I BOUGHT ONLINE.
SO WHEN YOU HEAR THE GREAT MACHINE WAS REALLY JUST SOME CUSTOMER WHO ONCE SHOPPED HERE, YOU CAME TO BELIEVE ANYONE COULD DO WHAT HE DID?
LISTEN, WHEN BATMAN DISAPPEARED, AZRAEL STEPPED TO THE PLATE. WHEN SUPES DIED, STEEL TOOK THE REINS. WHEN THE MACHINE QUIT, SOMEONE HAD TO FILL THE VOID.
STEADY, FUNNY BOOKS. KEEP YOUR HANDS WHERE I CAN--
SOMEONE HAD TO BE THE GOOD GUY!

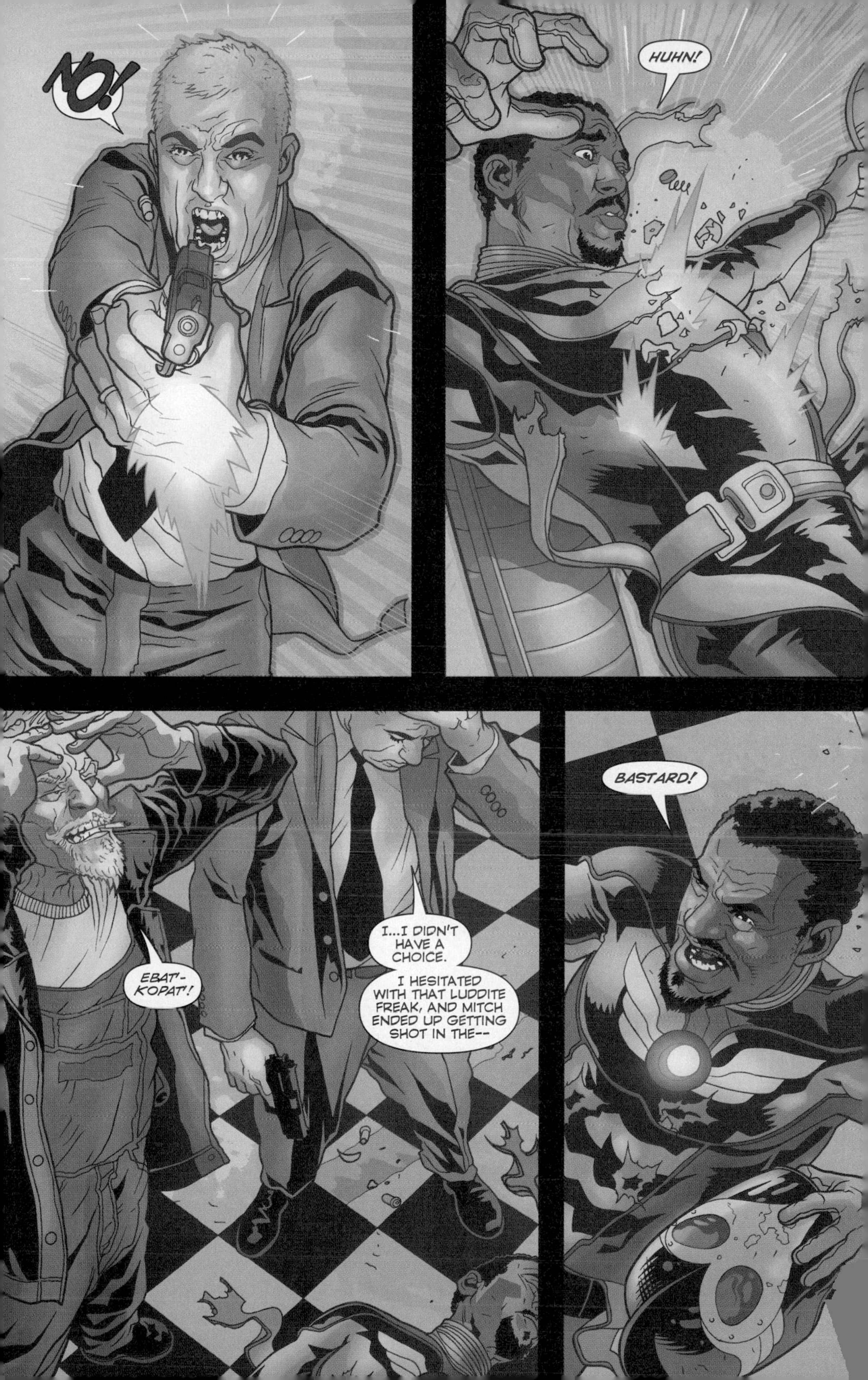
NO!
HUHN!
EBAT'-KOPAT'!
I...I DIDN'T HAVE A CHOICE.
I HESITATED WITH THAT LUDDITE FREAK, AND MITCH ENDED UP GETTING SHOT IN THE--
BASTARD!

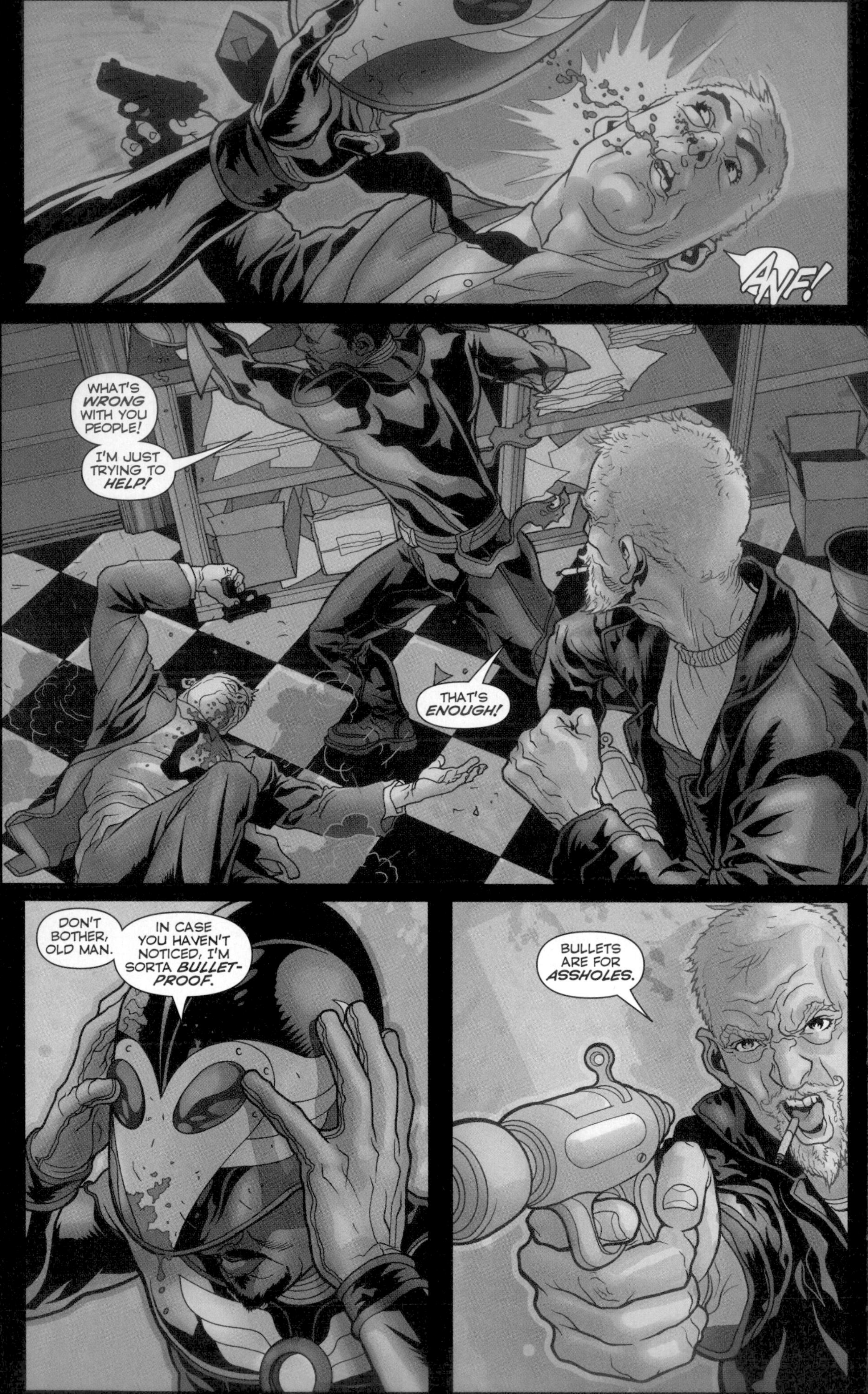
ANF!
WHAT'S WRONG WITH YOU PEOPLE!
I'M JUST TRYING TO HELP!
THAT'S ENOUGH!
DON'T BOTHER, OLD MAN.
IN CASE YOU HAVEN'T NOTICED, I'M SORTA BULLET-PROOF.
BULLETS ARE FOR ASSHOLES.

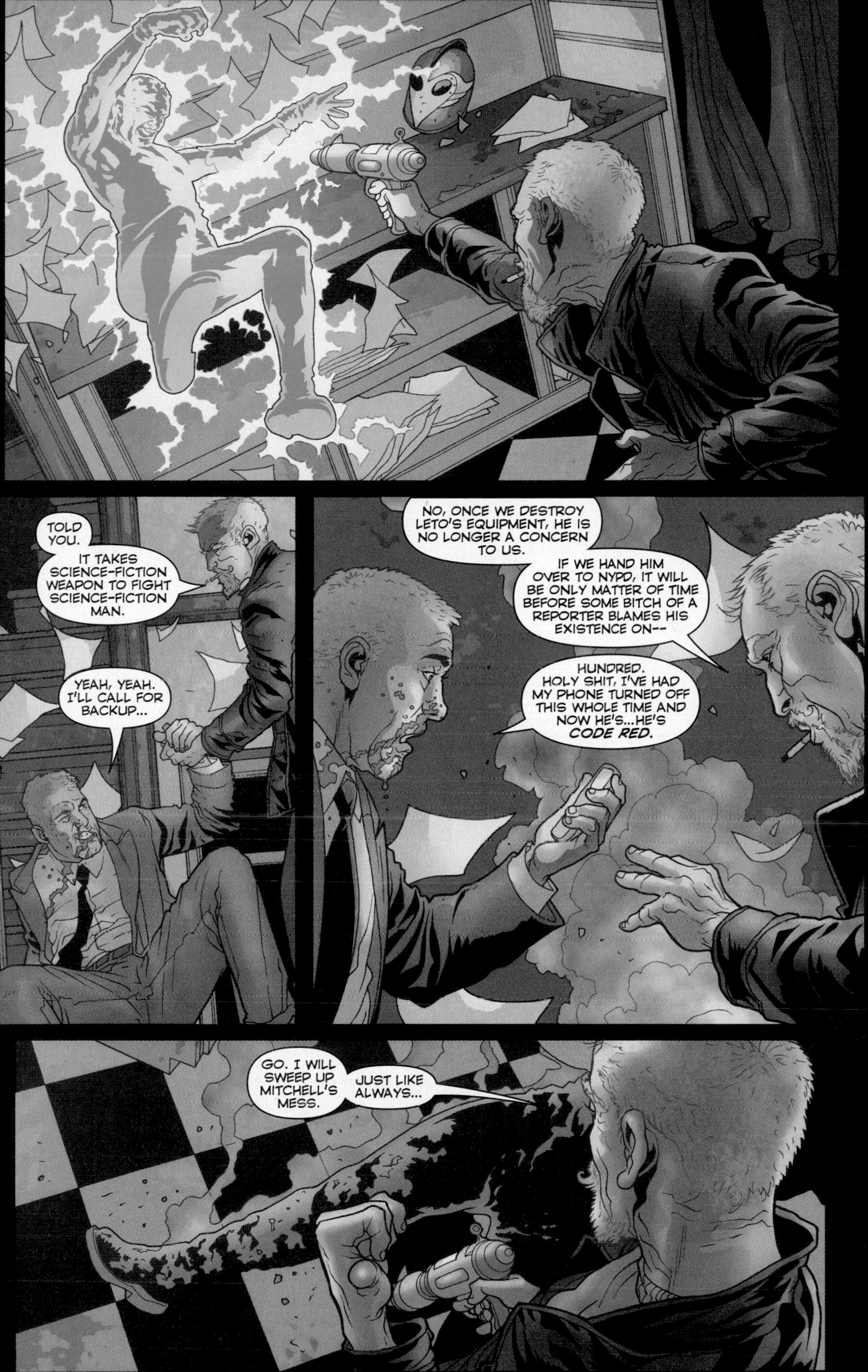
TOLD YOU.
IT TAKES SCIENCE-FICTION WEAPON TO FIGHT SCIENCE-FICTION MAN.
YEAH, YEAH. I'LL CALL FOR BACKUP...
NO, ONCE WE DESTROY LETO'S EQUIPMENT, HE IS NO LONGER A CONCERN TO US.
IF WE HAND HIM OVER TO NYPD, IT WILL BE ONLY MATTER OF TIME BEFORE SOME BITCH OF A REPORTER BLAMES HIS EXISTENCE ON--
HUNDRED. HOLY SHIT, I'VE HAD MY PHONE TURNED OFF THIS WHOLE TIME AND NOW HE'S...HE'S *CODE RED*.
GO. I WILL SWEEP UP MITCHELL'S MESS.
JUST LIKE ALWAYS...

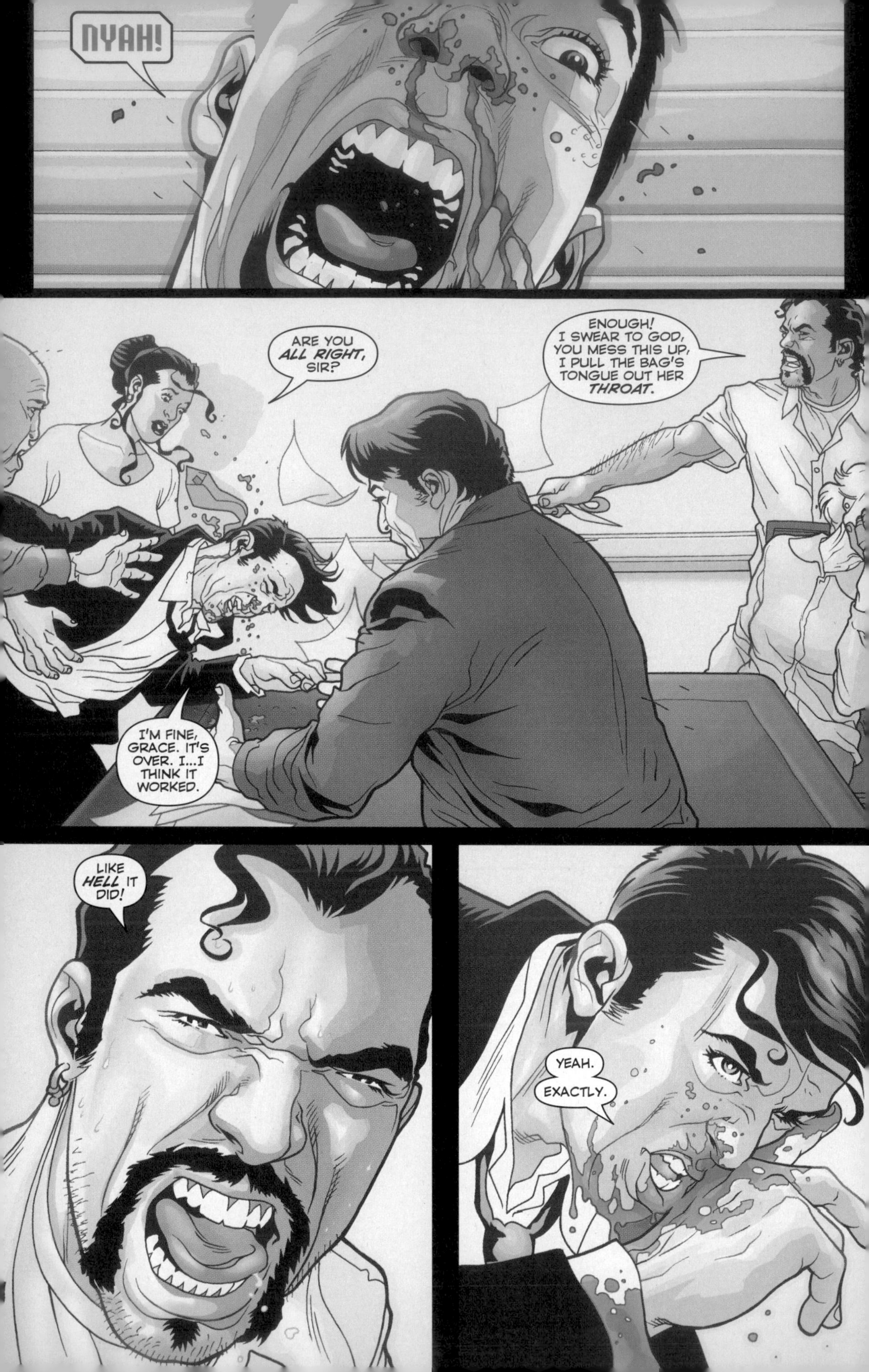
NYAH!
ARE YOU *ALL RIGHT,* SIR?
ENOUGH! I SWEAR TO GOD, YOU MESS THIS UP, I PULL THE BAG'S TONGUE OUT HER *THROAT.*
I'M FINE, GRACE. IT'S OVER. I...I THINK IT WORKED.
LIKE *HELL* IT DID!
YEAH.
EXACTLY.

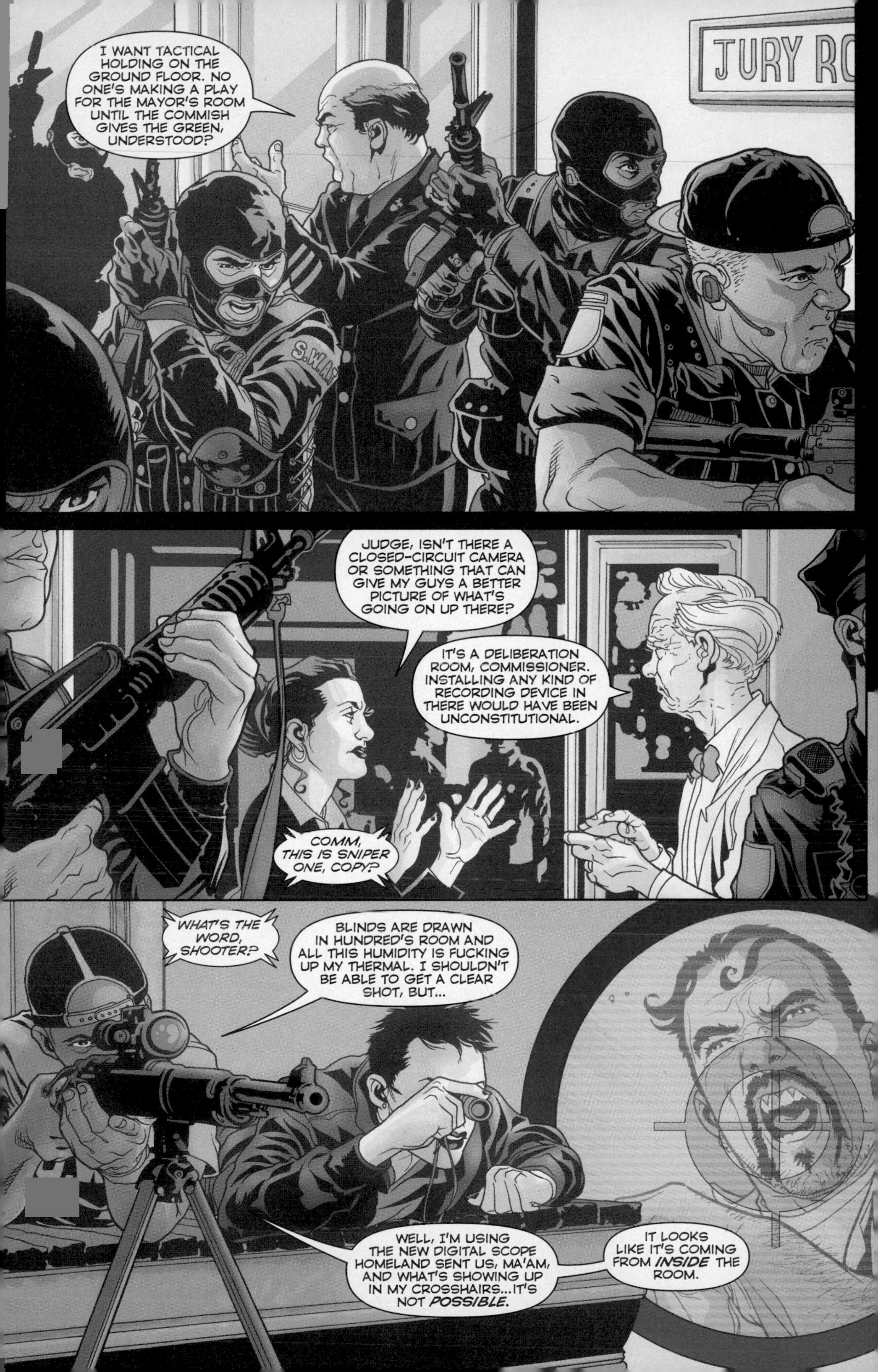
JURY RO
I WANT TACTICAL HOLDING ON THE GROUND FLOOR. NO ONE'S MAKING A PLAY FOR THE MAYOR'S ROOM UNTIL THE COMMISH GIVES THE GREEN, UNDERSTOOD?
S.W.A
JUDGE, ISN'T THERE A CLOSED-CIRCUIT CAMERA OR SOMETHING THAT CAN GIVE MY GUYS A BETTER PICTURE OF WHAT'S GOING ON UP THERE?
IT'S A DELIBERATION ROOM, COMMISSIONER. INSTALLING ANY KIND OF RECORDING DEVICE IN THERE WOULD HAVE BEEN UNCONSTITUTIONAL.
COMM, THIS IS SNIPER ONE, COPY?
WHAT'S THE WORD, SHOOTER?
BLINDS ARE DRAWN IN HUNDRED'S ROOM AND ALL THIS HUMIDITY IS FUCKING UP MY THERMAL. I SHOULDN'T BE ABLE TO GET A CLEAR SHOT, BUT...
WELL, I'M USING THE NEW DIGITAL SCOPE HOMELAND SENT US, MA'AM, AND WHAT'S SHOWING UP IN MY CROSSHAIRS...IT'S NOT *POSSIBLE*.
IT LOOKS LIKE IT'S COMING FROM *INSIDE* THE ROOM.

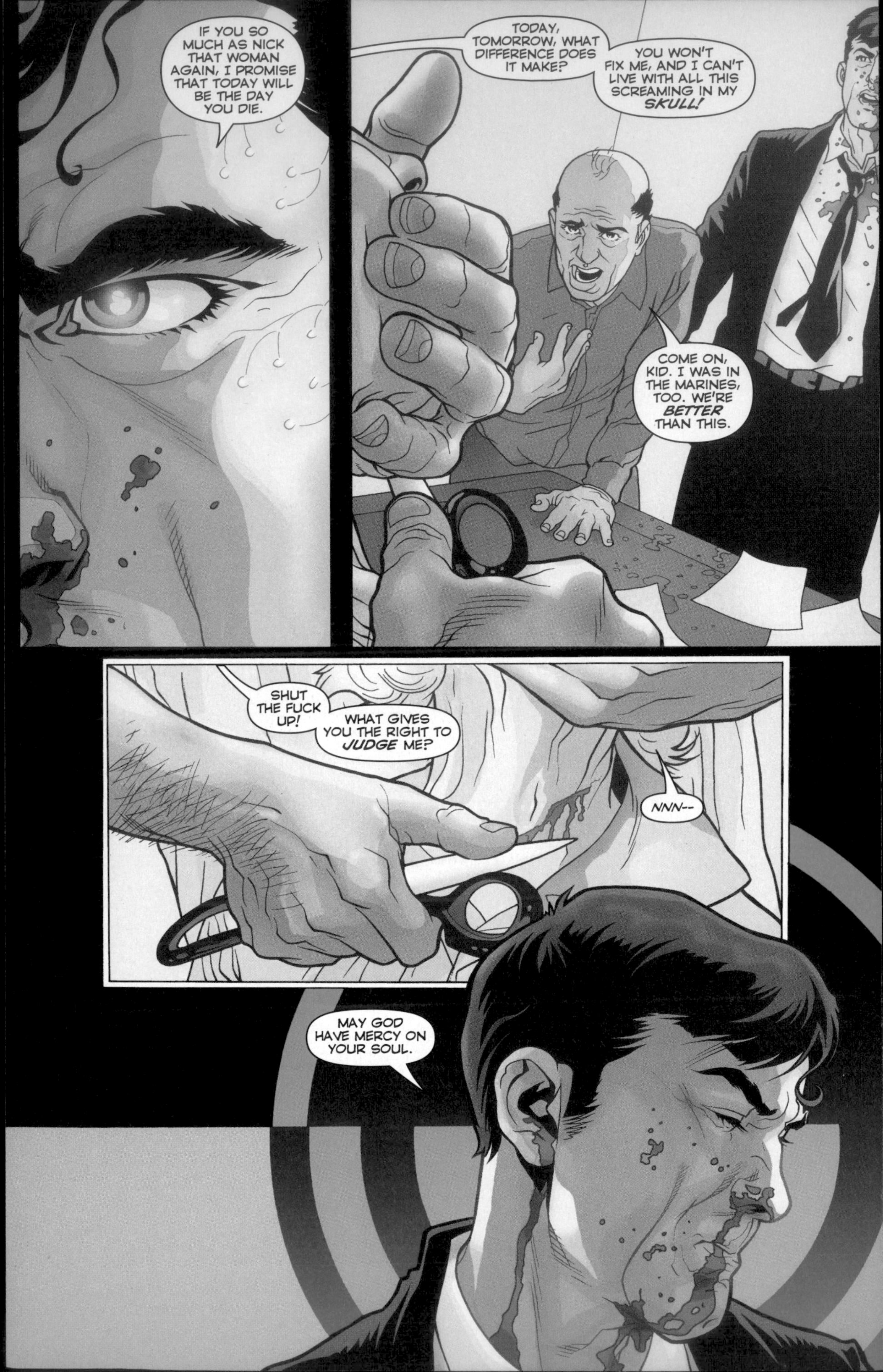
IF YOU SO MUCH AS NICK THAT WOMAN AGAIN, I PROMISE THAT TODAY WILL BE THE DAY YOU DIE.
TODAY, TOMORROW, WHAT DIFFERENCE DOES IT MAKE?
YOU WON'T FIX ME, AND I CAN'T LIVE WITH ALL THIS SCREAMING IN MY SKULL!
COME ON, KID. I WAS IN THE MARINES, TOO. WE'RE BETTER THAN THIS.
SHUT THE FUCK UP!
WHAT GIVES YOU THE RIGHT TO JUDGE ME?
NNN--
MAY GOD HAVE MERCY ON YOUR SOUL.

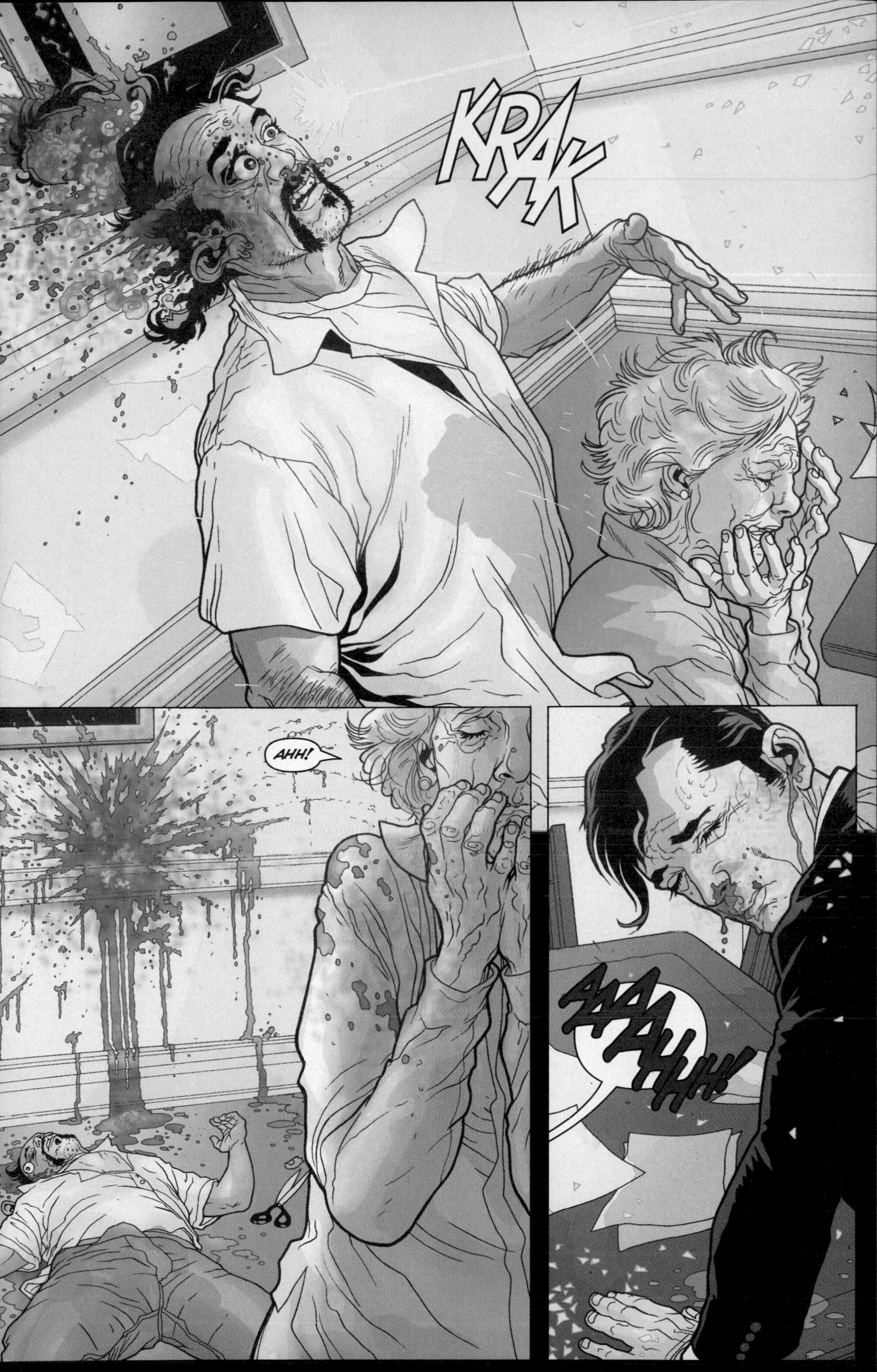
KRAK
AHH!
AAAAHHH!

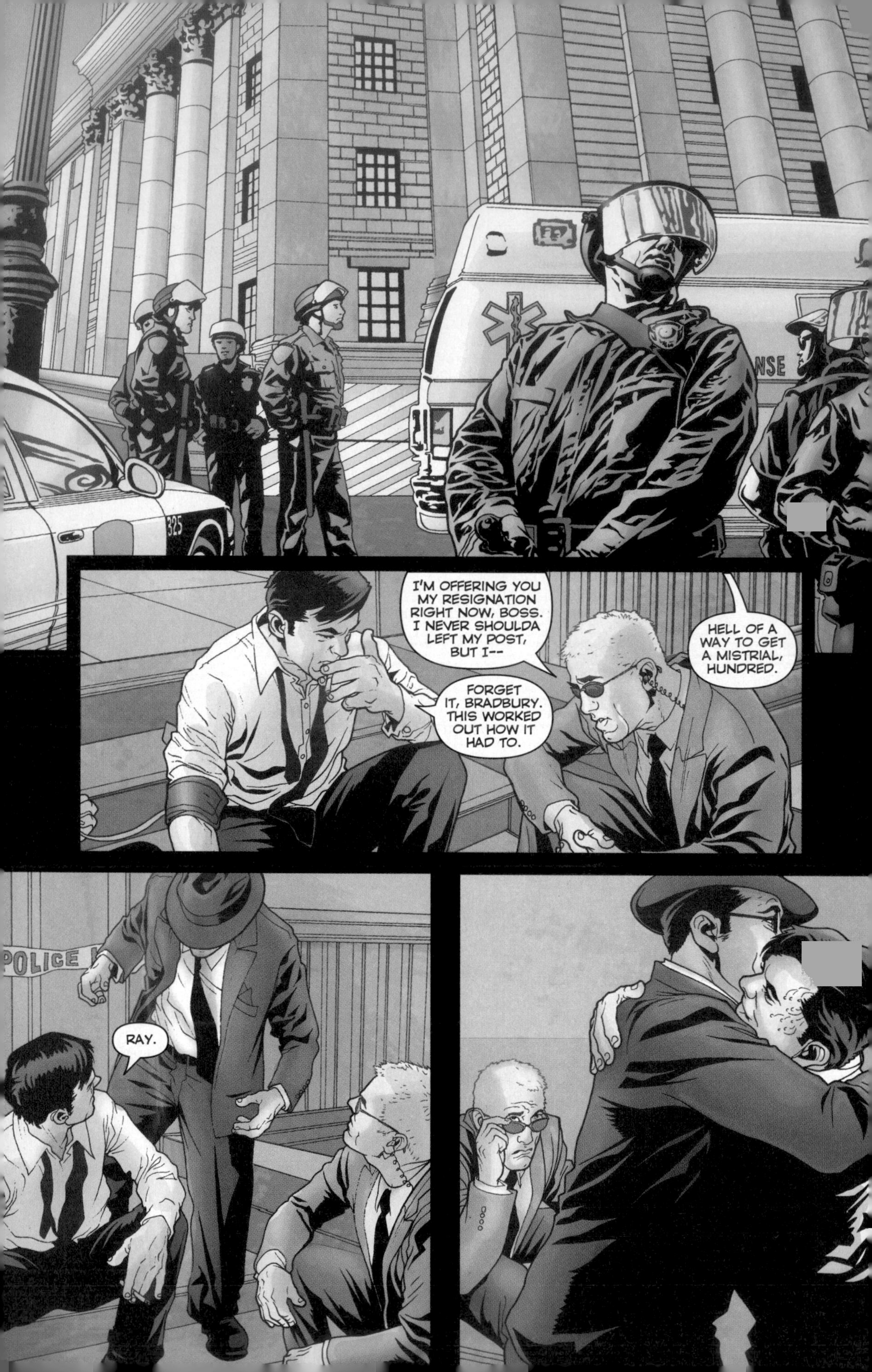
NSE
325
I'M OFFERING YOU MY RESIGNATION RIGHT NOW, BOSS. I NEVER SHOULDA LEFT MY POST, BUT I--
HELL OF A WAY TO GET A MISTRIAL, HUNDRED.
FORGET IT, BRADBURY. THIS WORKED OUT HOW IT HAD TO.
POLICE
RAY.

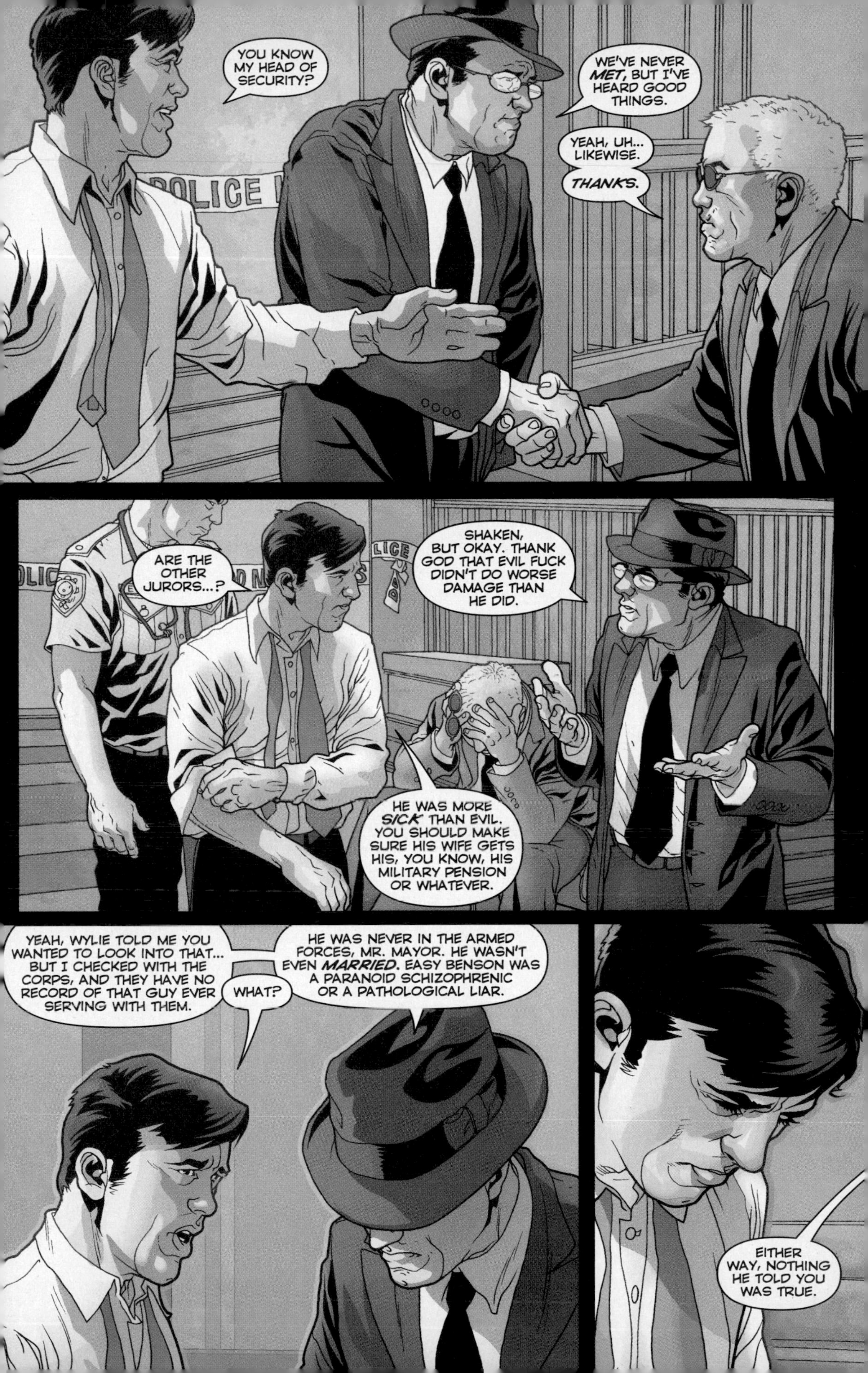
YOU KNOW MY HEAD OF SECURITY?
WE'VE NEVER MET, BUT I'VE HEARD GOOD THINGS.
YEAH, UH... LIKEWISE.
THANKS.
POLICE
ARE THE OTHER JURORS...?
SHAKEN, BUT OKAY. THANK GOD THAT EVIL FUCK DIDN'T DO WORSE DAMAGE THAN HE DID.
HE WAS MORE SICK THAN EVIL. YOU SHOULD MAKE SURE HIS WIFE GETS HIS, YOU KNOW, HIS MILITARY PENSION OR WHATEVER.
YEAH, WYLIE TOLD ME YOU WANTED TO LOOK INTO THAT... BUT I CHECKED WITH THE CORPS, AND THEY HAVE NO RECORD OF THAT GUY EVER SERVING WITH THEM.
WHAT?
HE WAS NEVER IN THE ARMED FORCES, MR. MAYOR. HE WASN'T EVEN MARRIED. EASY BENSON WAS A PARANOID SCHIZOPHRENIC OR A PATHOLOGICAL LIAR.
EITHER WAY, NOTHING HE TOLD YOU WAS TRUE.

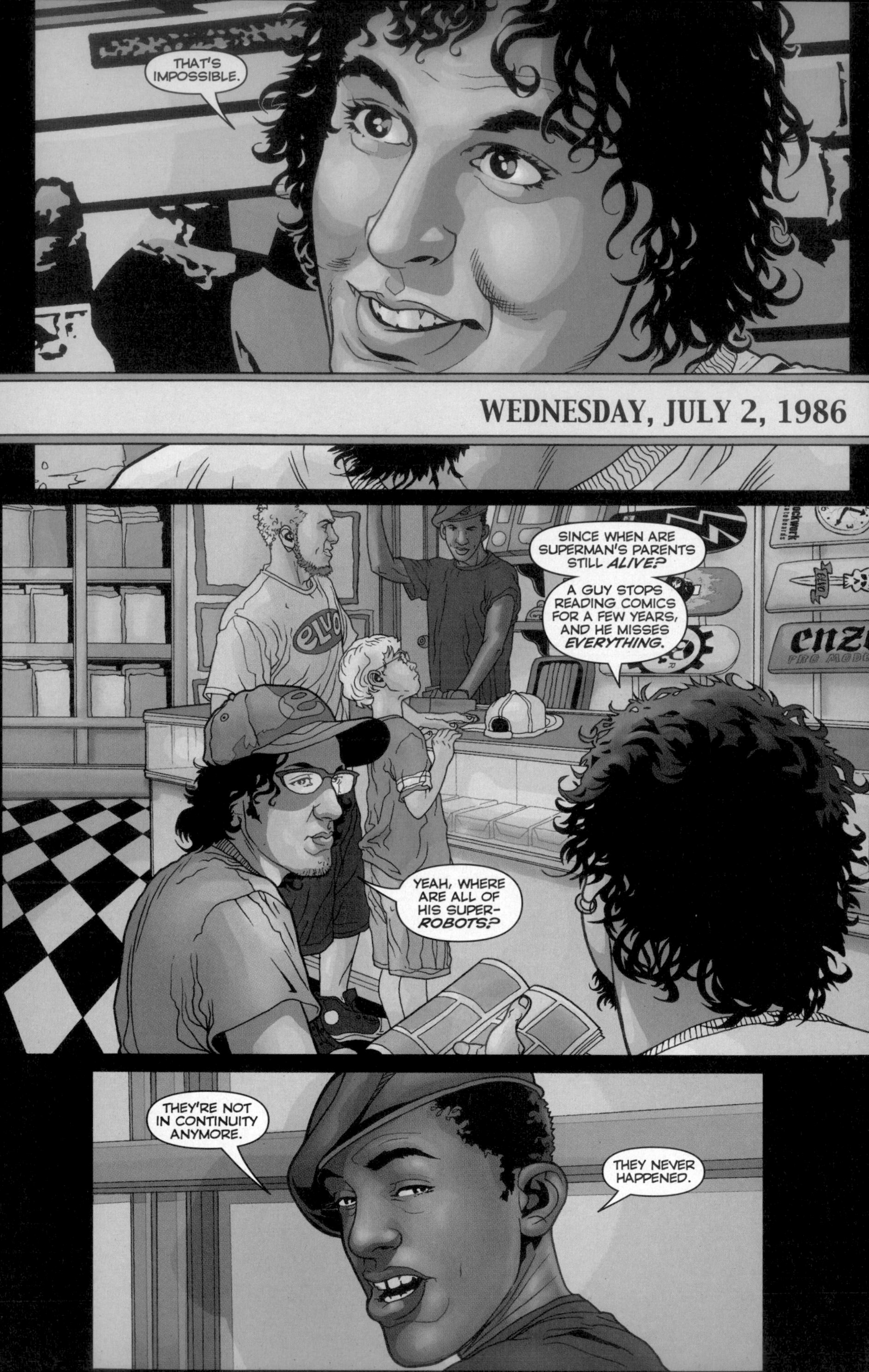
THAT'S IMPOSSIBLE.
WEDNESDAY, JULY 2, 1986
SINCE WHEN ARE SUPERMAN'S PARENTS STILL ALIVE?
A GUY STOPS READING COMICS FOR A FEW YEARS, AND HE MISSES EVERYTHING.
YEAH, WHERE ARE ALL OF HIS SUPER-ROBOTS?
THEY'RE NOT IN CONTINUITY ANYMORE.
THEY NEVER HAPPENED.

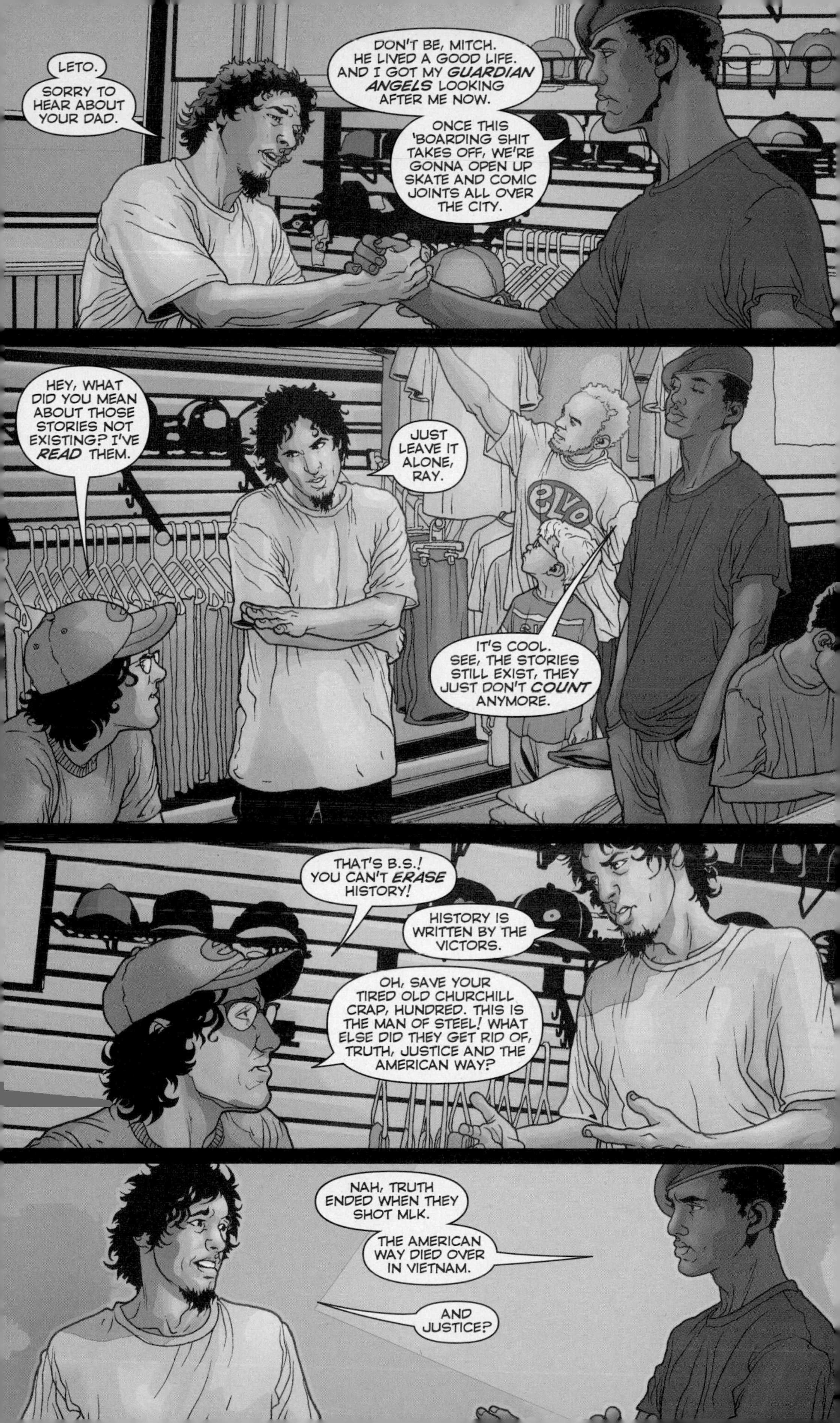
LETO.
SORRY TO HEAR ABOUT YOUR DAD.
DON'T BE, MITCH. HE LIVED A GOOD LIFE. AND I GOT MY GUARDIAN ANGELS LOOKING AFTER ME NOW.
ONCE THIS 'BOARDING SHIT TAKES OFF, WE'RE GONNA OPEN UP SKATE AND COMIC JOINTS ALL OVER THE CITY.
HEY, WHAT DID YOU MEAN ABOUT THOSE STORIES NOT EXISTING? I'VE READ THEM.
JUST LEAVE IT ALONE, RAY.
IT'S COOL. SEE, THE STORIES STILL EXIST, THEY JUST DON'T COUNT ANYMORE.
THAT'S B.S.! YOU CAN'T ERASE HISTORY!
HISTORY IS WRITTEN BY THE VICTORS.
OH, SAVE YOUR TIRED OLD CHURCHILL CRAP, HUNDRED. THIS IS THE MAN OF STEEL! WHAT ELSE DID THEY GET RID OF, TRUTH, JUSTICE AND THE AMERICAN WAY?
NAH, TRUTH ENDED WHEN THEY SHOT MLK.
THE AMERICAN WAY DIED OVER IN VIETNAM.
AND JUSTICE?

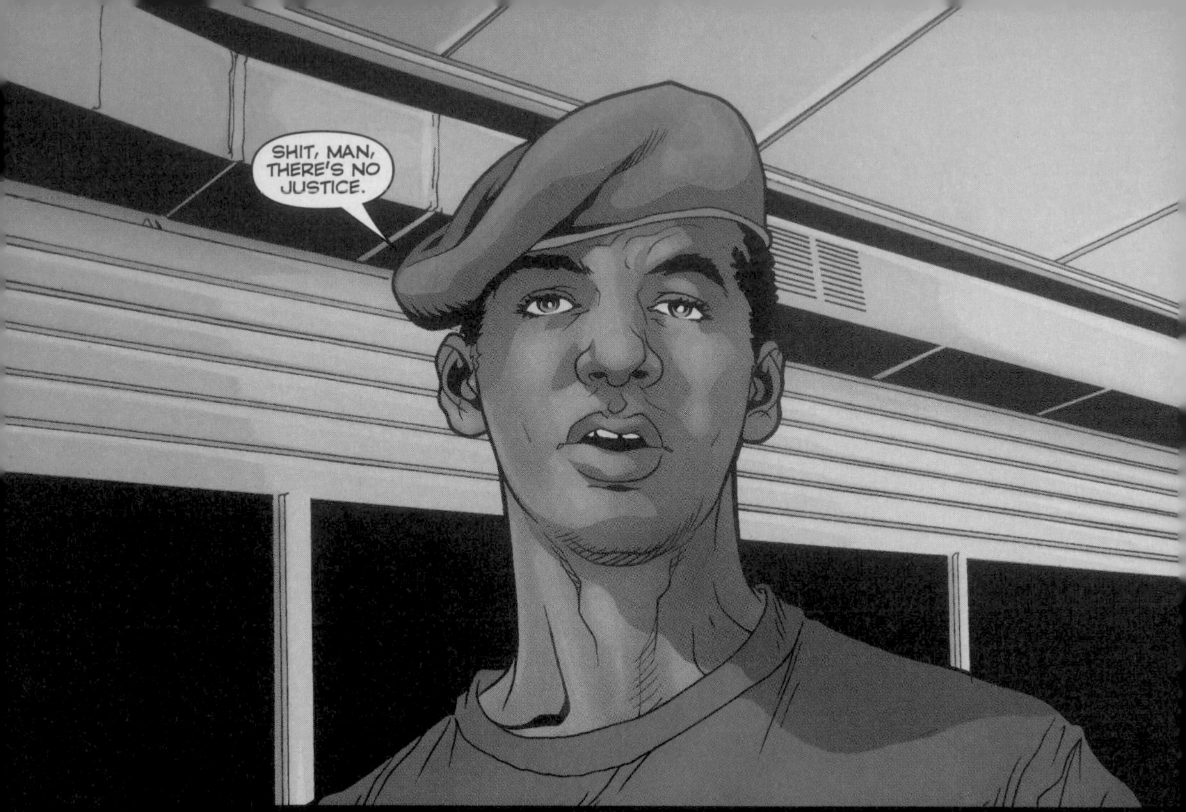
SHIT, MAN, THERE'S NO JUSTICE.

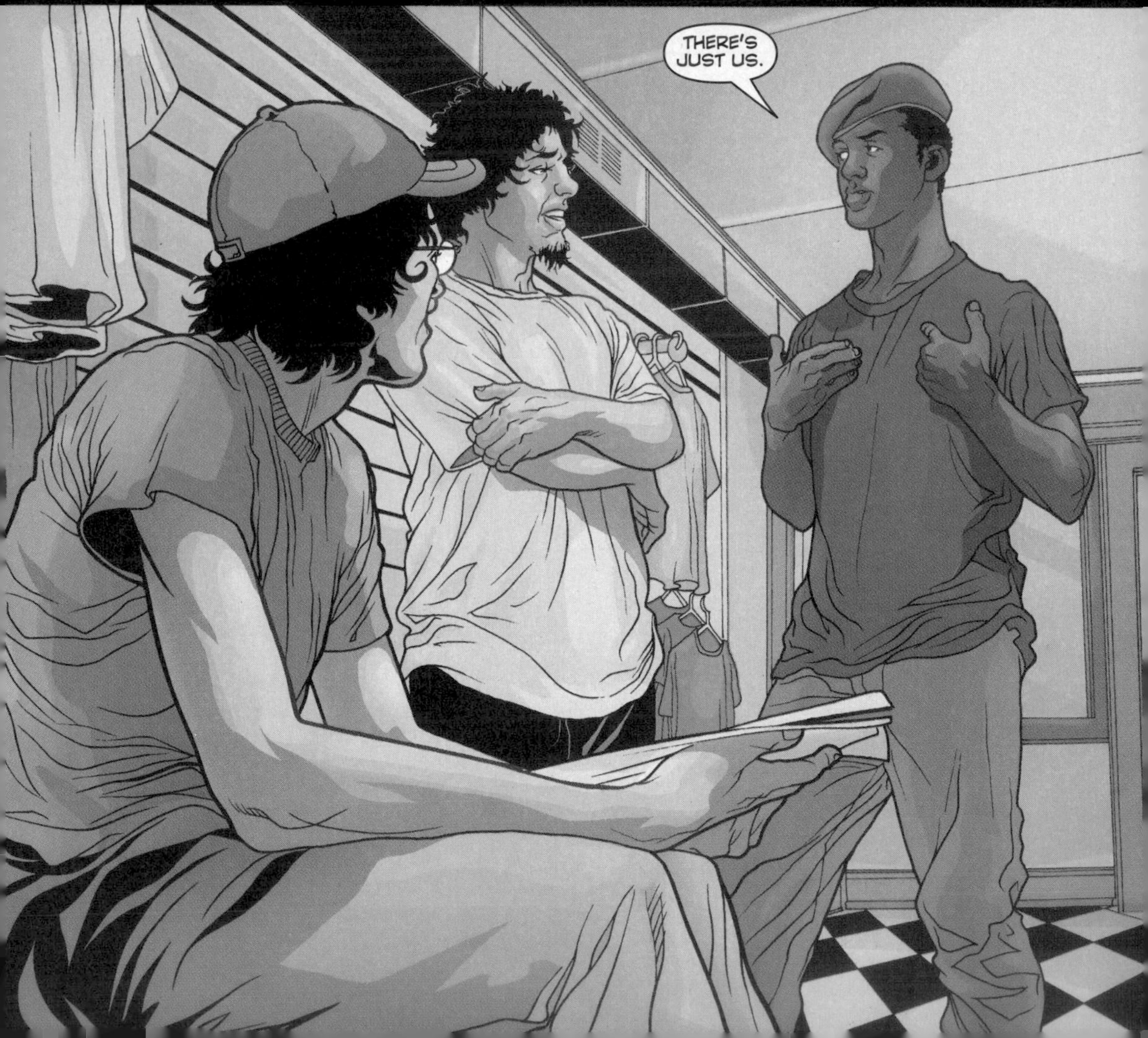
THERE'S JUST US.

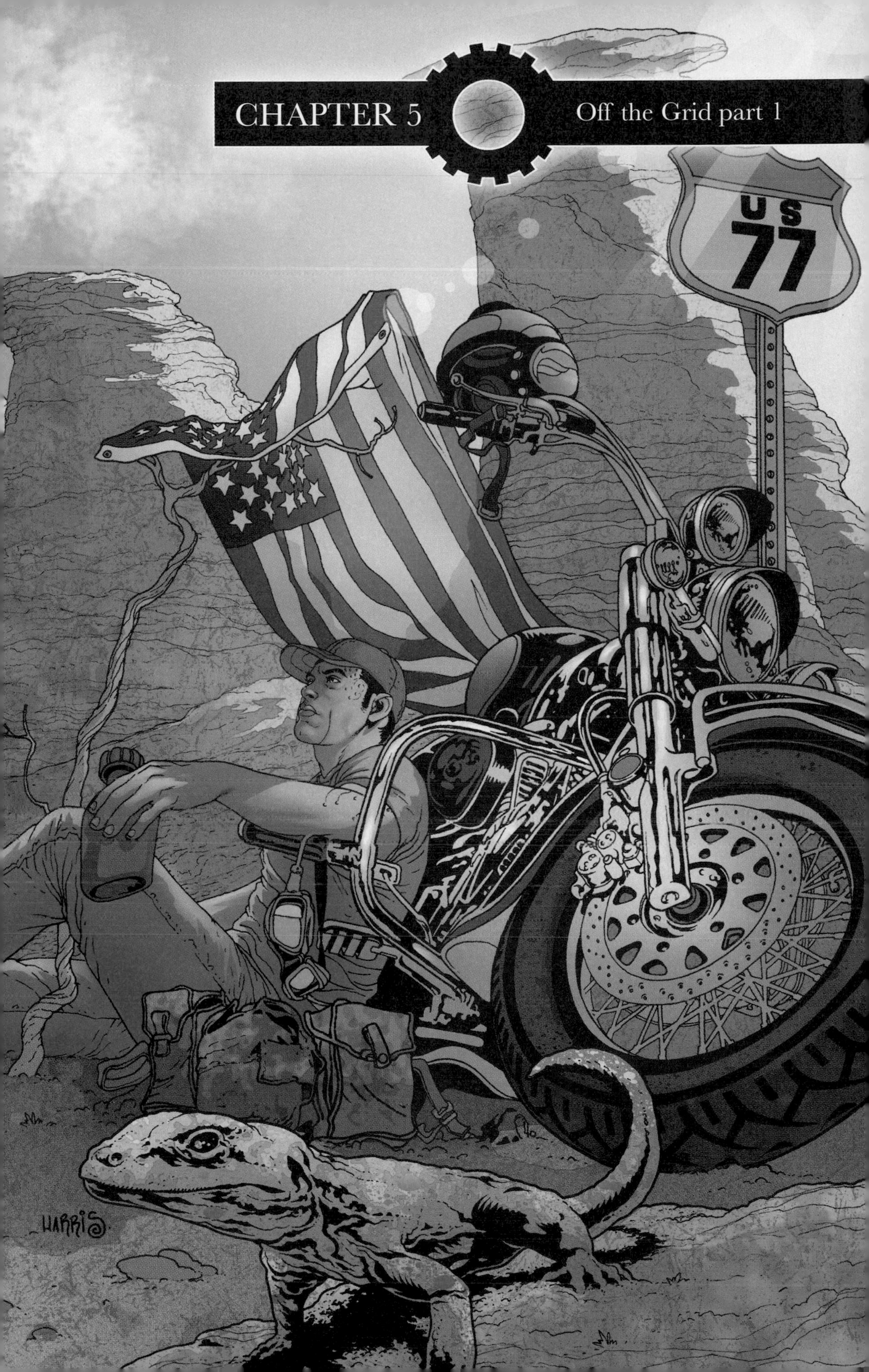
CHAPTER 5
Off the Grid part 1
US
77
HARRIS

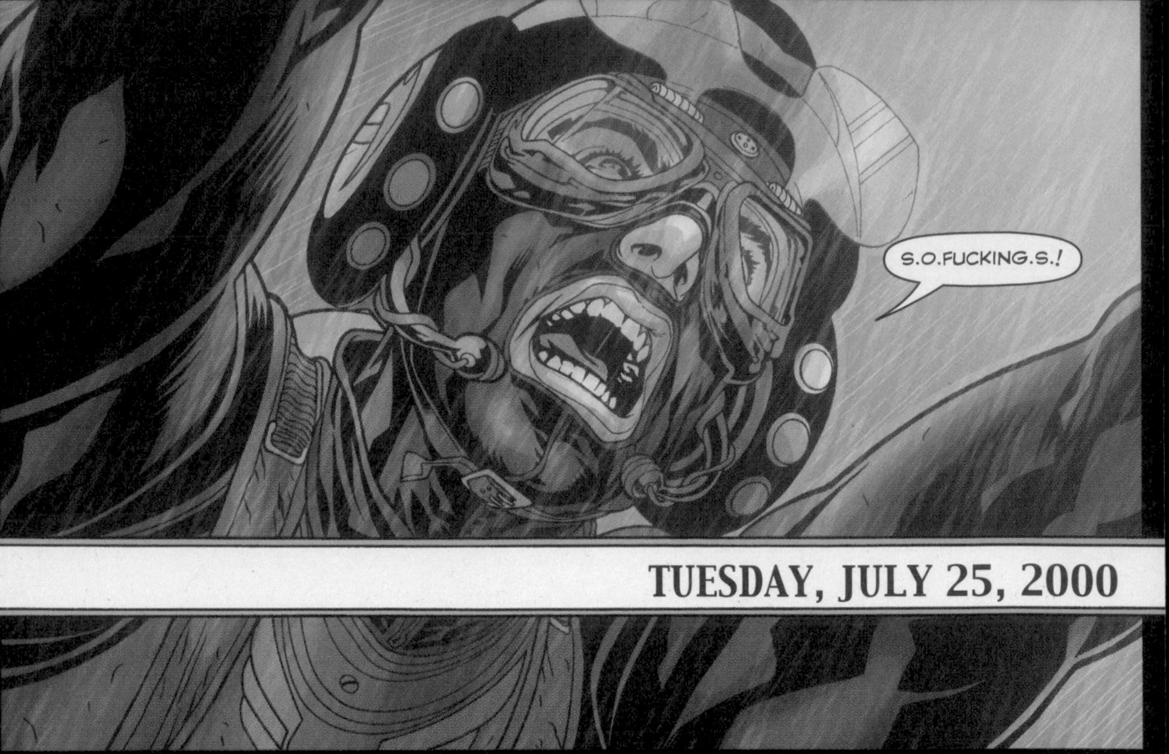
S.O.FUCKING.S.!
TUESDAY, JULY 25, 2000

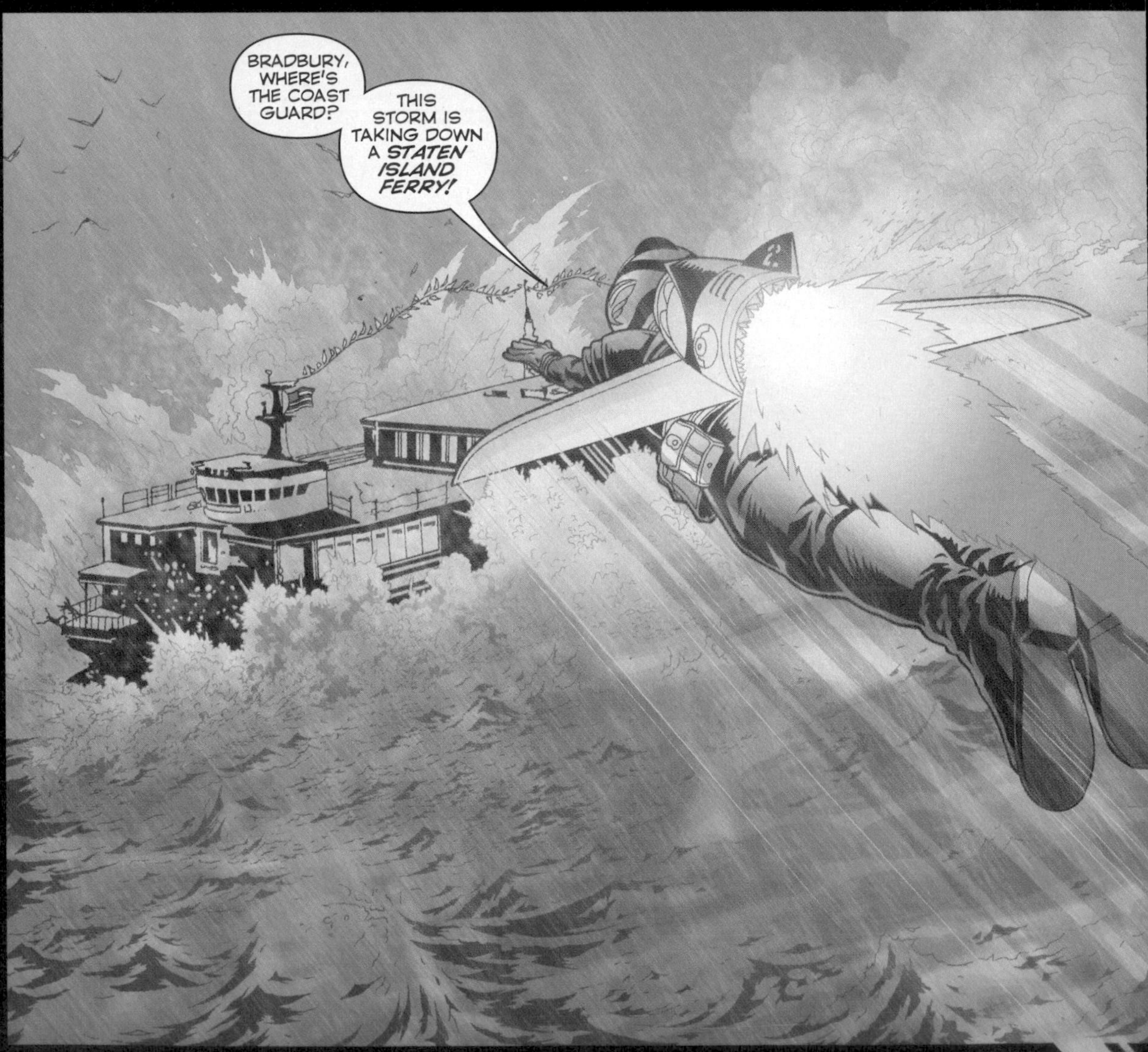
BRADBURY, WHERE'S THE COAST GUARD?
THIS STORM IS TAKING DOWN A *STATEN ISLAND FERRY!*

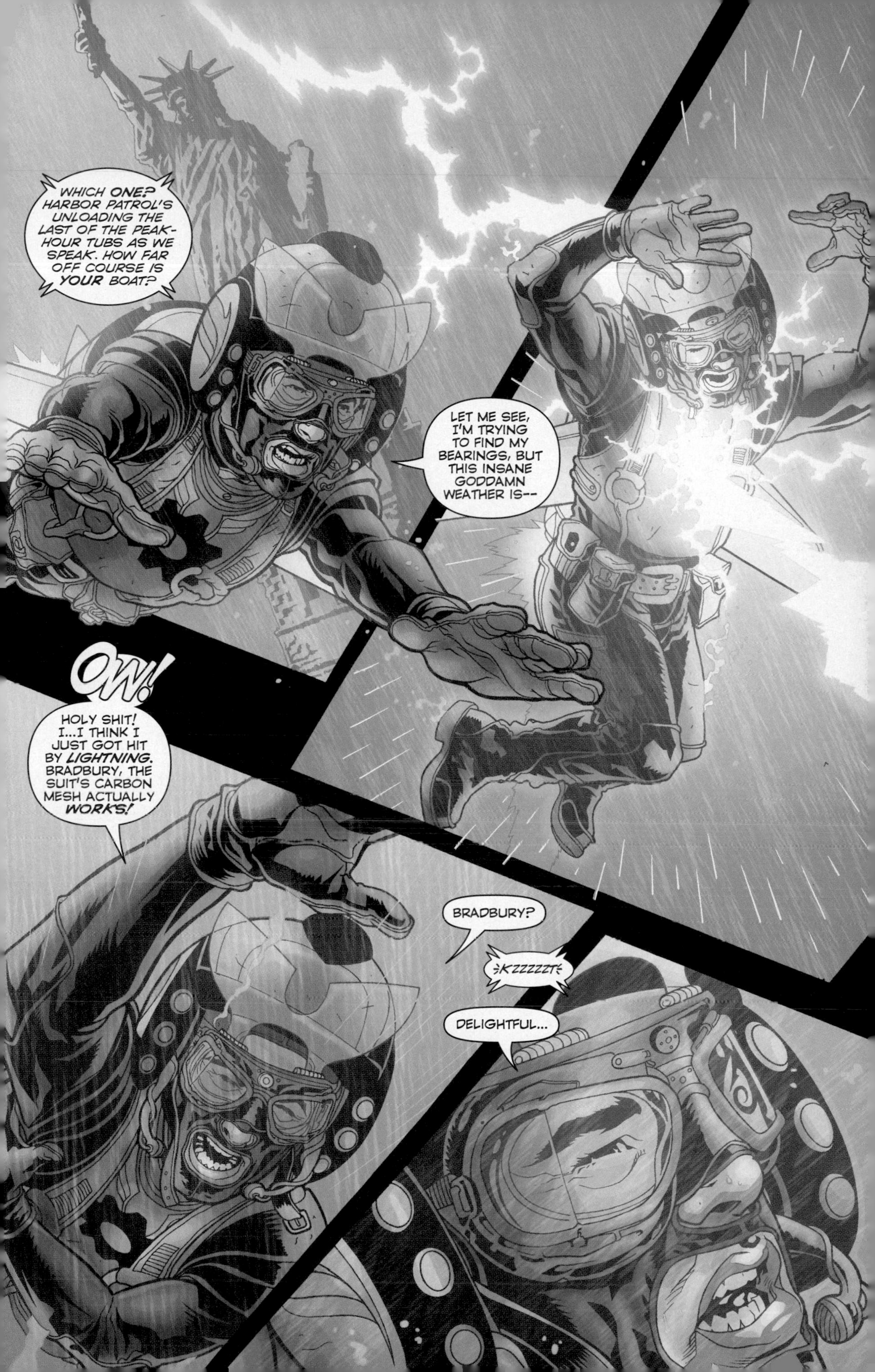
WHICH ONE? HARBOR PATROL'S UNLOADING THE LAST OF THE PEAK-HOUR TUBS AS WE SPEAK. HOW FAR OFF COURSE IS YOUR BOAT?
LET ME SEE, I'M TRYING TO FIND MY BEARINGS, BUT THIS INSANE GODDAMN WEATHER IS--
OW!
HOLY SHIT! I...I THINK I JUST GOT HIT BY LIGHTNING. BRADBURY, THE SUIT'S CARBON MESH ACTUALLY WORKS!
BRADBURY?
KZZZZZT
DELIGHTFUL...

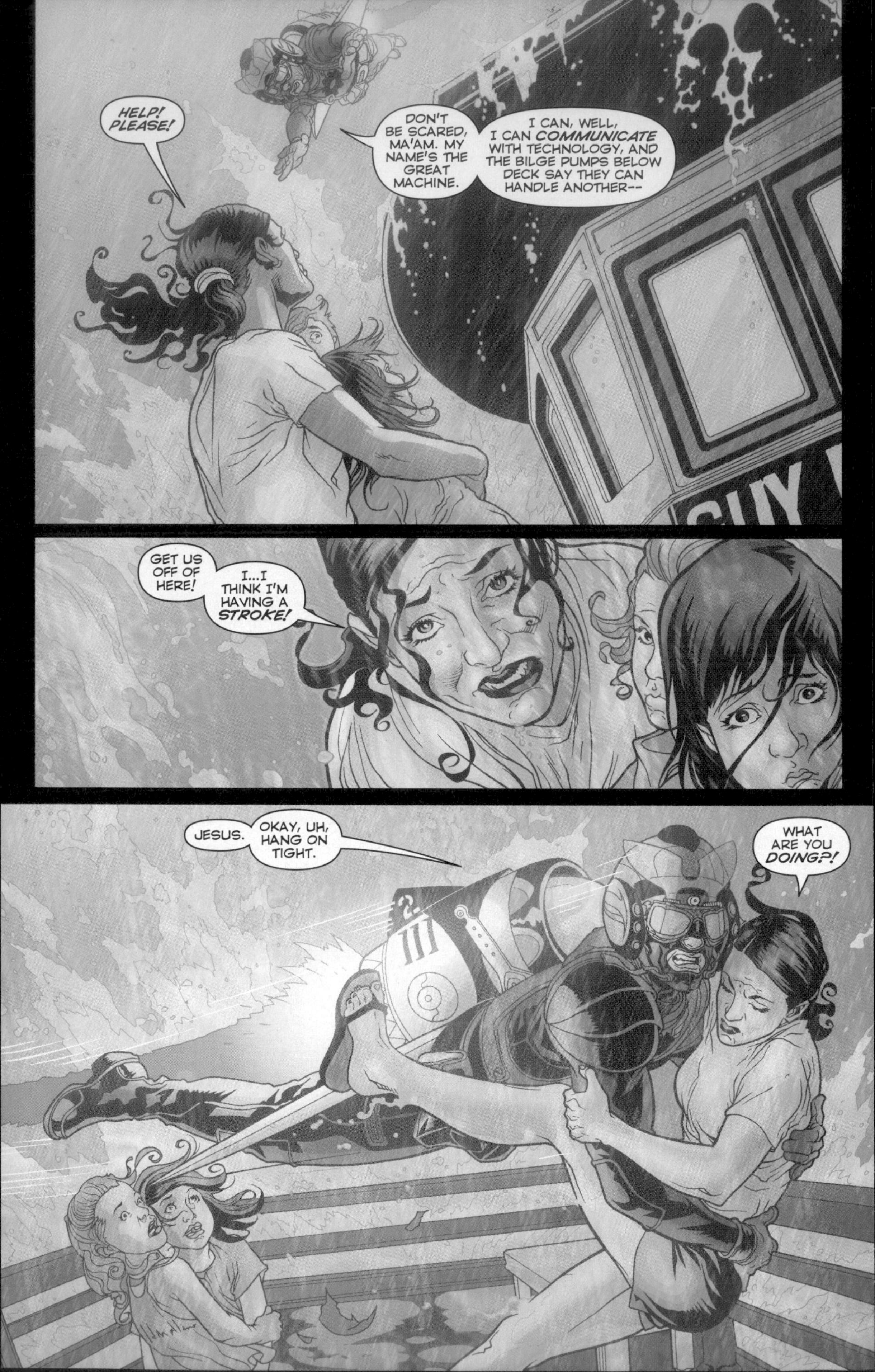
HELP! PLEASE!
DON'T BE SCARED, MA'AM. MY NAME'S THE GREAT MACHINE.
I CAN, WELL, I CAN COMMUNICATE WITH TECHNOLOGY, AND THE BILGE PUMPS BELOW DECK SAY THEY CAN HANDLE ANOTHER--
GET US OFF OF HERE!
I...I THINK I'M HAVING A STROKE!
JESUS.
OKAY, UH, HANG ON TIGHT.
WHAT ARE YOU DOING?!

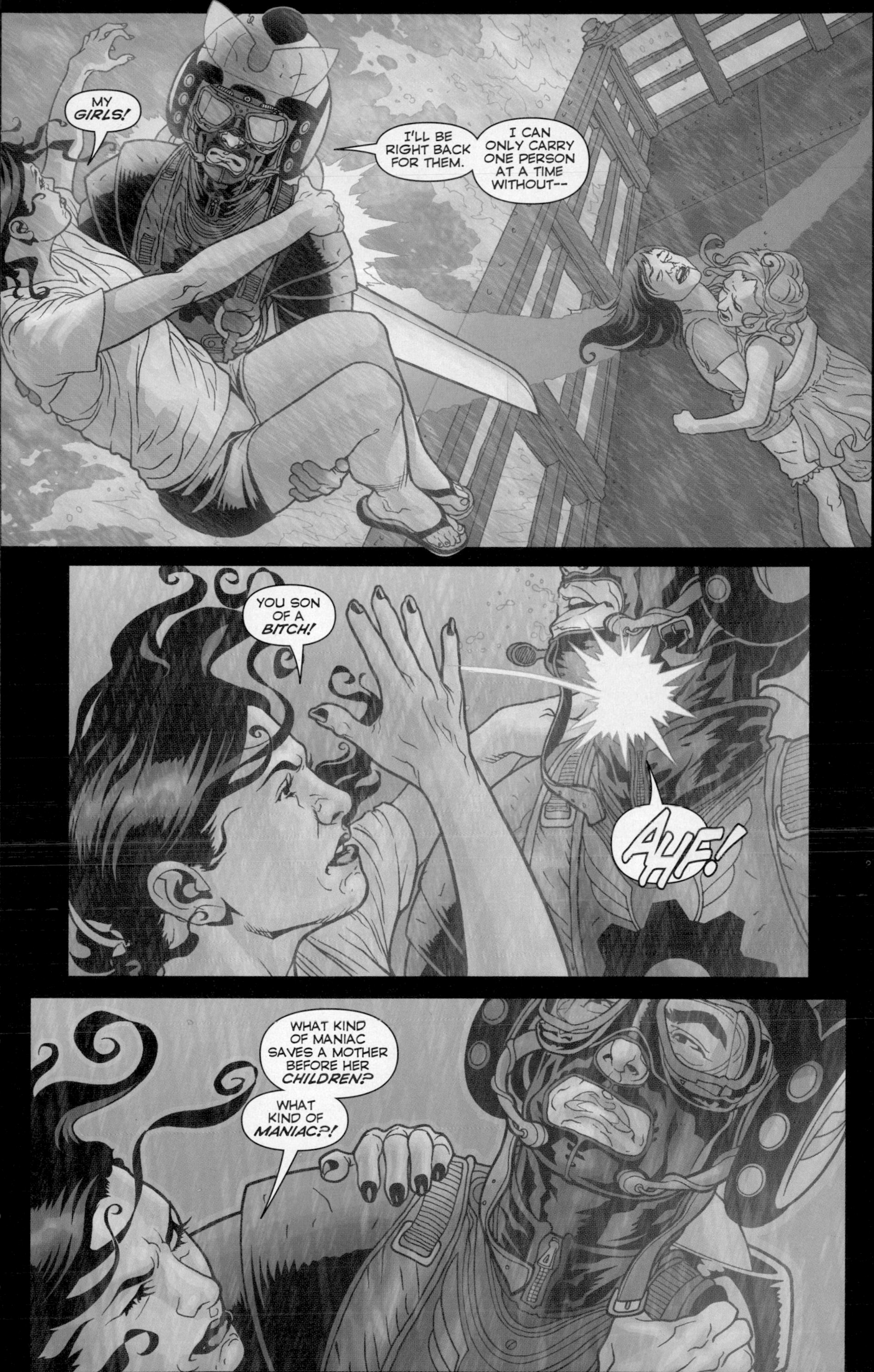
MY GIRLS!
I'LL BE RIGHT BACK FOR THEM.
I CAN ONLY CARRY ONE PERSON AT A TIME WITHOUT--
YOU SON OF A BITCH!
AHF!
WHAT KIND OF MANIAC SAVES A MOTHER BEFORE HER CHILDREN?
WHAT KIND OF MANIAC?!

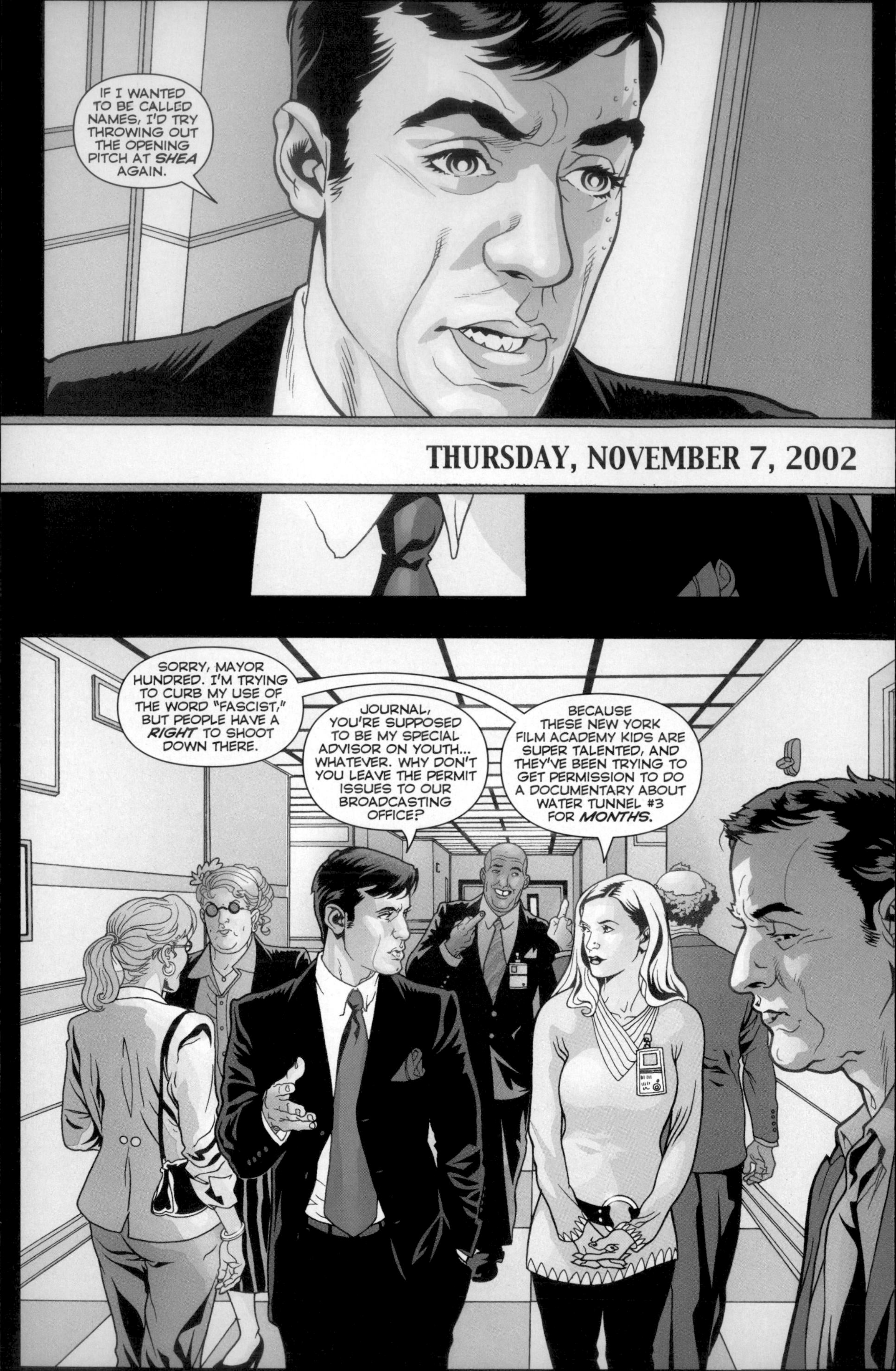
IF I WANTED TO BE CALLED NAMES, I'D TRY THROWING OUT THE OPENING PITCH AT *SHEA* AGAIN.
THURSDAY, NOVEMBER 7, 2002
SORRY, MAYOR HUNDRED. I'M TRYING TO CURB MY USE OF THE WORD "FASCIST," BUT PEOPLE HAVE A *RIGHT* TO SHOOT DOWN THERE.
JOURNAL, YOU'RE SUPPOSED TO BE MY SPECIAL ADVISOR ON YOUTH... WHATEVER. WHY DON'T YOU LEAVE THE PERMIT ISSUES TO OUR BROADCASTING OFFICE?
BECAUSE THESE NEW YORK FILM ACADEMY KIDS ARE SUPER TALENTED, AND THEY'VE BEEN TRYING TO GET PERMISSION TO DO A DOCUMENTARY ABOUT WATER TUNNEL #3 FOR *MONTHS*.

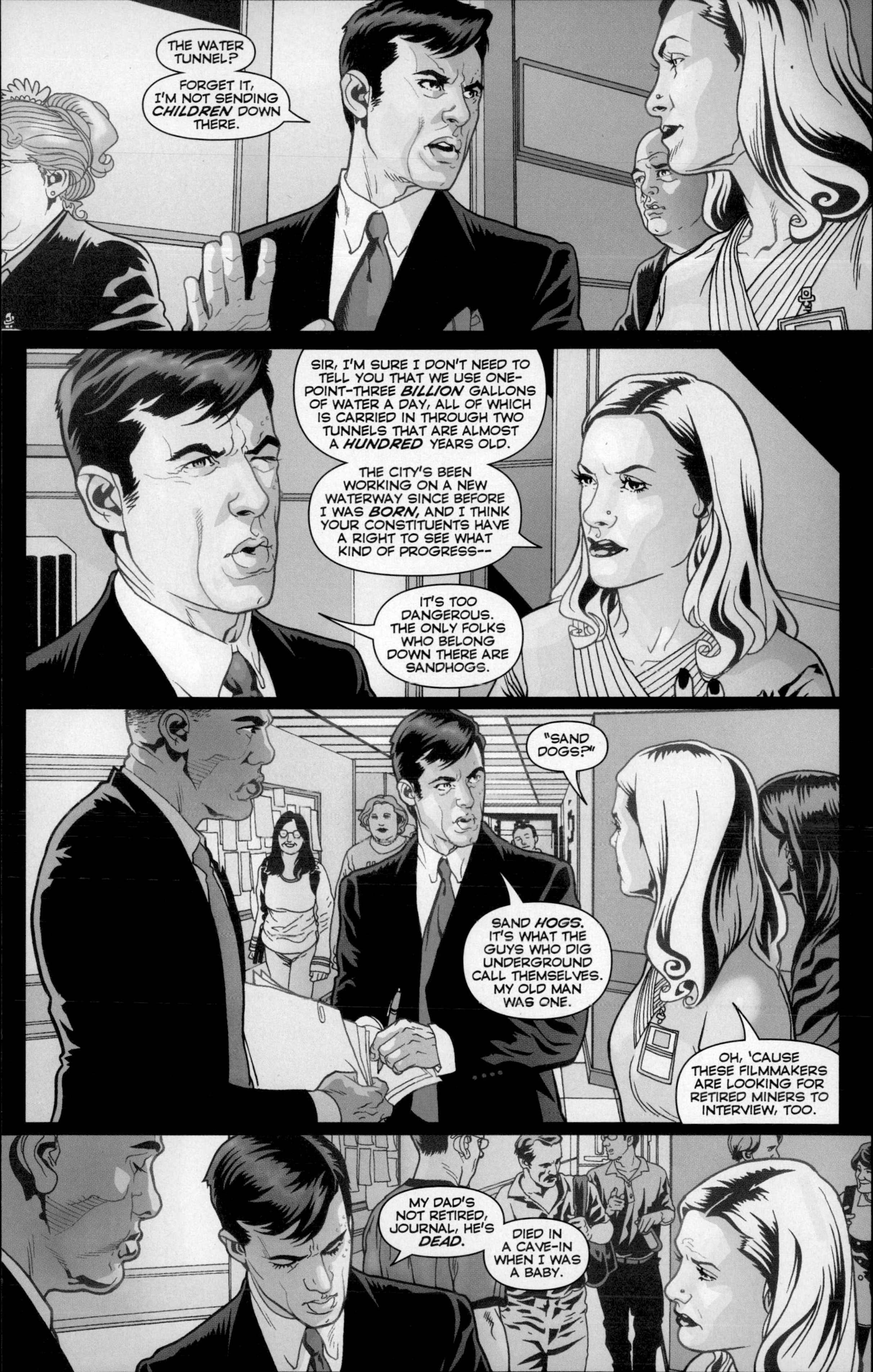
THE WATER TUNNEL?
FORGET IT, I'M NOT SENDING *CHILDREN* DOWN THERE.
SIR, I'M SURE I DON'T NEED TO TELL YOU THAT WE USE ONE-POINT-THREE *BILLION* GALLONS OF WATER A DAY, ALL OF WHICH IS CARRIED IN THROUGH TWO TUNNELS THAT ARE ALMOST A *HUNDRED* YEARS OLD.
THE CITY'S BEEN WORKING ON A NEW WATERWAY SINCE BEFORE I WAS *BORN,* AND I THINK YOUR CONSTITUENTS HAVE A RIGHT TO SEE WHAT KIND OF PROGRESS--
IT'S TOO DANGEROUS. THE ONLY FOLKS WHO BELONG DOWN THERE ARE SANDHOGS.
"SAND DOGS?"
SAND *HOGS.* IT'S WHAT THE GUYS WHO DIG UNDERGROUND CALL THEMSELVES. MY OLD MAN WAS ONE.
OH, 'CAUSE THESE FILMMAKERS ARE LOOKING FOR RETIRED MINERS TO INTERVIEW, TOO.
MY DAD'S NOT RETIRED, JOURNAL, HE'S *DEAD.*
DIED IN A CAVE-IN WHEN I WAS A BABY.

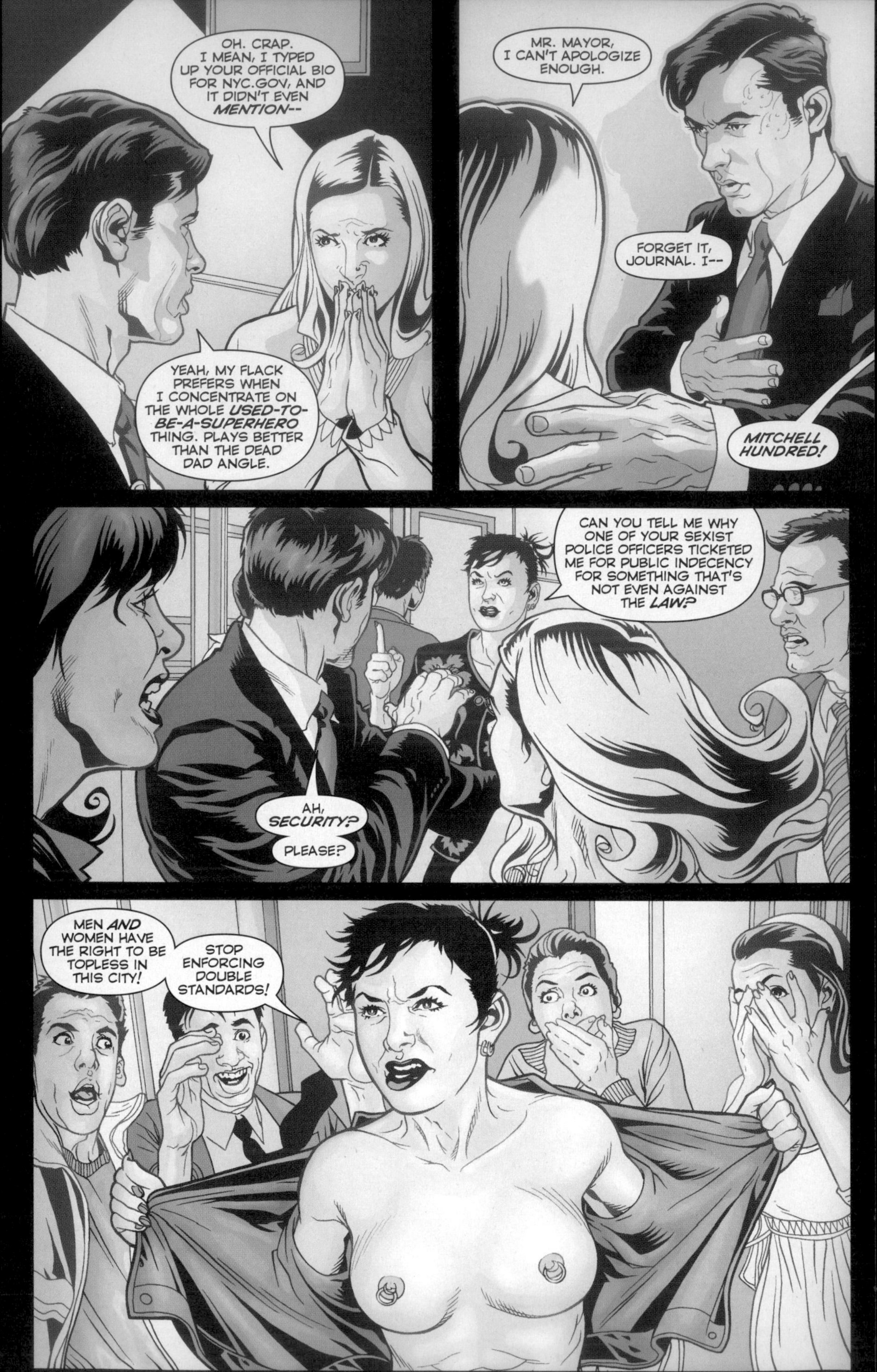
OH. CRAP. I MEAN, I TYPED UP YOUR OFFICIAL BIO FOR NYC.GOV, AND IT DIDN'T EVEN *MENTION*--
YEAH, MY FLACK PREFERS WHEN I CONCENTRATE ON THE WHOLE *USED-TO-BE-A-SUPERHERO* THING. PLAYS BETTER THAN THE DEAD DAD ANGLE.
MR. MAYOR, I CAN'T APOLOGIZE ENOUGH.
FORGET IT, JOURNAL. I--
MITCHELL HUNDRED!
CAN YOU TELL ME WHY ONE OF YOUR SEXIST POLICE OFFICERS TICKETED ME FOR PUBLIC INDECENCY FOR SOMETHING THAT'S NOT EVEN AGAINST THE *LAW?*
AH, *SECURITY?*
PLEASE?
MEN *AND* WOMEN HAVE THE RIGHT TO BE TOPLESS IN THIS CITY!
STOP ENFORCING DOUBLE STANDARDS!

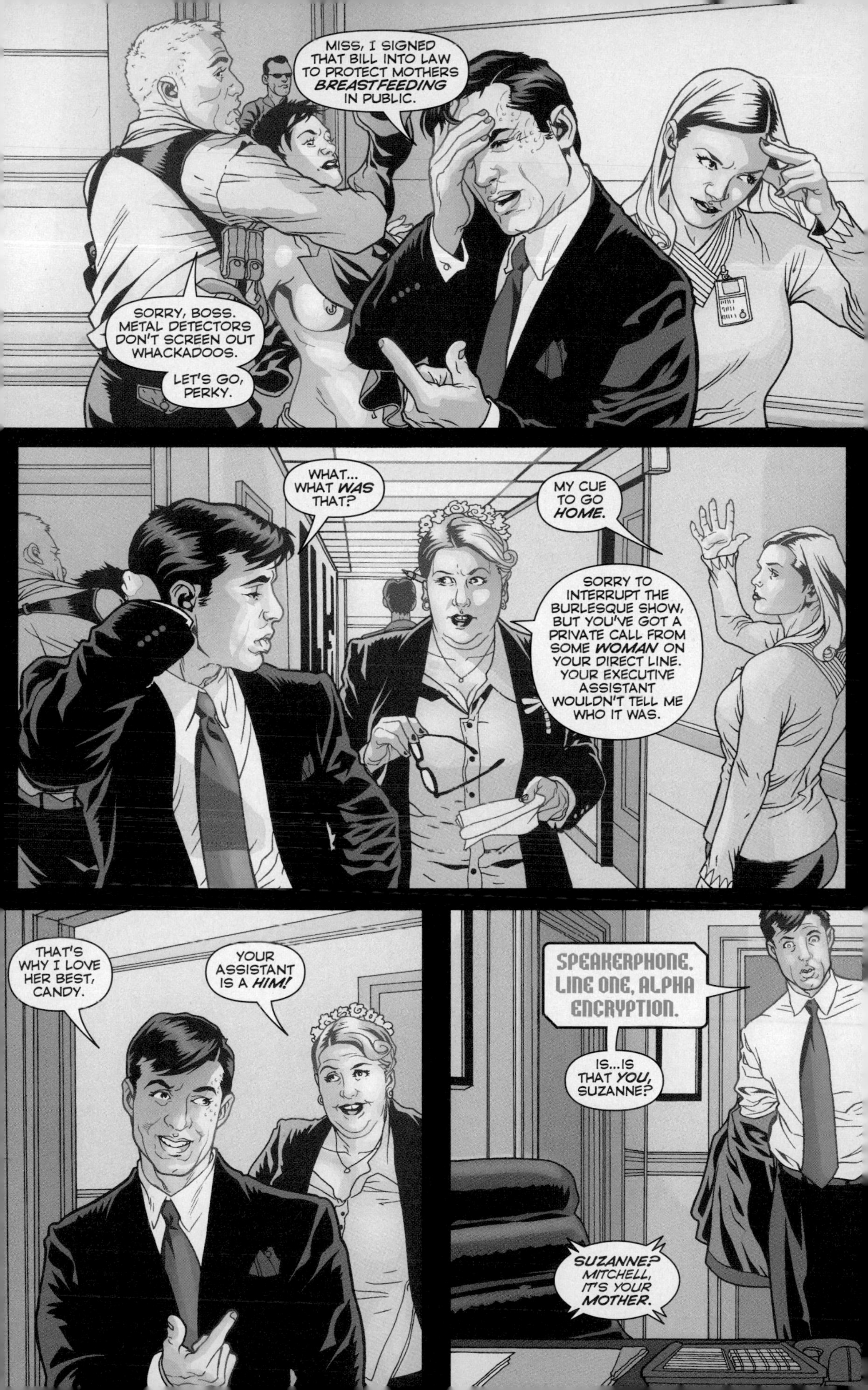

MISS, I SIGNED THAT BILL INTO LAW TO PROTECT MOTHERS *BREASTFEEDING* IN PUBLIC.
SORRY, BOSS. METAL DETECTORS DON'T SCREEN OUT WHACKADOOS.
LET'S GO, PERKY.
WHAT... WHAT *WAS* THAT?
MY CUE TO GO *HOME*.
SORRY TO INTERRUPT THE BURLESQUE SHOW, BUT YOU'VE GOT A PRIVATE CALL FROM SOME *WOMAN* ON YOUR DIRECT LINE. YOUR EXECUTIVE ASSISTANT WOULDN'T TELL ME WHO IT WAS.
THAT'S WHY I LOVE HER BEST, CANDY.
YOUR ASSISTANT IS A *HIM!*
SPEAKERPHONE. LINE ONE, ALPHA ENCRYPTION.
IS...IS THAT *YOU,* SUZANNE?
SUZANNE? MITCHELL, IT'S YOUR *MOTHER*.

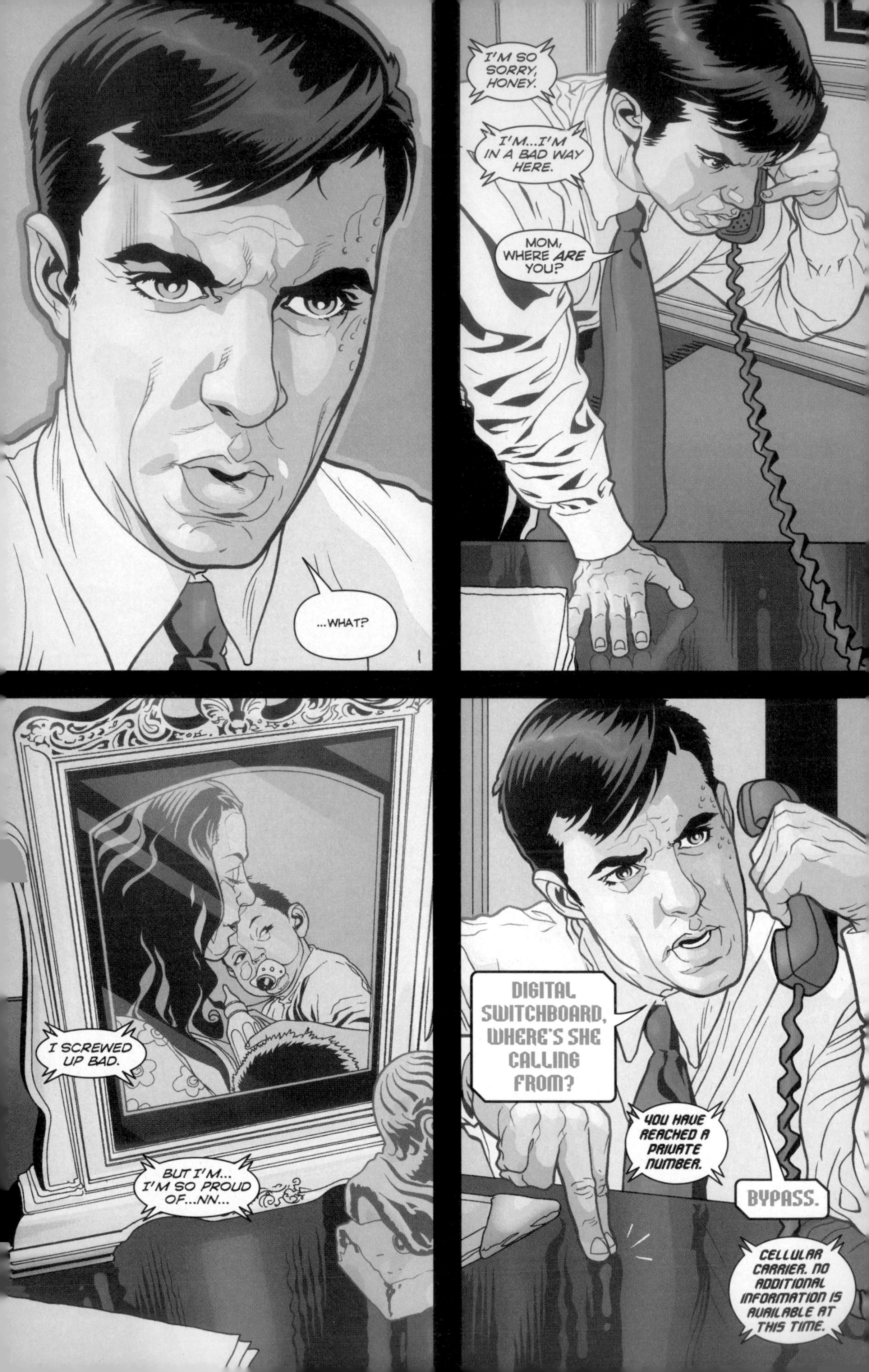
...WHAT?
I'M SO SORRY, HONEY.
I'M...I'M IN A BAD WAY HERE.
MOM, WHERE ARE YOU?
I SCREWED UP BAD.
BUT I'M... I'M SO PROUD OF...NN...
DIGITAL SWITCHBOARD, WHERE'S SHE CALLING FROM?
YOU HAVE REACHED A PRIVATE NUMBER.
BYPASS.
CELLULAR CARRIER. NO ADDITIONAL INFORMATION IS AVAILABLE AT THIS TIME.

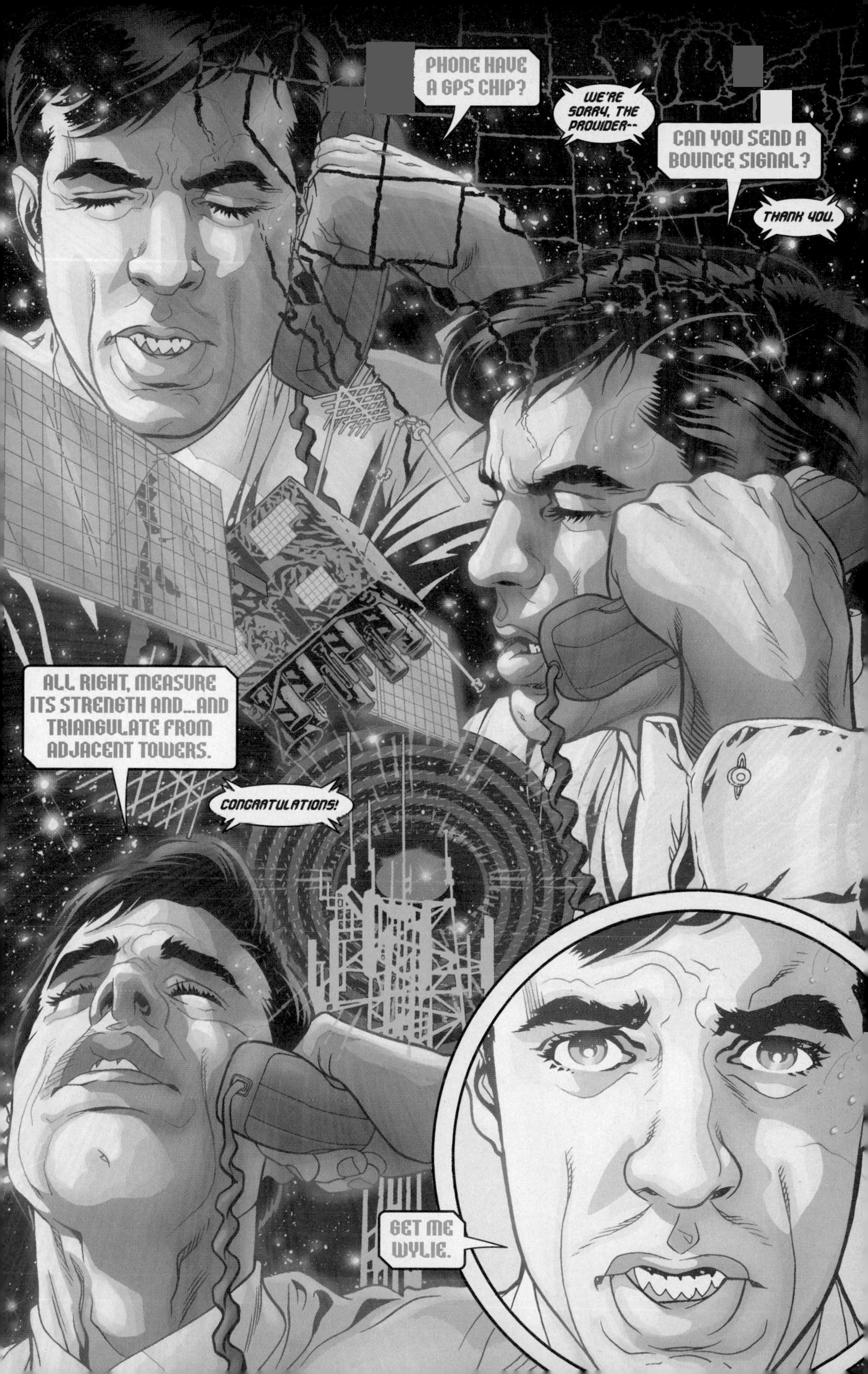
PHONE HAVE A GPS CHIP?
WE'RE SORRY, THE PROVIDER--
CAN YOU SEND A BOUNCE SIGNAL?
THANK YOU.
ALL RIGHT, MEASURE ITS STRENGTH AND...AND TRIANGULATE FROM ADJACENT TOWERS.
CONGRATULATIONS!
GET ME WYLIE.

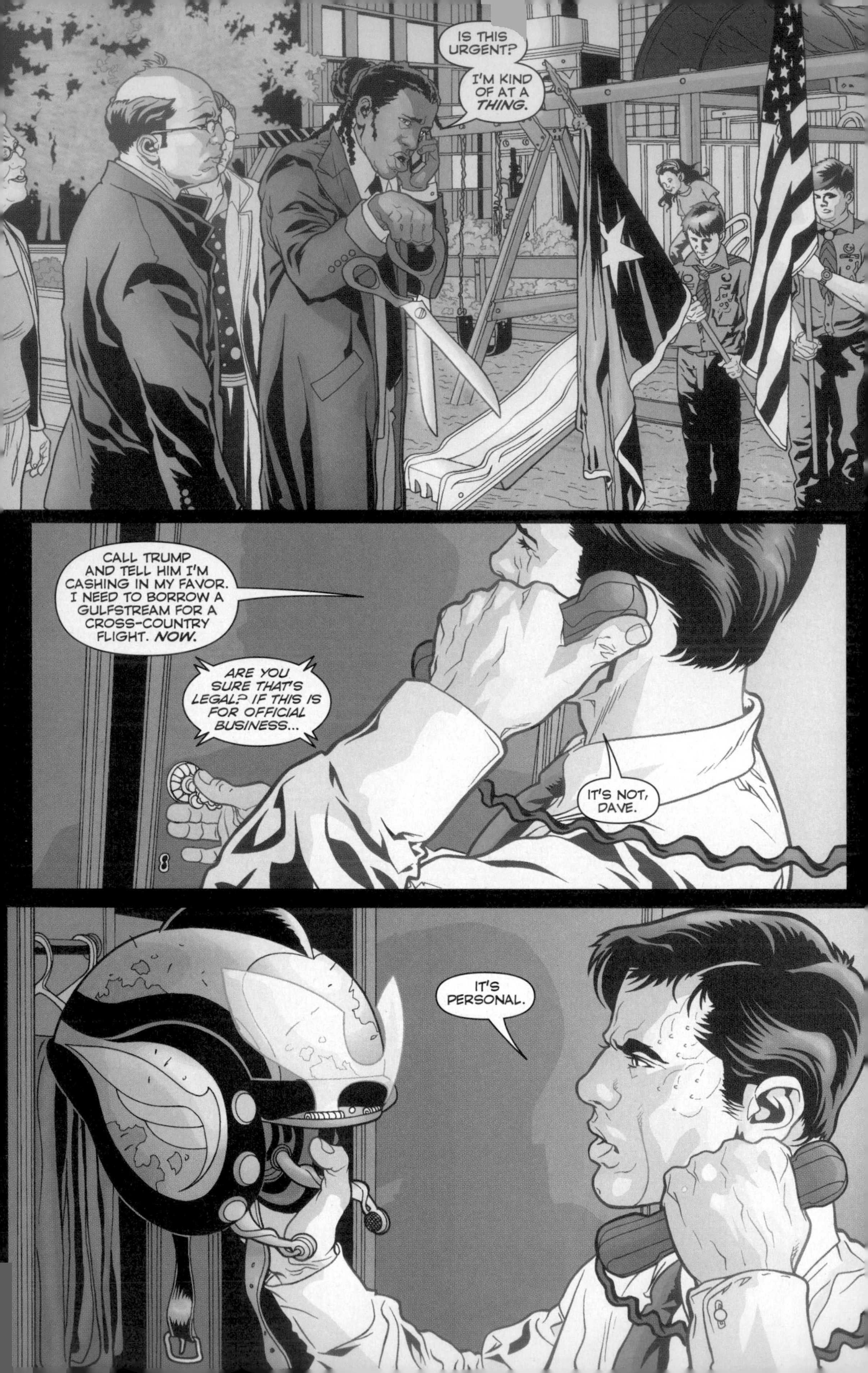
IS THIS URGENT?
I'M KIND OF AT A *THING*.
CALL TRUMP AND TELL HIM I'M CASHING IN MY FAVOR. I NEED TO BORROW A GULFSTREAM FOR A CROSS-COUNTRY FLIGHT. *NOW*.
ARE YOU SURE THAT'S LEGAL? IF THIS IS FOR OFFICIAL BUSINESS...
IT'S NOT, DAVE.
IT'S PERSONAL.

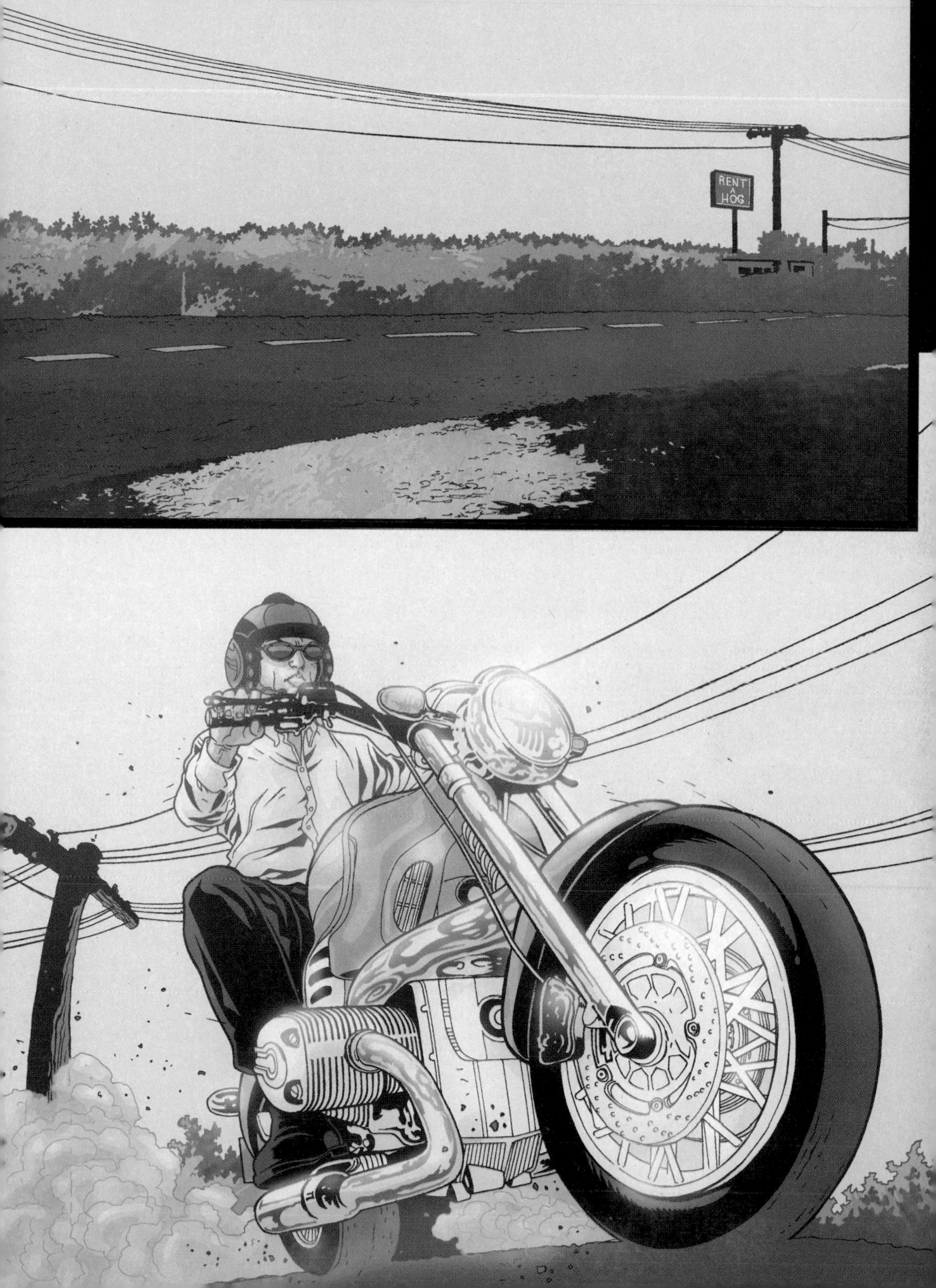
RENT A HOG

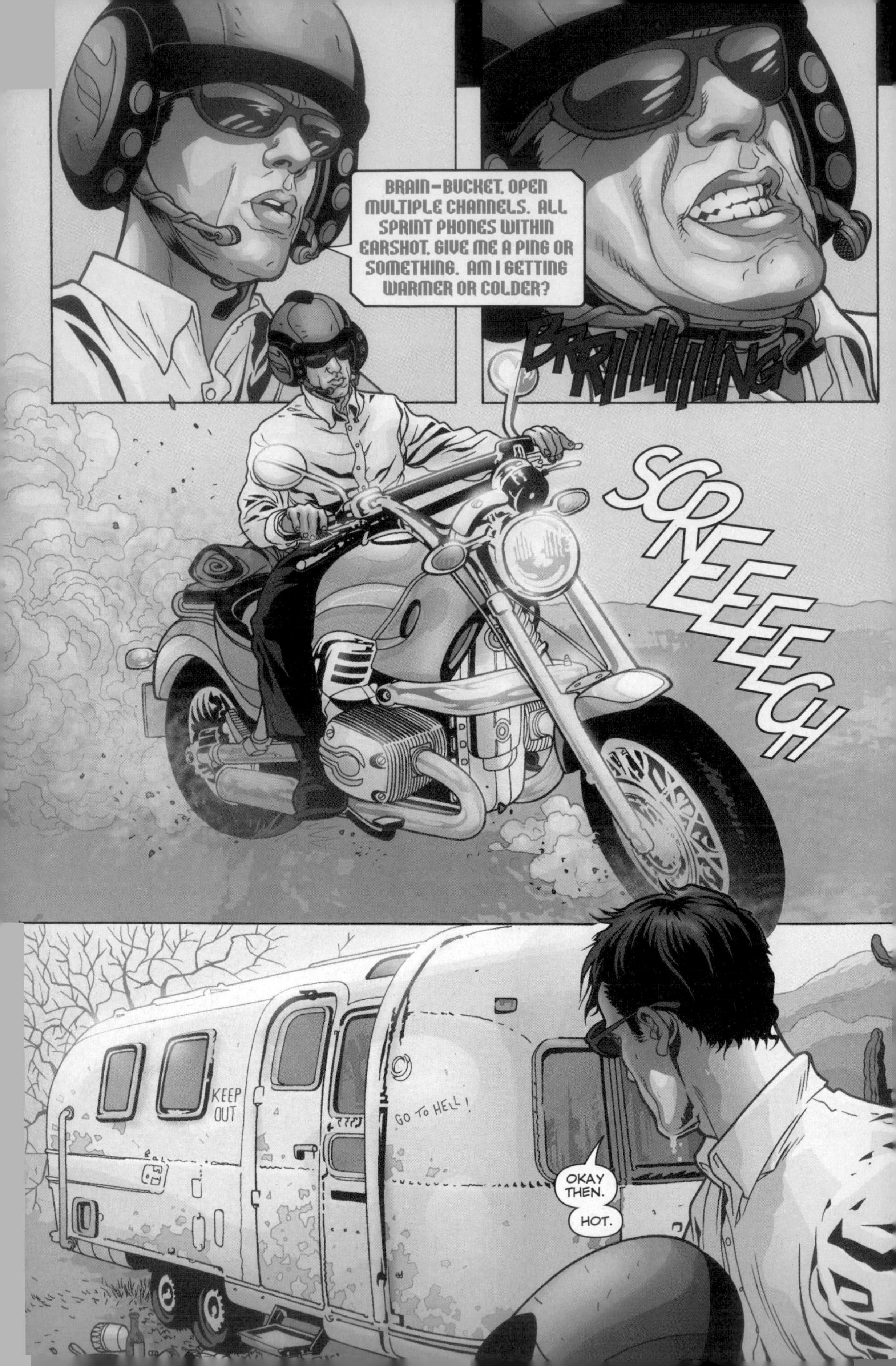
BRAIN-BUCKET, OPEN MULTIPLE CHANNELS. ALL SPRINT PHONES WITHIN EARSHOT, GIVE ME A PING OR SOMETHING. AM I GETTING WARMER OR COLDER?
BRRIIIIIIIIIING?
SCREEEEECH
KEEP OUT
GO TO HELL!
OKAY THEN.
HOT.

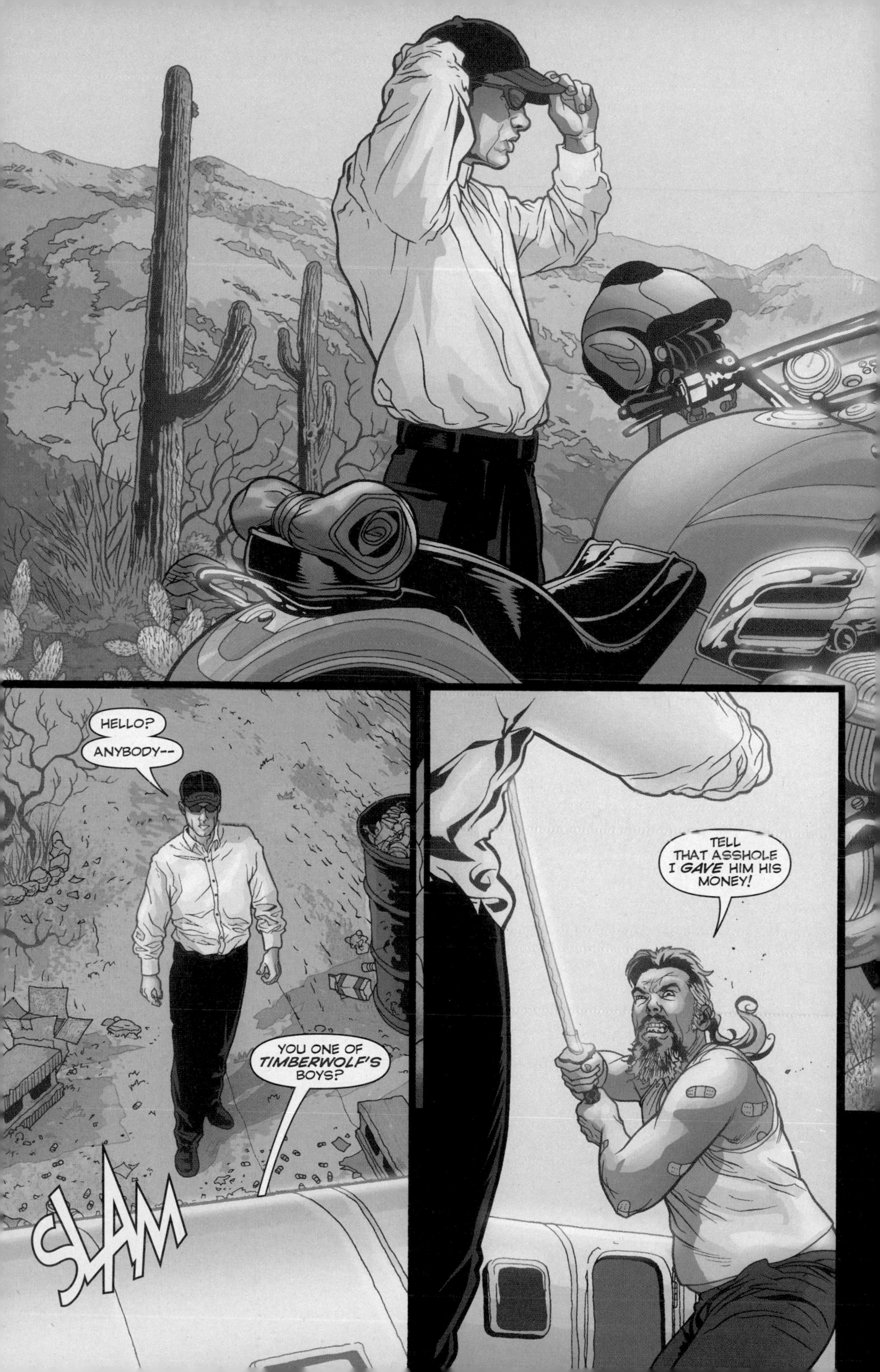
HELLO?
ANYBODY--
YOU ONE OF TIMBERWOLF'S BOYS?
SLAM
TELL THAT ASSHOLE I GAVE HIM HIS MONEY!

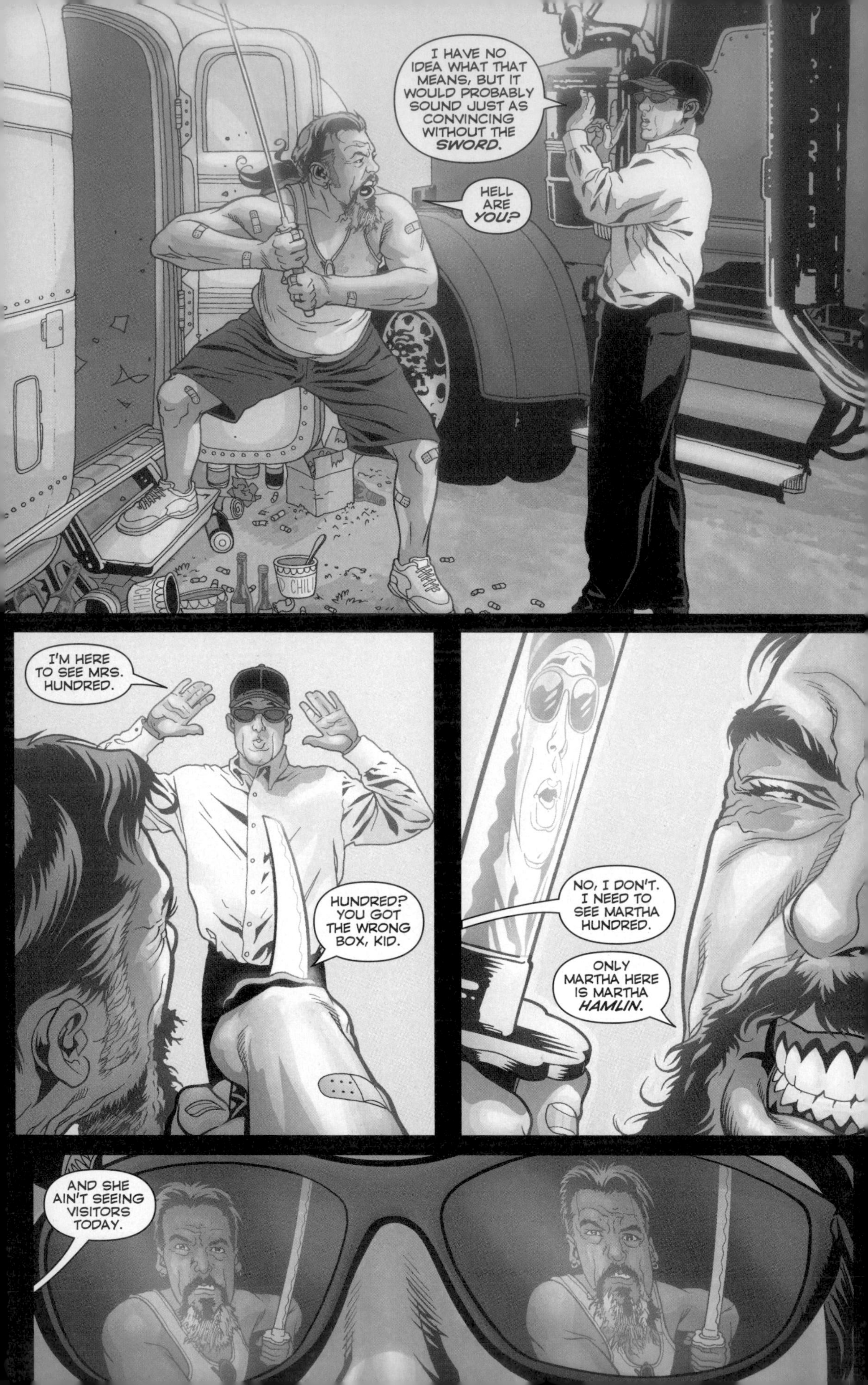
I HAVE NO IDEA WHAT THAT MEANS, BUT IT WOULD PROBABLY SOUND JUST AS CONVINCING WITHOUT THE SWORD.
HELL ARE YOU?
I'M HERE TO SEE MRS. HUNDRED.
HUNDRED? YOU GOT THE WRONG BOX, KID.
NO, I DON'T. I NEED TO SEE MARTHA HUNDRED.
ONLY MARTHA HERE IS MARTHA HAMLIN.
AND SHE AIN'T SEEING VISITORS TODAY.

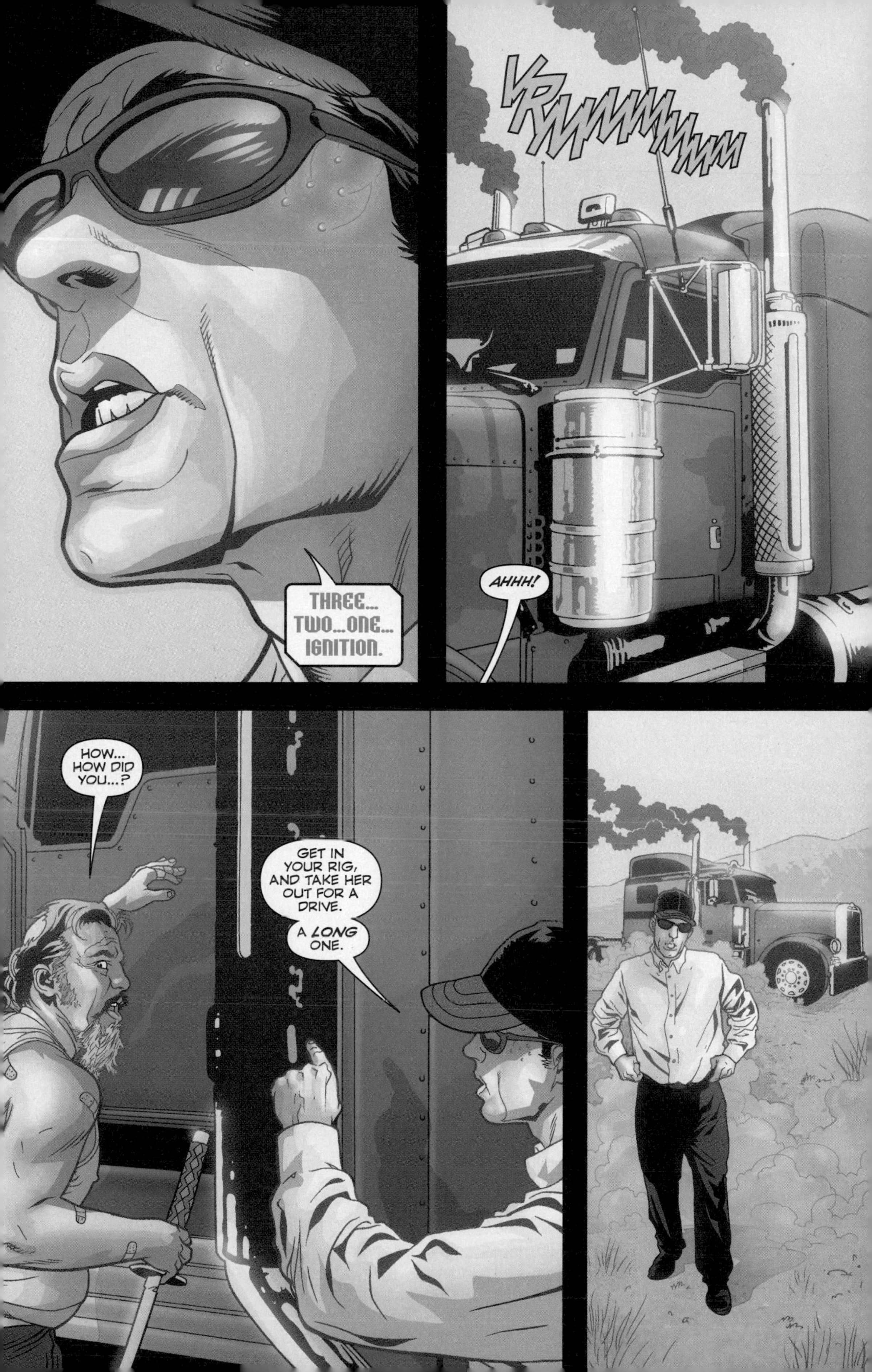
THREE... TWO...ONE... IGNITION.
VRMMMMMMM
AHHH!
HOW... HOW DID YOU...?
GET IN YOUR RIG, AND TAKE HER OUT FOR A DRIVE.
A *LONG* ONE.

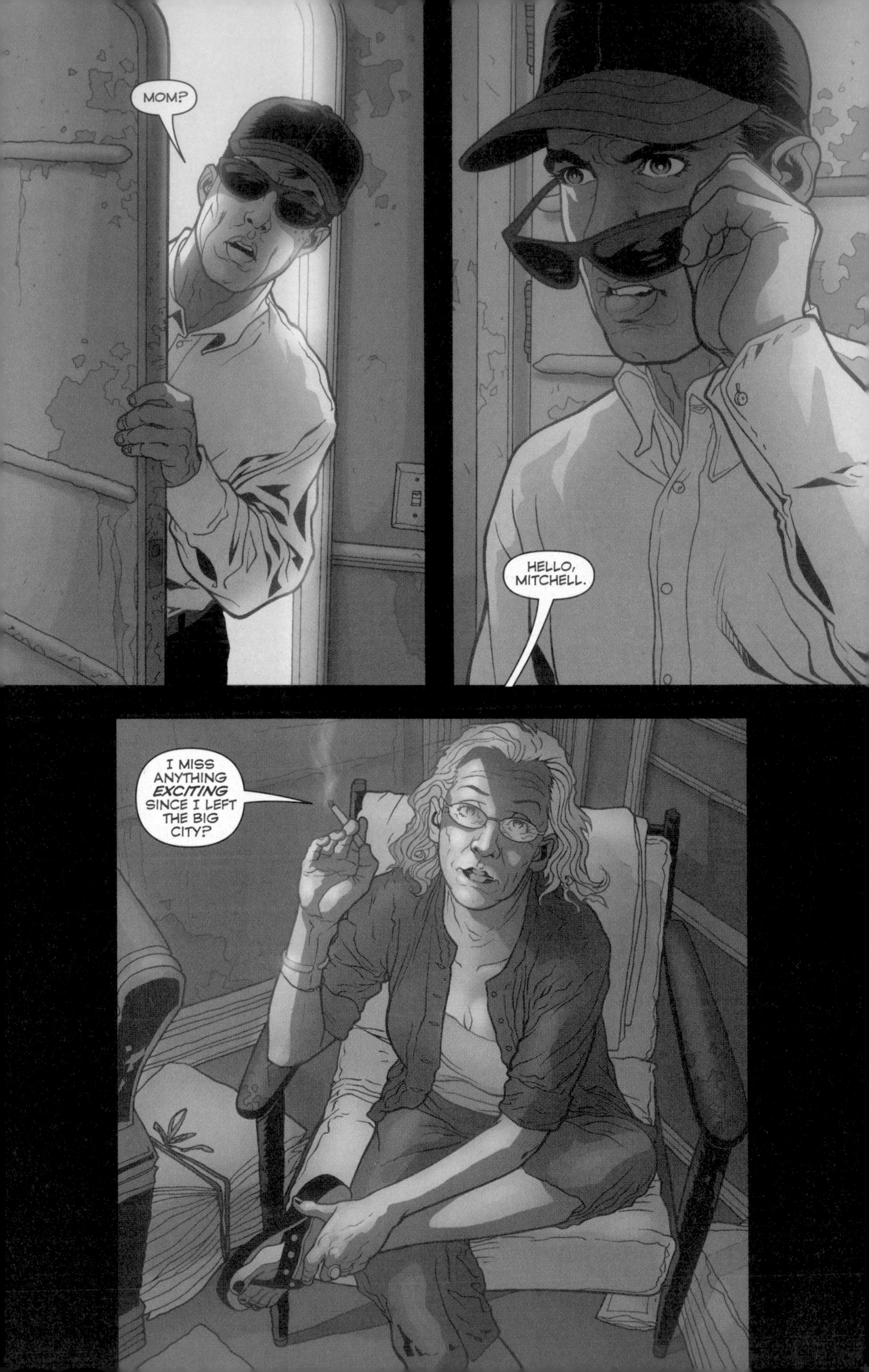
MOM?
HELLO, MITCHELL.
I MISS ANYTHING *EXCITING* SINCE I LEFT THE BIG CITY?

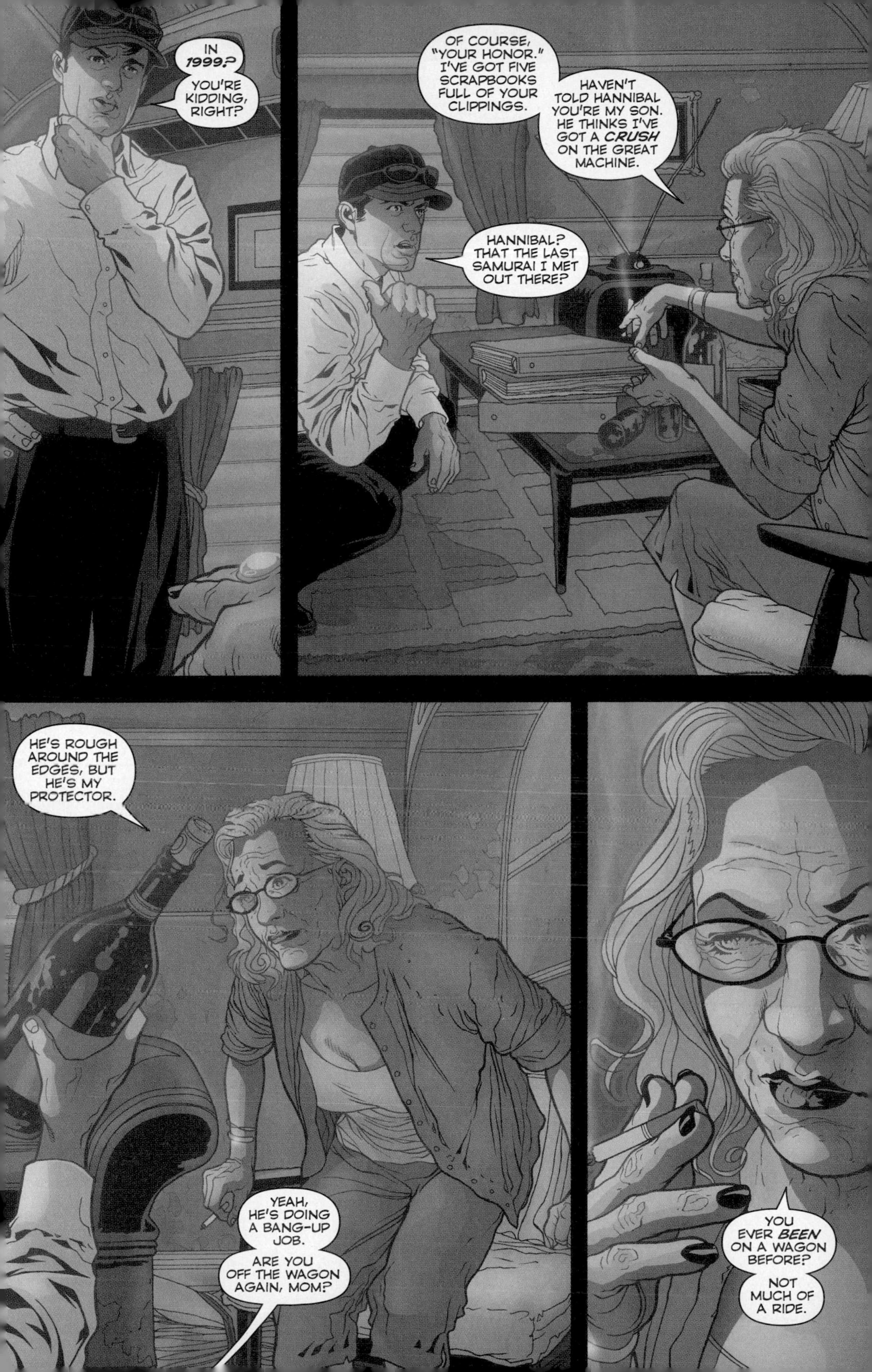
IN 1999? YOU'RE KIDDING, RIGHT?
OF COURSE, "YOUR HONOR." I'VE GOT FIVE SCRAPBOOKS FULL OF YOUR CLIPPINGS.
HAVEN'T TOLD HANNIBAL YOU'RE MY SON. HE THINKS I'VE GOT A CRUSH ON THE GREAT MACHINE.
HANNIBAL? THAT THE LAST SAMURAI I MET OUT THERE?
HE'S ROUGH AROUND THE EDGES, BUT HE'S MY PROTECTOR.
YEAH, HE'S DOING A BANG-UP JOB.
ARE YOU OFF THE WAGON AGAIN, MOM?
YOU EVER BEEN ON A WAGON BEFORE?
NOT MUCH OF A RIDE.

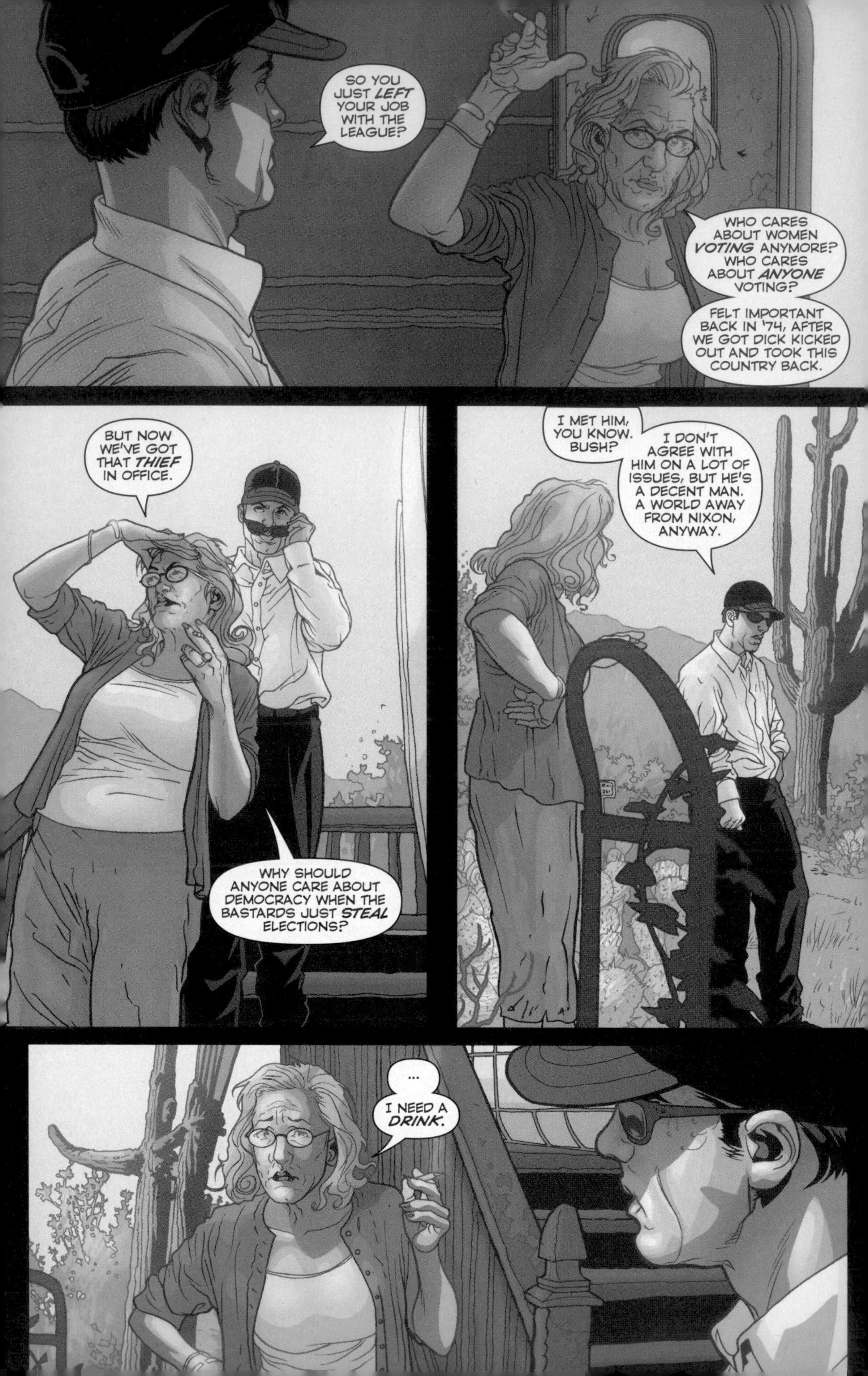
SO YOU JUST LEFT YOUR JOB WITH THE LEAGUE?
WHO CARES ABOUT WOMEN VOTING ANYMORE? WHO CARES ABOUT ANYONE VOTING?
FELT IMPORTANT BACK IN '74, AFTER WE GOT DICK KICKED OUT AND TOOK THIS COUNTRY BACK.
BUT NOW WE'VE GOT THAT THIEF IN OFFICE.
WHY SHOULD ANYONE CARE ABOUT DEMOCRACY WHEN THE BASTARDS JUST STEAL ELECTIONS?
I MET HIM, YOU KNOW. BUSH?
I DON'T AGREE WITH HIM ON A LOT OF ISSUES, BUT HE'S A DECENT MAN. A WORLD AWAY FROM NIXON, ANYWAY.
...
I NEED A DRINK.

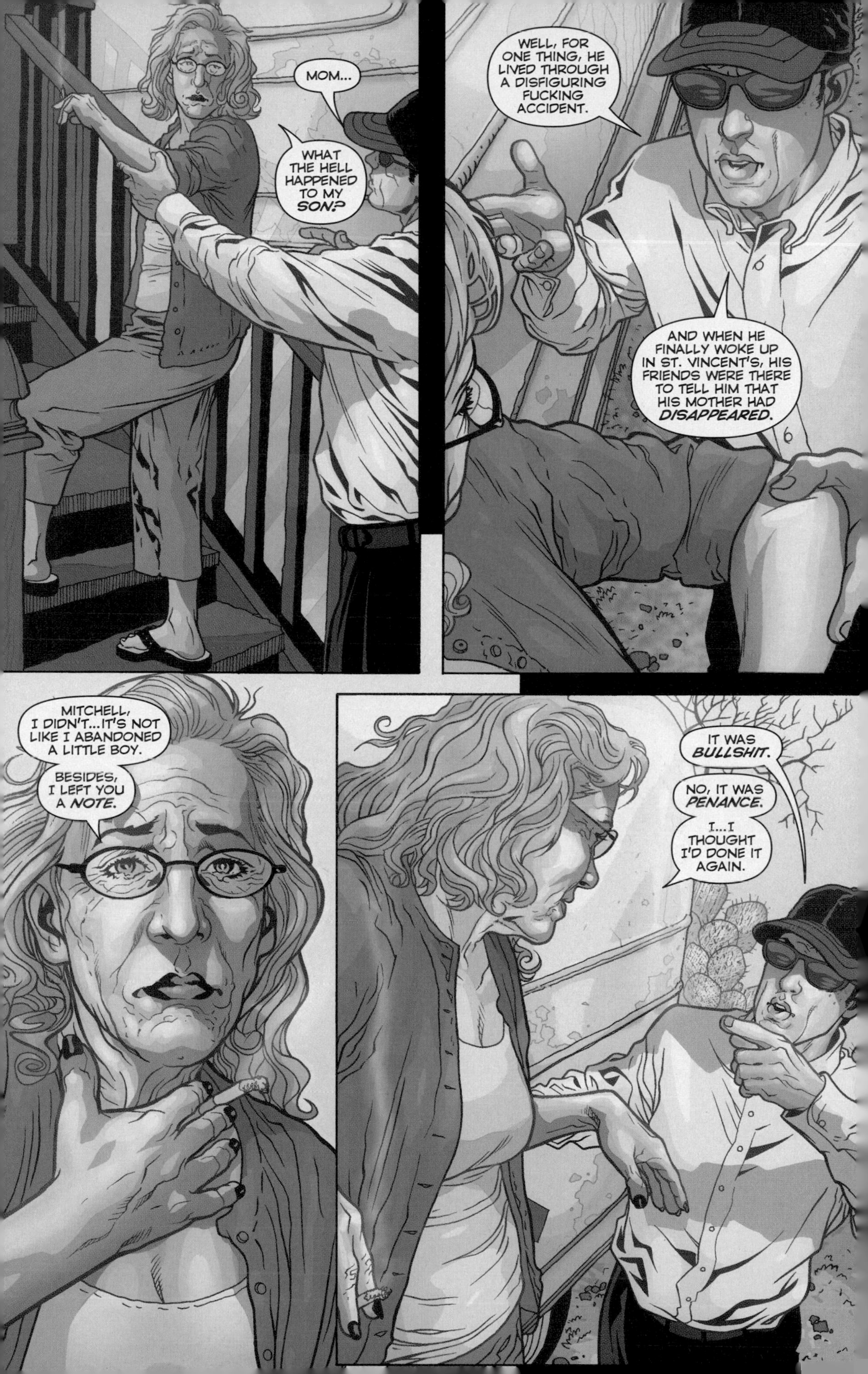
MOM...
WHAT THE HELL HAPPENED TO MY *SON?*
WELL, FOR ONE THING, HE LIVED THROUGH A DISFIGURING FUCKING ACCIDENT.
AND WHEN HE FINALLY WOKE UP IN ST. VINCENT'S, HIS FRIENDS WERE THERE TO TELL HIM THAT HIS MOTHER HAD ***DISAPPEARED.***
MITCHELL, I DIDN'T...IT'S NOT LIKE I ABANDONED A LITTLE BOY.
BESIDES, I LEFT YOU A *NOTE.*
IT WAS ***BULLSHIT.***
NO, IT WAS *PENANCE.*
I...I THOUGHT I'D DONE IT AGAIN.

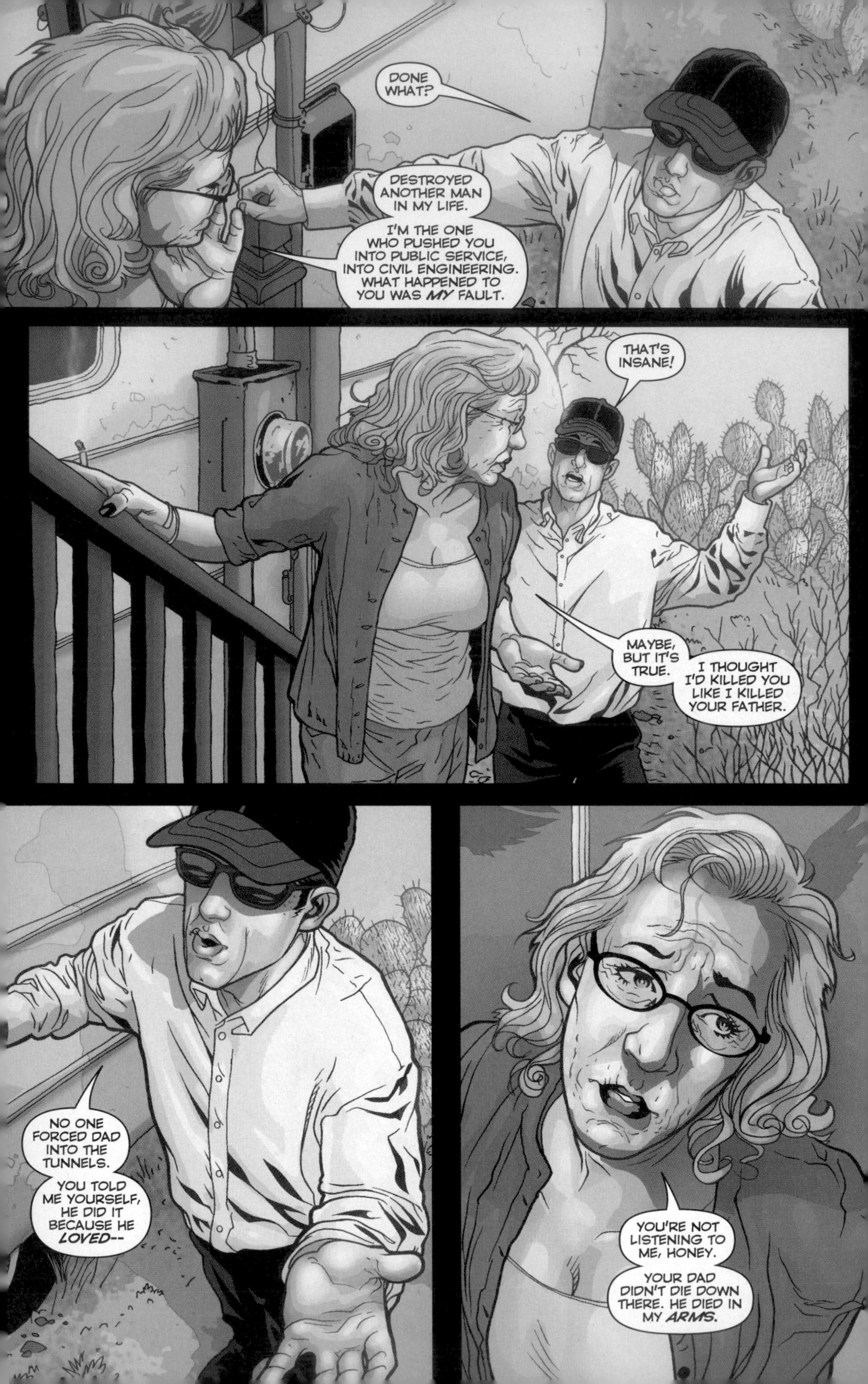
DONE WHAT?
DESTROYED ANOTHER MAN IN MY LIFE.
I'M THE ONE WHO PUSHED YOU INTO PUBLIC SERVICE, INTO CIVIL ENGINEERING. WHAT HAPPENED TO YOU WAS *MY* FAULT.
THAT'S INSANE!
MAYBE, BUT IT'S TRUE.
I THOUGHT I'D KILLED YOU LIKE I KILLED YOUR FATHER.
NO ONE FORCED DAD INTO THE TUNNELS.
YOU TOLD ME YOURSELF, HE DID IT BECAUSE HE *LOVED*--
YOU'RE NOT LISTENING TO ME, HONEY.
YOUR DAD DIDN'T DIE DOWN THERE. HE DIED IN MY *ARMS*.

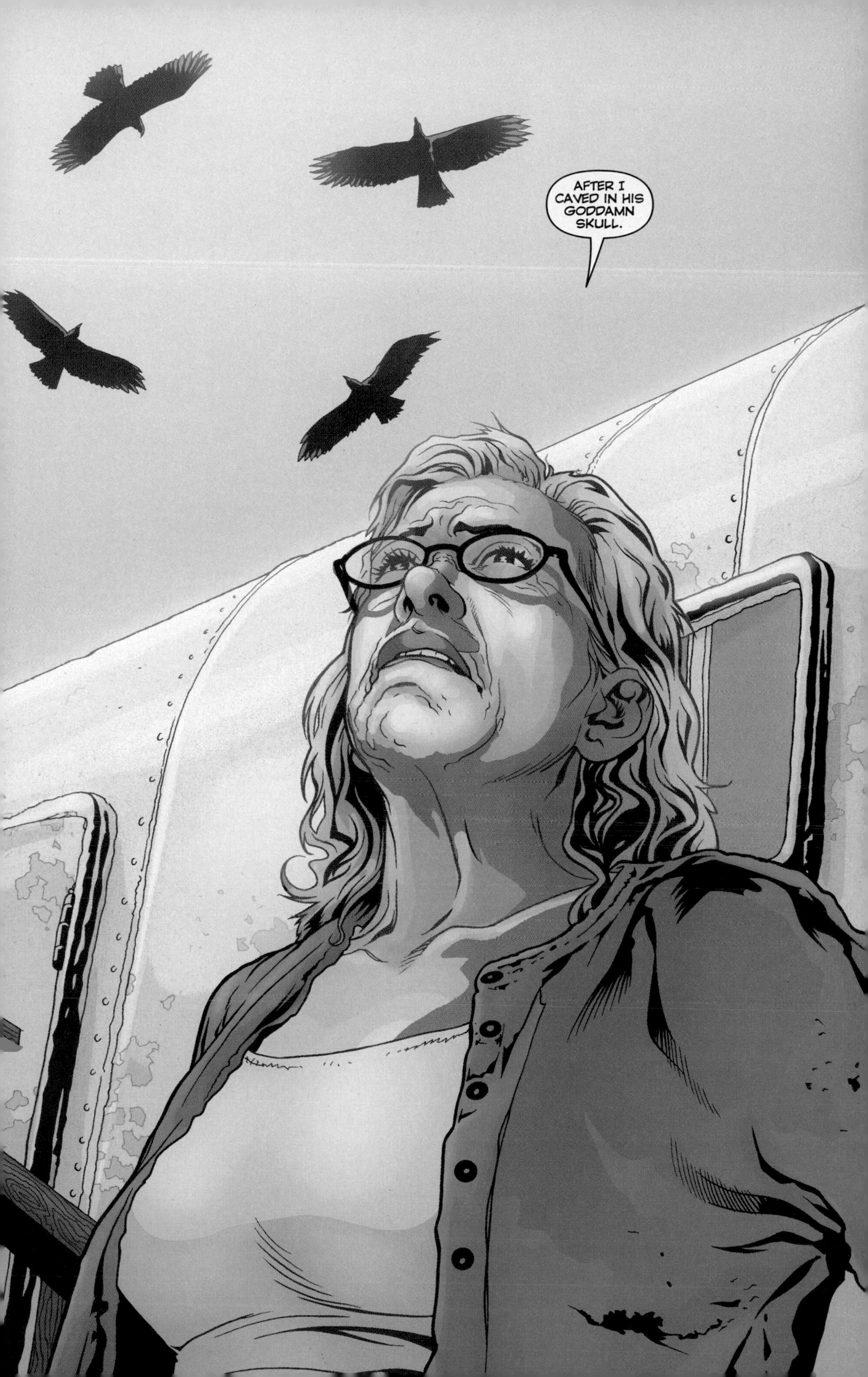
AFTER I CAVED IN HIS GODDAMN SKULL.

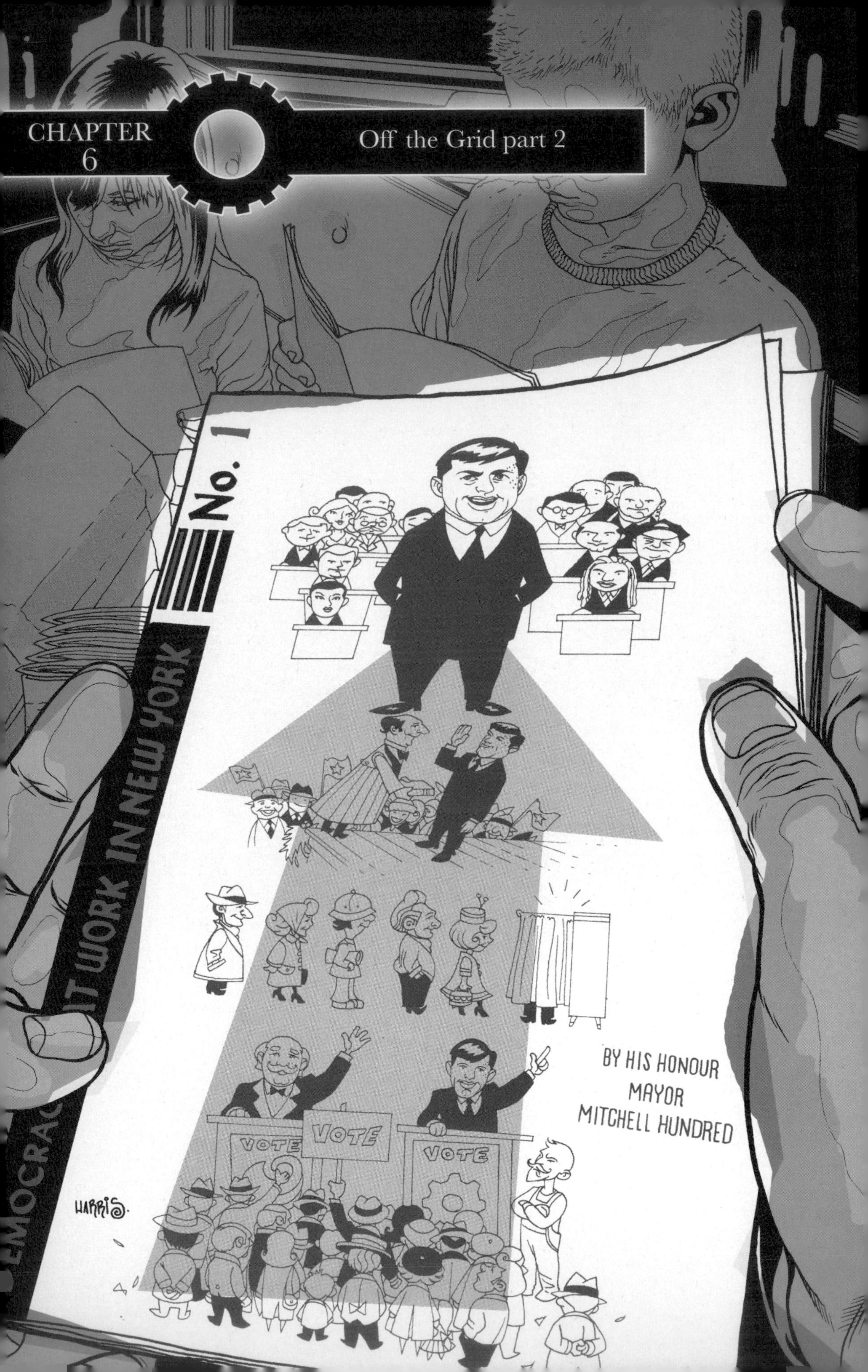
CHAPTER 6
Off the Grid part 2
No. 1
EMOCRAC
IT WORK IN NEW YORK
BY HIS HONOUR
MAYOR
MITCHELL HUNDRED
VOTE
VOTE
VOTE
HARRIS.

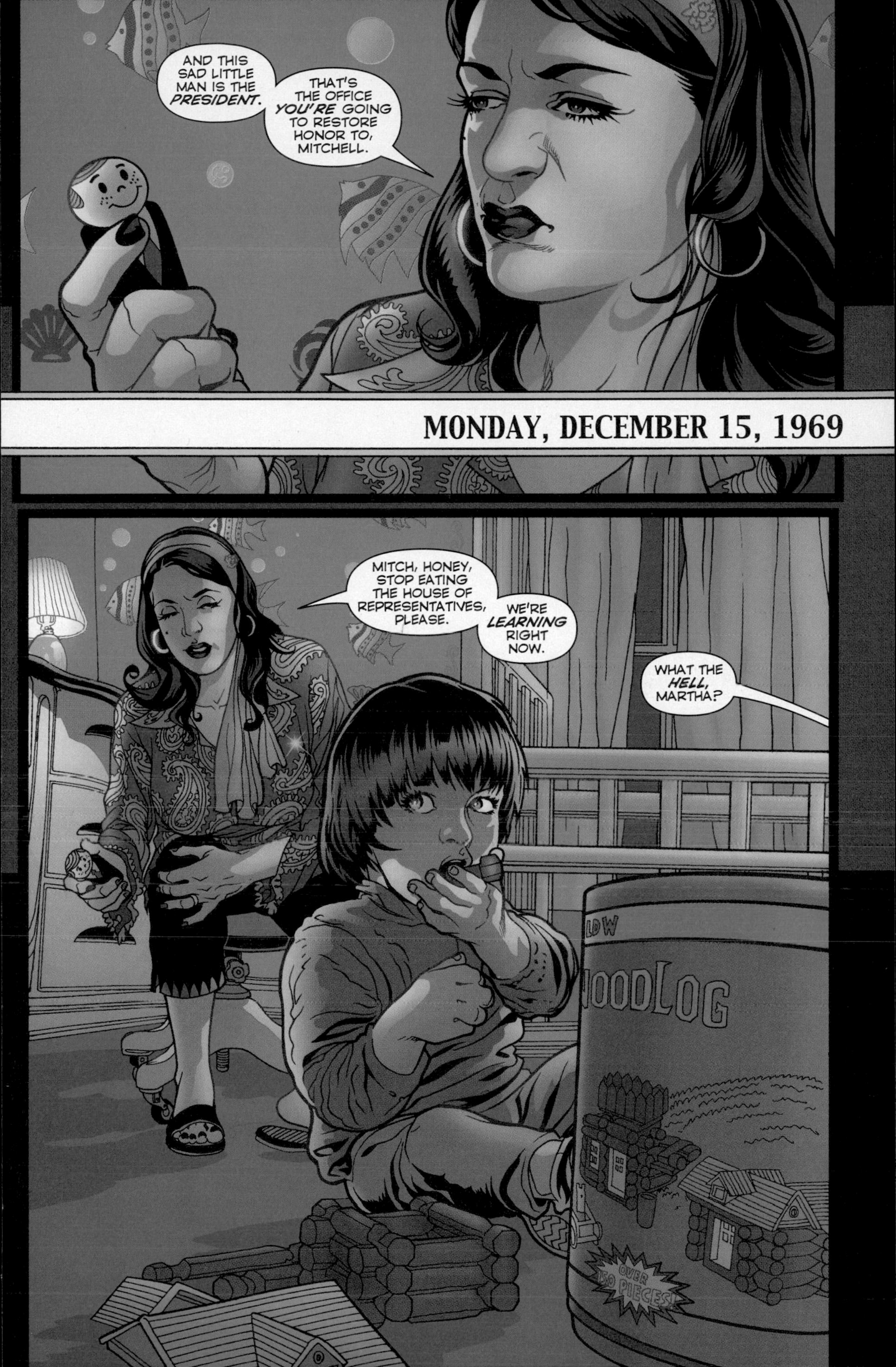
AND THIS SAD LITTLE MAN IS THE *PRESIDENT*.
THAT'S THE OFFICE *YOU'RE* GOING TO RESTORE HONOR TO, MITCHELL.
MONDAY, DECEMBER 15, 1969
MITCH, HONEY, STOP EATING THE HOUSE OF REPRESENTATIVES, PLEASE.
WE'RE *LEARNING* RIGHT NOW.
WHAT THE *HELL*, MARTHA?
OVER 150 PIECES!

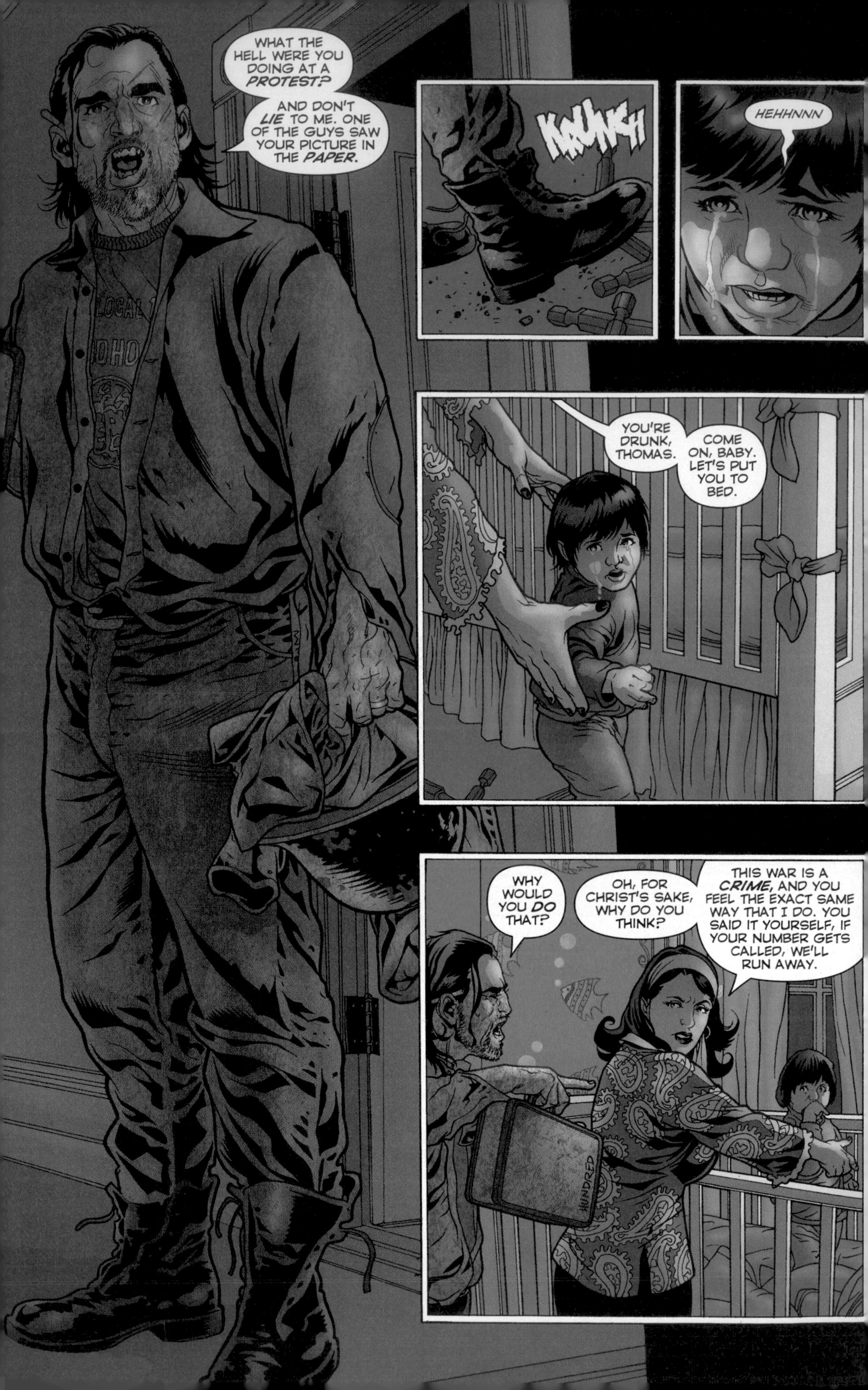
WHAT THE HELL WERE YOU DOING AT A *PROTEST?*
AND DON'T *LIE* TO ME. ONE OF THE GUYS SAW YOUR PICTURE IN THE *PAPER*.
KRUNCH
HEHHNNN
YOU'RE DRUNK, THOMAS.
COME ON, BABY. LET'S PUT YOU TO BED.
WHY WOULD YOU *DO* THAT?
OH, FOR CHRIST'S SAKE, WHY DO YOU THINK?
THIS WAR IS A *CRIME,* AND YOU FEEL THE EXACT SAME WAY THAT I DO. YOU SAID IT YOURSELF, IF YOUR NUMBER GETS CALLED, WE'LL RUN AWAY.
HUNDRED

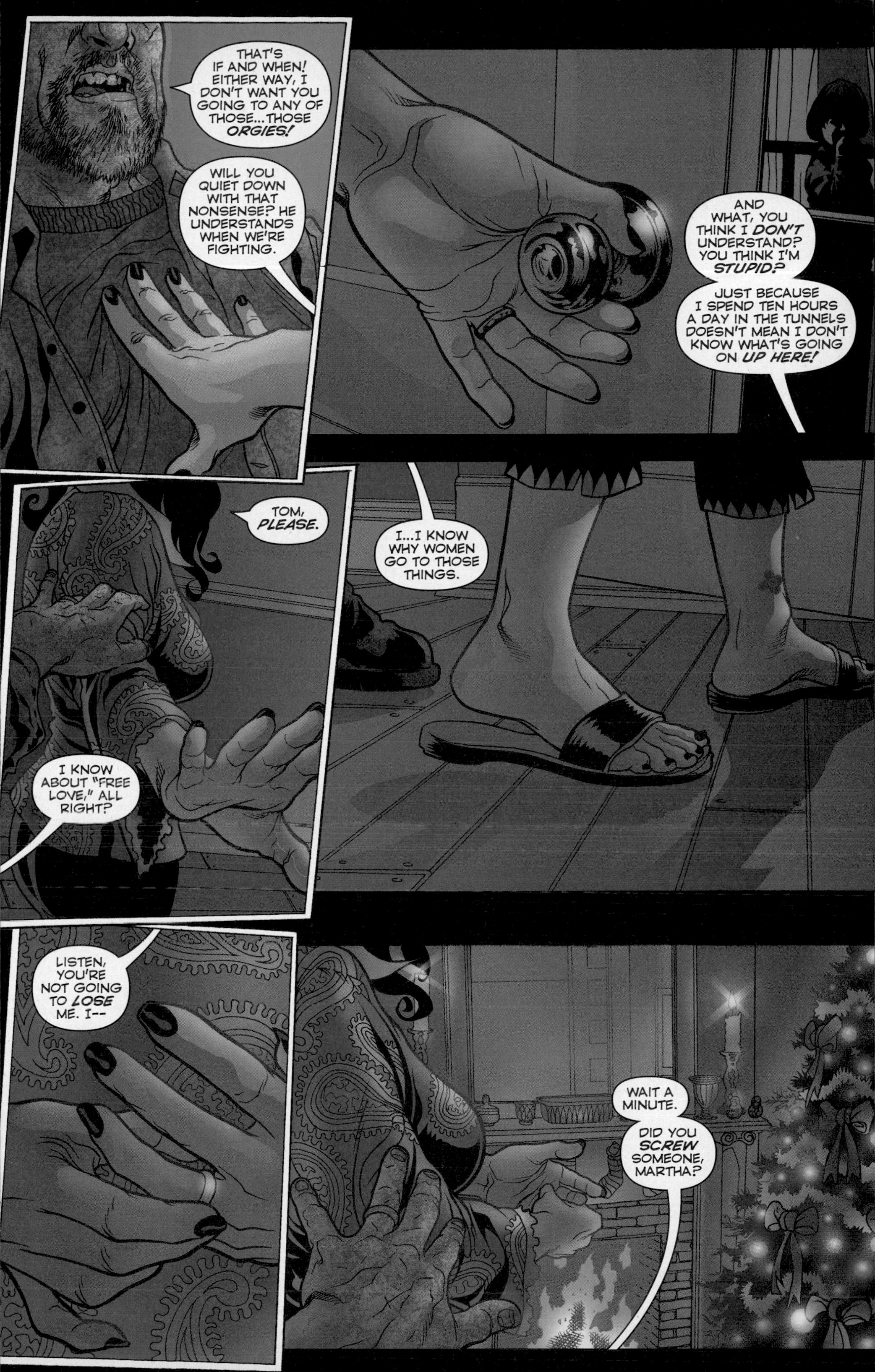
THAT'S IF AND WHEN! EITHER WAY, I DON'T WANT YOU GOING TO ANY OF THOSE...THOSE ORGIES!
WILL YOU QUIET DOWN WITH THAT NONSENSE? HE UNDERSTANDS WHEN WE'RE FIGHTING.
AND WHAT, YOU THINK I DON'T UNDERSTAND? YOU THINK I'M STUPID?
JUST BECAUSE I SPEND TEN HOURS A DAY IN THE TUNNELS DOESN'T MEAN I DON'T KNOW WHAT'S GOING ON UP HERE!
TOM, PLEASE.
I...I KNOW WHY WOMEN GO TO THOSE THINGS.
I KNOW ABOUT "FREE LOVE," ALL RIGHT?
LISTEN, YOU'RE NOT GOING TO LOSE ME. I--
WAIT A MINUTE.
DID YOU SCREW SOMEONE, MARTHA?

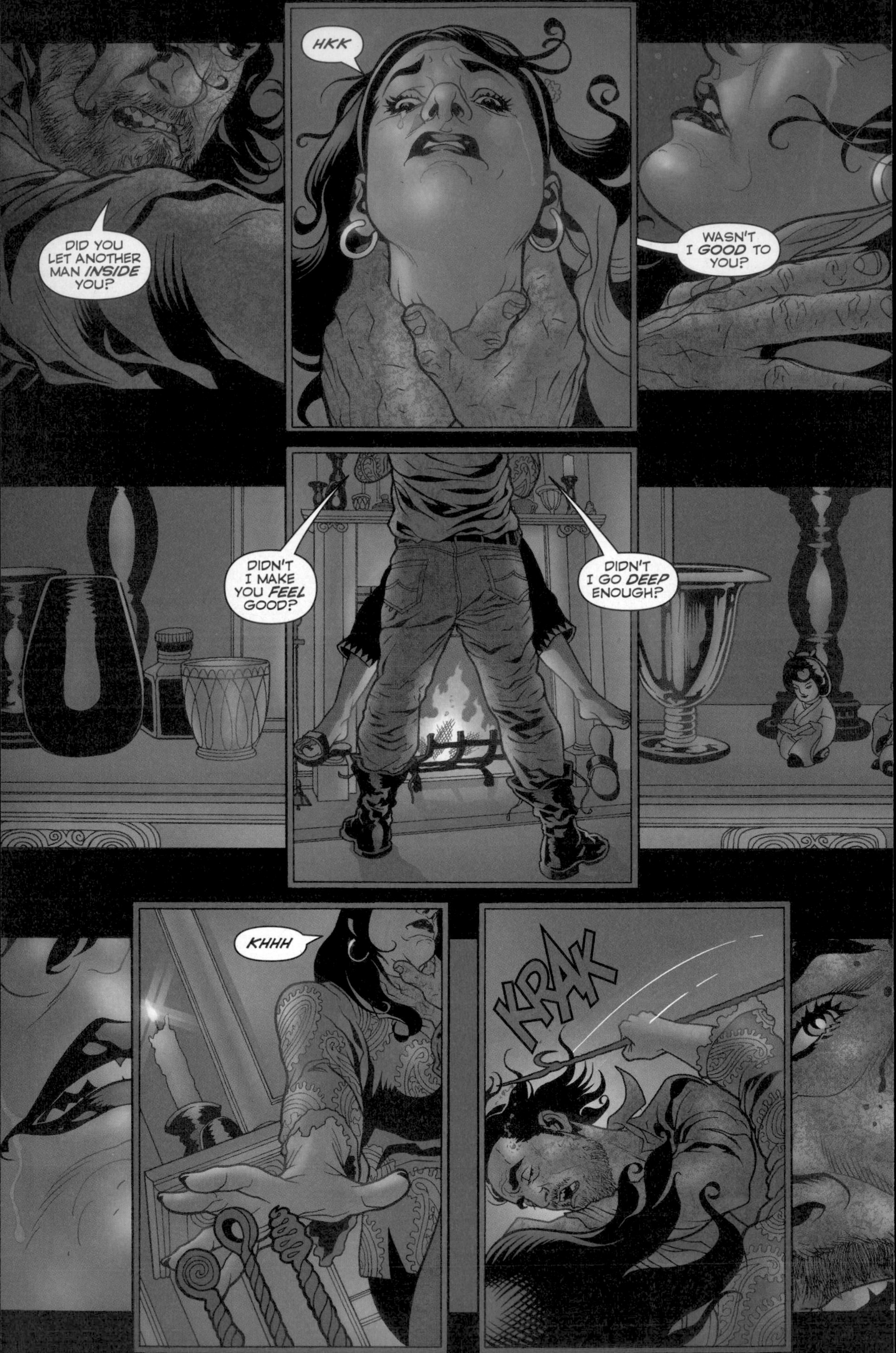
HKK
DID YOU LET ANOTHER MAN INSIDE YOU?
WASN'T I GOOD TO YOU?
DIDN'T I MAKE YOU FEEL GOOD?
DIDN'T I GO DEEP ENOUGH?
KHHH
KRAK

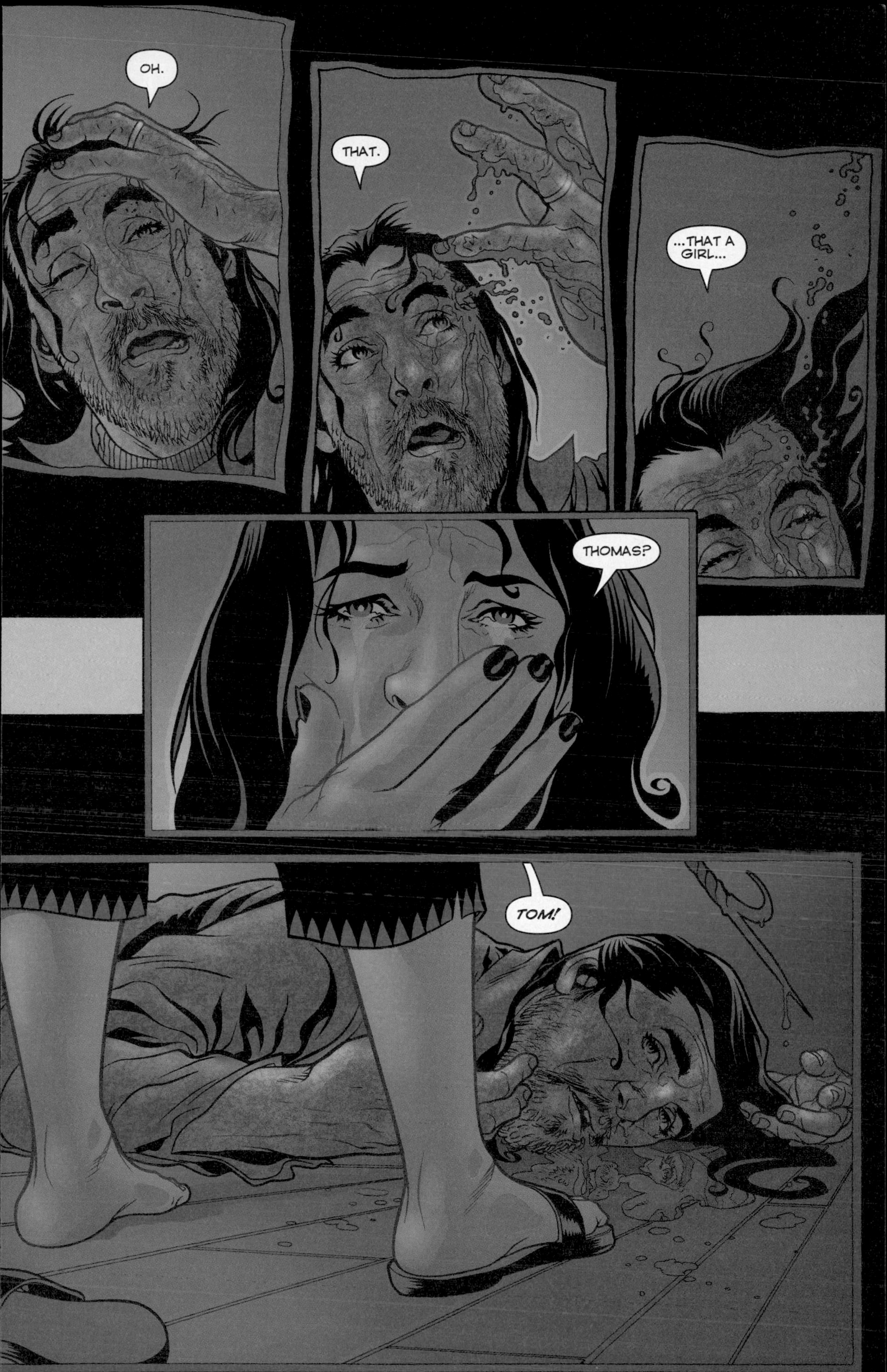
OH.
THAT.
...THAT A GIRL...
THOMAS?
TOM!

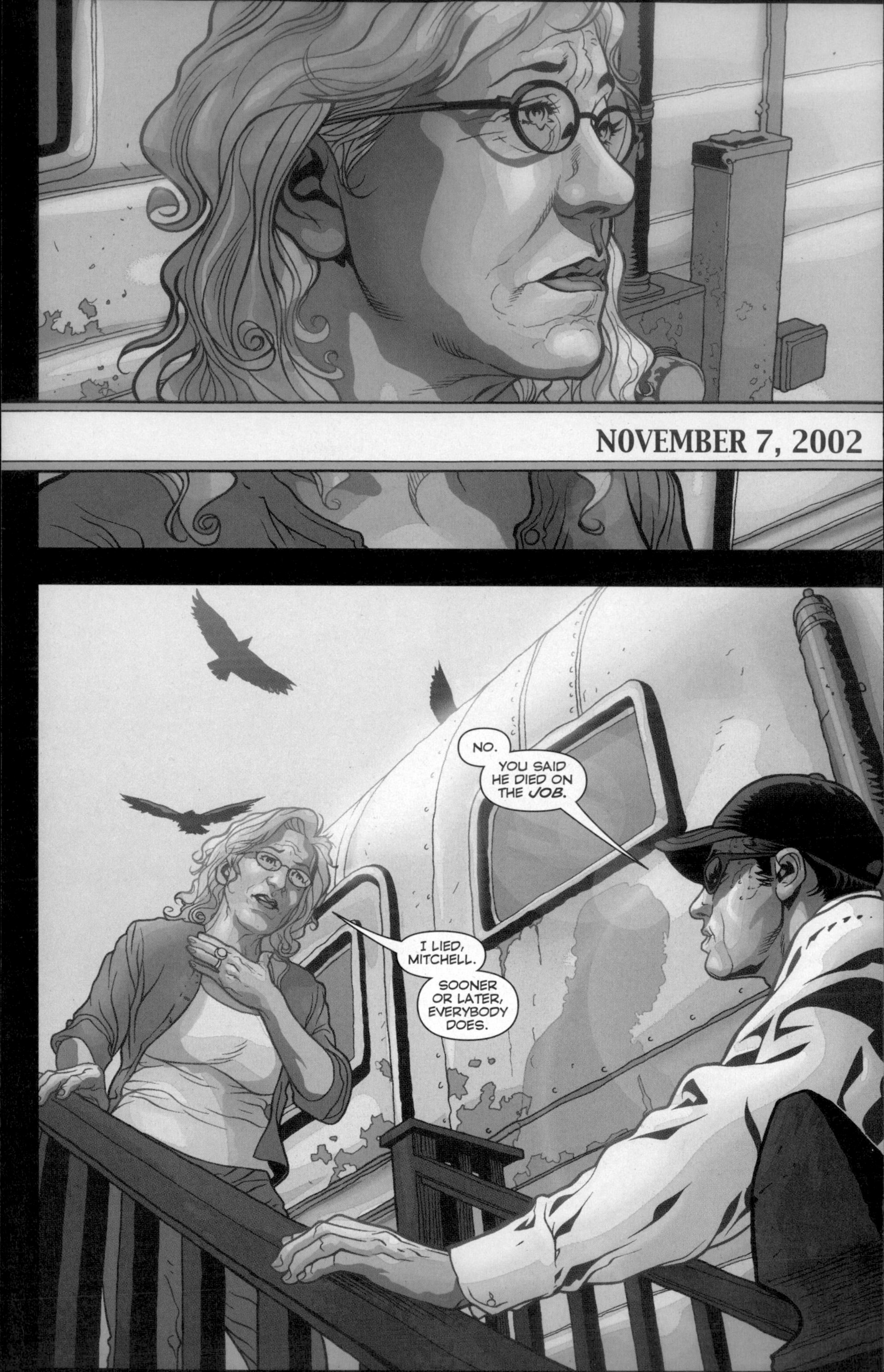
NOVEMBER 7, 2002
NO.
YOU SAID HE DIED ON THE JOB.
I LIED, MITCHELL.
SOONER OR LATER, EVERYBODY DOES.

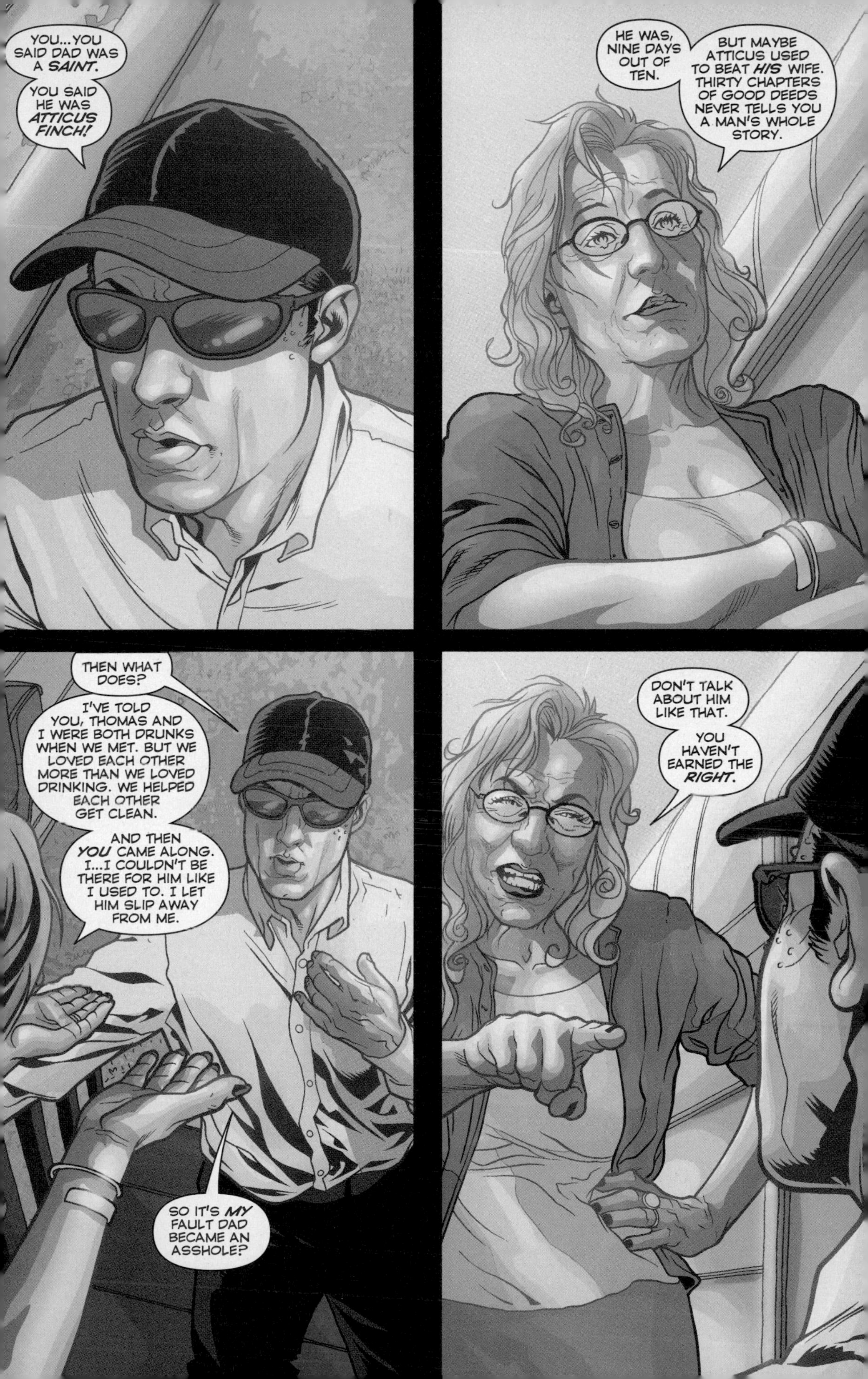
YOU...YOU SAID DAD WAS A *SAINT*.
YOU SAID HE WAS *ATTICUS FINCH!*
HE WAS, NINE DAYS OUT OF TEN.
BUT MAYBE ATTICUS USED TO BEAT *HIS* WIFE. THIRTY CHAPTERS OF GOOD DEEDS NEVER TELLS YOU A MAN'S WHOLE STORY.
THEN WHAT DOES?
I'VE TOLD YOU, THOMAS AND I WERE BOTH DRUNKS WHEN WE MET. BUT WE LOVED EACH OTHER MORE THAN WE LOVED DRINKING. WE HELPED EACH OTHER GET CLEAN.
AND THEN *YOU* CAME ALONG. I...I COULDN'T BE THERE FOR HIM LIKE I USED TO. I LET HIM SLIP AWAY FROM ME.
SO IT'S *MY* FAULT DAD BECAME AN ASSHOLE?
DON'T TALK ABOUT HIM LIKE THAT.
YOU HAVEN'T EARNED THE *RIGHT*.

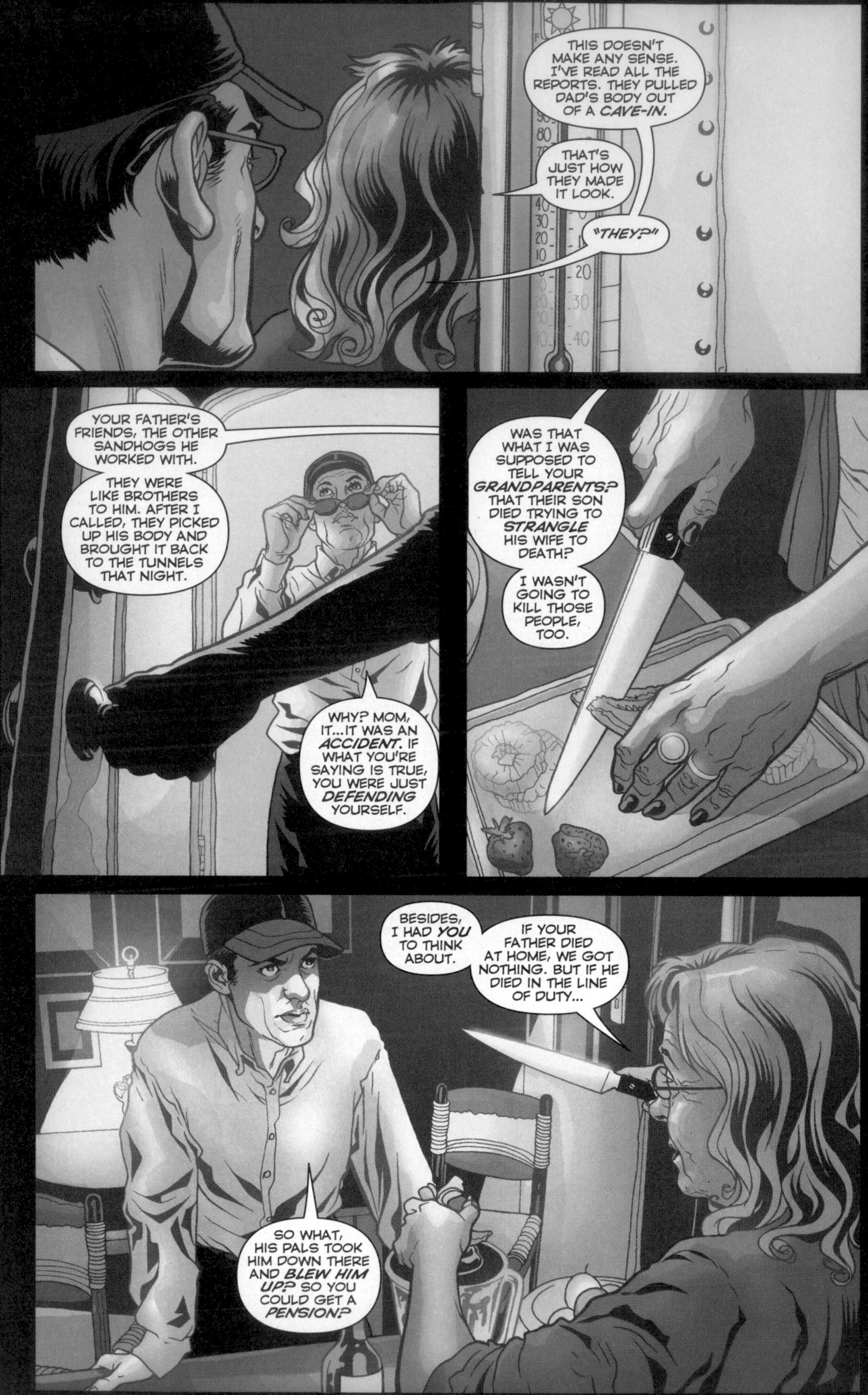
THIS DOESN'T MAKE ANY SENSE. I'VE READ ALL THE REPORTS. THEY PULLED DAD'S BODY OUT OF A CAVE-IN.
THAT'S JUST HOW THEY MADE IT LOOK.
"THEY?"
YOUR FATHER'S FRIENDS, THE OTHER SANDHOGS HE WORKED WITH.
THEY WERE LIKE BROTHERS TO HIM. AFTER I CALLED, THEY PICKED UP HIS BODY AND BROUGHT IT BACK TO THE TUNNELS THAT NIGHT.
WHY? MOM, IT...IT WAS AN ACCIDENT. IF WHAT YOU'RE SAYING IS TRUE, YOU WERE JUST DEFENDING YOURSELF.
WAS THAT WHAT I WAS SUPPOSED TO TELL YOUR GRANDPARENTS? THAT THEIR SON DIED TRYING TO STRANGLE HIS WIFE TO DEATH?
I WASN'T GOING TO KILL THOSE PEOPLE, TOO.
BESIDES, I HAD YOU TO THINK ABOUT.
IF YOUR FATHER DIED AT HOME, WE GOT NOTHING. BUT IF HE DIED IN THE LINE OF DUTY...
SO WHAT, HIS PALS TOOK HIM DOWN THERE AND BLEW HIM UP? SO YOU COULD GET A PENSION?

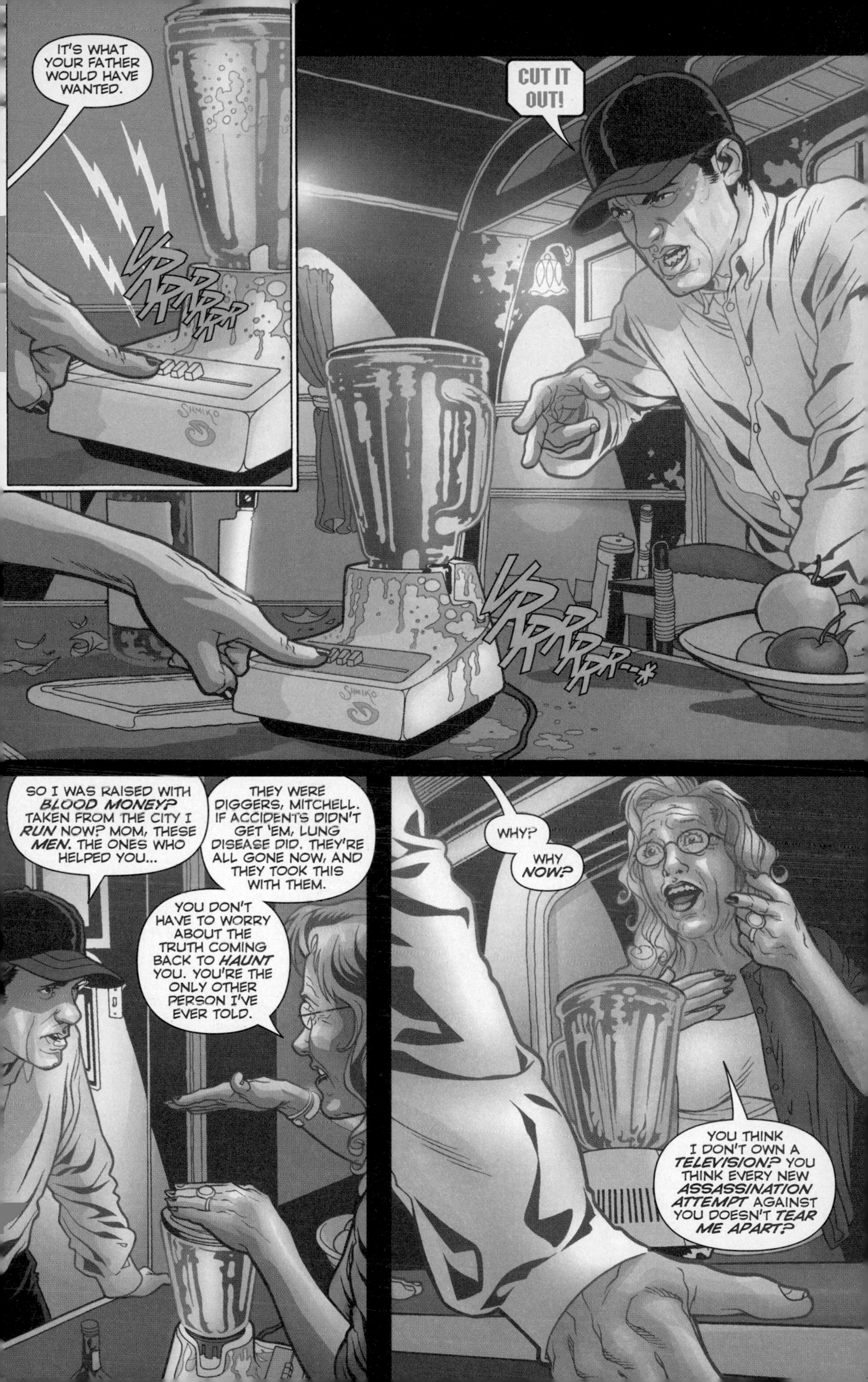
IT'S WHAT YOUR FATHER WOULD HAVE WANTED.
VRRRRRR
SHMIKO
CUT IT OUT!
VRRRRRRR--*
SHMIKO
SO I WAS RAISED WITH *BLOOD MONEY?* TAKEN FROM THE CITY I *RUN* NOW? MOM, THESE *MEN*. THE ONES WHO HELPED YOU...
THEY WERE DIGGERS, MITCHELL. IF ACCIDENTS DIDN'T GET 'EM, LUNG DISEASE DID. THEY'RE ALL GONE NOW, AND THEY TOOK THIS WITH THEM.
YOU DON'T HAVE TO WORRY ABOUT THE TRUTH COMING BACK TO *HAUNT* YOU. YOU'RE THE ONLY OTHER PERSON I'VE EVER TOLD.
WHY?
WHY *NOW?*
YOU THINK I DON'T OWN A *TELEVISION?* YOU THINK EVERY NEW *ASSASSINATION ATTEMPT* AGAINST YOU DOESN'T *TEAR ME APART?*

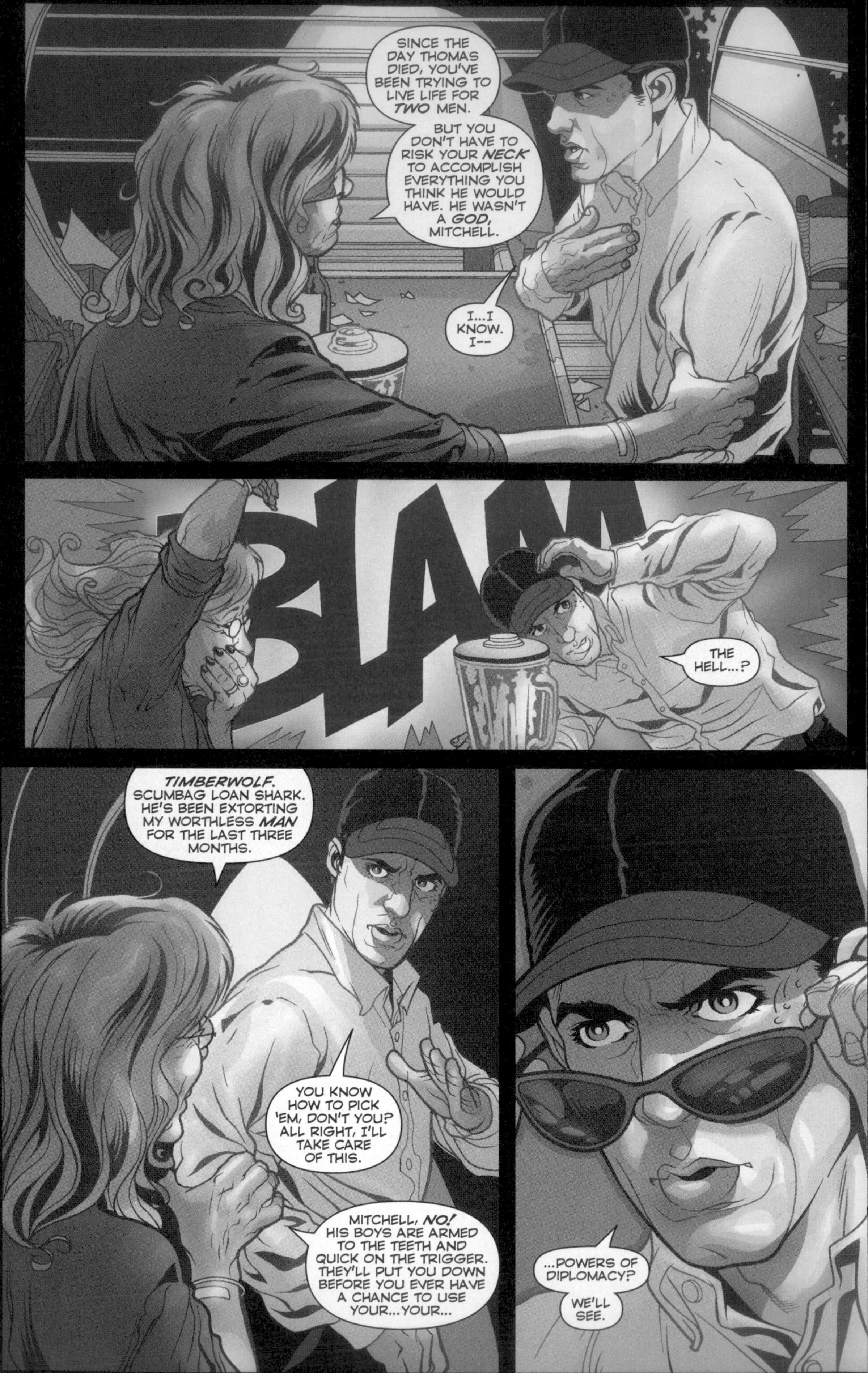
SINCE THE DAY THOMAS DIED, YOU'VE BEEN TRYING TO LIVE LIFE FOR *TWO* MEN.
BUT YOU DON'T HAVE TO RISK YOUR *NECK* TO ACCOMPLISH EVERYTHING YOU THINK HE WOULD HAVE. HE WASN'T A *GOD,* MITCHELL.
I...I KNOW. I--
BLAM
THE HELL...?
TIMBERWOLF. SCUMBAG LOAN SHARK. HE'S BEEN EXTORTING MY WORTHLESS *MAN* FOR THE LAST THREE MONTHS.
YOU KNOW HOW TO PICK 'EM, DON'T YOU? ALL RIGHT, I'LL TAKE CARE OF THIS.
MITCHELL, *NO!* HIS BOYS ARE ARMED TO THE TEETH AND QUICK ON THE TRIGGER. THEY'LL PUT YOU DOWN BEFORE YOU EVER HAVE A CHANCE TO USE YOUR...YOUR...
...POWERS OF DIPLOMACY?
WE'LL SEE.

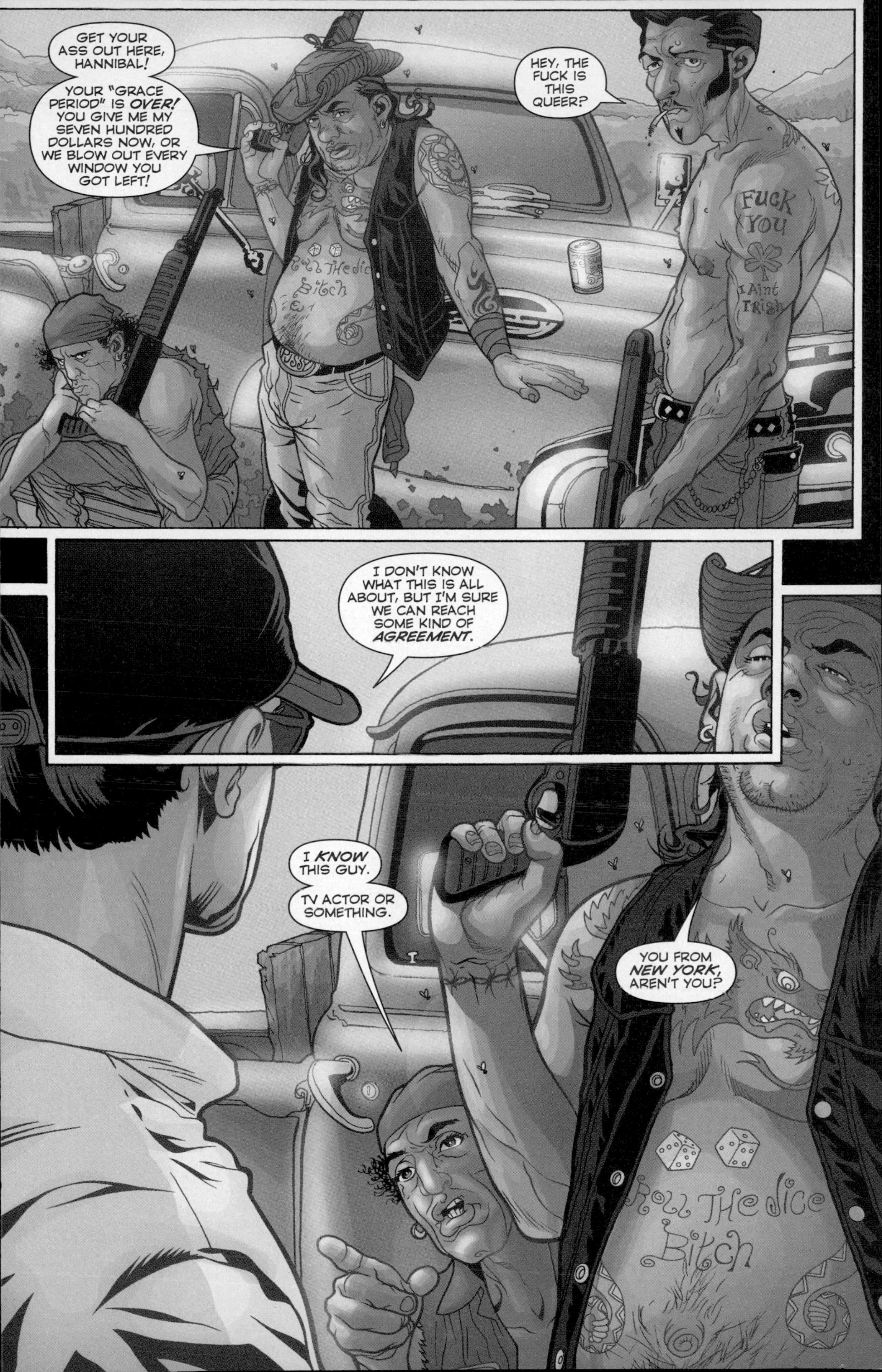
GET YOUR ASS OUT HERE, HANNIBAL!
YOUR "GRACE PERIOD" IS OVER! YOU GIVE ME MY SEVEN HUNDRED DOLLARS NOW, OR WE BLOW OUT EVERY WINDOW YOU GOT LEFT!
HEY, THE FUCK IS THIS QUEER?
I DON'T KNOW WHAT THIS IS ALL ABOUT, BUT I'M SURE WE CAN REACH SOME KIND OF AGREEMENT.
I KNOW THIS GUY.
TV ACTOR OR SOMETHING.
YOU FROM NEW YORK, AREN'T YOU?

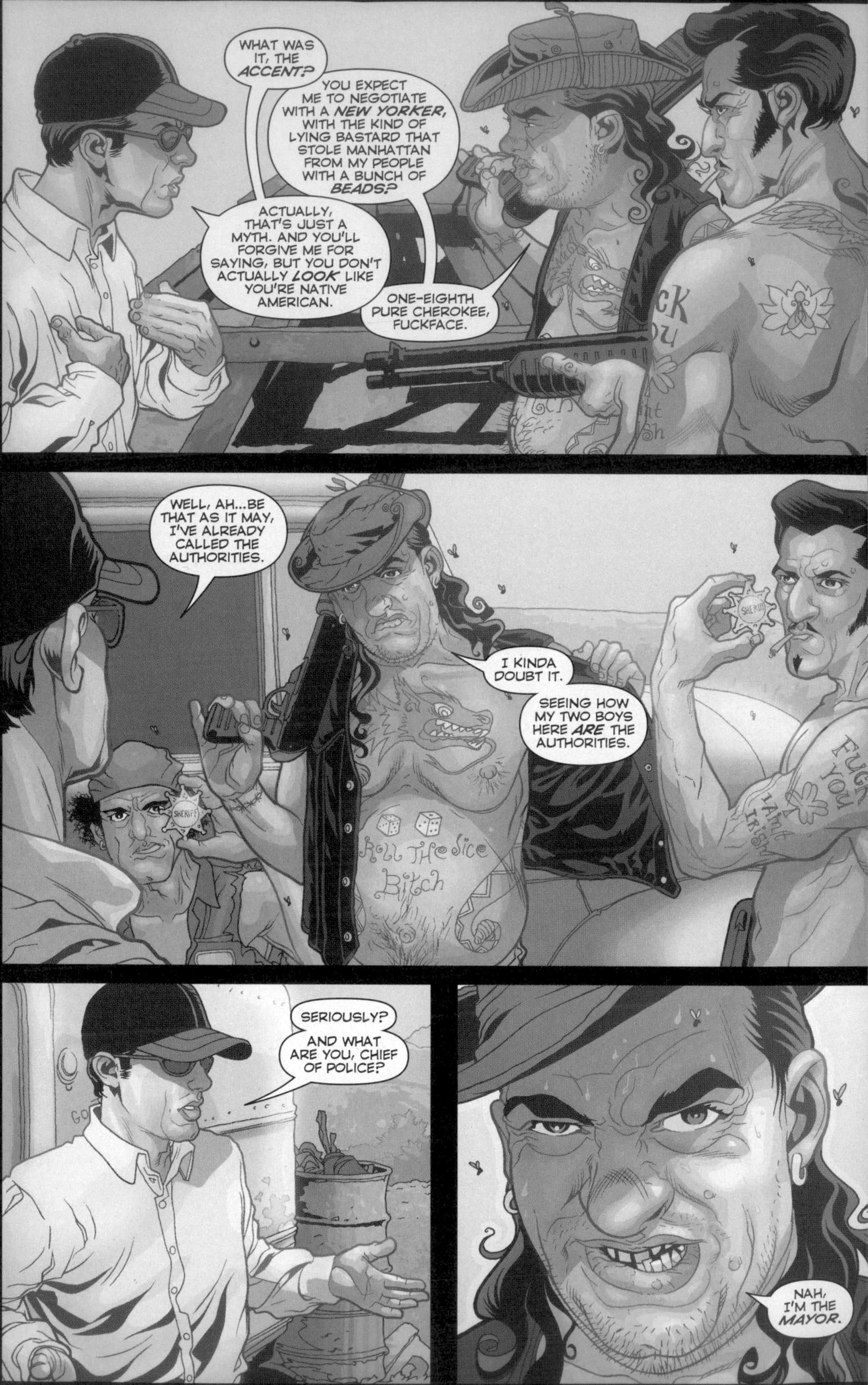
WHAT WAS IT, THE ACCENT?
YOU EXPECT ME TO NEGOTIATE WITH A NEW YORKER, WITH THE KIND OF LYING BASTARD THAT STOLE MANHATTAN FROM MY PEOPLE WITH A BUNCH OF BEADS?
ACTUALLY, THAT'S JUST A MYTH. AND YOU'LL FORGIVE ME FOR SAYING, BUT YOU DON'T ACTUALLY LOOK LIKE YOU'RE NATIVE AMERICAN.
ONE-EIGHTH PURE CHEROKEE, FUCKFACE.
WELL, AH...BE THAT AS IT MAY, I'VE ALREADY CALLED THE AUTHORITIES.
I KINDA DOUBT IT.
SEEING HOW MY TWO BOYS HERE ARE THE AUTHORITIES.
SHERIFF
SHERIFF
ROLL THE DICE BITCH
FUCK YOU
SERIOUSLY?
AND WHAT ARE YOU, CHIEF OF POLICE?
NAH, I'M THE MAYOR.

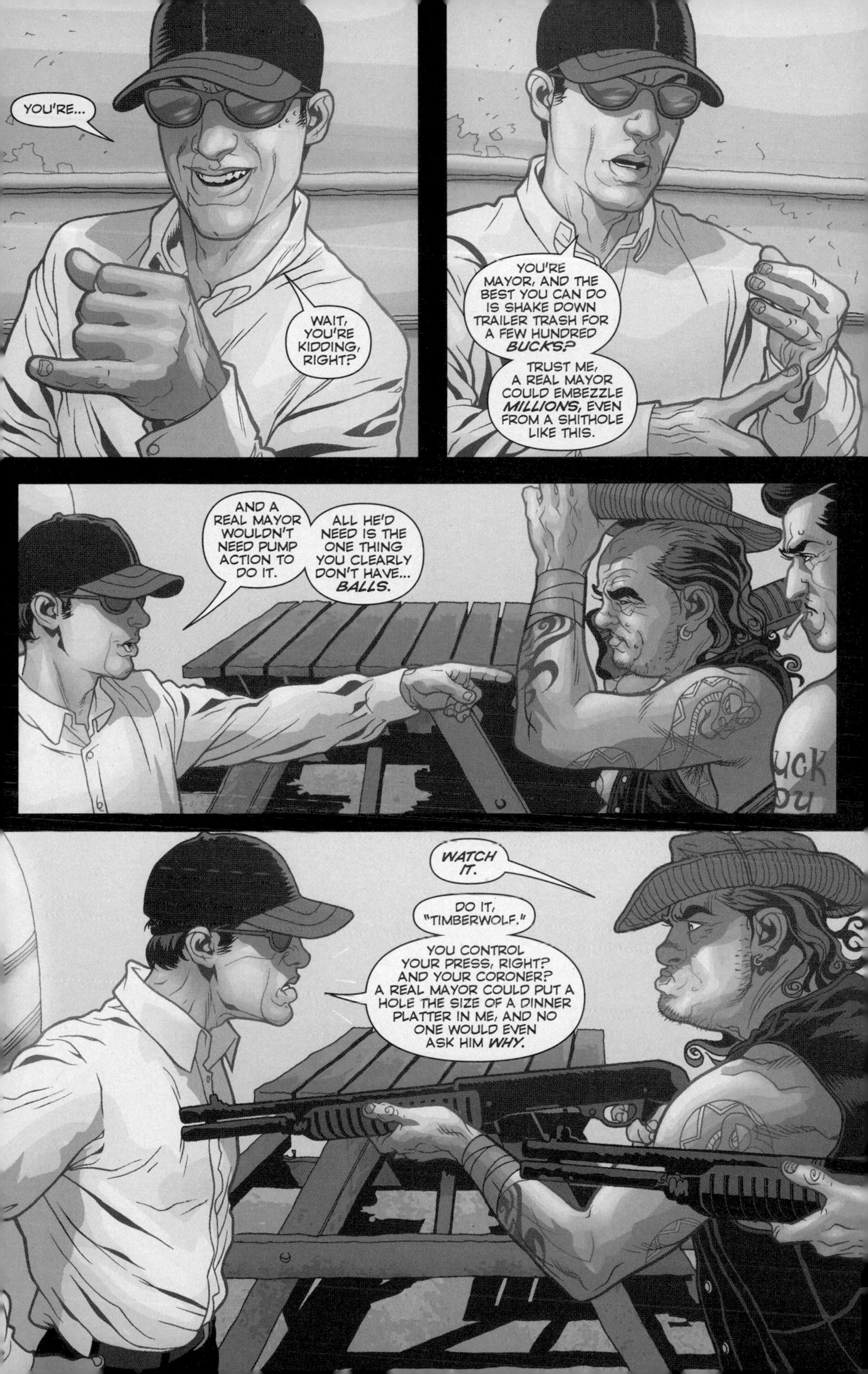
YOU'RE...
WAIT, YOU'RE KIDDING, RIGHT?
YOU'RE MAYOR, AND THE BEST YOU CAN DO IS SHAKE DOWN TRAILER TRASH FOR A FEW HUNDRED BUCKS?
TRUST ME, A REAL MAYOR COULD EMBEZZLE MILLIONS, EVEN FROM A SHITHOLE LIKE THIS.
AND A REAL MAYOR WOULDN'T NEED PUMP ACTION TO DO IT.
ALL HE'D NEED IS THE ONE THING YOU CLEARLY DON'T HAVE... BALLS.
WATCH IT.
DO IT, "TIMBERWOLF."
YOU CONTROL YOUR PRESS, RIGHT? AND YOUR CORONER? A REAL MAYOR COULD PUT A HOLE THE SIZE OF A DINNER PLATTER IN ME, AND NO ONE WOULD EVEN ASK HIM WHY.

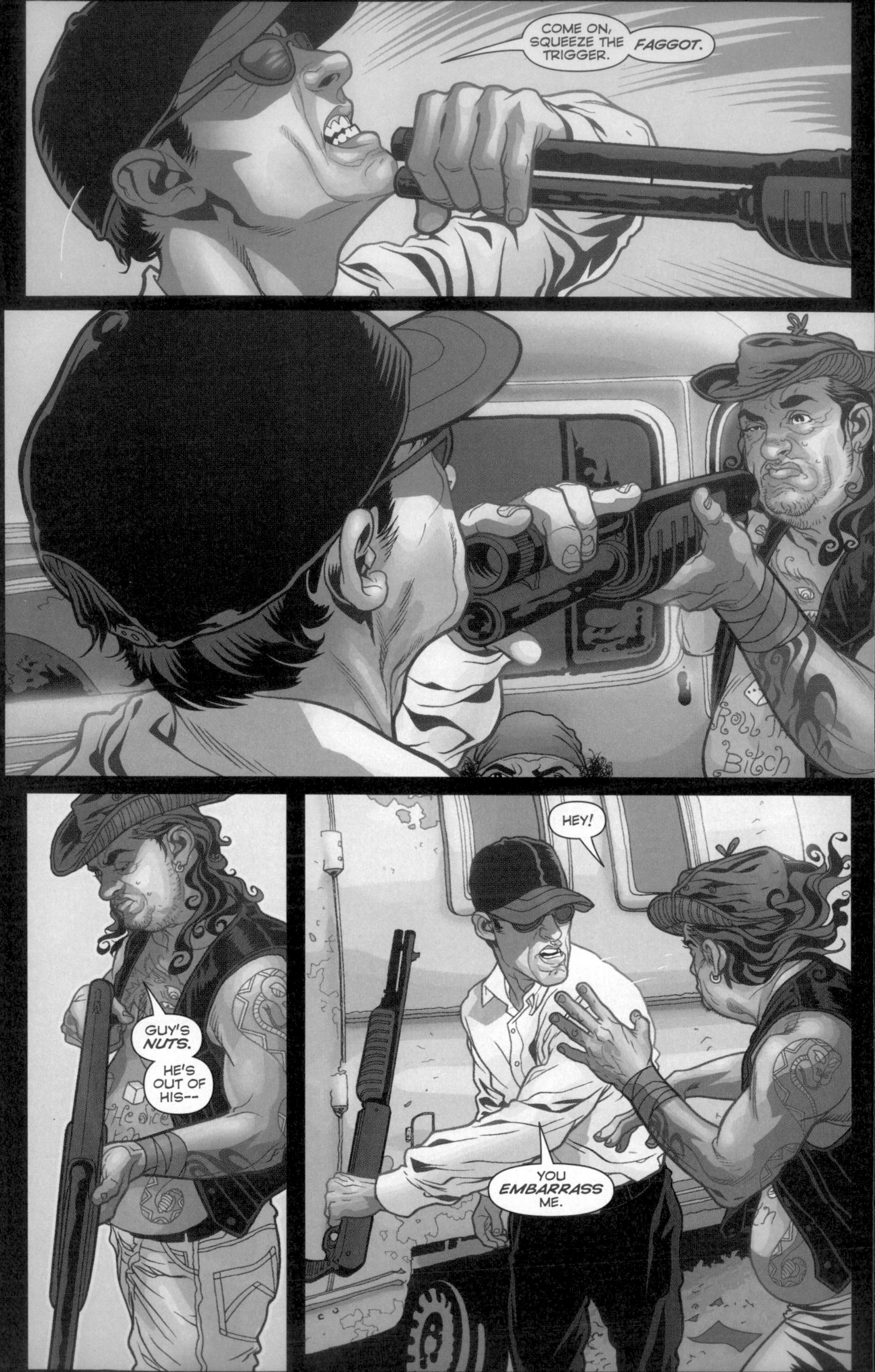
COME ON, SQUEEZE THE TRIGGER.
FAGGOT.
GUY'S *NUTS.*
HE'S OUT OF HIS--
HEY!
YOU *EMBARRASS* ME.

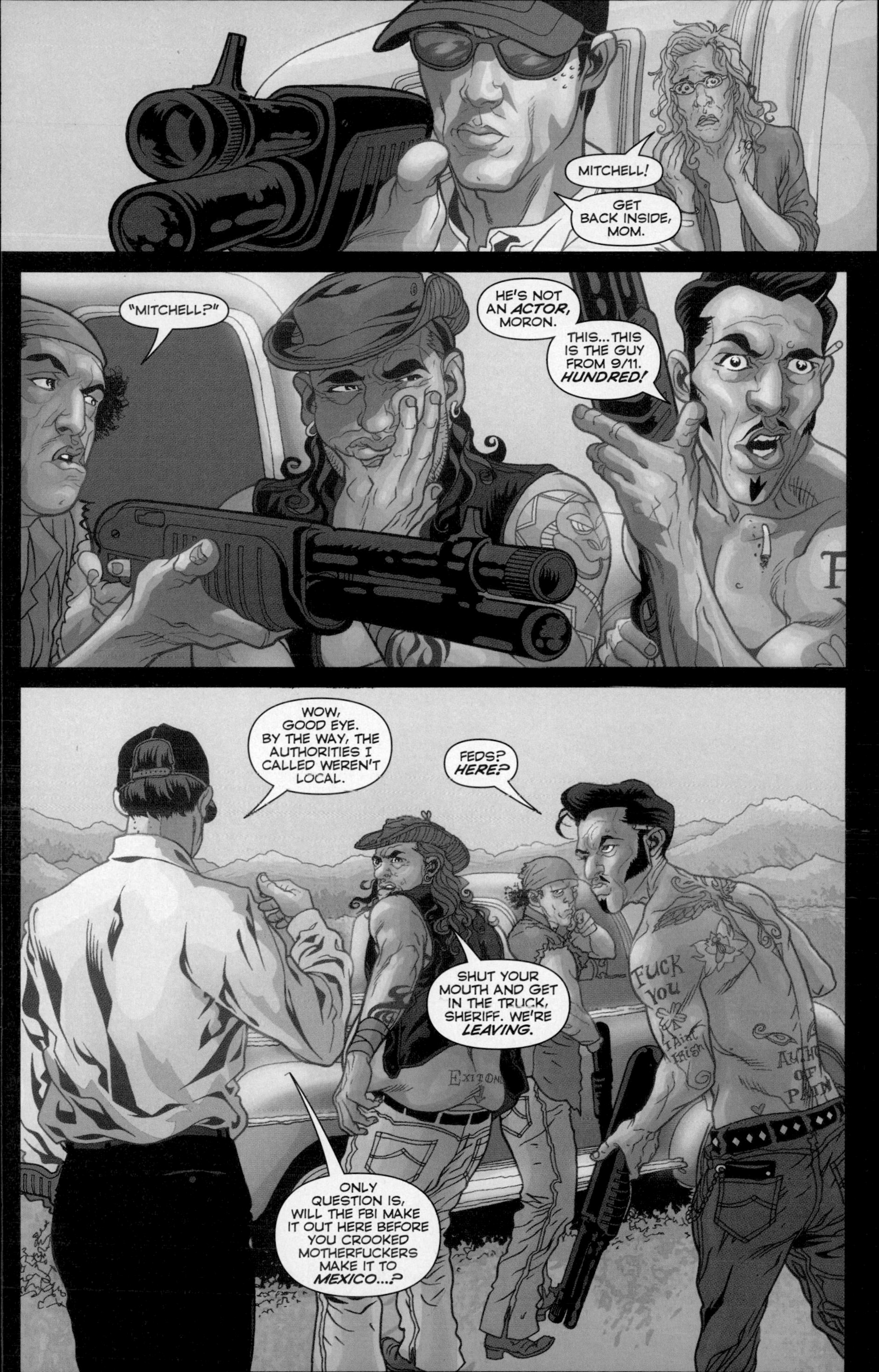
MITCHELL!
GET BACK INSIDE, MOM.
"MITCHELL?"
HE'S NOT AN ACTOR, MORON.
THIS... THIS IS THE GUY FROM 9/11. HUNDRED!
WOW, GOOD EYE. BY THE WAY, THE AUTHORITIES I CALLED WEREN'T LOCAL.
FEDS? HERE?
SHUT YOUR MOUTH AND GET IN THE TRUCK, SHERIFF. WE'RE LEAVING.
ONLY QUESTION IS, WILL THE FBI MAKE IT OUT HERE BEFORE YOU CROOKED MOTHERFUCKERS MAKE IT TO MEXICO...?

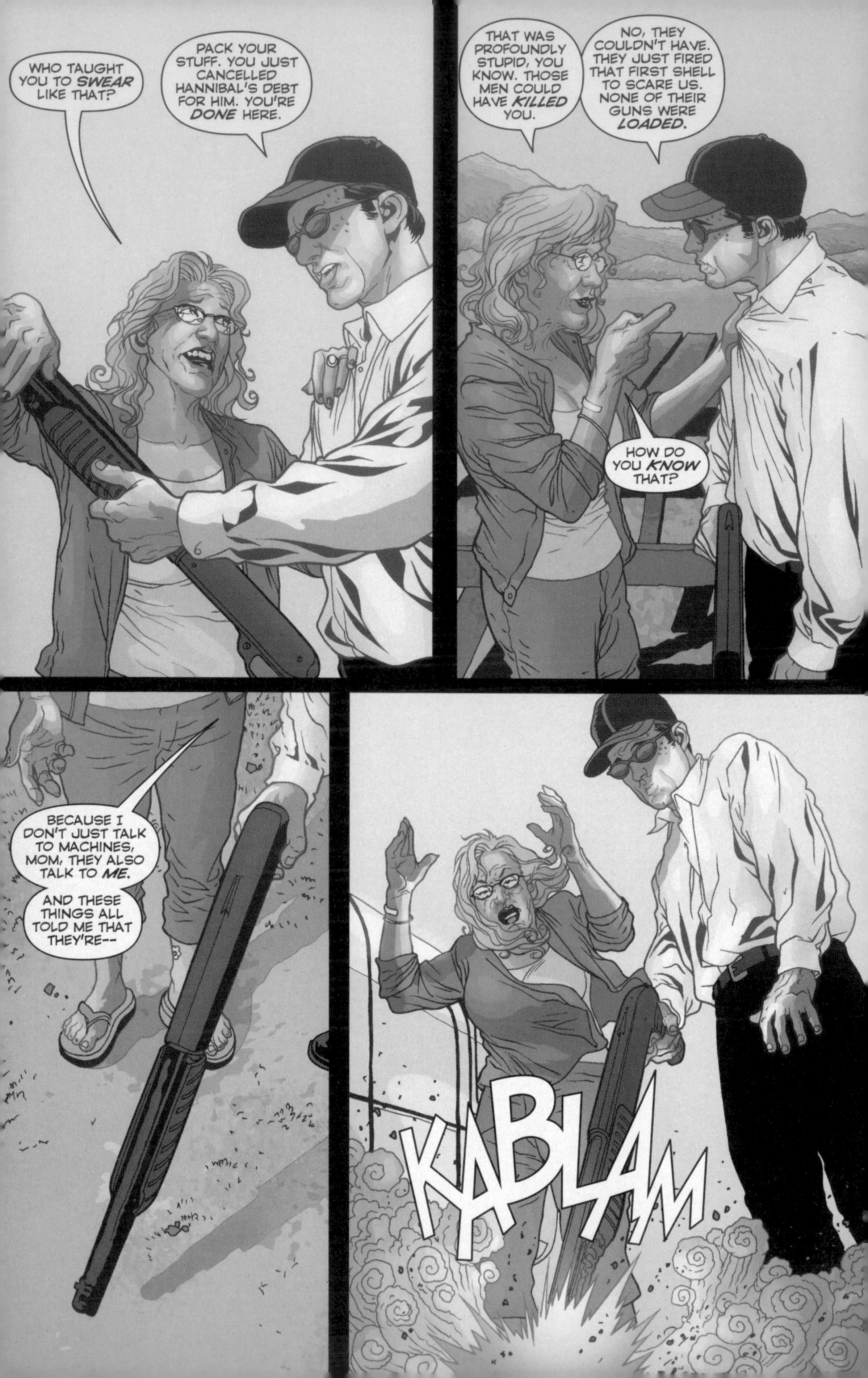
WHO TAUGHT YOU TO SWEAR LIKE THAT?
PACK YOUR STUFF. YOU JUST CANCELLED HANNIBAL'S DEBT FOR HIM. YOU'RE DONE HERE.
THAT WAS PROFOUNDLY STUPID, YOU KNOW. THOSE MEN COULD HAVE KILLED YOU.
NO, THEY COULDN'T HAVE. THEY JUST FIRED THAT FIRST SHELL TO SCARE US. NONE OF THEIR GUNS WERE LOADED.
HOW DO YOU KNOW THAT?
BECAUSE I DON'T JUST TALK TO MACHINES, MOM, THEY ALSO TALK TO ME.
AND THESE THINGS ALL TOLD ME THAT THEY'RE--
KABLAM

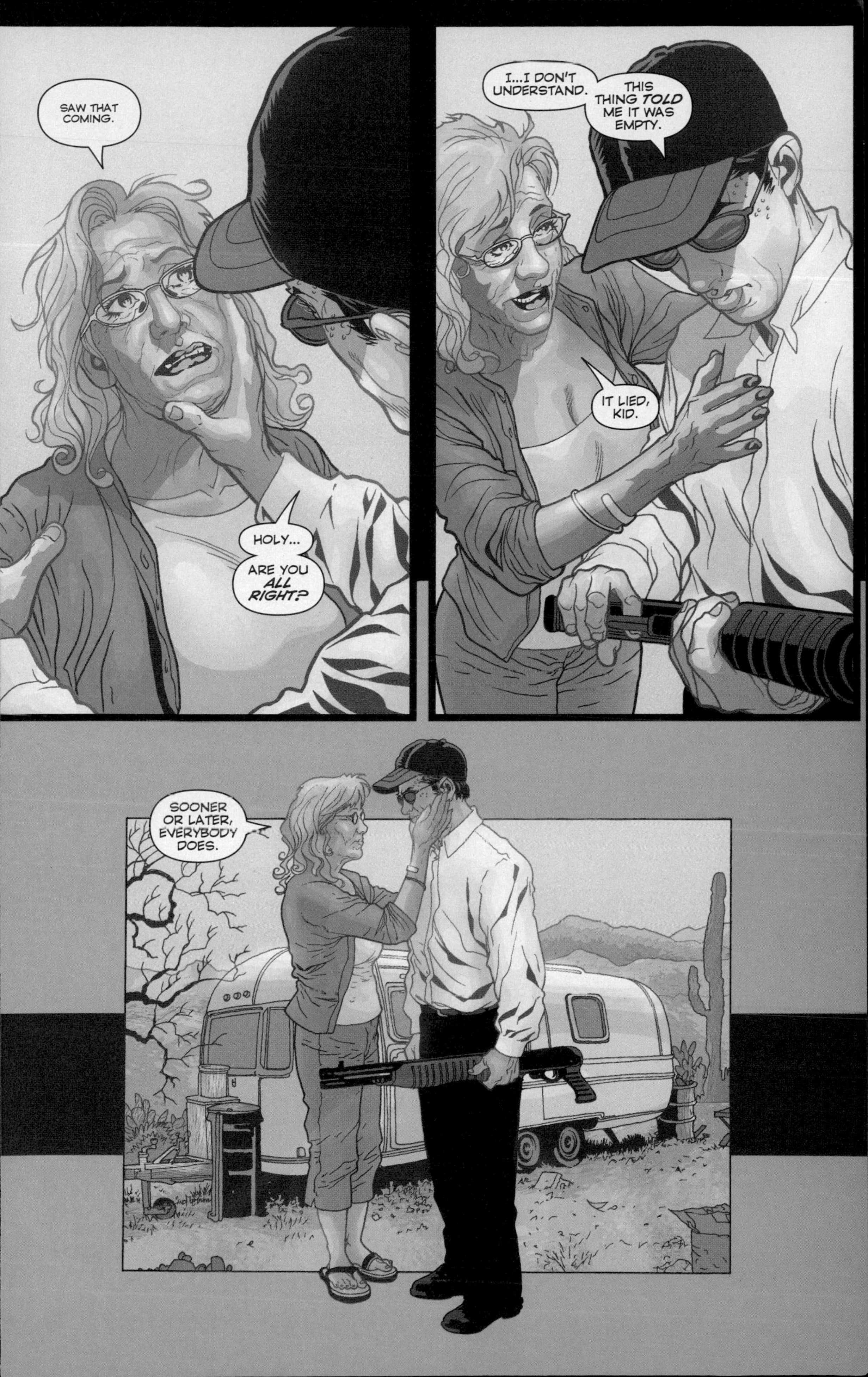
SAW THAT COMING.
HOLY...
ARE YOU ALL RIGHT?
I...I DON'T UNDERSTAND.
THIS THING TOLD ME IT WAS EMPTY.
IT LIED, KID.
SOONER OR LATER, EVERYBODY DOES.

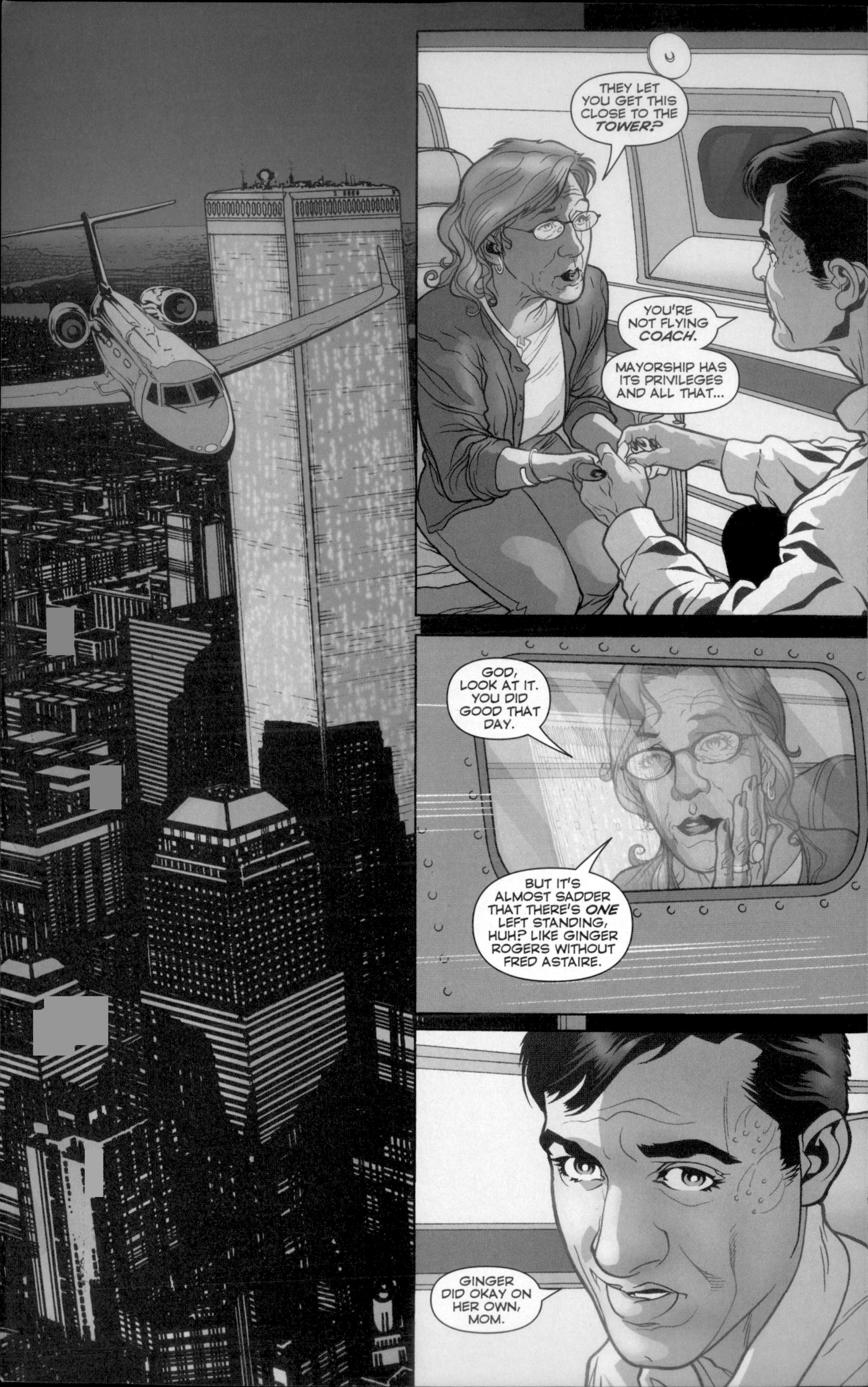
THEY LET YOU GET THIS CLOSE TO THE TOWER?
YOU'RE NOT FLYING COACH.
MAYORSHIP HAS ITS PRIVILEGES AND ALL THAT...
GOD, LOOK AT IT. YOU DID GOOD THAT DAY.
BUT IT'S ALMOST SADDER THAT THERE'S ONE LEFT STANDING, HUH? LIKE GINGER ROGERS WITHOUT FRED ASTAIRE.
GINGER DID OKAY ON HER OWN, MOM.

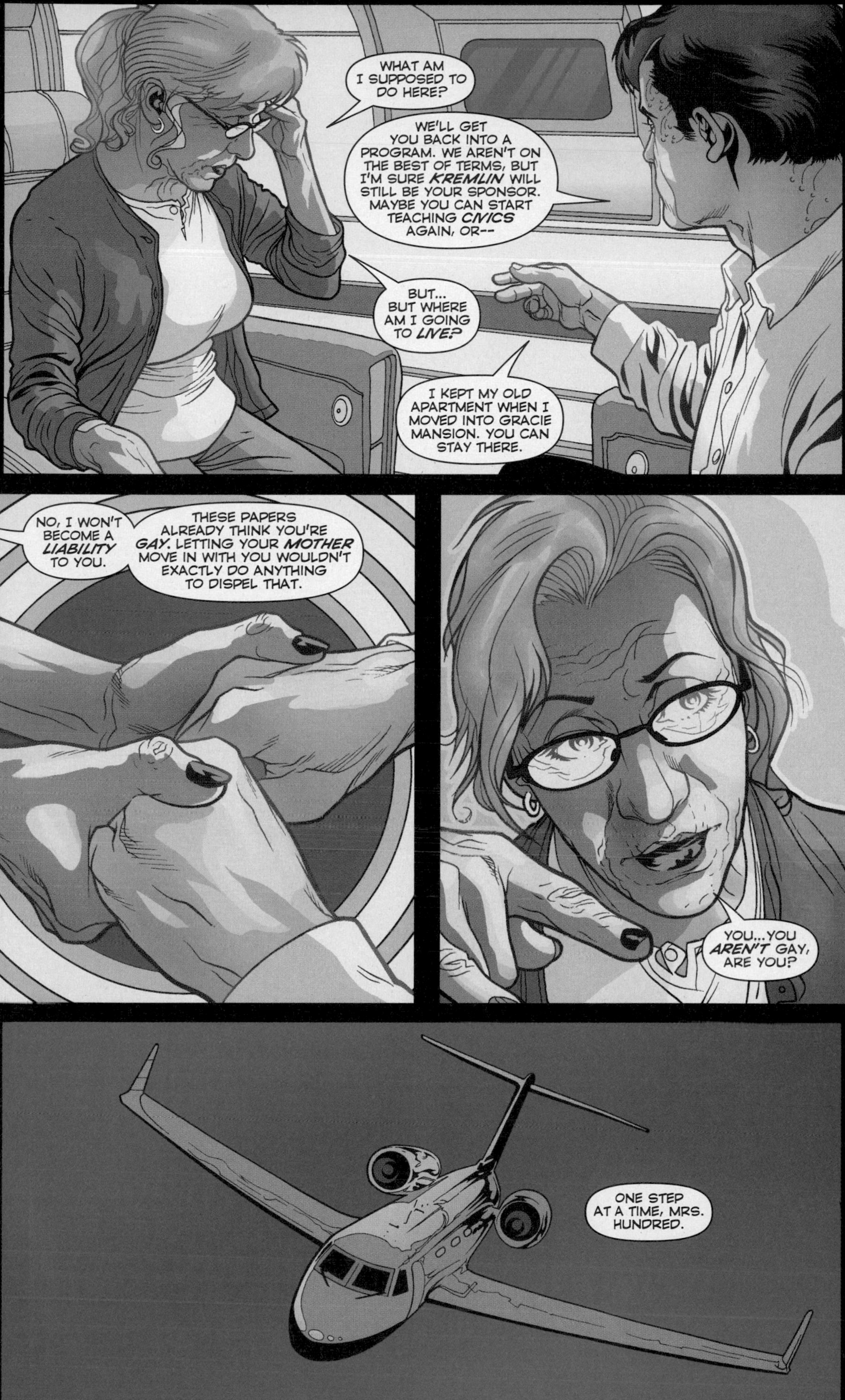
WHAT AM I SUPPOSED TO DO HERE?
WE'LL GET YOU BACK INTO A PROGRAM. WE AREN'T ON THE BEST OF TERMS, BUT I'M SURE KREMLIN WILL STILL BE YOUR SPONSOR. MAYBE YOU CAN START TEACHING CIVICS AGAIN, OR--
BUT... BUT WHERE AM I GOING TO LIVE?
I KEPT MY OLD APARTMENT WHEN I MOVED INTO GRACIE MANSION. YOU CAN STAY THERE.
NO, I WON'T BECOME A LIABILITY TO YOU.
THESE PAPERS ALREADY THINK YOU'RE GAY. LETTING YOUR MOTHER MOVE IN WITH YOU WOULDN'T EXACTLY DO ANYTHING TO DISPEL THAT.
YOU...YOU AREN'T GAY, ARE YOU?
ONE STEP AT A TIME, MRS. HUNDRED.

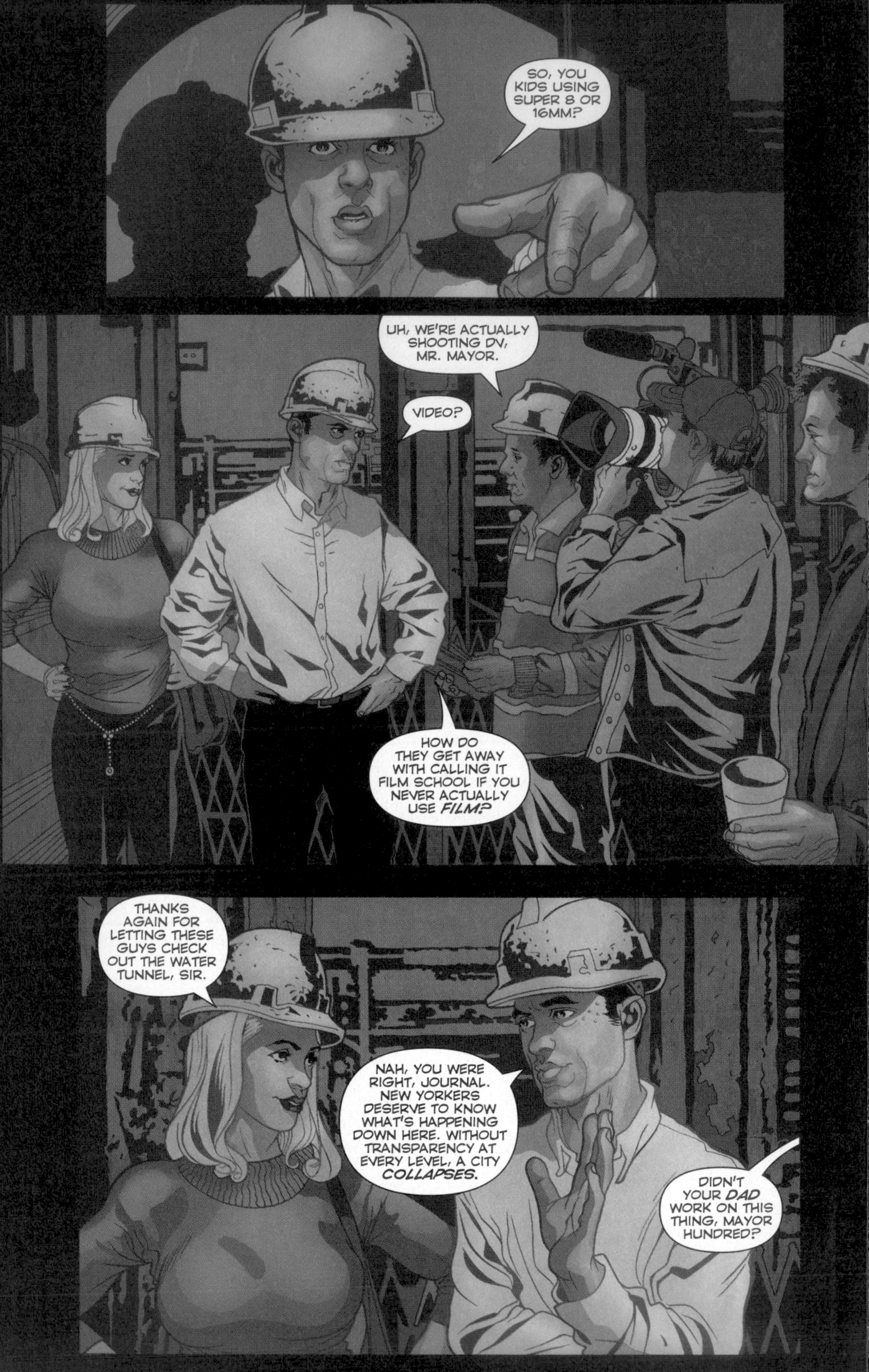
SO, YOU KIDS USING SUPER 8 OR 16MM?
UH, WE'RE ACTUALLY SHOOTING DV, MR. MAYOR.
VIDEO?
HOW DO THEY GET AWAY WITH CALLING IT FILM SCHOOL IF YOU NEVER ACTUALLY USE FILM?
THANKS AGAIN FOR LETTING THESE GUYS CHECK OUT THE WATER TUNNEL, SIR.
NAH, YOU WERE RIGHT, JOURNAL. NEW YORKERS DESERVE TO KNOW WHAT'S HAPPENING DOWN HERE. WITHOUT TRANSPARENCY AT EVERY LEVEL, A CITY COLLAPSES.
DIDN'T YOUR DAD WORK ON THIS THING, MAYOR HUNDRED?

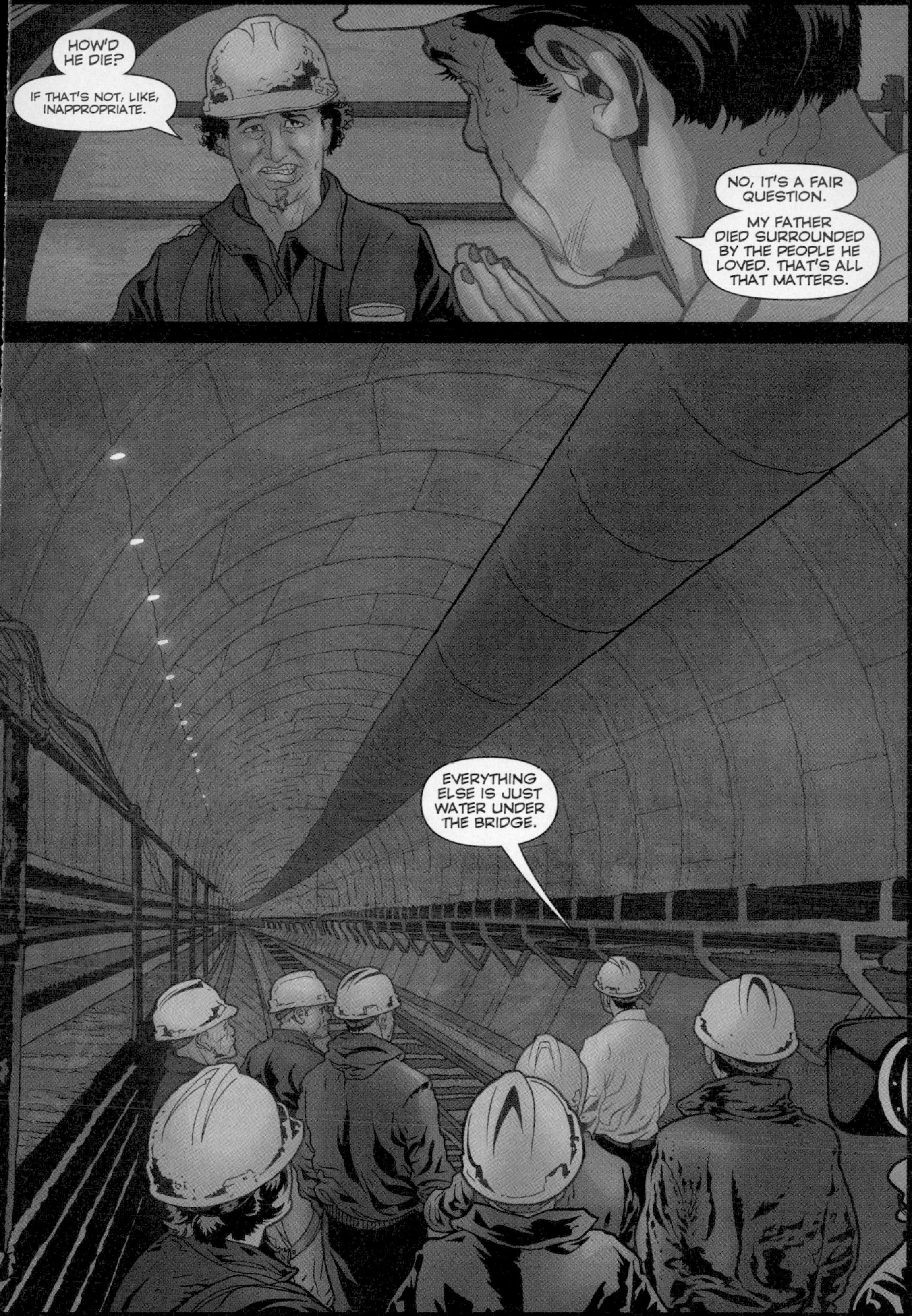
HOW'D HE DIE?
IF THAT'S NOT, LIKE, INAPPROPRIATE.
NO, IT'S A FAIR QUESTION.
MY FATHER DIED SURROUNDED BY THE PEOPLE HE LOVED. THAT'S ALL THAT MATTERS.
EVERYTHING ELSE IS JUST WATER UNDER THE BRIDGE.

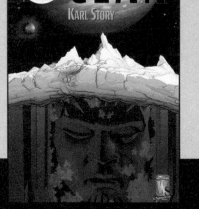